DISTINCT

Oritsesemisan Megbele

chipmunkapublishing
the mental health publisher

Published by
Chipmunkapublishing
United Kingdom

http://www.chipmunkapublishing.com

ISBN 978-1-78382-493-9

ABOUT THE AUTHOR:

This, is his sixth book where he express psychological and philosophical emotions, feelings, thoughts with backing from his believes associated with some personal life experiences. He is a diagnosed paranoid schizophrenia. As he endeavors to deal with ambiguity in a distinct nature about life in, and out with certain experience he exposes inner feelings and emotions some of which can lead to mental illness. But with self-motivation for example, the, thought and willingness of giving up smoking calls for some experience which cannot easily be narrative as he exposes some inner contours about life which frames every day psychology. To have written this book among other books he hopes to make a trademark instinctiveness of his own psychology. His is of an opinion people who, in any way feel irrational of his books should not take up care in psychiatrist.

Start

The Universe is full of unexplained mysteries, in the words of Aristotle, 'The more you know, and the more you know you don't know.' Mysteries drive us to explore, to search, to think and experiment. Mankind have been to the moon, explored our solar system and beyond; we've created computers we might feel are smarter than us, and we can store huge amount of data in tiny spaces. It is always intriguing when we solve mysteries, but in this category you will only find the solved varieties.

Uniqueness is a state or condition wherein someone or something is unlike anything else in comparison. When used in relation to humans, it is often in relation to a person's personality, or some specific characteristics of things, signaling if it is or unlike the personality traits that are prevalent in that individuals culture. Since cultures are widely known and accepted as being different in varied degree. This can make the study of personality difficult since, meaning and the expression of traits may be different within cultural groups. He wants an audience for the contents of this book. Trait theory uses a hierarchy of traits in order to separate culture from the traits, it can be said the culture is ignored in order to focus of the individual traits and how they are connected to the individual.

Gordon Allport's trait theory not only served as a foundational approach within personality psychology, but also is continued to be viewed and discussed by other disciplines such as anthropology because of how he approached culture within trait theory. Every smoker or alcoholic ought to read this book some of you, do not like what you do but you do it. He would also like to know much of other people's experience in relation to smoking and intake of alcohol. It would be considerate to understand the myth behind smoking and drinking excessive alcohol.
The author of this book has an opinion that if money is the root of all evil then, money is also a root of what unveils evil. Our world is full of mysterious events which in some cases defies explanation. Each tail tells the story of one incredible phenomenon and investigates every possible explanation

from the anchor of logic to the far end of the supernatural. It will be considerate to examine the contents of this book to see if, they seem superficial.

In psychology, trait theory (also called dispositional theory) is an approach to the study of human personality. Trait theorists are primarily interested in the measurement of *traits*, which can be defined as habitual patterns of behavior, thought, and emotion. According to this perspective, traits are aspects of personality that are relatively stable over time, differ across individuals (e.g. some people are outgoing whereas others are not), are relatively consistent over situations, and influence behavior. Traits are in contrast to states, which are more transitory dispositions.

In some theories and systems, traits are something a person either has or does not have, but in many others traits are dimensions such as extraversion vs. introversion, with each person rating somewhere along this spectrum.

There are two approaches to define traits: as internal causal properties or as purely descriptive summaries. The internal causal definition states that traits influence our behaviors, leading us to do things in line with that trait. On the other hand, traits as descriptive summaries are descriptions of our actions that don't try to infer causality.

An axiom or postulate is a statement that is taken to be true, to serve as a premise or starting point for further reasoning and arguments the word, comes from the Greek, 'that which is thought worthy or fit' or 'that which commends itself as evident.'

The term has subtle differences in definition when used in the context of different fields of study. As defined in classic philosophy, an axiom is a statement that is so evident or well-established, that it is accepted without controversy or question. As used in modern logic, an axiom is simply a premise or starting point for reasoning. This book would make sense and concreate meaning to you if you understand or the word axiom and postulate mean something to you.

Meaning 'being in balance', and hence 'having (the same) value (as)', 'worthy', 'proper'. Among the ancient Greek philosophers an axiom was a claim which could be seen to be true without any need for proof.

I do not know much of what this means medically about procrastination but it will help in reflecting distinct meaning based on the content of this book on why and how it has been written, what are the real effect of the emotion, feeling or psychology even traits I went through, to have written this book. In short could I have been procrastinating to have written such a book? Please read on let's see if it sounds as if I have been procrastinating.

Trait theory tends to focus on the individual over the situation in which they are in. This focus has relaxed within modern studies allowing for a consideration of the external factors outside of the self. As the focus becomes more relaxed (but still prominent as it is a main part of the theory) research expands.

Gordon Willard Allport (November 11, 1897 – October 9, 1967) was an American psychologist. Allport was one of the first psychologists to focus on the study of the personality, and is often referred to as one of the founding figures of personality psychology. He contributed to the formation of values scales and rejected both a psychoanalytic approach to personality, which he thought often was too deeply interpretive, and a behavioral approach, which he thought did not provide deep enough interpretations from their data. He emphasized the uniqueness of each individual, and the importance of the present context, as opposed to past history, for understanding the personality.

Allport had a profound and lasting influence on the field of psychology, even though his work is cited much less often than that of other well-known figures. Part of his influence stemmed from his knack for exploring and broadly conceptualizing important and interesting topics (e.g. rumor,

<u>prejudice</u>, <u>religion</u>, traits). Another part of his influence resulted from the deep and lasting impression he made on his students during his long teaching career, many of whom went on to have important careers in psychology.

Procrastination: It's pretty much all in the mind 26 August 2018:

To procrastinate or not: the answer may be down to differences in how our brains are wired, a study suggests.
It identified two areas of the brain that determine whether we are more likely to get on with a task or continually put it off.
Researchers used a survey and scans of 264 people's brains to measure how proactive they were.
Experts say the study, in Psychological Science, underlines procrastination is more about managing emotions than time.

Big clue:
It found that the amygdala - an almond-shaped structure in the temporal (side) lobe which processes our emotions and controls our motivation - was larger in procrastinators.
In these individuals, there were also poorer connections between the amygdala and a part of the brain called the dorsal anterior cingulate cortex (DACC).

The DACC uses information from the amygdala and decides what action the body will take. It helps keep the person on track by blocking out competing emotions and distractions.
'Individuals with a larger amygdala may be more anxious about the negative consequences of an action - they tend to hesitate and put off things,' says Erhan Genç, one of the study authors, based at Ruhr University Bochum.

The researchers suggest that procrastinators are less able to filter out interfering emotions and distractions because the connections between the amygdala and the DACC in their brains are not as good as in proactive individuals.

Mindfulness control:

Prof Tim Pychyl, from Carleton University, Ottawa, who has been studying procrastination for the past few decades, believes it is a problem with managing emotions rather than time.

'This study provides physiological evidence of the problem procrastinators have with emotional control,' he says.
'It shows how the emotional centres of the brain can overwhelm a person's ability for self-regulation.'
Dr Pychyl is optimistic about the potential for change. He said: 'Research has already shown that mindfulness meditation is related to amygdala shrinkage, expansion of the pre-frontal cortex and a weakening of the connection between these two areas'.

He said this showed that changing the brain was possible.
Dr Caroline Schluter, the lead author of the study, said: 'The brain is very responsive and can change throughout the lifespan.'

Tips for procrastinators:

Productivity expert Moyra Scott thinks we need to take personality into account when motivating ourselves.
'We need to recognise when we are procrastinating and have 'tricks' we can employ to get us doing something,' she said.

Her top tips are:

- If you don't have an external deadline, use a timer to focus for set periods - for example, 25 minutes at a time with 5 minute breaks and a longer break every 90 minutes.
- Write a list of tasks but break it down into smaller, more specific ones. This makes them easier to action and complete.
- Try to minimise interruptions like email notifications. Putting your phone on airplane mode or going somewhere to work where you won't be disturbed will also help.

- Being 'busy' is easier than doing the thing we are avoiding. Instead of doing the task at hand, we do other stuff instead and kid ourselves that we don't have the time. You do have the time. You just need to make it.

Have you ever thought or wondered what life and the future holds for you and your family dose it promises riches, ruin, love, loneliness, contentment did it promise you live long life or that, your life will be cut short. We always have speculations about such things and we will probably be for thousands of years to come our life might still be based on speculations about such issues.

Experts have been studying, making research on global trends, making projections for the future how are many of the forecasts becoming true some have been successful others have failed while, some are still in progress. Meanwhile some of us have been turning to the supernatural for clues about such issues for example, to address some of the complications or to demonstrate our own understanding and readiness. Some of us are becoming our own astrologers, read our horoscopes or regulate our future we are naturally becoming our own psychologist through such process.

In the process and efforts of discerning our future, since our ancient world still in several ways remains with us we, consult oracles, priest or priestesses passing on information from God or the gods to us. Astrology has always been a form of divination holding the stars our future, the moon, sun infarct our planet as a whole and the entire Universe for some of us if not outwardly it will always influence our life inwardly.

On another level dose it seems we are finding it difficult to walk in our Godly ways or are we finding it easier? The precision in which we walk knowing God is in us in some ways are not being quenched this book has been written by a diagnosed paranoid schizophrenic. This is out of a question of being right or wrong or if am a schizophrenic or not. I mean, it as in a spiritual sense if God is actually leading us in our ways. Things are not only just cantered on us but even if it does it's the will of God. Or probably other things are not, the will of God for us. Dose it not seem these days we are rounding things up to be centered on ourselves, what we want, how we are going to do this or that, what it will mean to us, how it will put a smile on our face or is it the other way round.

Astrology claims the position of the celestial bodies at the time of one's birth shapes his or her personality and future though the root of astrology can be traced to ancient Babylon if we are good observers of such related issue's it more seems its becoming scientific while creatures are in multitude are now being used for scientific purpose what should we expect.

The planet and stars emit no force that could affect humans the way astrologers say they do probably to them. Astrological calculations toady are made according to the ancient beliefs the planet revolves around the earth in fact, the planets revolves around the sun. Predictions made by different astrologers for the same people do not match.

In my opinion the Zodiac signs are said to give clues to a person's character in reality, people who have the same birth day do not have the same traits; ones birthday date reveals something of the persons personality astrologers judge a person's behaviour and character by sets of assumptions it's the case or they as the astrologers have no personality. There is evil, pain and suffering they do not tell you much about if God exist or not. What seem to be the symbols of astrologers related to that of medical science if not, religious', spiritual infusion or diffusion it could even lead to spiritual warfare. We are of the same star am still being primitive you are being civilized. We are of the same star am still being heartfelt about a situation you are enjoying it.

If two people are of the same star someone dose them good are you sure both of them would definably use the good in turn not to hurt someone else? Are you God who can establish this?

What are schools, employers using details of our data's to do astrology is becoming a state of scientific prospect.

If we are of the same star does this mean we would both be good at computing? We might both be good with our hands but probably on other different things.

The making of God is all around us unfolding it-self. Each day what do we make out of the making of our own hands on this planet it would be good to address our future at the same time consider this.

Lions feed on creatures which misbehave in the wild Tigers feed on the once which doesn't misbehave. Doesn't Tigers look more serene than Lions? I mean in a spiritual sense of having good or evil intent.

The tiger (*Panthera tigris*) is the largest cat species, most recognizable for its pattern of dark vertical stripes on reddish-orange fur with a lighter underside. The species is classified in the genus *Panthera* with the lion, leopard, jaguar, and snow leopard. It is an apex predator, primarily preying on ungulates such as deer and bovids think of Tigers having creatures outside these scopes. It is territorial and generally a solitary but social predator, often requiring large contiguous areas of habitat that support its prey requirements. This coupled with the fact that it is indigenous to some of the more densely populated places on Earth, has caused significant conflicts with humans.

Talking about education and its recent undertakings, the issues involved have been very huge but should not be made conflicting what most children have now apart from education in their class room might be family problems this holds a significant aspect in a child's life if they would do well, at school. Teachers do not actually take notice of this except something about it happens tragically and it comes out in the open.

Am of an opinion Jesus Christ has a part to play as the author of all religion because he holds a position of an arrest in every religion in a way which, is very vital and should be significant to every religion. He addressed most of the things life holds in our relationship as part of the living e.g. love, peace, do not hate , be kind to others we should avoid sin. He did not tell us much on how to progress in life when it comes to our material life but how to justify it with rightness with the love which come from God who gave us purpose, to look up to him and our wellbeing with righteousness and peace as our amour.

He invited the Gentiles, Pharisee's to be part of his heavenly call that we hold righteousness' dear to our hearts he even invited sinners. He did not invite us to be slaves but to be our own master as the world progresses. To be ourselves when it comes to goodness e.g. for us to be good to one another to bear good fruits how we would bear the fruits at the same time, redeem ourselves from the slavery of evil and sin.

Something may go wrong; a person has a problem he or she doesn't know how to go about solving the problem. Having the initiative to think through it is one thing; another aspect is how to think things through on the right path. It pleases you, God in your mind and heart and e.g. another person if be the case someone else is involved.

Christ endorsed us as much as he could with prayers and thanks giving on how, we should bear the fruit at the same time redeem our souls making, ourselves children of God rather than being children of evil who transgress against God. He told us about brotherly and sisterly love forgiveness if your brother or sister offends you and about compassion for one another because in so doing, we are one together in unity with God.

How would one do a thing out of annoyance which can be put as basically true?

Since, we humans on earth have more than one religion or belief system the sword he brought is for us sorting out our indifference or we still need to realize love is stronger than hate. Good and evil can't join hands this needs to be addressed. Realizations of this and the continuation of our existence on earth brought about God's message through Christ among other prophets before him and after him. Am yet to come across any other religion that gives more detail into this than that of Christ observing how humans had overtime progress we talk each day of governance, human laws, family, welfare, wellbeing, reducing pain and suffering how to compose ourselves in times of heartfelt issues all in the name of God. If some of us have not been believing in God lots of these issues would have driven us out of our hearts and mind.

I always wish things will get along fine with me when it comes to dealing or managing my illness of paranoid schizophrenia. Most of us always think things will get along fine when it comes to business matters, finance, education, work, raising children. We have over time become very advance much, still has to be done as our world has become very complex at the same time delicate. Most of us should know about what is or might be coming for us when it comes to science, religion, engineering, technology, politically, socially and the way we tend to live our lives.

Such issues or there occurrences comes with anomalies sometimes it's all part of life based on its beauty, ugliness and the hassles it brings we, being who we are, have ways to give ourselves advice based on the way our mind, hearts and brains work. On how we can do much better than our present circumstances or on how to do better things in life why does it seems to fad things get out of control at certain times could it be its because our world is being driven by money or a sort of arrogance towards the way we do things? Its part of what is affecting health care all around the world one would expect our lives should not be becoming complicated due to human advancement.

Meanwhile at the moment certain aspects of our world seems to be going worse off as much as we put efforts towards what we want out of life to better ourselves if that, is the case why is our world getting bad or out of control our world is now in a delicate position it needs to be addressed.

In view of this as part of human efforts going into space mission it might have some religious inference in relation to God and his creation. We have always been going on about building a better world, making our planet a better place for the need to enhance ourselves spiritually, psychologically, in the things we do, can it all be done mostly economically I mean, financially. Now is the time! Now is the real time to consider building a better mind, consideration of making the most of anything that is good now and towards, the future based on positive emotional psychology or it will lead more into a state of needing more psychiatrics.

2011 annual report on keeping to commitment to tenants Greenwich council was pleased it had been able to maintain its commitment in improving its quality of service for tenants over the last twelve months as a new Woolwich service centre and library opened in July offering range of services from one location, helping to achieve its £3.7m efficiency savings per year for reinvestment in services for local people.

Two hundred and twenty-nine of the four thousand new homes being developed in Kidbrooke Village formerly Ferrier Estate were completed. On its completion, one thousand five hundred and twenty-five affordable homes would have been delivered.

Tenants on Borough Wide Panel agreed on local offer with the council identifying six key areas for improvement considerations were on tenant involvement, quality of housing, repair and maintenance, house allocation, effective use of resources and estate cleanliness.

Over two hundred tenants took the opportunity on discussions on housing and related services through formal council meetings, estate walkabout, focus groups, local tenant and resident association housing panel activities.

They were commitment in working together for better services keeping us informed of services we can expect and working in partnership to ensure future housing services reflects priorities of local people. Woolwich is well served by a hundred of fifty tenants representatives involved in local borough wide housing panels which are strongly supported by thirty-three tenant associations.

By working together they have made a difference in a new local estate inspection system involving tenants, council officers and local councilors so everyone identifies the issues concerned and agree what improvements can be made.

Improve the way empty properties are inspected and prepared for new tenants. More tenants had become mystery shoppers, testing council services to highlight areas for improvement and recognizing excellent services. Develop communal land to create vegetable plots. Proving tenants with computer training to promote benefits of the internet and to access full range of council services online, working together in refurbishing a range of play sites and design new play facilities on three housing estates.

Using local play sites in creating local sports teams for children and young people, ensuring the views of tenants are listened to in consultation plans for the 2012 London game. Proving long lasting London 2012 legacy benefits such as outdoor gyms, as well as Olympic theme local community gardening and art projects.
Councilor Steve Offord, Greenwich Cabinet Member for housing looks to the future there had been many achievements to celebrate over the past year he said, he would like to thank tenants' representative organization for helping develop housing services.

As a council we have a duty to balance our responsibilities as managers of properties together, with the need to be efficient social landlords he says. He added this means we need to continue driving efficiency when delivering services ensuring tenants and residents live harmoniously in well maintained homes and communities. The challenges' are well underway much, has been achieved and they are committed to the followings.

Continue to meet regularly with housing panels to gain feedback from tenants and residents to help deliver good services. Continue to come down hard on tenants who continue to ignore terms of their tenancy. Priorities to reducing rent arrears, set up dedicated teams to tackle illegal subletting.

Provide incentives to encourage rather than force under occupiers to move out of their homes. Create two hundred and fifty extra care properties built in high standard to replace existing sheltered blocks. They would create forty-six new family homes to meet the needs of serious overcrowding and seven new bungalows for older or disable residents. Replace all existing communal TV aerials with digital system before April 2012 digital switchover.

Invest in keeping estates safe including investment of over £500,000 to provide new secure entry system. The whole communities were told to keep up to date and get involved.

Humans generally have the powers or abilities towards something more advance each day of their lives but some of us could waste it because some of us do fail to build towards our inner self or why not do, greater things or good yet they waste it or the life of opportunity to do so. In short it's those who feel they are in need who should do greater good they should stand for integrity, uprightness and honesty before all mankind and God an honour we place on ourselves here or display is also an honor it would be for us in heaven.

Some people have abilities to think fast and rightly they have all they need in such aspects so most things might be at their disposal. A problem is it's what some people in such position want in their own terms that interest them most. It is therefore good for them to reverend God so when they act, they are acting in the name of God towards their fellow human beings the more it would empower those around them that it's their interest but in the name of God because they seek to do right within themselves before God.

Most people who know or understand their own worth listen to their conscience therefore having a tendency to care for their own interest and those of others so invariably, am implying this that we understand, the present issues of being careless in the interest of other people when it comes to social science e.g. when it comes to world issues. Our world should not just become complex it should have a sense of direction at this stage, chaos can easily be triggered by just a fish in the pond.

Caring less to understand this and not taking it into consideration, advantages can be taken in any works of life rather than working towards a common goal life could easily be disrupted. That's what happens when a world or a life you once know is no longer as it used to be. It has changed all of a sudden or it's gradually changing to our own disadvantage. That's what is driving some of us into having mental health issues, prison, crime, becoming anti-social. At the same time all this is taking place working towards a common goal, should be acknowledged since it's a very vital prospect for every state of mind or nation.

It's time to us inner vision rather than being vulnerable to inner vision. Inner perspectives are what make life experience worth having. Our misgiving or misfortunes are all anomalies. But they seek to address our inner visions in a way that spells who we are. It gives insight God is in us and within the things we do so we either have the fear of God or we do not like God in us. Inner vision and perspectives always correlate something worthwhile because they assist life from a higher perspective not of our own making yet in it, we are not deluded or is it based on illusions.

Humans can endure in all stages of their life until death when life is no more they are prone to using inner vision, inner vision is what makes their life experiences meaningful while their misgiving or misfortune are all mere anomalies. They could have inner vision and perspectives to correlate to something worthwhile or meaningful because, they accept life from a higher perspectives nothing of their own making they endure in all stage of their life. Experience for the good of all mankind it's what God has created us for a greater unification of all mankind within beauty ugliness and death.

Using inner vision and being constructive are abilities most suited for when we are down as much as its need to display our abilities in decency towards life in the things we do and how we do it. Why is therefore evil, pain and suffering in our world to put us in check, to display who or the kind of person we truly are. To understand a Universal theory there is a supreme deity. If we understand our abilities and worth we would also know he did not leave us as just mere humans under evil, pain and suffering. For he created us in a way we would understand ourselves and the things we go through.

Smart, digital bins are helping chefs to reduce the amount of ingredients they throw away. How Starbucks hopes to end staff racism. The coffee chain is giving all its US staff 'unconscious bias' training after protests against the treatment of black customers at some of its stores. But how do such courses identify biases, and then try to change behaviour? They went to a training session for charity workers held in Richmond, Virginia, to find out.

South African 'world's oldest man' wants to stop smoking Fredie Blom spent most of his life as a labourer - on a farm and in the construction industry - in apartheid South Africa but he might soon be recognised as the world's oldest man, as the BBC's Mohammed Allie reports from Cape Town. Although he gave up drinking many years ago, Fredie Blom is still a regular smoker. 'Every day I still smoke two to three 'pills',' - local slang for tobacco tightly rolled into a cigarette-length piece of newspaper. 'I use my own tobacco because I don't smoke cigarettes'. The urge to smoke is so strong. Sometimes I tell myself I'm going to stop but it's just me lying to myself. My chest chases me to have a puff and I'm then forced to make a 'pill'. 'I blame the devil for that because he's so strong,' he says with mischievous grin.

If our planet is really moving into a state of civilization out of primitiveness, reaching towards an understanding of each other, I see no reason why children need to be spanked physically in other for them to do well at school, spanking them to do well at school or for behaving inappropriately or when to study at home. Speaking to them letting them know when to study at school or at home should be enough. Children who are treated with respect at the same time cautioned when they are young grow up; to be decent naturally since we all have feelings, emotions and thoughts nobody grows up taking things too easily for granted it will catch up with them in the future negatively then we feel sorry for ourselves then, it bears on us 'then we feel asking ourselves if, we had known'.

Since it's a situation as such, I feel parents or teachers who spank their children or pupils' do not want to take the blame in such times in a person's life. At such an age doing so dramatically below such age, the child might not understand. 12 years of age is when I feel we get to know children they want to be themselves if there had been a lot of spanking going on parent and teachers might find things much difficult at that age taking not at that age they may hit back.

They would grow up faced with ups and down in the presence of evil, pain and suffering as they grow up reasoning with them right from when they are young is what every good child wants at such level parents, teachers pupils tend to understand each other. It is one reason some parts of the world are much more advance. I do not feel anybody needs to beat me up to be successful in life it sounds primitive. Now within misunderstanding or conflict spanking children even treating them unfairly with words and changes might disturb their sense if its severe, it could make them grow up becoming cruel or grow up with cruelty in their mind showing understanding at all level to children would make them more regrettable for their downfall or for their stupidity. Be nice to them and they would be more mindful of suffering, pain and evil. Mind you some evil mind do not always regret at the end of the day. How dose and evil mind develop?
How Satan Gains Control Of The Mind: Therefore be careful how you walk, not as unwise men, but as wise, making the most of your time, because the days are evil. Where do evil desires and thoughts that arise in a Christian's mind and heart come from? ... The evil desires and thoughts in human beings come from our flesh. How Children Develop the Idea of Free Will Young children develop the concept of free will

in the short period between ages 4 and 6. But if free will doesn't exist, why do we believe so strongly that it does? Where does that belief come from? Spiritual warfare is real, difficult, and sometimes dangerous.

For a good child or person the presence and problem of evil, pain and suffering are enough for them having a better approach to life so how best is it to make children understand life, to do well in life or to be good is not by inflicting cruelty on them. So how, did God turn education into doing right and a person turning deaf ears to evil?
Ear piercing is one of the oldest known forms of body modification, with artistic and written references from cultures around the world dating back to early history. Gold, silver and bronze hoop earrings were prevalent in the Minoan Civilization (2000–1600 BCE) and examples can be seen on frescoes on the Aegean island of Santorini, Greece. During the late Minoan and early Mycenaean periods of Bronze Age Greece hoop earrings with conical pendants were fashionable.

By the late 1950s or early 1960s, the practice re-emerged, but since a large commercial market did not exist, most ear piercings were done at home. Teenage girls were known to hold *ear piercing parties*, where they performed the procedure on one another. Such an event is depicted in the 1978 motion picture *Grease* (set in 1959), where Sandy (Olivia Newton-John), the leading lady, is pierced by her friends.

In the late 1960s, ear piercing began to make inroads among men through the hippie and gay communities, although they had been popular among sailors for decades (or longer). Traditionally, a right-side piercing identified a man as gay and left-side as straight. Both sides pierced is commonly denoted as bisexual, though this has modified somewhat over the past decade.

By the early 1970s, ear piercing was common among women, thus creating a broader market for the procedure. Department stores throughout the country would hold ear piercing events, sponsored by earring manufacturers. At these events, a nurse or other trained person would perform the procedure, either pushing a sharpened and sterilized starter earring through the earlobe by hand, or using an ear-piercing instrument modified from the design used by physicians.

According to Hindu dharmic tradition, most girls and some boys (especially the 'twice born') get their ears pierced as part of a Dharmic rite known as Karnavedha before they are about five years old. Infants may get their ears pierced as early as several days after their birth.
Similar customs are practiced in other Asian countries, including Nepal, Sri Lanka, and Laos, although traditionally most males wait to get their ears pierced until they have reached young adulthood.

Ear piercing is mentioned in the Bible in several contexts. The most familiar refers to a Hebrew slave who was to be freed in the seventh year of servitude but wishes to continue serving his master and refuses to go free: '...his master shall take him before God. He shall be brought to the door or the doorpost, and his master shall pierce his ear with an awl; and he shall then remain his slave for life'.

The health risks with conventional earlobe piercing are common but tend to be minor, particularly if proper technique and hygienic procedures are followed. One study found that up to 35 percent of persons with pierced ears had one or more complications, including minor infection (77 percent of pierced ear sites with complications), allergic reaction (43 percent), keloids (2.5 percent), and traumatic tearing (2.5 percent). Pierced ears are a significant risk factor for contact allergies to the nickel in jewelry. Earlobe tearing, during the healing period or after healing is complete, can be minimized by not wearing earrings, especially wire-based dangle earrings, during activities in which they are likely to become snagged, such as while playing sports. Also, larger gauge jewelry will lessen the chance of the earring being torn out.

With cartilage piercing, the blunt force of an ear piercing instrument will traumatize the cartilage, and therefore make healing more difficult. Also, because there is substantially less blood flow in ear cartilage than in the earlobe, infection is a much more serious issue. There have been several documented cases of severe infections of the upper ear following piercing with an ear piercing instrument, which required courses of antibiotics to clear up. There are many ways that an infection can occur: the most common way is when the person that got pierced decides to take out the piercing too early. According to the A.M.A the proper waiting period to change or take out a piercing with substantially less risk of infection would be three weeks.

For all ear piercings, the use of a sterilized hollow piercing needle tends to minimize the trauma to the tissue and minimize the chances of contracting a bacterial infection during the procedure. As with any invasive procedure, there is always a risk of infection from blood borne pathogens such as hepatitis and HIV. However, modern piercing techniques make this risk extremely small (the risk being greater to the piercer than to the pierced due to the potential splash-back of blood). There has never been a documented case of HIV transmission due to ear/body piercing or tattooing, although there have been instances of the Hepatitis B virus being transmitted through these practices.

Negative effects of wearing earrings in light of researches:

The most frequent complications connected with wearing earrings are:

- inflammation
- keloids
- loss of tissue by tearing
- mechanical division of earlobes.
-

Researchers observed a correlation between the piercing of young girls' earlobes and subsequent development of allergies.

In Professor Ewa Czarnobilska's view (the manager of research team) the main reason of allergy (listed by allergists) is presence of nickel as a component of alloys used in the production of earrings – however the ingredients declared by producer is not significant, because nickel is a standard component of jewelry.

Symptoms of allergy are visible as eczema. This symptom is often justified to be food allergy (e.g. to milk), meanwhile the reason is contact with the earring (precisely Ni ions) with Lymphatic system. Ceasing of wearing earrings by children doesn't result in vanishing allergy symptoms. Immune system remembers the presence of Ni ions which existed in someone's blood and lymph.

Even though the children ceased wearing earrings, it can appear as an allergic reaction to:

- metal parts of wardrobe
- dental braces
- dental prosthesis
- orthotics
- meals cooked in pots with addition of nickel
- margarine (nickel is a catalyst in hydrogenation of unsaturated fats)
- coins
- chocolate
- nuts
- leguminous vegetables
- wine
- beer.

Researchers studying a sample of 428 pupils, age seven and eight, and 16 and 17 noticed that:

- thirty percent of population were allergic to nickel
- allergy occurred for many girls who had started wearing earrings in early childhood.

Other symptoms of allergy to nickel are:

- recurring infections
- asthma attacks

- chronic larynxis.

Regret is a negative conscious and emotional reaction to one's personal decision-making, a choice resulting in action or inaction. Regret is related to perceived opportunity. Its intensity varies over time after the decision, in regard to action versus action, and in regard to self-control at a particular age. The self-recrimination which comes with regret is thought to spur corrective action and adaptation. In Western societies adults have the highest regrets regarding choices. Regret has been defined by psychologists in the late 1990′s as a 'negative emotion predicated on an upward, self-focused, counterfactual inference'. Regret lingers where opportunity existed, with self-blame being a core element to ultimately spur corrective action in decision-making. Another definition is 'an aversive emotional state elicited by a discrepancy in the outcome values of chosen vs. unchosen actions'.

Regret is distinct from disappointment; both are negative emotional experiences relating to a loss outcome, and both have similar neuronal correlates. However, they differ in regard to feedback about the outcome, comparing the difference between outcomes for the chosen vs. unchosen action; in regret, full feedback occurs and with disappointment partial feedback. They also differ in regard to agency (self in regret versus external in disappointment).
There are conceptual models of regret in regret (decision theory) mostly in theoretical economics and finance under a field called behavioral economics. The term buyer's remorse, also called buyer's regret which is assumed to be the cause for regret aversion.

Anticipated regret or how much regret one thinks one will feel in the future, appears to be overestimated for actions and choices. This appears to be, in part, due to a tendency to underestimate the extent to which people attribute bad outcomes to external factors rather than to internal factors (i.e., themselves). It can lead to inaction or inertia and omission bias.

Existential regret has been specifically defined as 'a profound desire to go back and change a past experience in which one has failed to choose consciously or has made a choice that did not follow one's beliefs, values, or growth needs'.

Instruments to measure regret in people having to make medical decisions have failed to address current concepts of regret and failed to differentiate regret from disappointment. They have also not looked for positive impacts of regret. Process regret may occur, if a person does not consider information about all available choices before making a decision.
In a 2002 study, high intensity of regret and intrusive thoughts in older adults was related to self-control, and low internal control was expected to be self-protective and help to decrease regret. In younger adults, internal-control facilitated active change and was associated with low intensity of regret. There is interplay between action versus inaction and time. Regrets of an action are more intense in the short term, whereas regrets of inaction are more intense over the long term.

People's biggest regrets occur where they perceive the greatest and most important opportunity for corrective action. When no opportunity exists to improve conditions, thought processes mitigate the cognitive dissonance caused by regret, e.g. by rationalization, and re-construal. Regret pushes people toward revised decision making and corrective action as part of learning that may bring improvement in life circumstances. A 1999 study measured regret in accordance to negative reviews with service providers. Regret was an accurate predictor of who switched providers. As more intense regret is experienced, the likelihood of initiating change is increased. Consequently, the more opportunity of corrective action available, the larger the regret felt and the more likely corrective action is achieved. Feeling regret spurs future action to make sure other opportunities are taken so that regret will not be experienced again. People learn from their mistakes.

With a lost opportunity regret should intensify, not diminish, when people feel that they could have made better choices in the past but now perceive limited opportunities to take corrective action in the future. 'People who habitually consider future consequences (and how they may avoid future negative outcomes) experience less, rather than more, intense regret after a negative outcome.' This principle offers another reason as to why education is the most regretted aspect in life. Education becomes a more limited opportunity as time passes. Aspects such as making friends, becoming more spiritual, and community involvement tend to be less regrettable which makes sense because these are also aspects in life that do not become limited opportunities. As the opportunity to remedy a situation passes, feelings of hopelessness may increase. An explanation of the lost opportunity principle can be seen as a lack of closure: Low closure makes past occurrences feel unresolved. Low closure is associated with 'reductions in self-esteem and persistent negative affect over time' and with the realization and regret of lost opportunity. High closure is associated with acceptance of lost opportunity.
The lost opportunity principle suggests that regret does not serve as a corrective motive (which the opportunity principle suggests). Instead, regret serves as a more general reminder to seize the day.

Parents, teachers ought to educate children to understand evil, pain and suffering yes every child would grow up understanding if they place their hands on a boiling kettle they would get hurt as part of facing challenges in life as they grow up being spanked, ridiculed from childhood is not good since there is much more to come as they grow up what effigies dose this hold since there is pain and suffering. It's good to understand pain and suffering in reasonable ways then it becomes rational dealing with pain, suffering or evil.

This is something having to do with creation. But does anyone as part of God's creation where there is pain and suffering need contribute more to your suffering or pain we often talk of living a reasonable life we talk of making the world a better place, don't we? We hear of child sex abuse, children at school or orphanages being bullied, in some parts of the world without food, clean water or clothing.

Standard of living in the developing world:

Surveys information about quality of life in the developing world the purpose, is primarily to answer the question, 'If a donor's funds save a live, what sort of life is saved?' We make fewer attempts to fully convey what life is like; instead, we focus on what facts are available from relatively broad, large-sample, plausibly representative. Restricting ourselves to basic questions such as 'What health problems are common and how common are they?', 'What problems do people in the developing world generally list as particularly important?' For someone seeking a more qualitative and less representative picture, I suggest a visit to the developing world.

- Income and self-reported well-being.
- Are people in poor countries less satisfied with their lives?
- Income and assets.
- Global poverty rates.
- What does it mean to live on under $1 or $2 per day?
- Mortality and Morbidity: what are the major health problems in the developing world?
- Non-fatal health problems.
- What problems do people in the developing world believe are most pressing?
- Self-reported life satisfaction: People in poor countries report that they are on average less satisfied with their lives than people in rich countries. The average resident of a low-income country rated their satisfaction as 4.3 using a subjective 1-10 scale, while the average was 6.7 among residents of G8 countries. We interpret this as a large satisfaction gap.
- Incomes: A large proportion of the population in developing countries live on under $1 or $2 per day. The poor spend a large proportion of their incomes

on food, may lack access to basic infrastructure, and own few productive assets. However, they do make consumption choices that involve spending on things other than food and use a variety of instruments to manage erratic income streams. Ownership of televisions and radios and access to electricity and sanitation varies widely.

- Mortality: On one hand, people in Sub-Saharan Africa are much worse off, and much more likely to die prematurely, than people in wealthier parts of the world. On the other hand, those who live past the age of 5 have strong chances of living to age 60 or so; saving a life even from a single cause of death means saving a person who is likely to live quite a while longer.
- Morbidity: A third of children under five in developing countries show evidence of long-term malnutrition. Malnutrition can cause low energy, diarrhea, anemia, hypothyroidism, poor vision, and pneumonia, as well as increased susceptibility to many other diseases. Prevalence of parasitic worm infection is very high in many poor regions. Malaria causes frequent sickness among children under 5, who average over 4 days of sickness with the disease per year.
- Development Priorities: Sub-Saharan Africans rank reducing poverty and hunger as the two most pressing Millennium Development Goals. Health goals are also prioritized.

These are enough to make a child feel sad, regret some of them are being spanked in other for them to do well at school. This results to partly where the get rich syndromes comes in, We want to be better than each other but it should be on a reasonable level not mostly based on material things or on issues which would create unnecessary conflicts, bias or misunderstanding. Do we know of the amount of witchcraft, native doctors parent go to for these to occur, politics and cult groups involved in just education alone?

They would grow up to work have children, do other things not every one of them will fit in one category or the other. It's what might have resulted to some classless society or a society being less pragmatic in one direction among other groups leading to each other's downfall in several ways that hardly surfaces but is stinging a whole country within nations. Why don't we all become individuals who are guided more by practical considerations and by ideals?

Anti-reification of concepts and theories:

Dewey, in *The Quest for Certainty*, criticized what he called 'the philosophical fallacy':- philosophers often take categories (such as the mental and the physical) for granted because they don't realize that these are merely nominal concepts that were invented to help solve specific problems. This causes metaphysical and conceptual confusion. Various examples are the 'ultimate Being' of Hegelian philosophers, the belief in a 'realm of value', the idea that logic, because it is an abstraction from concrete thought, has nothing to do with the act of concrete thinking, and so on David L. Hildebrand sums up the problem: 'Perceptual inattention to the specific functions comprising inquiry led realists and idealists alike to formulate accounts of knowledge that project the products of extensive abstraction back onto experience.'

Naturalism and anti-Cartesianism:

From the outset, pragmatists wanted to reform philosophy and bring it more in line with the scientific method as they understood it. They argued that idealist and realist philosophy had a tendency to present human knowledge as something beyond what science could grasp. They held that these philosophies then resorted either to a phenomenology inspired by Kant or to correspondence theories of knowledge and truth. Pragmatists criticized the former for its a priorism, and the latter because it takes correspondence as an unanalyzable fact. Pragmatism instead tries to explain the relation between *knower* and *known*.

In 1868, C.S. Peirce argued that there is no power of *intuition* in the sense of cognition unconditioned by inference, and no power of introspection, intuitive or otherwise, and that awareness of an internal world is by hypothetical inference from external facts. Introspection and intuition were staple philosophical tools at least since Descartes. He argued that there is no absolutely first cognition in a cognitive process; such a process has its beginning but can always be analyzed into finer cognitive stages.

That which we call introspection does not give privileged access to knowledge about the mind—the self is a concept that is derived from our interaction with the external world and not the other way around (De Waal 2005, pp. 7–10). At the same time he held persistently that pragmatism and epistemology in general could not be derived from principles of psychology understood as a special science: what we *do* think is too different from what we *should* think; in his 'Illustrations of the Logic of Science' series, Peirce formulated both pragmatism and principles of statistics as aspects of scientific method in general. This is an important point of disagreement with most other pragmatists, who advocate a more thorough naturalism and psychologism.
Richard Rorty expanded on these and other arguments in *Philosophy and the Mirror of Nature* in which he criticized attempts by many philosophers of science to carve out a space for epistemology that is entirely unrelated to—and sometimes thought of as superior to—the empirical sciences. W.V. Quine, instrumental in bringing naturalized epistemology back into favor with his essay *Epistemology Naturalized* (Quine 1969) also criticized 'traditional' epistemology and its 'Cartesian dream' of absolute certainty. The dream, he argued, was impossible in practice as well as misguided in theory, because it separates epistemology from scientific inquiry.

While pragmatism started out simply as a criterion of meaning, it quickly expanded to become a full-fledged epistemology with wide-ranging implications for the entire philosophical field. Pragmatists who work in these fields share a common inspiration, but their work is diverse and there are no received views.

Philosophy of science:

In the philosophy of science, instrumentalism is the view that concepts and theories are merely useful instruments and progress in science cannot be couched in terms of concepts and theories somehow mirroring reality. Instrumentalist philosophers often define scientific progress as nothing more than an improvement in explaining and predicting phenomena. Instrumentalism does not state that truth doesn't matter, but rather provides a specific answer to the question of what truth and falsity mean and how they function in science.
One of C.I. Lewis' main arguments in *Mind and the World Order: Outline of a Theory of Knowledge* was that science does not merely provide a copy of reality but must work with conceptual systems and that those are chosen for pragmatic reasons, that is, because they aid inquiry. Lewis' own development of multiple modal logics is a case in point. Lewis is sometimes called a 'conceptual pragmatist' because of this. (Lewis 1929).
Another development is the cooperation of logical positivism and pragmatism in the works of Charles W. Morris and Rudolf Carnap. The influence of pragmatism on these writers is mostly limited to the incorporation of the pragmatic maxim into their epistemology. Pragmatists with a broader conception of the movement don't often refer to them.
W. V. Quine's paper 'Two Dogmas of Empiricism', published 1951, is one of the most celebrated papers of twentieth-century philosophy in the analytic tradition. The paper is an attack on two central tenets of the logical positivists' philosophy. One is the distinction between analytic statements (tautologies and contradictions) whose truth (or falsehood) is a function of the meanings of the words in the statement ('all bachelors are unmarried'), and synthetic statements, whose truth (or falsehood) is a function of (contingent) states of affairs. The other is reductionism, the

theory that each meaningful statement gets its meaning from some logical construction of terms which refers exclusively to immediate experience. Quine's argument brings to mind Peirce's insistence that axioms aren't a priori truths but synthetic statements.

Philosophy of mind:

Both John Dewey in *Experience and Nature* (1929) and half a century later Richard Rorty in his *Philosophy and the Mirror of Nature* (1979) argued that much of the debate about the relation of the mind to the body results from conceptual confusions. They argue instead that there is no need to posit the mind or mind stuff as an ontological category.

Pragmatists disagree over whether philosophers ought to adopt a quietist or a naturalist stance toward the mind-body problem. The former (Rorty among them) want to do away with the problem because they believe it's a pseudo-problem, whereas the latter believe that it is a meaningful empirical question.

Pragmatism sees no fundamental difference between practical and theoretical reason, nor any ontological difference between facts and values. Both facts and values have cognitive content: knowledge is what we should believe; values are hypotheses about what is good in action. Pragmatist ethics is broadly humanist because it sees no ultimate test of morality beyond what matters for us as humans. Good values are those for which we have good reasons.

Moral questions immediately present themselves as questions whose solution cannot wait for sensible proof. A moral question is a question not of what sensibly exists, but of what is good, or would be good if it did exist.

We all wants to be better in life we want or hope to do one good thing or the other in our life time if it's not all about making the world a better place what then, is this great issue of civilization, moral values, integrity, loyalty at the moment isn't it all being pushed aside for personal self. Reasonably we all need to do things with other people therefore we make friends have business partners for example while; we all have our own drives. Who, do we owe it all to if not God is there anything wrong in demonstrating it that way? You have you do; I have mine within beauty and ugliness. It's very easy to find truth, true or false?

If you are cheating at school, you move with pupils who also cheat. If you go to school always siting down quietly studying, being a good student not much people notice you if they do its being said you are a clever person or contributing to this you are being bullied or other student making faces at you.

Pupils come from different background, homes, family under different situation or circumstances. Who among them wants to be a realist, a pragmatist and how did the philosopher narrated their thoughts? Hardliners, open, skeptical, critics they all have their place in philosophy, psychology or sociology as well as life of their own. Their background would spell a lot about their thoughts and personal feelings. Why do we have life if not to understand life or its paradigms?

Purpose is a double edged sword. The moment we do not stop abandoning the notion of purpose instead, of certain narrow tracks we can tread depending on how 'important' they are, we realize life simply is, and are freer to wander the field at will.

Are you frustrated of your life? Are you questioning yourself, 'why do I live?' Then you are in the right place. If life is all about failures, loss, fear, distress, pain and tears, why should we live? This is what our mind immediately thinks.

Moving with friends who know our parents is good the feeling is good and could be comforting especially when we are down or up. We all need to have knowledge of why there is pain and suffering in this world. I feel, its one reason God brought us all together from different race, background and creed. If we understand evil, then we have less problem understanding pain or suffering. Understanding Gods wish and commandments is also good. I feel it's even at this complex and delicate time of our planet we need most to have had knowledge of Gods through his commandments for all mankind.

Harmony is good it might be a quest for God in his own way that justifies his own creation. How do parents fill when their children drift away from them within all these I am pouring out my feeling since there is a need for each and every one of us in existence to justify ourselves, to value ourselves, humble ourselves before man and God. For we to show understanding about life, as much as he has created all things bright and beautiful within ugliness, beauty and death. We all find pleasure in one way or another in life, there is always something we want since, it pleases us.

When atheist say God does not exist if he does, he will not allow pain or suffering how then evil did came into our world. Since there is evil, pain and suffering in the world it does not necessarily mean he does not exist. Not even in their own sense do they say likely he does exist but, that he does not exist. If it's a relationship having to do within him and the fallen angels what about us within the presence of evil, pain and suffering what is it about this with them that God does not exist? What do some of us hope to achieve from this? When some people say God does not exist because of this; I might have a feeling, they just jumped down from the sky into this planet or they rose from below the earth and become critics they are new born who are just taking form from the light of which our world is today. Not from centuries ago or from the beginning.

How do you know if somebody is seating next to you and it's as if you are not there could someone seat next to you and it's as if you are not there? They are basis for the philosopher stone the throne of astrologers, mediums yet some believe in the spiritual or spirit world. Religion should not be stigmatized in any way God made us come this far with progress and intelligence e.g. science, technology, engineering look at man going to planet Mars yet, take a real view on the conflicts within men. Nations, business consumers are in a state of confusion.

To those who believe in God in the way he has created things he gives them worthy trust, wisdom to understand things better in the real light. So they can adjust and take things calmly because they do not trust in their own whip but in God. They will wait for God until the grace is given to them by God they might suffer it's to make them even greater, stronger and worthier in a world of beauty, ugliness and death, in a world of the good the bad and the ugly. With God every evil leads to greater good. An outlandish mind cannot understand God not even their fellow human beings. I am not being a critic you need an understanding of other people to understand God while at the same time you need an understanding of God to understand those around you.

Your father likes you he does not know how to explain his ways to you his hands are into lot of things there are family situation like this all around the world. He probably feels in time you will understand him and the things around his back. Hoping, you should do all you can to live your own life amicably regardless if some people will distort him or you from doing the right things.

The illness schizophrenia prevents sufferer from doing the right things they wish to do most cares call it lethargy its more than that paranormal are involved which could lead to paranoias. If care is not taken, phobias, negative speculations, our instincts could sometimes be distorted. Sufferer sense unusual things as well things that could involve the body, mind, soul and the things around them if care is not taken a sufferer can lose each of these bit by bit.

Things people say might mean something heartfelt or less to them or the whole issues bothers them to detail. Their mind is always preoccupied. Sometimes, it might mean the body and mind are no longer a unified whole thoughts, of all kind jumping into a sufferers mind or head. One aspect cares should note is that there consciousness can constantly be or not be in motion. When it's likely they suffer e.g. from back pain, swaying or dizzy spells. Then and only then are they more conscious of themselves. For some of them who tend to be in constant worries, fatigue might sometimes set in. People around them, should not make them feel unusual because it's part of their symptoms I take them all as a spiritual warfare.

Some of us often worry about lots of things we could do little or nothing about it might be it is due to these nature in mental health sufferers are easily triggered to do negative or positive things. Some of us worry ourselves to a state leaving us helpless based on nothing or little we can do anything about. While at the same time putting ourselves together in relation to the symptoms we go through as sufferers bothers us if, a patient brings an issue bothering them to care about worries, fear, uncertainty which probably is affecting them into a state of depression words cannot recount, something should be done about it cares are there to notice such signs. If some of them do not have their bath, wash their teeth in the morning and at night it does not mean they are not worried about being unable to do so. Stigmatizing them might only inflame the situation or drive them more depress looking for way out drinking alcohol, taking more drugs which they then depend on cares know what harm they entail. It does not mean, they do not warry about these things and the harm, loss of dignity its causes them.

These negative things people or cares say about mental health sufferers but in line of care because they have negative inferences thus affect them really. These are people who, experience unusual things and sometimes feel unusual. Seeing a red colored shirt might sometimes mean seeing it as blue but when it comes to relating it to reality it makes them aware something is wrong in their observation at least they might come to realize it's actually a red shirt. Mental health has a lot to do with thought, feeling and emotional processing it could linger on for days, weeks or for months.

In such reverie cares or family members and friends just making them feel good about something positive could means a lot to them it means, you have no problem with them it makes them feel welcome, open to tell you as a care their real problems. Sometimes if you make them feel negative, they withdraw if other contact needs to be made they still feel negative or you are bias. The inference is; they might make body language try to read their body language the tone of their voice when they speak to you.

Pushing for them to understand you might make them feel relax, confident or even open. Address different subjects with them this does not mean you cannot stick to the points you want to definably address. Make them feel there is an important thing you want them to be aware of. Loosen up their mind or thought process it seems we have been drifting from our cares recently it's been calm no suicide or murder in late 2017 to mid-2018 probably because of past incidents of such occurrence.

Their suffering needs to be soothed like dressing a wound because there could be certain areas it hurts it should not be left buried in the minds of sufferers even trying to make them understand what they are going through can help or be comforting to them.

Thought also called thinking the mental **process** in which beings form psychological associations and models of the world. Thinking is manipulating information, as when we form concepts, engage in problem solving, reason and make decisions. **Thought**, the act of thinking produces **thoughts**.

Psychology projections not mind sets.

Mental process or mental functions are all the things that individuals can do with their minds. These include perception, memory, thinking (such as ideation, imagination, belief, reasoning, etc.), volition, and emotion.
Sometimes the term cognitive function is used instead.
A specific instance of engaging in cognitive process is a mental event. The event of perceiving something is different from the entire process, or capacity of perception one's ability to perceive things. In other words, an instance of perceiving is different from the ability that makes those instances possible.

A mental event is anything which happens within the mind or mind substitute of a conscious individual. Examples include thoughts, feelings, decisions, dreams, and realizations.
Some believe that mental events are not limited to human thought but can be associated with animals and artificial intelligence as well. Whether mental events are identical to complex physical events, or whether such an identity even makes sense, is central to the mind-body problem.

Relation to mind-body problem:

Some state that the mental and the physical are the very same property which causes any event(s). This view is known as substance monism. An opposing view is substance dualism which claims that the mental and physical are fundamentally different and can exist independently.
Physicalism, a form of substance monism, states that everything that exists is either physical or depends on that which is physical. The existence of mental events has been used by philosophers as an argument against physicalism. For example, in his 1974 paper *What Is it Like to Be a Bat?*, Thomas Nagel argues that physicalist theories of mind cannot explain an organism's subjective experience because they cannot account for its mental events.

A psychedelic experience (or 'trip') is a temporary altered state of consciousness induced by the consumption of psychedelic drugs (such as mescaline, LSD, psilocybin, and DMT). For example, the term acid trip refers to psychedelic experiences brought on by the use of LSD.
The term 'psychedelic' derives from Greek words meaning 'mind revealing'. Psychedelic experiences are interpreted in exploratory, learning, recreational, religious/mystical and therapeutic contexts.
A psychedelic experience is a temporary altered state of consciousness induced by the consumption of psychedelic drugs (the best known of which are LSD and psilocybin 'magic' mushrooms). The psychedelic altered state of consciousness is commonly characterized as a higher (elevated or transcendent) state relative to ordinary (sober) experience; for example, the psychologist Benny Shanon

observed from ayahuasca trip reports: 'the assessment, very common with ayahuasca, that what is seen and thought during the course of intoxication defines the real, whereas the world that is ordinarily perceived is actually an illusion.'
Similarly, psychologist Stanislav Grof described the LSD experience as: 'complex revelatory insights into the nature of existence... typically accompanied by a sense of certainty that this knowledge is ultimately more relevant and 'real' than the perceptions and beliefs we share in everyday life.'
The philosopher Alan Watts likened psychedelic experiencing to the transformations of consciousness that are undertaken in Taoism and Zen, which he says is, 'more like the correction of faulty perception or the curing of a disease... not an acquisitive process of learning more and more facts or greater and greater skills, but rather an unlearning of wrong habits and opinions.'

The LSD experience was described by Alan Watts as, 'revelations of the secret workings of the brain, of the associative and patterning processes, the ordering systems which carry out all our sensing and thinking.'
The term 'psychedelic' was coined in 1953 by the psychiatrist Humphrey Osmond, during written correspondence with Aldous Huxley. 'Psychedelic' derives from two Ancient Greek words, 'psyche' meaning mind or soul and 'delos' meaning reveal or manifest. The psychedelic experience is said to reveal aspects of the mind that are normally hidden.
The term 'trip' was first coined by US Army scientists during the 50s when they were experimenting with LSD.

Mystical/religious experience:

Psychedelic experience includes the full range of mystical or religious experiential phenomena. Two scientific studies have concluded that psilocybin (a typical psychedelic compound that occurs naturally in psilocybin mushrooms) reliably triggers mystical-type experiences. The more recent study at Johns Hopkins University identified mystical experiences by means of several questionnaires designed to

categorize altered state 'non-ordinary' experiences, including one questionnaire called 'the mysticism scale'.
Furthermore, psychedelic drugs have a long history of religious use across the world; they are often called entheogens because of their propensity to induce these kinds of experiences.
Several modern religions exists today that base their religious activities and beliefs around psychedelic experiencing, such as Santo Daime and the Native American Church. In this context, the psychedelic experience is interpreted as a way of communicating with the realm of spirits or ancestors.

Psychedelic psychotherapy:

Psychedelic therapy refers to therapeutic practices involving the use of psychedelic drugs to facilitate beneficial emotional processing and exploration of the psyche. In contrast to conventional psychiatric medication which is taken by the patient regularly or as-needed, in psychedelic therapy, patients remain in an extended psychotherapy session during the acute activity of the drug and spend the night at the facility. In the sessions with the drug, therapists are nondirective and support the patient in exploring their inner experience. Patients participate in psychotherapy before the drug psychotherapy sessions to prepare them and after the drug psychotherapy to help them integrate their experiences with the drug.

An early practitioner of psychedelic drug based psychiatry was Humphrey Osmond, a British psychiatrist who was responsible for coining the word 'psychedelic' in the first place. Osmond claimed that his own personal use of LSD had helped him to understand the inner mental states of his schizophrenic patients.
Another important practitioner in this field is Stanislav Grof, who pioneered the use of LSD in psychotherapy. Grof characterized psychedelic experiencing as 'non-specific amplification of unconscious mental processes', and he analyzed the phenomenology of the LSD experience (particularly the experience of psychospiritual death and

rebirth) in terms of Otto Rank's theory of the unresolved memory of the primal birth trauma.
The use of psychedelic drugs can allow terminally ill patients (e.g. those with end-stage cancer) to deal with the difficult emotions (fear and anxiety) resulting from their illness. Trials have demonstrated that psychedelic experiencing is capable of causing the pains associated with imminent, unavoidable death to become manageable and understandable; realizing that the passage from life to death is simply another step in living.

An altered state of consciousness (ASC), also called altered state of mind or mind alteration, is any condition which is significantly different from a normal waking state. By 1892, the expression was in use in relation to hypnosis although an ongoing debate about hypnosis as an ASC based on modern definition exists. The next retrievable instance, by Dr. Max Mailhouse from his 1904 presentation to conference, does however, as it was in relation to epilepsy, and is still used today.

In academia, the expression was used as early as 1966 by Arnold M. Ludwig and brought into common usage from 1969 by Charles Tart. It describes induced changes in one's mental state, almost always temporary. A synonymous phrase is 'altered state of awareness'.
There is no general definition of an altered state of consciousness, as any definitional attempt would firstly have to rely on a definition of a normal state of consciousness. Attempts to define the term can however be found in Philosophy, Psychology and Neuroscience. There is no final consensus what the most accurate definition for what purpose is. In the following, the best established and latest definitions are provided:

Arnold M. Ludwig attempted a first definition in 1966.
'An altered state is any mental state(s), induced by various physiological, psychological, or pharmacological maneuvers or agents, which can be recognized subjectively by the individual himself (or by an objective observer of the individual) as representing a sufficient deviation in subjective

experience of psychological functioning from certain general norms for that individual during alert, waking consciousness.' Starting from this Charles Tart focuses his definition on the subjective experience of a state of consciousness and its deviation from a normal waking state.

'Altered states of consciousness are alternate patterns or configurations of experience, which differ qualitatively from a baseline state.'

Farthing's definition of an altered state of consciousness (ASC) is based on Charles Tart's terminology. Charles Tart described an altered state of consciousness as a profound change in the 'overall pattern of subjective experiences'. In order to define an ASC Tart focuses on the importance of subjective experience.

Farthing adds to his definition that an ASC is short-termed or at least reversible and that it might not even be recognized as an ASC at that moment. His definition relies only on subjective experience, leaving aside behavioral changes and physiological response.

'An altered state of consciousness (ASC) may be defined as a temporary change in the overall pattern of subjective experience, such that the individual believes that his or her mental functioning is distinctly different from certain general norms for his or her normal waking state of consciousness'.

He lists fourteen dimensions of changed subjective experience. To account for an ASC multiple dimensions need to be altered.

A recent working definition for empirical research is based on these previous definitions and provided by Schmidt.

Translated from German as a working definition for neuroscientific research, it might suffice to presume that most people have a strong intuition concerning which variability in their everyday wakeful state feels normal to them. This variability of experience is considered as normal fluctuation, while any state that is experienced to diverge significantly from it can be called an ASC. From an experimental perspective, it is also reasonable to compare ASC conditions to a baseline state – a state subjectively judged as average, or normal.

The comparison with a 'normal' baseline requires that the ASC under investigation is of relatively short duration (minutes to hours), which differentiates ASCs from most pathological conditions. Importantly, it has been emphasized that an ASC is not a mere quantitative change in a single cognitive function (e.g. elevated arousal).
Instead, it is a multidimensional phenomenon. Thereby, the relative intensity of multiple consciousness aspects constitutes a 'phenomenological pattern' characterizing a particular state. Such 'patterns' have also been referred to as relative changes in the '(basic) dimensions of consciousness'. For empirical research, such patterns correspond to a multivariate combination of independent 'consciousness factors', which can be quantified via questionnaires.

The 'phenomenological pattern' results from the factor structure of the applied psychometric assessment, i.e. individual ratings, or factor scores, of a questionnaire.
History of utilization of ASCs:

ASCs might have been employed by humans as early as 30,000 years ago. Fields of application were mainly religion and spirituality. Mind-altering plants and/ or excessive dancing were used in order to attain an ecstatic or mystic state. Examples of early religious use are the rites of Dionysos and the Eluisian Mysteries, as well as Yoga and Meditation. To the recent day, followers of various shamanic traditions 'enter altered states of consciousness in order to serve their community'.

One rather speculative theory by McKenna suggests that the use of psychedelic mushrooms in prehistoric times has led to the 'evolution of human language and symbol use'. Furthermore, some theorists argue that mind-altering substances might have pushed the formation of some of the world's main religions (See also: Soma). The book Altering Consciousness (Etzel Cardeña, Michael Winkelman) summarizes multiple of these theories'.

Meditation in its various forms is being rediscovered by modern psychology because of its therapeutic potential and its ability to 'enable the activity of the mind to settle down'. In Psychotherapy techniques like hypnosis, meditation, support psychological processes.
History of the science and theoretical-modelling:
Due to the behaviorist paradigm in psychology altered states of consciousness were dismissed as a field of scientific inquiry during the early 20th century. They were pathologized and merely seen as symptoms of intoxication or demonic possession.

Their return into psychology began with Wiliam James' interest into a variety of altered states such as 'mystical experiences and drug-induced states' James' investigations into first-person subjective experience contributed to the reconsideration of introspection as a valuable research method in the academic community.
The social change of the turbulent 1960s has decisively led to a change of the scientific perspective to the point that introspection as a scientific method and ASCs as valid realms of experience became more widely accepted. Foundations for the research have been laid out by various scientists such as Abraham Maslow, Walter N. Pahnke, Stanislav Grof and Charles Tart. They focused on seemingly beneficial aspects of ASCs such as their potential to 'promote creativity or treat addiction'. Rather oppressive states such as dissociation from trauma were neglected.
The findings of the famous Good Friday Experiment by Pahnke suggest that mystical experiences can be triggered by psilocybin. Later investigations by Rick Doblin found that participants valued those experiences as 'spiritual high points of their lives'. In the midst of the rise of new-age subculture Stanislav Grof and others formed the new field of transpersonal psychology, which emphasized 'the importance of individual human experience, validity of mystical and spiritual experience, interconnectedness of self with others and the world and potential of self-transformation'.

Abraham Maslow's research on peak experiences as, moments of 'highest happiness and fulfillment', further contributed to the depathologization of altered states.
A first summary of the existing literature was carried out by Charles T. Tart in his book *Altered the States of Consciousness*, which led to a more common use of the term. Tart coined the key terms discrete and baseline states of consciousness and thought about a general classification system for ASCs. He also called for 'state specific sciences' in which researchers should do science on ASCs from within such states.

Pharmacological:

An altered state of consciousness may be defined as a short-term change in the general configuration of one's individual experience, such that the rational functioning is clearly altered from one's usual state of consciousness. (Revonsuo, Kallio & Sikka, 2009) There are many ways that one's consciousness can be altered, and drug use is one of them. Psychoactive drugs aid in altering the state of consciousness. Psychoactive drugs can be defined by a chemical substance that passes through the blood and disturbs brain function, causing changes in awareness, attitude, consciousness, and behavior.

Marijuana is a psychoactive drug that is known to alter the state of consciousness. Marijuana alters mental activity, memory, and pain perception. One who is under the influence of marijuana may experience degrees of paranoia, increased sensitivity, and delayed reactions not normal for their usual conscious state.
MDMA (ecstasy) is a drug that also alters one's state of consciousness. The state of consciousness brought about by MDMA ingestion includes a rise in positive feelings and a reduction in negative feelings (Aldridge, D., & Fachner, J. ö. 2005). Users' emotions are increased and inhibitions lowered, often accompanied by a sensation of intimacy or connection with other people.

Opiates are a class of drugs that alter consciousness. Examples of opiates include heroin, morphine, hydrocodone, and oxycodone. Opiates produce analgesia and often feelings of euphoria in users. Opiate abuse may result in decreased production of endorphins in the brain, natural pain relievers whose effects may be heightened by drugs. If one takes a large dose of opiates to compensate for the lack of natural endorphins, the result may be death (Berridge, V. 2001).

Cocaine alters one's state of consciousness. Cocaine affects the neurotransmitters that nerves use to communicate with each other. Cocaine inhibits the reuptake of norepinephrine, serotonin, dopamine, and other neurotransmitters in the synapse, resulting in an altered state of consciousness.
Lysergic acid diethylamide, or LSD, activates serotonin receptors (the amine transmitter of nerve urges) in brain matter. LSD acts on certain serotonin receptors, and its effects are most prominent in the cerebral cortex, an area involved in attitude, thought, and insight, which obtains sensory signs from all parts of the body. LSD's main effects are emotional and psychological. The ingester's feelings may alter quickly through a range from fear to ecstasy. (Humphrey, N. 2001) This may cause one to experience many levels of altered consciousness. Alcohol alters consciousness by shifting levels of neurotransmitters.

Neurotransmitters are endogenous chemicals that transmit signals across a synapse from one neuron (nerve cell) to another 'target' cell (often another neuron). Neurotransmitters can cause inhibitory or excitatory effects on the 'target' cell they are affecting. Alcohol increases the effect of the neurotransmitter GABA (gamma-Aminobutyric acid) in the brain. GABA causes slow actions and inaudible verbal communication that often occur in alcoholics (Berridge, V 2001). Alcohol also decreases the excitatory neurotransmitter glutamate. Suppressing this stimulant results in a similar type of physiological slowdown in addition to increasing the GABA and decreasing the glutamate in the brain, alcohol increases the amount of the chemical dopamine in the brain, which is one of the addictive causes of alcoholism.

Non-pharmacological:

Altered states of consciousness may also be induced by:

- Meditation
- Spiritual experience
- Learning
- Insight
- Understanding
- Emotional development
- Sensitivity training
- Mental development
- Recreational.
-

Emotions influence behavior that alters the state of consciousness. Emotions can be influenced by various stimuli.

Pathologies/other:

Pathological or accidental induction may refer to unforeseen events or illnesses. According to Dr. Jeffrey R. Avner, professor of clinical pediatrics, a crucial element to understanding accidental and pathological causes to altered states of consciousness (ASC) is that it begins with reduced self-awareness followed by reduced awareness in the environment (2006). Those with personal experience of conditions such as Depersonalization often cite the opposite, which is an increased awareness of the environment and the self that results in altered states of consciousness. When the reduction of self-awareness and environmental awareness take effect, they produce altered states of consciousness. The specific conditions below provide clarity on the types of conditions compromise accidental and pathological causes.

Traumatic experience:

The first condition, traumatic experience, is defined as a lesion caused by an external force Trauma. In Merriam-Webster Dictionary online, 2013 examples include impact to the brain caused by blunt force (i.e., a car accident). The reason a traumatic experience causes altered states of consciousness is that it changes how the brain works. The external impact diverts the blood flow from the front of the brain to other areas. The front of the brain is known as the prefrontal cortex responsible for analytical thought (Kunsman, 2012). When the damage becomes uncontrollable, the patient experiences changes in behavior and impaired self-awareness. This is exactly when an ASC is experienced.

Epilepsy:

Another common cause is epilepsy. According to Medlineplus epilepsy can be described as a brain disorder that causes seizures (2013). During the seizure it is said that the patient will experience hallucinations and loss of mental control (Revonsuo, Chaplin, and Wedlund, 2008) causing temporary dissociation from reality. A study that was conducted with six epileptic patients and used the functional magnetic resonance imaging (fMRI) detected how the patients did indeed experience hallucinations while a seizure is occurring (Korsnes M, Hugdahl K, Nygard M, Bjornæs H, 2010). This not only altered the patient's behavioral pattern but also made them dissociate from reality during that particular time frame.

Oxygen deficiency:

The next item of interest is oxygen deficiency, questioning how oxygen deficiency impacts the brain is an important part of comprehending why ASC occurs when there is oxygen deprivation in an environment.

Infections:

In addition to oxygen deprivation or deficiency, infections are a common pathological cause of ASC. A prime example of an infection includes meningitis. The medical website WEBMD states that meningitis is an infection that causes the coverings of the brain to swell. This particular infection occurs in children and young adults. This infection is primarily viral. Viral meningitis causes ASC and its symptoms include fevers and seizures (2010). The Impairment becomes visible the moment seizures begin to occur, this is when the patient enters the altered state of consciousness.

Sleep deprivation:

Sleep deprivation is also associated with ASC, and can provoke seizures due to fatigue. Sleep deprivation can be chronic or short-term depending on the severity of the patient's condition. Many patients report hallucinations because sleep deprivation impacts the brain. An MRI study conducted at Harvard Medical School in 2007, found that a sleep-deprived brain was not capable of being in control of its sensorimotor functions, leading to impairment to the patient's self-awareness. Patients were also prone to be a lot clumsier than if had they not been experiencing sleep deprivation.

Fasting:

Coupled with deprivation of sleep and oxygen, another form of deprivation includes fasting. Fasting can occur because of religious purposes or from psychological conditions such as anorexia. Fasting refers to the ability to willingly refrain from food and possibly drinks as well. Anorexia, as previously mentioned, is psychological disorder in which the patient is irrationally afraid of gaining weight. Therefore, he or she restricts the intake of calories on a daily basis. Anorexia can lead to seizures due to malnutrition (Hockenbury, Don, and Hockenbury, Sandra, 2008). The dissociation caused by fasting is not only life-threatening but it is the reason why extended fasting periods can lead to ASC. Thus, the temporary dissociation from reality allows fasting to fall into the category of an ASC following the definition provided by Dr. Avner (2006).

Psychosis:

Another pathological cause is psychosis, otherwise known as a psychotic episode. In order to comprehend psychosis, it is important to determine what symptoms it implies. Psychotic episodes often include delusions, paranoia, de-realization, depersonalization, and hallucinations (Revonsuo et al., 2008). Studies have not been able to clearly identify when a person is reaching a higher level of risk for a psychotic episode (Schimmelmann, B., Walger, P., & Schultze-Lutter, F., 2013), but the earlier people are treated for psychosis the more likely they are to avoid the devastating consequences which could lead to a psychotic disorder (Schimmelmann, B., Walger, P., & Schultze-Lutter, F., 2013). Unfortunately, there are very few studies which have thoroughly investigated psychotic episodes, and the ability to predict this disorder remains unclear.
Reviewing the previous conditions for accidental and pathological causes, we can come to understand that all of these accidental or pathological causes share the component of reduced self-awareness. Therefore, ASCs cannot only be caused naturally but they can be induced intentionally with methods including hypnosis meditation, amongst others. There are also ASCs which are caused by less recreational purposes; people who utilize illegal substances, or heavy dosages of medications, as well as large amounts of alcohol, can indeed comply with the definition of an ASC (Revonsuo et al., 2008).

Set and setting describes the context for psychoactive and particularly psychedelic drug experiences: one's mindset (shortened to 'set') and the physical and social environment (the setting) in which the user has the experience. This is especially relevant for psychedelic experiences in either a therapeutic or recreational context. The term was coined by Timothy Leary in 1961, and became widely accepted by researchers in psychedelic therapy. Norman Zinberg has also discussed this in Drug, Set, And Setting: The Basis for Controlled Intoxicant Use (1984).

'Set' is the mental state a person brings to the experience, like thoughts, mood and expectations. 'Setting' is the physical and social environment. Social support networks have shown to be particularly important in the outcome of the psychedelic experience. They are able to control or guide the course of the experience, both consciously and subconsciously. Stress, fear, or a disagreeable environment, may result in an unpleasant experience (bad trip). Conversely, a relaxed, curious person in a warm, comfortable and safe place is more likely to have a pleasant experience.

Of course, the drug dose does not produce the transcendent experience. It merely acts as a chemical key it opens the mind, frees the nervous system of its ordinary patterns and structures. The nature of the experience depends almost entirely on set and setting. Set denotes the preparation of the individual, including his personality structure and his mood at the time. Setting is physical the weather, the rooms atmosphere; social feelings of persons present towards one another; and cultural prevailing views as to what is real. It is for this reason that manuals or guide-books are necessary. Their purpose is to enable a person to understand the new realities of the expanded consciousness, to serve as road maps for new interior territories which modern science has made accessible.

Timothy Leary, the Psychedelic Experience: A Manual Based on the Tibetan Book of the Dead.
In 1966, Timothy Leary conducted a series of experiments with dimethyltryptamine (DMT) with controlled set and setting. The aim was to see whether DMT, which had then been mostly thought of as a terror-inducing drug, could produce pleasant experiences under a supportive set and setting. It was found that it could.

Set and setting has also been investigated from a religious perspective.

I also considered:

- Altered state of consciousness
- Counterculture of the 1960s
- Psychedelic psychotherapy

- Responsible drug use
- Sensory deprivation
- Out-of-body experience.

In decision theory and general systems theory, a mindset is a set of assumptions, methods, or notations held by one or more people or groups of people.
A mindset can also be seen as incident of a person's world view or philosophy of life.
A mindset may be so firmly established that it creates a powerful incentive within these people or groups to continue to adopt or accept prior behaviors, choices, or tools. The latter phenomenon is also sometimes described as *mental inertia*, 'groupthink', and it is often difficult to counteract its effects upon analysis and decision making processes.
In cognitive psychology, a mindset represents the cognitive processes activated in response to a given task (French, 2016).

It would appear that some of the earliest empirical explorations of mindset originated in the early 1900s (Gollwitzer 1990, 2012). These studies are identified as foundational to and precursory for the study of cognition (Gollwitzer 1990, 2012). The attention to mindset within the study of cognitive psychology has continued relatively unabated In addition to the field of cognitive psychology, the use of mindset is evident within the social sciences and several other fields (e.g., positive psychology). Interestingly, a characteristic of this area of study, in all its various manifestations, is the fragment use of mindset throughout the academy (e.g. French, 2016).

A well-known example is the 'Cold War mindset' prevalent in both the U.S. and USSR, which included absolute trust in two-player game theory, in the integrity of command chain, in control of nuclear materials, and in the mutual assured destruction of both in the case of war. Although most consider that this mindset usefully served to prevent an attack by either country, the assumptions underlying deterrence theory have made assessments of the efficacy of the Cold War mindset a matter of some controversy.

Most theorists consider that the key responsibility of an embedded power group is to challenge the assumptions that comprise the group's own mindset. According to these commentators, power groups that fail to review or revise their mindsets with sufficient regularity cannot hold power indefinitely, as a single mindset is unlikely to possess the flexibility and adaptability needed to address all future events. For example, the variations in mindset between Democratic Party and Republican Party Presidents in the U.S. may have made that country more able to challenge assumptions than the Kremlin with its more static bureaucracy.

Modern military theory attempts to challenge entrenched mindsets in dealing with asymmetric warfare, terrorism, and the proliferation of weapons of mass destruction. In combination, these threats represent 'a revolution in military affairs' and require very rapid adaptation to new threats and circumstances. In this context, the cost of not implementing adaptive mindsets cannot be afforded.

Naturally, the question regarding the embodiment of a collective mindset comes to mind. Erikson's (1974) analysis of group-identities and what he calls a life-plan seems relevant here. He recounts the example of American Indians, who were meant to undergo a reeducation process meant to imbue a modern 'life-plan' that aimed for a house and a richness expressed by a filled bank account. Erikson writes that the Indians' collective historic identity as buffalo hunters was oriented around such fundamentally different reasons/goals that even communication about the divergent 'life plans' was itself difficult.

There is a double relation between the institution embodying for example an entrepreneurial mindset and its entrepreneurial performance. Firstly, an institution with an entrepreneurial philosophy will set entrepreneurial goals and strategies as a whole, but maybe even more importantly, it will foster an entrepreneurial milieu, allowing each entity to pursue emergent opportunities. In short, philosophical

stance codified in the mind, hence as mindset, lead to a climate that in turn causes values that lead to practice.
Collective mindsets in this sense are described in such works as Hutchin's 'Cognition in the wild' (1995), who analyzes a whole team of naval navigators as the cognitive unit or as computational system, or Senges' Knowledge entrepreneurship in universities (2007). There are also parallels to the emerging field of 'collective intelligence' (e.g. (Zara, 2004)) and exploiting the 'Wisdom of the crowds' (Surowiecki, 2005) of stakeholders. Zara notes that since collective reflection is more explicit, discursive, and conversational, it therefore needs certain good percepts especially when it comes to information and communication technology.

Most historians use the concept of mentality or mindset to denote very slowly changing mental dispositions active over longer periods of time, but occasionally there have been efforts to also apply it to much more rapidly changing historical situations such as the French revolution (Michel Vovelle) or the short period of Allied occupation of Germany after World War II (Hentschel 2007).
As previously alluded to, there is a great deal of variation within the study of mindsets. This variation includes how to define, measure, and conceptualize a mindset as well as the types of mindset identified. Even amongst scholars within the same disciple studying the same mindset, substantial variations exist (French, 2016). Nevertheless, any discussion of mindset should include recognition concerning the numerous, varied, and growing number of mindsets and mindset theories that receive attention in multiple disciplines throughout the academy.

Fixed and growth:

According to Carol Dweck, individuals can be placed on a continuum according to their implicit views of 'where ability comes from'.

Dweck states that there are two categories (growth mindset versus fixed mindset) that can group individuals based on their behavior, specifically their reaction to failure. Those with a 'fixed mindset' believe that abilities are mostly innate and interpret failure as the lack of necessary basic abilities, while those with a 'growth mindset' believe that they can acquire any given ability provided they invest effort or study. Dweck argues that the growth mindset 'will allow a person to live a less stressful and more successful life'.

In a 2012 interview, Dweck defined both fixed and growth mindsets:

In a fixed mindset students believe their basic abilities, their intelligence, their talents, are just fixed traits. They have a certain amount and that's that, and then their goal becomes to look smart all the time and never look dumb. In a growth mindset students understand that their talents and abilities can be developed through effort, good teaching and persistence. They don't necessarily think everyone's the same or anyone can be Einstein, but they believe everyone can get smarter if they work at it.
A large part of Dweck's research on mindsets has been done in the field of education, and how these mindsets affect a student's performance in the classroom. The growth mindset is clearly the more desirable of the two for students. In particular, an individual's mindset impacts how they face and cope with challenges, such as the transition into junior high school from elementary school or losing your job. According to Dweck, individuals with a 'growth' theory are more likely to continue working hard despite setbacks. Individuals' theories of intelligence can be affected by subtle environmental cues. For example, children given praise such as 'good job, you're very smart' are much more likely to develop a fixed mindset, whereas if given compliments like 'good job, you worked very hard' they are likely to develop a growth mindset.

While elements of our personality such as sensitivity to mistakes and setbacks can make us predisposed towards holding a certain mindset, we are able to develop and reshape our mindset through our interactions. In multiple studies, Dweck and her colleagues noted that alterations in mindset could be achieved through 'praising the process

through which success was achieved', 'having [college aged students] read compelling scientific articles that support one view or the other', or teaching junior high school students 'that every time they try hard and learn something new, their brain forms new connections that, over time, make them smarter'. These studies all demonstrate how framing and discussing students' work and effort play a considerable role in the type of mindset students develop and students' conceptions of their own ability.
Carol Dweck and Jo Boaler have done extensive research on the topics of fixed and growth mindset. However, studies on mindset depict results that show that there is a disparity in the fixed and growth mindsets of females and males. In Boaler's Ability and Mathematics: the Mindset Revolution that is Reshaping Education, she notes that fixed mindset beliefs lead to inequalities in education and are a main reason for low achievement and participation amongst minorities and female students. Boaler's research shows that many women feel as though they are neither smart enough nor capable enough to continue in certain subjects, such as STEM areas of academia. Boaler uses Carol Dweck's research showing 'gender differences in mathematics performance only existed among fixed mindset students' (Boaler, 2013).

In addition, there have been tests administered by L.S. Blackwell to see if the fixed mindset of women can be changed to a growth mindset (Boaler, 2013). This is the mindset in which Boaler and Dweck believe people can gain knowledge. Boaler said, 'The key growth mindset message was that effort changes the brain by forming new connections, and that students control this process. The growth mindset intervention halted the students' decline in grades and started the students on a new pathway of improvement and high achievement' (Boaler, 2013). Educational systems focusing on creating a growth mindset environment allows for girls to feel like their intelligence is moldable rather than constant.

Dweck's research and theory of growth and fixed mindsets has been useful in intervention strategies with at risk students, dispelling negative stereotypes in education held by teachers and students, understanding the impacts of self-theories on resilience, and understanding how process praise can foster a growth mindset and positively impact students' motivation levels.

Benefit:

In 2015, Ashley Buchanan proposed a complimentary evolution to the fixed and growth mindset – the benefit mindset.

The benefit mindset describes society's everyday leaders who promote wellbeing on both an individual and a collective level. People who discover their strengths to make valuable contributions to causes that are greater than the self they question why they do what they do, positioning their actions within a purposeful context.
Buchanan argues 'creating cultures of contribution and everyday leadership could be one of the best points of leverage we have for simultaneously bringing out the best in people, organizations and the planet.'
Every so often a truly groundbreaking idea comes along.

This is one. Mindset explains:

- Why brains and talent don't bring success.
- How they can stand in the way of it.
- Why praising brains and talent doesn't foster self-esteem or accomplishment, but jeopardizes them.
- How teaching a simple idea about the brain raises grades and productivity.
- In a fixed mindset, people believe their basic qualities, like their intelligence or talent, are simply fixed traits. They spend their time documenting their intelligence or talent instead of developing them. They also believe that talent alone creates success without effort. They're wrong.
- In a growth mindset, people believe that their most basic abilities can be developed through dedication and hard work brains and talent are just the starting

point. This view creates a love of learning and a resilience that is essential for great accomplishment. Virtually all great people have had these qualities.

Repeatedly bringing awareness to body and breathe can improve mood and relieve stress. Explore mindfulness exercises and tools to help train your attention.

Discover methods of addressing thoughts, emotions and beliefs with exercises through Cognitive Behavioral Therapy.

Beat your inner negativity bias by recognizing and celebrating good things, and watch a pattern of positivity start to form in your life.

The thoughts in our mind, head and the way we feel about things are not always the same or else why do we need to compromise. If you have an open mind you can easily understand other people's feelings or emotions in some ways how negative things occur through such process and why. If you have an open mind with understanding of people without negative bias you are the right person to care for people with mental health issues do not make your patients feel negative or bias but point to them relevance that could help them. Your real feelings as a care means a lot to them if some people could read your leaps others can read your emotion its customary of what parents do to their children do they really need to be spanked. Dealing with mental health issue today might seems difficult it's not the case but very complex.

If you make your patients feel bias they would react, there are always signs to show this taking place some of them who are sure of themselves would seem motionless even open minded those are the once who should not be easily triggered, made to feel like a fool. Some of them can be hard tempered while it's not very easy to correct such circumstances with exuberance but just e.g. reacting open minded as well if they tell lies you can easily spot this out because such people would not speak straight right from their heart or mind.

Patients themselves know about negative things they experience probably every single day its part of their symptoms before they get to you at an appointment, meeting or you visit them at their homes or in social gathering how they are dressed, insight of their homes notice anything unusual some of us have already known through hearing voices while, they were wearing this or that clothing, if they haven't had their bath, if the accommodation looks untidy voices telling them about it.

Could it not often be true cares fail to show concern for sufferers who display positive signs? Care for sufferers who show negative signs at the same time display bias on those who display positive signs. Some of us are in constant augment within ourselves on how we walk, talk, feel, trying each day, to adjust I might be displaying a response towards something at the same time other people are showing their response through my hearing voice on the same topic. Even when am seating down talking to my GP.

How many cares encourage patient with things well noticed which they have done for themselves towards positive health? Sometimes a sufferer might just be going out on his on her own feeling sulky and can easily be termed wondering on the street. For some of us going out to the shops sometimes is wondering encourage patients to see such an experience as going out to take fresh air. Take it that at such times they are partly adjusting to their symptoms.

For some of us, whatever is being said about mental health sufferers after living within two or three different continents might have explanations.

What are the correlations within?
Experience
Explanation and
Compromise
Experience is the knowledge or mastery of an event or subject gained through involvement in or exposure to it. Terms in philosophy such as 'empirical knowledge' or '*a*

posteriori knowledge' are used to refer to knowledge based on experience. A person with considerable experience in a specific field can gain a reputation as an expert. The concept of experience generally refers to know-how or procedural knowledge, rather than propositional knowledge: on-the-job training rather than book-learning.
The interrogation of experience has a long term tradition in continental philosophy. Experience plays an important role in the philosophy of Søren Kierkegaard. The German term *Erfahrung*, often translated into English as 'experience', has a slightly different implication, connoting the coherency of life's experiences.

Certain religious traditions (such as Buddhism, Surat Shabd Yoga, mysticism and Pentecostalism) and educational paradigms with, for example, the conditioning of military recruit-training (also known as 'boot camps'), stress the experiential nature of human epistemology. This stands in contrast to alternatives: traditions of dogma, logic or reasoning. Participants in activities such as tourism, extreme sports and recreational drug-use also tend to stress the importance of experience.

The history of the word experience aligns it closely with the concept of experiment.

An explanation is a set of statements usually constructed to describe a set of facts which clarifies the causes, context, and consequences of those facts. This description of the facts ecetera may establish rules or laws, and may clarify the existing rules and/or laws in relation to any objects, or phenomena examined. The components of an explanation can be implicit, and be interwoven with one another.
An explanation is often underpinned by an understanding or norm that can be represented by different media such as music, text, and graphics. Thus, an explanation is subjected to interpretation, and discussion.
In scientific research, explanation is one of several purposes for empirical research. Explanation is a way to uncover new knowledge, and to report relationships among different aspects of studied phenomena. Explanation attempts to answer the 'why' and 'how' questions. Explanations have

varied explanatory power. The formal hypothesis is the theoretical tool used to verify explanation in empirical research.

To compromise is to make a deal between different parties where each party gives up part of their demand. In arguments, compromise is a concept of finding agreement through communication, through a mutual acceptance of terms often involving variations from an original goal or desires.
Extremism is often considered as antonym to compromise, which, depending on context, may be associated with concepts of balance and tolerance. In the negative connotation, compromise may be referred to as capitulation, referring to a 'surrender' of objectives, principles, or material, in the process of negotiating an agreement. In human relationships, 'compromise' is frequently said to be an agreement with which no party is happy because the parties involved often feel that they either gave away too much or that they received too little.
Why do we need to compromise In short, a psychological solution is the exact answers to the compromise situation where we need support for our resilience to compromise and encouragement to be agreeable. Focusing on getting people to compromise should runs into further difficulties where long standing social biases have existed.

We have to make compromises in our lives because we simply don't live for ourselves. We have our family to look after. In India, people mostly sacrifice their happiness or compromise because they simply don't wish to hurt their parents.

Related Searches for Why do we need to compromise:

Why do we need government?
Why do we need information?
Why do we need water?
Why do we need time?
Why do we need people?
What do we need?

Why do we need food?
Why do we need rules?
Why do we respond to a **concession with another concession reciprocity and compromise** in order to shed light on how **we live, why do we have life, what dose tomorrow hold for us**?

We all know or hear about heartfelt issues it's just that some people like trouble they do not get into trouble but are intrigue when they experience problematic situation. You as a care is the one who chose to do the job you ought to know when the time comes for the unexpected within patients under you care. You should be under premonition of problematic situation when it comes to issues concerning mental health as it could be related to any other thing or a given situation. Very observant of your patients in dealing with them cares who do not have, such tendencies are only doing their own thing regardless of negative issues related to mental health you should keep an open mind and know when to be very prepared. We all have our own private lives your tendency and private life could make a real difference e.g. the way you view life and how watchful you are of the outside world.

Sufferers sometimes find it hard to eat, cloth or to care for themselves you, might know all the good things that is right for you this does not mean you do not have, your own life problems. Relate it to societal issues and you will know why and how to help them. We all view life, behave differently, no wonder in certain cases action speaks louder than voice as life continues we tend to know what is really right for us. You have taken a job in such domain. Some of us do not even care for what matters most we do not know how to say it's not the food, clothing, drugs, alcohol that matters must but something else matters we can feel it but cannot explain it but its inside and part of us. Nobody should be meant to feel this way yet it saddens our hearts, mind and brains every one of us, should want to do well in life. There is nobody who doesn't want to do well in life which has certain recollective negative effect.

Sadness is an emotional pain associated with, or characterized by, feelings of disadvantage, loss, despair, grief, helplessness, disappointment and sorrow. An individual experiencing sadness may become quiet or lethargic, and withdraw themselves from others. An example of severe sadness is depression. Crying can be an indication of sadness.

Sadness is one of the six basic emotions along with happiness, anger, surprise, fear, and disgust.

Nobody should be meant to live under just being sad, feeling regret or anger its one reason we have cares. Finding out the real issues of their problem is very important it can't all be about drugs, anti-social behaviors. Find out what triggers them in a societal context then you can easily work with the government. As a care you should be gifted with initiatives just like any good politician to register what could be the cause of such related issues within your community why should some people get along and some cannot what are the reasons for such failures what is all this taking it out on each other.

You are working with your patients to reach concepts about not only life related issues but also problems related to existence. It's quite an important role you might even need the help of the spiritualist. Cares need to give them inner vision of what lies before them how they can outlive their illness or manage it if not it might all simply be put down to the educational system right from while they were children the educational system has not been doing enough for them but only to those for example who become cares.

Under the pace of educational inclusion at the secondary level, how families organize themselves internally to produce well-being is an unavoidable topic for countries to address when seeking to broaden the effective opportunities of access to, retention in and graduation from the secondary education. Therefore, the construction of a new policy, the adolescent and the young person at school, is an acknowledgement of what is happening in reality and shapes a mutually beneficial alliance between the state and families to generate dynamics where young people can become exclusive recipients of care at least until completion of their secondary schooling. Dropping out means leaving high school, college, university or another group for practical reasons, necessities, or disillusionment with the system from which the individual in question leaves.

We know certain things are expected of life those who cares observe as managing their illness related to mental health issues even slightly positively should be treated with encouragement as doing something interesting, something good has been noticed because as far as I know as a schizophrenia sufferer myself its quite a contentious, contemptuous illness. A sufferer can feel regret, sorrow or sadness for the rest of their life. Sometimes I feel am writing this book under premonition. The most common method to receive premonition visions is by way of your dreams. Our dreams provide us with awareness and understanding in spite of the fact that our conscious mind does as well. These sometimes uncomfortable experiences are frequent vehicles of premonitions, either direct or symbolic, as well as in real dreams. I can understand it's not everything you have to or can explain to people but taking notice or details of things as they occur is good infarct it's a very good quality in any human being.

We all have different views about life what should be and what shouldn't be of what we make out of the world the same thing applies to how the illness affects us what should be, what should not be and if it should be, what could be the cause. Cares have a huge task on their hands they are dealing with humans yet it doesn't seem easy. It's quite a delicate role in a situation not very predictable. Cares should know themselves very well before they put themselves forward as cares for the mentally unwell. So should priests or priestess.

You should have an understanding of origin, background, the family, likes and disliked what could be tolerated and what shouldn't be tolerated what could cause hat, malice or contempt. What cause anger, frustration, sadness or sorrow. I come from both parents who were separated just after I was born as far as the patient is concern both parent have gone their own separate ways having children with two other different opposite sex am all on my own. Cares should have good solid family background profiles you can't be caring for such people while the issues are like flies all around you. As a care on the other hand I might feel the more you can handle such a given situation nicely with understanding and thoroughness I as a patient would be rest assured.

Why are some of us on hard drugs it stimulates us is not fully enough to explain this when correlated with other things. We humans can do better than having hard drugs probably each day. Most of us ought to understand our world is now filled with social diffusion even if some of us do not agree or its viewed with skepticism which should not be the case if we are at the real verge of solving world and social problems. Our world should not be getting bad where negativity is being used to give guidance where dose this lead us to if not more into contrast which could lead us to far more worse outcomes in dealing with e.g. work and health for example those in care and the people who care for them should be aware of these things it does not make neither party happy being part of a negative social outpouring we should rather be faced with grace outpouring.

Those in care are embarrassed at the way care is now being handled cares say they need more money from the government some of us feel we talk about things with our cares they already actually know about. We open avenues for them to see us in the real view which they sometimes keep private to themselves its good having two cares not just one care involved in our care so, we can in retrospect understand where we stand when it comes to such related issues of uncertainty in our care.

In Western Christian theology, grace has been defined, not as a created substance of any kind, but as 'the love and mercy given to us by God because God desires us to have it, not necessarily because of anything we have done to earn it', 'Grace is favor, the free and undeserved help that God gives us to respond to his call to become children of God, adoptive sons, partakers of the divine nature and of eternal

life.' It is understood by Christians to be a spontaneous gift from God to people 'generous, free and totally unexpected and undeserved' that takes the form of divine favor, love, clemency, and a share in the divine life of God.
It is an attribute of God that is most manifest in the salvation of sinners. Christian orthodoxy holds that the initiative in the relationship of grace between God and an individual is always on the side of God.

In Eastern Christianity too, grace is the working of God completely, not a created substance of any kind that can be treated like a commodity.
The question of the means of grace has been called 'the watershed that divides Catholicism from Protestantism, Calvinism from Arminianism, modern [theological] liberalism from [theological] conservatism.' The Catholic Church holds that it is because of the action of Christ and the Holy Spirit in transforming into the divine life what is subjected to God's power that 'the sacraments confer the grace they signify': 'the power of Christ and his Spirit acts in and through [each sacrament], independently of the personal holiness of the minister.
Nevertheless, the fruits of the sacraments also depend on the disposition of the one who receives them.' the Sacred Mysteries (sacraments) are seen as a means of partaking of divine grace because God works through his Church. Catholics, Eastern Orthodox and Protestants agree that faith is a gift from God. Ephesians 2:8; 'For by grace you have been saved through faith, and that not of yourselves; it is the gift of God'. Protestants almost universally believe that grace is given by God based on the faith of the believer. Lutherans hold that the means of grace are 'the gospel in Word and sacraments'.

That the sacraments are means of grace is also the teaching of John Wesley, who described the Eucharist as 'the grand channel whereby the grace of his Spirit was conveyed to the souls of all the children of God'. Calvinists emphasize 'the utter helplessness of people apart from grace.' But God reaches out with 'first grace' or 'prevenient grace'. The Calvinist doctrine known as irresistible grace states that, since all persons are by nature spiritually dead, no one desires to accept this grace until God spiritually enlivens them by means of regeneration. God regenerates only individuals whom he has predestined to salvation.

Arminians understand the grace of God as cooperating with one's free will in order to bring an individual to salvation. According to Evangelical theologian Charles C. Ryrie, modern liberal theology 'gives an exaggerated place to the abilities of people to decide their own fate and to effect their own salvation entirely apart from God's grace.' He writes that theological conservatives maintain God's grace is necessary for salvation is not therefore inevitable that there should be pain and suffering in this world? Let's wait and see as man travels to outer space mission if there would be another form of life out there.

Second, God may be letting evil run its course in order to prove that evil is malignant and that suffering, which is the unfortunate product of evil, is further proof that anything contrary to God's will is bad, harmful, painful, and leads to death. God gave Adam dominion over the world.

The sociological theory of diffusion is the study of the diffusion of innovations throughout social groups and organizations. The topic has seen rapid growth since the 1990s, reflecting curiosity about the process of social change and 'fueled by interest in institutional arguments and in network and dynamic analysis.' The theory uses a case study of the growth of business computing to explain different mechanisms of diffusion.

Infusion is the process of extracting chemical compounds or flavors from plant material in a solvent such as water, oil or alcohol, by allowing the material to remain suspended in the solvent over time (a process often called steeping). An infusion is also the name for the resultant liquid. The process of infusion is distinct from both decoction a method of extraction involving boiling the plant material and percolation, in which water is passed through the material (as in a coffeemaker).

A contrast effect is the enhancement or diminishment, relative to normal, of perception, cognition or related performance as a result of successive (immediately previous) or simultaneous exposure to a stimulus of lesser or greater value in the same dimension. (Here, normal perception, cognition or performance is that which would be obtained in the absence of the comparison stimulus i.e., one based on all previous experience.)

Perception example: A neutral gray target will appear lighter or darker than it does in isolation when immediately preceded by, or simultaneously compared to, respectively, a dark gray or light gray target. Cognition example: A person will appear more or less attractive than that person does in isolation when immediately preceded by, or simultaneously compared to, respectively, a less or more attractive person. Performance example: A laboratory rat will work faster, or slower, during a stimulus predicting a given amount of reward when that stimulus and reward are immediately preceded by, or alternated with, respectively, different stimuli associated with either a lesser or greater amount of reward.
Social contract: An implicit agreement among the members of a society to cooperate for social benefits, for example by sacrificing some individual freedom for state protection. Theories of a social contract became popular in the 16th, 17th, and 18th centuries among theorists such as Thomas Hobbes, John Locke, and Jean-Jacques Rousseau, as a means of explaining the origin of government and the obligations of subjects.

How do I explain this whilst trying to manage my illness I might, eat well within certain two or three day and not eat anything the following day except drink tea on that particular day? It comes as something of a phenomena to me before something of such nature might occur e.g. heavy rainfall, thunderstorm within this, my mood might change probably more of being myself, being certain of myself. My negative moods might become calm as if they are not there anymore but within me the symptoms is there may be just a sensation that it might occur again or it's something that is part of me that would not go away. I do not want to relate this experience to my subconscious because at least not yet I want to be easily understood in my writing.

How do you explain this a care comes into your flat to administer you injection or hand prescriptions over to you after months or years, you begin to feel the care is inside you talking to you or you could hear the cares voice from far away talking to you.

Based on this a sufferer might stay indoors for up to three days without going out at all were they happy during such periods, do they just feel that way without anything bothering them? Most cares hardly shear any sort of attachment with us could this be part of their own doing or ours?

During this period did the sufferer listened to music for a while, tidy up, clean the flat how often did they watch TV during this period of shutting themselves indoors for three days did they at any point, felt relaxed did they sleep much during the day or at night very well if they did not sleep well how did they felt for not being able to sleep well.

Were they just indoors because they did not like the way they felt could it be a protest e.g. we now live in a world where we hardly recognize dignity or that no man should be left to sleep on the street. When situation like this occurs rainfall, sunshine or a tendency to shut oneself indoors what could be the problem, what could be the right solution. If you are a care and you experience this within a patient what should you do? The patient is not being violent or anti-social and had a lot to say to you.

What if the sufferer explains to you the experience comes like an 'Imogi' call it omen if you like shutting once self-indoors might have been because some people make themselves at the disposal of an Imogi to do something a sufferer chooses to be involved in or they do not want to be part of e.g. it's like a voodoo spell please whatever voodoo you want to do to me please do not do it or it occurred on a period a certain sufferer runs rampaged and it's all over the news on radio and on television.

Did the patient mention they go into phase they are someone very powerful Imogi or they are being influence by just an Imogi or Imago.

Related to:
Influence
Human association
Human disposition
Likes and dislike
Peace and love

Now Associate these above with:
Work and play
Human feelings
Psychology
Rituals
Magic
Juju
Voodoo

Now they are generated feelings of an infusion probably may be its one reason we have rainfall and sunshine at the same time because they are the infusion of the Imogi's, of moody weather reflecting moody feelings from the way it rains at the same time as the sun shines.

In some origin it is believed if you were walking and you kicked a stone or pavement as you were walking, your will run into luck. Some mental health issues relates to this e.g. walking with quick steps how do sufferers feel during walking with quick step if they stumble once or twice on the same day? Dose it leave them in a state after such an experience they would run into luck or e.g. become moody when they walk back indoors.

How do human reactions evolve and develop coming from within two different background if your fathers origin feeds on pigs while your mothers background from the same part of the same nation do not feed on pigs your parents separated long time ago. During such times living with your father his other wives and children you had to eat pig flesh after which, later on you had to go and live with your mother within her own origin which doesn't eat pigs?

What kind of juju, rituals is your mother likely to use on you? How do rituals evolve and develop it would have to be a juju which doesn't involve pigs while the worst juju anyone could do for any of your mothers children for example is to have given them dog flesh to eat if your mothers origin doesn't eat dogs.

How do humans respond to something termed as unclean, a myth or attached to religious' beliefs. They have practiced various beliefs' and will still do and they will go on doing so for more centuries to come. In certain attributes as a native of Africa from Nigeria this is where my beliefs originate from with my beliefs in Christ, I need to realize, need answer and to correlate why Africa is widely arrayed as a ritualist ground why and for what reason did God made it that way?

Before and after the time of Christ witchcraft, magic had probably been practiced in Israel, Rome or Jerusalem but Christ came to address us about love, peace, to strengthen our beliefs in God at the same time abide by his will. To live in a world like ours, having love for God our creator in our hearts and mind who can be very dear and comforting in this world of pain and suffering. Bearing in mind at least we have to know where suffering comes from, why we suffer or why we need to address our life with pain or suffering.

Christ healed the sick did miracles to end the suffering of some people even in his teaching how do miracles develop it's because you have been given the grace by God to do miracle or to experience miracle. Now those kind of miracles are not what we seldom use or they occurs through human advancement but now by the grace of God we are experiencing a new life, new ways in the words of God and the teaching of Christ and through human advancement. Some of us feel miracles do no longer occur anymore.

It has changed in its manifestation because humans have moved on. Its wickedness, cruelty, self-centeredness for our own selfish needs that drives us in this present time something needs to be done about. It now needs to change while those who actually believe in God it's the kind of miracle they expect they would receive the modern way will guide them into it to satisfy their needs. Nevertheless we still believe in miracles that they occur but how do we address this in relation to how we live our lives as of today compared to the time and kind of miracles Christ did?

Some kind of food we eat in one part of the world might not be in other parts of the world for some people to see food and eat in a day in some parts of the world is termed as a miracle do you believe this? It's true.

How do humans apply secrets of secrets and crafts of crafts it's through the grace of God based on what it holds or would unfold for the future it will customarily address human ways in different dimensions within the present and future generation in, a way that we feel the grace. They would always feel the presence through which the grace has been given and how it applies to them as they think or reason about the things around them at the same time, the things they think about God. If more and more people become religious' in the right path most of us will think in the right direction, do lots of good things, like to see each other happy, we will care more for each other and so on we will not like to see each other suffer.

We would always believe in God even a wicked mind would want to believe in God but will probably not admit it. How do we save our souls to be under Gods shelter and protection if not through life experience? Each day people from opposite sex are giving birth and raising up children. It's good to believe what God holds in store for you is the best for you continue to find your level as far as you do ṣo and believe or have the feeling God is with you that's how it is.

In Retrospect's:

- How dose mysticism starts.
- The first step is to get hold of your life.
- How do we address life issues in good and hard time?
- Do we wait until it struck us before we react or take action as everything proceeds?
- Within this there is Gods manifestation because he is our author whether we like it or not he is with us then, we are ourselves in the long run, being who we are.
- We all know to some extent why things happen I would take it it's because of different reasons or we would not be who we are or would not be experiencing the things we do which are all part of our own education.
- We often hear that the sky is always the limit mind you, it's for the taking whether you are the good the bad or the ugly.
- This is what our world has turned into.
- Now is a time to consider and take precautions in relations to human ways understand how far our world has over time become complex, what it means and where it might be heading to. Basically this ought to be done by each and every one of us irrespective of who we are where we come from or our status.
- We should take time to consider not leaving our self into worse predicaments.
- The illness schizophrenia in my opinion is a form of predicament bondage but based on life issues. If a sufferer, is to outlive or manage the illness he or she should learn or be in constant motion of taking precautions.
- A care saying this to a sufferer could send shiver or thrill through the nerves or their body it might even 'Stager lee them' out of hard drugs sometimes! Or to think twice or rather than having a fag they feel like eating something.

- It's how to keep this world of ours alive since as we exist, it's a living planet in a way that best buttress what we stand for, what our aims are and the moral duties we are obliged to hold dear to our hearts.

Anyone who could educate you at something is always a star teachers are stars. Those who are creative at something create something in or from their star. Some people could get hold of their star it's not something one could easily get hold off, if gotten hold off it should not be used as a vice or its been granted by a fake Genie you must be very wise, clever and intelligent getting hold of a Genie's worth. Being able to use it wisely, it means you must be very good at heart.

Using mythical or religious object based on vice should not be made easy it could result to having a child with physical disability, epilepsy, suzerain etc. those who get hold of their star not for mythical gain based on material wealth display certain wisdom very unique in a way that they have prolong life, live happy lives regardless of pain or suffering. They could still carry on even if they have time and time again been let down. When mythical or religious objects begin to create positive sensation it means they are working but think of what to do with them if they create negative sensation. It's always good to first of all meditate on it e.g. confronting the object spiritually from your mind. Your mind will tell you if you should keep it or get rid of it. These are the kind of things you can know through people who have mental health issues.

Letting go at an early stage if they emit negative sensation some resultant effect could be getting off lightly with premature birth even at things we do we use religious objects to seek spiritual essence not the once that would use us. Such objects always want what's in the inside. A good religious object for example should spell out the correct timing to our everyday work and play not, the once which would seek our time as it goes by. It should spell a lot about our life experience when we look at them, touch them or reflect on them it should relate to our time of doing anything right not in a way, that it is following us on a negative side of action. Or it might be its being used on us if we are clear about its intentions then it's alright. It's good to consider such things because these days material things use us negatively.

Most people just tend to do things and time just goes by as things occur in their lives they should spells a lot about our life experience within the past, present and what's in the future e.g. related to a time of doing certain things or when certain things had occurred if you come about a religious object reflecting to you in such way, it's good and it confirms or confer to your define or Devine order, lifts you up when you are down, you can communicate with your mind, soul, thoughts, feelings and emotions. Your sub-consciousness unveils you to deep meaning about life.

People who tend to experience such outcome depending if they are letting go or holding on to something now relating this with people suffering from mental health issues by studying its nature, symptoms might help understand mental health, as well as the spiritual world. If a mental health sufferer is walking in the street he or she raises their hand in gesticulation and talk out loud from their mouth to nobody in particular what does it mean?

- How much do we know about spiritual warfare?
- How much do we know about letting go or holding something back
- Why do birds fly?
- How do we relate to anything as unclean what is the meaning and difference of unclean and sin.

How do we know if and when we have been spiritually called upon taking an initiative of the experience to have confronted a spiritual warfare would have been enough. Everyone has got their own personal feelings from which they deduct right, wrong in a way which leads to conformity to their hopes, dreams, and beliefs. We are all bound at one point or another to confirm to something. Why would some of us not easily allow ourselves to be drawn into religion or discus religious topics?

You had been drinking alcohol excessively for a while with efforts at some point you gave it up at the same time, trying not to go back at it but that's when, you walk into a store at this same point in time you were on welfare benefit which had been reduce for reasons beyond your control you were just trying to live up your life to expectation you even took-up drinking Coca-Cola and tea more often that it takes over the need for you, going back in a position where you start drinking alcohol excessively once again.

Then you began hearing voices as if the voice bearers if more than one ware cautioning you not to drink alcohol excessively. If the voice bearers do not want you to drink alcohol would they at the same time make bald remarks, sort of turning your own personal initiative's inside out at least all you could have expected from the voice bearer is well done lad, keep it up, you can spend the money on something else look at that beautiful shirt there buy it instead of alcohol. At this point you might be getting worried you have recently been drinking too much tea and Coca-Cola at this point, were the voice bearers complaining you were drinking too much e.g. Coca-Cola it's good to find out or to be aware of what the voice bearers intentions are.

One thing you could consider is how do voices come to you with the intention that the voice bearers intention is to help you when you are down could it be through suspicious mind, portrayal of understanding, giving reassurance or encouragement for the positive move you make?

It's surprising it's when some sufferers go through complete breakdown which occurs so very often that's when cares turn up. Cares do not have to wait until their mind and body screams. Cares ought to show an initiative of understanding. They should want to rock the world of sufferers they have nothing negative in their own life that causes other people to suffer from mental health issues. This can be used as an experiment on sufferers not lots of us consider such to be the case whenever there is an outburst coming from a patient. If you can rock other people's world it must be at a level of understanding e.g. they understand the things you go through when it comes to mental health. Issue such as these involves most people, organization even the government sending people all around the world for better understanding of such issues.

I know we might not have too much in common, such is life you as a care ought to understand this more than I do some of you are found to be setting the barriers not we. One for the money, two for the base three is for keeping you going so loosen-up or we would be busting each other's lips. Let's talk or discus things this way it should not, get any physical. In my opinion it had always been triggered when things go terribly wrong all over the news. This has been going on for far too long because we are not surprised why we have been drifting apart. Differentiating each other our relationship goes bust sometimes in somewhat unusual times. It must all stop. We need action and the voice to come out un-intimidated base on issues' surrounding us when it comes to mental health. It seems mental health issues are in a vibe to take over the planet not us some of us see ourselves in smoke while others see themselves as if their life is out of luck.

Friday 17th August 2018, E-cigarettes can be key weapon against smoking, say MPs
Rules around e-cigarettes should be relaxed so they can be more widely used and accepted in society, says a report by a committee of MPs.
Vaping is much less harmful than normal cigarettes and e-cigarettes should be made available on prescription to help more people quit smoking, it said.
The report also calls on the government to consider their use in public places.
There is no evidence e-cigarettes are a gateway into smoking for young people, Public Health England said.
The report on e-cigarettes, by the science and technology MPs' committee, said they were too often overlooked by the NHS as a tool to help people stop smoking.
For example, it said it was 'unacceptable' that a third of the 50 NHS mental health trusts in England had a ban on e-

cigarettes on their premises, when there was a 'negligible health risk' from second hand e-cigarette vapours.
What else do the MPs say?

In the report they call for:

- greater freedom for industry to advertise e-cigarettes
- relaxing of regulations and tax duties on e-cigarettes to reflect their relative health benefits
- an annual review of the health effects of e-cigarettes, as well as heat-not-burn products
- a debate on vaping in public spaces
- e-cigarettes licensed as medical devices
- a rethink on limits on refill strengths and tank sizes
- an end to the ban on snus - an oral tobacco product which is illegal in the UK under EU rules

How popular has vaping become?

Around 2.9 million people in the UK are currently using e-cigarettes.

It is estimated that about 470,000 people are using them as an aid to stop smoking and tens of thousands are successfully quitting smoking each year as a result.

- Vaping - the rise in five charts
- E-cigarettes 'should be on prescription'
- Vaping 'can damage vital immune system cells's

Although the report recognized the long-term health effects of vaping were not yet known, it said e-cigarettes were substantially less harmful than conventional cigarettes because they contained no tar or carbon monoxide.
Norman Lamb, chairman of the science and technology committee, said: 'Current policy and regulations do not sufficiently reflect this and businesses, transport providers and public places should stop viewing conventional and e-cigarettes as one and the same.
'There is no public health rationale for doing so,' he said.

'Concerns e-cigarettes could be a gateway to conventional smoking, including for young non-smokers, have not materialised.

'If used correctly, e-cigarettes could be a key weapon in the NHS's stop-smoking arsenal.'
Mr Lamb said medically licensed e-cigarettes 'would make it easier for doctors to discuss and recommend them as a stop-smoking tool to aid those quitting smoking'.
'Stub' it out or puff away? The debate on e-cigarettes:
The report was the latest in a long-running debate about e-cigarettes and their harm.
It comes days after a small study suggested vaping can damage vital immune system cells.
The small experimental study, led by Prof David Thickett, at the University of Birmingham, found it can damage the lungs although further research is needed to better understand the long-term health impact.
A survey in Scotland found young people who use e-cigarettes could be more likely to later smoke tobacco.
And in Wales, concern have been raised about young people using e-cigarettes on a regular basis.
But elsewhere, a six month trial at an Isle of Man jail found allowing inmates to smoke e-cigarettes made them calmer and helped them quit smoking.

Where are you not allowed to vape?

E-cigarettes are not covered by the smoking legislation which bans the use of cigarettes in all enclosed public and work places.

In fact, to encourage smokers to switch to vaping, Public Health England recommends e-cigarettes should not be treated the same as regular cigarettes when it comes to workplaces devising smoking policies.
'Vaping,' the authority said, 'should be made a more convenient as well as safer option'.
But some places have banned vaping.

For example, Transport for London forbids the use of e-cigarettes on all buses and the Underground, including at stations.

Big cinema chains such as Cineworld, Odeon and Empire also ban smoking e-cigarettes anywhere on their premises while most theatres similarly forbid their use.
Most airlines and airports also ban vaping apart from in designated smoking areas.

What is the response to the MPs' report?

Public Health England estimates that e-cigarettes are 95% less harmful than normal cigarettes.
Duncan Selbie, chief executive of PHE, said: 'E-cigarettes are not without harm but are way safer than the harms of tobacco.
'There is no evidence that they are acting as a gateway into smoking for young people.
'We want to see a tobacco-free generation within 10 years and this is within sight.'

The charity Action on Smoking and Health welcomed the report but said it had some concerns over rule changes on advertising, which could mean tobacco companies being allowed to market their e-cigarettes in packs of cigarettes.
George Butterworth, from Cancer Research UK, said any changes to current e-cigarette regulations 'should be aimed at helping smokers to quit whilst preventing young people from starting to use e-cigarettes'.
On the other hand nobody seems to notice all these voice making bald remarks at us which makes us go more into some of our negative symptoms. What I would remind sufferers is that the experience we go through serves more into what we know and should do to get our priorities rights.
Some of these meetings we attend how many of our cares have put us together and say let's get our priorities right do not suffer in silence let people or cares know our feelings wouldn't a remark such as this be very encouraging?
All these times most of us had listened to words of advice to have stayed off drinking alcohol or excessive smoking nobody thought the remarks they make through hearing

voices we should instead play the national lottery instead of drinking or smoking then, go and play the lottery instead of drinking alcohol or smoking and then listen to what the voice bearers say.

This would be part of going through feelings to ascertain if the voice bearer is inside you or outside you. Sometimes being worried of why you hear voices what the voice say if negative of course it makes you feel bad but what are your responses?

Giving up for example smoking it might surprise you; you had begun taking something else to substitute its place e.g. drinking too much tea in a way which seems addictive. Talk to your cares at an early stage if this occurs and do not listen to anybody or voices which say take e-cigarettes or e-pipes as an alternative.

I told one of my cares that it's easy to give up smoking than giving up hard drugs. Hard drugs in my opinion other than cigarettes or tobacco kill the system faster than can be easily realised, faster before you can know how to give it up, your ability to see life in the clear is often blared. I felt hard drugs are more terrible and so do most people who still continue to smoke there is nothing wrong in feeling the same way about e-cigarettes.

Now if am going to give up smoking, I have no intention of taking up any hard drugs to my beliefs I do not see any reason why I should take up e-cigarettes. I should rather be thinking of giving up smoking and drinking alcohol at the same time. At this point in my life, I had stopped drinking alcohol excessively.

Those taking hard drugs do look terrible than most people who smoke while I must emphasize that there are perspectives to these e.g. how you represent yourself how you use, your common sense when it comes to any other related issues in life.

E.g. you cannot confront the fact that hard drugs are taking over your life if cigarettes and tobaccos can do worse as it seems for some of us what would hard drugs do if not make us even far more worse. Or lead us into while we are still yet to know some of the real dangers behind e-cigarettes?
It's good to worry sometimes; it's also good having an understanding of your worries. Worrying too much is not good for you but to live and not worry at all is not good for you because the more it spells who you are, the way you view life, the people around you through worrying you also get to understand yourself even better. If you are worried of not being able to word process but it comes to you to buy and play a piano please do so it might be what is going to trigger you to be good at word processing.

Being diagnosed with paranoid schizophrenia the way I felt and the symptoms I went through if I should say them all out and loud I might not be believed that I went through it all nevertheless, it was through the experiences I wrote my books because I wouldn't let go a lot it stand as a blockade but I showed resilience and a perseverance to move on.
At some point I felt I should hear voices saying one girl wants to have a fuck with you that's if you will give up smoking if you do, she would want to have a fuck with you but our world no longer care for keeping up with morals in such ways. Or that, I hear voices such as take a look at you in your situation there is water for you to bath yourself, there is food and a flat to live in yet you can't eat, you can't sleep well, you smoke, drink excessive alcohol.

You do not know where you stand in life cancer occur as a result of smoking it shortens your life you cannot do all these things yet you continue to smoke and drink too much alcohol what is it that is eating your life out of you? Try to make sense out of things.

We hear and talk about climate change, waste disposal yet you continue to think this way or hear voices in such direction what should be your response? If these are the case, there should be a level of understanding, reason behind it and knowledge to be gained or to be addressed e.g. the need to listen to positive impulse and most

importantly move away from the notion that you are being persecuted or if, all such thoughts, feelings and emotions comes to you count yourself as very lucky.
At certain points in our life its good and necessary comes a time to self-reflect or self-actualize.

Norman Triplett pioneered research on social facilitation in 1898. Triplett found that cyclists had faster race times when in the presence of other cyclists. Triplett theorized that the faster times were because the presence of others made individuals more competitive. Further research led Triplett to theorize that the presence of others increases individuals' performances in other situations as well. Floyd Allport coined the term 'social facilitation' for the first time in 1924.
Floyd Allport, commonly considered the founder of Social Psychology, conducted studies in which participants sat alone, or with other participants, and did a variety of tasks such as word association tasks and multiplication assessments. He found that people performed better when in a group setting than when alone for the majority of tasks. At this time, social facilitation simply meant an 'increase in response merely from the sight or sound of others making the same movement.'

Activation theory:

In 1965, Robert Zajonc proposed the first Activation Theory for social facilitation. Zajonc's Generalized Drive Hypothesis was the first theory that addressed why sometimes the presence of others increases performance, and sometimes the presence of others decreases performance. Zajonc argued that the presence of others serves as a source of arousal, and heightened arousal increases the likelihood of an organism to do well-learned or habitual responses.
For this reason, arousal improves performance on simple (well-learned) tasks, but impairs performance on complex (not well-learned) tasks (see Yerkes-Dodson law). Zajonc's reasoning was based on Yerkes-Dodson's law, which holds that performance works like an inverse 'U' function. This means that an individual's optimal drive is higher for simpler,

or well-practiced tasks and that the same individual's optimal drive is lower for more complex, or less-practiced tasks.
The presence of other people further arouses us and increases our drive level, so if a task is simple, an individual's performance will be enhanced because of the high levels of energy, but performance will be diminished on more complex tasks. Zajonc tested his theories by having people complete word association tasks alone and again in the presence of others.

Zajonc also learned that Social Facilitation was not a phenomenon restricted to human beings, since he found that cockroaches ran through easy mazes faster when other cockroaches were watching them or also running through the maze (coactors), than when the cockroaches ran through the maze alone. However, cockroaches ran slower through hard mazes when there were other cockroaches present or running through it than when they ran through it alone.

Other activation theories include the Alertness Hypothesis, the Monitoring Hypothesis and the Challenge and Threat Hypothesis. The Alertness Hypothesis says that people are uncertain of how observers will act while in the presence of others, so they become more alert (because the performer will be uncertain about how the observers will act in the situation) and the heightened alertness causes them to perform better on tasks.
The Monitoring Hypothesis posits that Social Facilitation effects do not occur when the performer is familiar with the observers or are familiar with the situation, because the performer will know how the observer will act or what the situational factors will do, so the performer's arousal will not increase.

So if the person is unfamiliar with the observers or the situation, he/she will experience uncertainty and arousal will increase, but not if he/she is familiar with them the Challenge and Threat Hypothesis states that people perform worse on complex tasks and better on simple tasks when in the presence of others.

Because of the type of cardio-vascular response to the task when, performing a simple task in the presence of others, people show a normal cardio-vascular response however, when performing a complex task in the presence of others, the cardio-vascular response is similar to that of a person in a threatening position. The normal cardio-vascular response serves to improve performance, but the threat-like cardiovascular response serves to impede performance.

Evaluation approach:

In 1968, Henchy and Glass proposed the first Evaluation Approach to social facilitation. They proposed the Evaluation Apprehension Hypothesis that says it is not the mere presence of others that increases individual activation/arousal, but rather the fear of being evaluated. An extension of the Evaluation Apprehension Hypothesis is the Learned Drive Hypothesis, which states that activation increases, not because of fear of evaluation, but from just the act of being evaluated, or associating evaluation with a certain activity.

Attention theories:

In the 1980s, explanations shifted from Activation Theories to Attention Theories. Activation Theories that explain social facilitation include the Distraction-Conflict Hypothesis, the Overload Hypothesis, the Feedback-Loop Model and the Capacity Model.
In his Distraction-Conflict Hypothesis, Robert Barron proposed that the level of performance on a task is predicted by the amount of distractions in the environment surrounding the task. The hypothesis states that distraction leads to arousal, so the presence of others always impedes performance on difficult tasks, but the number of distractions in the environment either improves or impedes the performance on simple tasks.
The Overload Hypothesis works off of the Distraction-Conflict Hypothesis, saying that distracters do not lead to increased arousal, but rather to cognitive overload, (when an individual is bombarded with excessive information on their

working memory), and while in cognitive overload, individuals will do worse on complex tasks and better on more simple tasks.

Performance increases on simple tasks because the performers focus their attention on the new stimuli, instead of the irrelevant stimuli that is characteristic of simple tasks. Performance decreases on complex tasks because the performers focus on the distracters, but also need to focus on the relevant stimuli that are characteristic of complex tasks, and they cannot handle all of the information they are being presented with.

The Feedback-Loop model postulates that when people feel they are being observed, they focus attention on themselves. While in this state, individuals become aware of the differences between their actual behavior and anticipated behavior. So, by Feedback-Loop Model, people do better in the performance of others because of this increased awareness about their behavior.

The Capacity Model of social facilitation focuses on the role of types of information processing on performance in front of an audience, rather than the performance on different type of tasks (simple or complex) in front of an audience.

The Capacity Model suggests that for tasks that require automatic information processing, the presence of others does not cause problems because the short-term memory is not required for automatic information processing, so performance quality increases. However, for tasks that require controlled information processing, the presence of others does impede the level of performance because the short-term memory is necessary to both focus attention on the audience, as well as the task at hand.

Other theories:

The Self-Presentation Approach argues that individuals want to appear competent in the presence of others. If the task is easy, the individual will want to make him/herself appear even more competent by doing exceptionally well on the task. However, if the task is difficult, they will fear that they will present themselves as incompetent, which will in turn make them embarrassed, and further impede their performance.

Major empirical findings:

In 1969, Zajonc, Heingartner, and Herman demonstrated that social facilitation occurs not only in humans, but also in species with limited or no cognitive processing. They observed that it takes a cockroach a longer time to complete a complex maze in the presence of other cockroaches than when alone.
They also observed that in a simple, straight runway, a cockroach reaches the end of the runway faster in the presence of other cockroaches than when alone. This experiment lends support to the theory that physiological arousal resulting from the presence of others leads to social facilitation effects.

In 1973, Chapman ran an experiment and found that levels of laughter among 7–8-year-old children were highest when two children listened to funny material together (coaction condition). Furthermore, levels of laughter were higher when one child listened to funny material in the presence of another child (audience condition) than when one child listened to the funny material alone (alone condition). These results indicate that laughter is also socially facilitated.
In June 1980, Forgas et al. conducted a field study of audience effects, looking at the performance of expert and novice squash players when observed by no audience, a male audience, and a female audience. Contrary to Zajonc's drive-arousal theory, it was found that novice players performed significantly better when there were audiences than when they were playing without audiences.
In contrast, expert players performed significantly worse when there were audiences than when they were playing without audiences. This indicates that the other factors, such as cognitive variables and players' interpretation of the audience's presence, also influence players' reactions to the presence of an audience in a natural setting.
In 1994, De Castro demonstrated that social facilitation affects food intake by extending the time spent eating a

meal. His results also showed that the presence of family and friends, in comparison with the presence of mere companions, increases food intake to a greater degree, possibly due to the 'release of inhibitory restraints on intake' that occurs when people feel more comfortable around people they are most familiar with.

Furthermore, males ate 36% more food when with other people than when alone, and females ate 40% more food when with other people than when alone. De Castro attributes this to the time-extension model of social facilitation, as the time spent at a meal increased when the meal was a social occasion.

In 2007, Rosenbloom *et al.* studied archival data from Jerusalem in 2004 and found that the presence of an additional person in the car during a driving license test decreased the likelihood that the testee would pass the driving test. Although the nature of the study made it impossible to distinguish one explanation of social facilitation from another, the findings generally support the basic premise of social facilitation theory.

In 2009, Dindo, Whiten, and de Waal studied the effect of social facilitation in capuchin monkeys. The monkeys in this study were required to complete a new foraging task, either alone or in a social group.
While both sets of monkeys completed the task, those in the social group completed it three times faster than those monkeys that were alone. This increase in speed was facilitated through 'observational learning and synchronization of behavior between group mates.'

In 2009, Thompson, Sebastienelli and Murray conducted an experiment to determine the effect of electronic monitoring on students who used web-based training to learn new online search skills.
They found that participants who were explicitly told that their training was being monitored performed markedly worse on a post-training skills test than participants who were unaware that their training was being monitored. These findings adhere to the basic premise of social facilitation and

reveal that the heightened awareness of evaluation on complex tasks significantly hinders performance.

Application:

Social facilitation is a widespread phenomenon in society. Social facilitation is the ability to excel on simple tasks and worse on complex tasks because of the presence of others. Many public tasks demonstrate the effects, both the costs and benefits, of social facilitation.
From taking exams in a high school or college environment to performing in sporting events, people may perform better or fall short depending on the task's complexity. In many experiments, people display signs of social facilitation even in everyday tasks, such as driving - increasing ability when others are present.
This effect can even be seen in animals, as displayed by Zajonc, Heingarter, and Herman's aforementioned study on cockroaches. Businesses can even use social facilitation to their advantage, through placing their employees in evaluated, group situations for simple tasks.
Students can also place themselves in group situations for simple tests to improve their performance, or conversely, sit farther away from other classmates on complex tasks.

Controversies:

Social facilitation's definition and explanations are not without controversy. Social psychologists first debate whether social facilitation in humans can be through mere presence effect, or whether it must be through evaluation. Many psychologists also question whether social facilitation and social loafing, an occurrence in which someone works less when in a group rather than by themselves, should be studied together, rather than separately, because of the overlap of conditions.
One of the greatest controversies surrounding social facilitation is its origination. Psychologists continue to debate whether social facilitation is adopted through the innate biology of humans and animals, social learning through interaction with society or individual interaction with other

people, and not society in general. Further research and expansion of experiments and theories may begin to resolve, or further complicate, these issues.

Conclusion:

Today, there are many different theories about why social facilitation occurs. Norman Tripplett initiated the research on the phenomenon, and many psychologists have followed suit. Despite the large number of theories on the topic, today, most social psychologists agreed that social facilitation were a result of increase arousal, distraction and awareness of evaluation.

As a whole, the study of Social Facilitation has the potential to explain why certain people perform the way that they do. This can be applied to public speakers, sports players, classroom performance, or really any evaluated social situation. Until now, most of the findings have reinforced the original theories that people either perform better on simple tasks and worse on complex tasks when in the presence of other people.

Many studies have also shown that the effects are not limited to humans, but have been displayed in other species like Capuchin primates. As research is becoming more extensive, the theories are starting to be applied to other cultures, adding validity to the theory in that it is not only true for Americans and Europeans.

Related concepts:

Social loafing is the tendency of individuals to slack in a group when work is pooled and individual performance is not being evaluated. A good example of social facilitation is a foot race (where the individual runs faster when there are other runners) as opposed to a group tug-of-war (where the work is pooled, and an individual's lack of performance is hard to notice).

Social Inhibition:

It was Floyd Allport (1920) who first used the term social inhibition, while also studying social facilitation. Social facilitation is the opposite of social inhibition. It is the ability of people to perform better when they have an audience, or when they are in a group. In his paper he talks about how it is the presence of other people that is the cause for both social facilitation and inhibition.
However, he found a vital difference between the two. Social facilitation could be caused in a relatively simple task like running or eating, however social inhibition takes control during relatively difficult tasks like math's or public speaking.
So from this we can say that either response could be invoked depending on the task complexity. After this initial theory came three main theories to describe social facilitation and inhibition and so we would look at all three and what the content of my books have contributed to it.

The Drive Theory:

The first is the drive theory that was put forward by Zajonic (1965). He states that the two responses can be attributed to psychological arousal. There are two parts to this theory. The first part says that the mere presence of other people around you will cause psychological arousal.
This stems from evolutionary factors which apply to all living beings, which mean that the presence of others either presents danger or a chance to reproduce. We cannot help but have this kind of response, however, perhaps these days there are different reasons behind these reactions, and this causes psychological arousal in us.
The second part of this theory is the assumption that this psychological arousal will cause our well-learned response tendencies to become dominant (Hull, 1943), be they to become more confident in what we are doing or to regress and protect ourselves.

This second part also makes sense when you consider that some types of arousal will cause us to narrow our field of focus and this in turn restricts our processing capacity

(Kahneman, 1973). So if our well learned response becomes dominant and that is the only thing we can focus on then that is what shows to the outside world and becomes our normative response to that particular situation (Crisp & Turner, 2007).

The important thing to note about drive theory is that it doesn't say social facilitation or inhibition occurs whether the task at hand is simple or complex but rather that either one will occur depending on the match between our dominant response and the task requirements.

For example, a correct match between these two would be social facilitation going with a task like running. Socially inhibited people often respond incorrectly in that their response to what should be a relatively relaxing time, in a group of friends, is to regress inwardly and remain quiet.

Evaluation Apprehension:

The theory of evaluation apprehension holds with the idea that it is psychological arousal that makes us turn to our well-learned responses. However it does differ from the Drive Theory in that it states that it may not be the mere presence of others that is the trigger of the arousal.

This theory instead claims that it is evaluation apprehension which causes the arousal. Evaluation apprehension is of course the concern that people have of being judged by the people around them and the fear that one may look a fool in front of an audience (Crisp & Turner, 2007). This idea of people clearly being worried about what others may think of them was clearly shown in the Asch Experiment:

As is stated in the video, humans by nature want to fit in with the group and are very aware of what the people around them are feeling. This experiment is a great example of how we will sometimes go completely against what we really think in order to avoid seeming ignorant even in front of people we may not even know.

Cottrell and his colleagues (1968) conducted an experiment in an attempt to show their theory of evaluation apprehension. In this experiment, participants were asked to pronounce out loud nonsense words that appeared on a screen every four seconds.

The participants were split into two groups; one group had to read the words while in front of a blindfolded audience, while the other groups audience was not blindfolded. Now according to drive theory (Zajonic, 1965), the mere presence of an audience would be enough to evoke psychological arousal and cause the participants to revert to the dominant reaction.

However what the evaluation apprehension theory says is that there should be a difference between the groups because one group knows that their audience can see them and judge them and the other group knows that their audience can't. The results of this experiment supported the evaluation apprehension theory.

There was found to be a large difference between the two groups and social facilitation was only found to occur within the group with the non-blindfolded audience. This shows that people need to actually know they are being watched and judged for the effects to be caused instead of just knowing that people are there.

Distraction Conflict:

Evaluation apprehension theory (Cottrell et al, 1968) directly contradicts drive theory's statement of mere presence being the cause of the psychological arousal and in turn social facilitation and inhibition. However evaluation apprehension theory does not explain the social facilitation and inhibition effects seen in animals (Chen, 1937). So one theory accounts for the effects seen in humans and the other can explain the effects in animals but neither can explain both and that is what distraction conflict theory attempts to do.

This theory puts forward the idea that neither mere presence nor evaluation apprehension is the cause of the psychological arousal. Instead it states that a conflict that is created between the tasks at hand and attending to others around you is the cause.

The effect of becoming psychologically aroused when trying to attend to multiple things is an effect that is well established in psychology. So this conflict is created from people first worrying about what they are doing and then worrying about the people around them.

This in turn causes psychological arousal which leads to social facilitation or inhibition. This theory does have great support because of the fact that it is the only theory so far that can explain the effects seen in both humans and animals (Crisp & Turner, 2007).

Therefore because distraction theory is the only theory that can explain both human and animal effects, should we take it as the one true theory or is there room for all the theories in explaining social facilitation and inhibition?

The truth is that there is yet to be any major supporting evidence in favor of distraction conflict theory and so for now it is best to say that the best explanation we can give to the effects seen is that it is sometimes the combination of two of these theories or even all three working together.

These theories are not mutually exclusive and it can be said, for now, that each main point of each theory all play a role in some way or another in making people either socially facilitated or inhibited (Crisp & Turner, 2007).

Changing One's Social Inhibition

Artificial Means:

An extreme lack of social inhibition may be seen as very antisocial, however on the other hand, a high level of inhibition may also create serious personal problems, including an inability to feel or express certain emotions. So everyone has some level of social inhibition, some more than others, but what if we were to take someone who normally has a healthy level of inhibition, and take it away from them? It may be quite difficult to predict their behavior but how might we do this in the first place?

Alcohol is of course the most common method of reducing a person's social inhibition. It has been well proven that alcohol will strip people of their inhibition to varying degrees and this does depend on the person.

Other drugs do have a similar effect but none are more readily available then alcohol and none is more responsible for a large percentage of antisocial behavior in our society. One of the most interesting effects of alcohol influencing a person's inhibition is that sometimes people don't even need the alcohol in the first place in order to change.

The classic 'alcohol: without alcohol' experiment shows how some people just need to think they are drinking or maybe just look like they are drinking in order to begin to change. This type of person already wants a chance to change for whatever reason and a chance to release the feelings inside them but because they are motivated by social norms to act in a certain way, they cannot do this during a normal day, in normal encounters with the people around them.

So they think alcohol is the best way to gain that chance for release and sometimes all they need is the illusion of drinking alcohol, which automatically gives them an excuse to start to act differently.

There are of course substances, such as stimulants, that can have the opposite effect to alcohol and actually strengthen people's inhibition. An abuse of these kinds of drugs can lead to heightened anxiety and inhibition and as a result of these effects have the potential to cause great mental issues for the people taking them and can also add to antisocial behavior in society.

Natural Means

There are more natural and less invasive methods of changing ones inhibition. There are many different methods of doing something like this and it is almost impossible to name them all, so we will just focus on two. The first is to train a person to respond differently to difficult situations.

This will not only show them that there is a different way but also start to train them to use the new response as their dominant one instead of the old response. So if both drive theory and evaluation apprehension theory hold true then when this person becomes psychologically aroused their new response will come into play instead of their old one and they will begin to feel more confident in their behavior.

The other method applies to people who are deeply afraid of being judged. It involves slowly beginning to show these people that those around them are not going to judge them in the way they think that they will be judged. If this were to happen they may begin to see that it is ok to speak up and be heard without being so afraid of the judgement of others.

These methods are of course not as easy as they sound and it does make it easy to understand why people turn to alcohol instead. As has already been stated these two methods are just two examples of many natural ways of changing a person's inhibition that can be used. They have been explored further as they are the most understandable and easy to explain.

Summary:

The list of motivations and reasons people have today to be socially inhibited is still endless, however we may be able to say they all somehow stem from at least one of the three theories discussed above.
For example, most people might say they are shy because they are afraid of being embarrassed which is of course evaluation apprehension. Some people might say they don't have the skills to work around other, this may be seen as drive theory because for these individuals their well learned response is to close up around others which is just what they will do when they become psychologically aroused.
So although these theories may not be motivations to be socially inhibited it is safe to say that the majority of people, who are socially inhibited, are so for some form of personal protection and that is a good motivation and there are of course others.
The best way we have to describe these motivations is with these three theories. When it comes to changing a person, unfortunately it is increasingly hard to do so the older a person becomes due to them becoming stuck in their ways and all their responses becoming so deeply ingrained in their personality. However it is possible, it takes time and effort and above all else, the individual must be willing to change.
According to the *Portland Business Journal*, people skills are described as:

- Understanding ourselves and moderating our responses
- Talking effectively and empathizing accurately
- Building relationships of trust, respect and productive interactions.

A British definition is 'the ability to communicate effectively with people in a friendly way, especially in business.'
The term people skills are used to include both psychological skills and social skills.

History:

Guidelines relating to people skills have been recorded from very early times. Two examples of early human guidelines can be found in the Old Testament. Firstly in Leviticus 19:18 it says: 'Do not seek revenge or bear a grudge against your people, but love your neighbor as yourself' and secondly from Solomon's wisdom in Proverbs 15:1 it says: 'A gentle answer turns away wrath, but a harsh word stirs up anger.' However the Bible also condemns 'flattery' (Psalms 5:9).
Human relations studies became a movement in the 1920s, as companies became more interested in the 'soft skills' and interpersonal skills of employees. In organizations, improving people skills became a specialized role of the corporate trainer. By the mid-1930s, Dale Carnegie popularized people skills in *How to Win Friends & Influence People* and *How to Stop Worrying & Start Living* throughout America and later throughout the world.
In the 1960s, US schools introduced people skills topics and methods—often as a way to promote better self-esteem, communication and social interaction. These encompassed psychologist Thomas Gordon's 'Effectiveness Training' variations as well as many other training programs.
A significant portion of deaths, pain and suffering can be attributed to psychosocial deficits in people skills for stress management and supportive social connection. Business, labor and government authorities should agree that wide-ranging people skills are necessary.
Resilience in psychology refers to the idea of an individual's tendency to cope with stress and adversity. This coping may result in the individual 'bouncing back' to a previous state of normal functioning, or using the experience of exposure to adversity to produce a 'steeling effect' and function better than expected (much like an inoculation gives one the capacity to cope well with future exposure to disease).

Resilience is most commonly understood as a process, and not a trait of an individual.

Recently there has also been evidence that resilience can indicate a capacity to resist a sharp decline in functioning even though a person temporarily appears to get worse. A child, for example, may do poorly during critical life transitions (like entering junior high) but experience problems that are less severe than would be expected given the many risks the child faces.

There is also controversy about the indicators of good psychological and social development when resilience is studied across different cultures and contexts. The American Psychological Association's Task Force on Resilience and Strength in Black Children and Adolescents, for example, notes that there may be special skills that these young people and families have that help them cope, including the ability to resist racial prejudice.

Researchers of indigenous health have shown the impact of culture, history, community values, and geographical settings on resilience in indigenous communities. People who cope may also show 'hidden resilience' when they don't conform to society's expectations for how someone is supposed to behave (in some contexts, aggression may be required to cope, or less emotional engagement may be protective in situations of abuse).

In all these instances, resilience is best understood as a process. It is often mistakenly assumed to be a trait of the individual, an idea more typically referred to as 'resiliency'. Most research now shows that resilience is the result of individuals being able to interact with their environments and the processes that either promote well-being or protect them against the overwhelming influence of risk factors.

These processes can be individual coping strategies, or may be helped along by good families, schools, communities, and social policies that make resilience more likely to occur. In this sense 'resilience' occurs when there are cumulative 'protective factors'. These factors are likely to play a more and more important role the greater the individual's exposure to cumulative 'risk factors'. The phrase 'risk and resilience' in this area of study is quite common.

Commonly used terms related within psychology are 'psychological resilience', 'emotional resilience', 'hardiness', 'resourcefulness', and 'mental toughness'. The earlier focus on individual capacity which is described as the 'invulnerable child' has evolved into a more multilevel ecological perspective that builds on theory developed focus in research has shifted from 'protective factors' toward protective 'processes'; trying to understand how different factors are involved in both promoting well-being and protecting against risk.

Definition of resilience:

Resilience is a dynamic process whereby individuals exhibit positive behavioral adaptation when they encounter significant adversity, trauma, tragedy, threats, or even significant sources of stress. It is different from strengths or developmental assets which are a characteristic of an entire population, regardless of the level of adversity they face.
Under adversity, assets function differently (a good school, or parental monitoring, for example, have a great deal more influence in the life of a child from a poorly resourced background than one from a wealthy home with other options for support, recreation, and self-esteem).
Resilience is a two-dimensional construct concerning the exposure of adversity and the positive adjustment outcomes of that adversity. This two-dimensional construct implies two judgments: one about a 'positive adaptation' and the other about the significance of risk (or adversity). One point of view about adversity could define it as any risks associated with negative life conditions that are statistically related to adjustment difficulties, such as poverty, children of mothers with schizophrenia, or experiences of disasters.
Positive adaptation, on the other hand, is considered in a demonstration of manifested behavior on social competence or success at meeting any particular tasks at a specific life stage, such as the absence of psychiatric distress after the September 11th terrorism attacks on the United States.
Ungar argues that this standard definition of resilience could be problematic because it does not adequately account for

cultural and contextual differences in how people in other systems express resilience.

Through collaborative mixed methods research in eleven countries, Ungar and his colleagues at the Resilience Research Centre have shown that cultural and contextual factors exert a great deal of influence on the factors that affect resilience among a population of youth-at-risk.

Resilience has been shown to be more than just the capacity of individuals to cope well under adversity. Resilience is better understood as the opportunity and capacity of individuals to navigate their way to psychological, social, cultural, and physical resources that may sustain their well-being, and their opportunity and capacity individually and collectively to negotiate for these resources to be provided and experienced in culturally meaningful ways.

Studies of demobilized child soldiers, high school drop-outs, urban poor, immigrant youth, and other populations at risk are showing these patterns. Among adults, these same themes emerge, as detailed in the work of Zautra, Hall and Murray (2010).

History of research on resilience:

Garmezy (1973) published the first research findings on resilience. He used epidemiology, which is the study of who gets ill, who doesn't, and why, to uncover the risks and the protective factors that now help define resilience. Garmezy and Streitman (1974) then created tools to look at systems that support development of resilience.

Emmy Werner (1982) was one of the early scientists to use the term resilience in the 1970s. She studied a cohort of children from Kauai, Hawaii. Kauai was quite poor and many of the children in the study grew up with alcoholic or mentally ill parents. Many of the parents were also out of work.

Werner noted that of the children who grew up in these very bad situations, two-thirds exhibited destructive behaviors in their later teen years, such as chronic unemployment, substance abuse, and out-of-wedlock births (in case of teenage girls).

However one-third of these youngsters did not exhibit destructive behaviors. Werner called the latter group 'resilient'. Resilient children and their families had traits that made them different from non-resilient children and families. Resilience emerged as a major theoretical and research topic from the studies of children of schizophrenic mothers in the 1980s. In Masten's (1989) study, the results showed that children with a schizophrenic parent may not obtain comforting caregiving compared to children with healthy parents, and such situations had an impact on children's development.

However, some children of ill parents thrived well and were competent in academic achievement, and therefore led researchers to make efforts to understand such responses to adversity.

In the onset of the research on resilience, researchers have been devoted to discovering the protective factors that explain people's adaptation to adverse conditions, such as maltreatment, catastrophic life events, or urban poverty. The focus of empirical work then has been shifted to understand the underlying protective processes. Researchers endeavor to uncover how some factors (e.g. family) may contribute to positive outcomes.

Expressions of resilience

Resilience can be described by viewing:

1. Good outcomes regardless of high-risk status
2. Constant competence under stress
3. Recovery from trauma, and
4. Using challenges for growth that makes future hardships more tolerable.

Resilience describes people who are expected to adapt successfully even though they experience risk factors that 'stack the odds' against them experiencing good development. Risk factors are related to poor or negative outcomes. For example, poverty, low socioeconomic status, and mothers with schizophrenia are coupled with lower academic achievement and more emotional or behavioral problems.

Risk factors may be cumulative, carrying additive and exponential risks when they co-occur. When these risk factors happen, according to a study conducted on children, resilient children are capable of resulting in no behavioral problems and developing well. Additionally, they are more active and socially responsive. These positive outcomes are attributed to some protective factors, such as good parenting or positive school experiences.

Resilience is also treated as an effective coping mechanism when people are under stress, such as divorce. In this context, resilience is relevant with sustained competence exhibited by individuals who experience challenging conditions. Most research built on this perspective focuses on the children's response to parents' divorce in terms of gender.

Boys show more conduct problems than do girls; girls obtain more support from mothers and are less exposed to family conflict than boys. Although divorce may have some negative impacts on children's development, it may help children in single households to become more responsible than those in dual-parents households because of helping with chores. Some protective factors attributing to resilient children in single-family, for example, are adults caring for children during or after major stressors (e.g., divorce), or self-efficacy for motivating endeavor at adaptation.

Finally, resilience can be viewed as the phenomenon of recovery from a prolonged or severe adversity, or from an immediate danger or stress. In this case, resilience is not related to vulnerability. People who experience acute trauma, for example, may show extreme anxiety, sleep problems, and intrusive thoughts. Over time, these symptoms decrease and recovery is likely.

This realm of research shows that age and the supportive qualities of the family influence the condition of recovery. The Buffalo Creek dam disaster, for example, had longer effects on older children than on younger. Additionally, children with supportive families show fewer symptoms (e.g., dreams of personal death) than children from troubled families, as revealed by a study on victims of the 1976 Chowchilla bus kidnapping.

Factors related to resilience:

Several factors are found to modify the negative effects of adverse life situations. Many studies show that the primary factor is to have relationships that provide care and support, create love and trust, and offer encouragement, both within and outside the family. Additional factors are also associated with resilience, like the capacity to make realistic plans, having self-confidence and a positive self-image, developing communications skills, and the capacity to manage strong feelings and impulses.

Another protective factor is related to moderating negative effects of environmental hazards or a stressful situation in order to direct vulnerable individuals to optimistic paths, such as external social support.

More specifically, Werner (1995) distinguished three contexts for protective factors: (1) personal attributes, including outgoing, bright, and positive self-concepts; (2) the family, such as having close bonds with at least one family member or an emotionally stable parent; and (3) the community, like receiving support or counsel from peers.

Besides the above distinction on resilience, research has also been devoted to discovering the individual differences in resilience. Self-esteem, ego-control, and ego-resiliency are related to behavioral adaptation. For example, maltreated children who feel good about themselves may process risk situations differently by attributing different reasons to the environments they experience and, thereby, avoid producing negative internalized self-perceptions.

Ego-control is 'the threshold or operating characteristics of an individual with regard to the expression or containment' (Block & Block, 1980, p. 43) of their impulses, feelings, and desires. Ego-resilience refers to 'dynamic capacity ...to modify his or her model level of ego-control, in either direction, as a function of the demand characteristics of the environmental context' (Block & Block, 1980)

Maltreated children, who experienced some risk factors (e.g., single parenting, limited maternal education, or family unemployment) showed lower ego-resilience and

intelligence than non-maltreated children (Cicchetti et al., 1993).
Furthermore, maltreated children are more likely than non-maltreated children to demonstrate disruptive-aggressive, withdraw, and internalized behavior problems (Cicchetti et al., 1993). Finally, ego-resiliency, and positive self-esteem were predictors of competent adaptation in the maltreated children (Cicchetti et al., 1993).

A number of other factors that promote resilience have been identified as:

- The ability to cope with stress effectively and in a healthy manner
- Having good problem-solving skills
- Seeking help
- Holding the belief that there is something one can do to manage your feelings and cope
- Having social support
- Being connected with others, such as family or friends
- Self-disclosure of the trauma to loved ones
- Spirituality
- Having an identity as a survivor as opposed to a victim
- Helping others
- Finding positive meaning in the trauma

Certain aspects of religions/spirituality may, hypothetically, promote or hinder certain psychological virtues that increase resilience. Research has not established connection between spirituality and resilience. According to the 4th edition of Psychology of Religion by Hood, et al., the 'study of positive psychology is a relatively new development...there has not yet been much direct empirical research looking specifically at the association of religion and ordinary strengths and virtues'.

In a review of the literature on the relationship between religiosity/spirituality and PTSD, amongst the significant findings, about half of the studies showed a positive relationship and half showed a negative relationship

between measures of religiosity/spirituality and resilience. The United States Army has received criticism for promoting spirituality in its new [Comprehensive Soldier Fitness] program as a way prevent PTSD, due to the lack of conclusive supporting data.
An emerging field in the study of resilience is the neurobiological basis of resilience to stress. For example, neuropeptide Y (NPY) and 5-Dehydroepiandrosterone (5-DHEA) are thought to limit the stress response by reducing sympathetic nervous system activation and protecting the brain from the potentially harmful effects of chronically elevated cortisol levels respectively. In addition, the relationship between social support and stress resilience is thought to be mediated by the oxytocin system's impact on the hypothalamic-pituitary-adrenal axis.

Resilience building

The American Psychological Association suggests '10 Ways to Build Resilience', which are: (1) maintaining good relationships with close family members, friends and others; (2) to avoid seeing crises or stressful events as unbearable problems; (3) to accept circumstances that cannot be changed; (4) to develop realistic goals and move towards them; (5) to take decisive actions in adverse situations; (6) to look for opportunities of self-discovery after a struggle with loss; (7) developing self-confidence; (8) to keep a long-term perspective and consider the stressful event in a broader context; (9) to maintain a hopeful outlook, expecting good things and visualizing what is wished; (10) to take care of one's mind and body, exercising regularly, paying attention to one's own needs and feelings and engaging in relaxing activities that one enjoys. Learning from the past and maintaining flexibility and balance in life are also cited.
The Young Foundation's work on wellbeing in the UK emphasizes 'subjective wellbeing', what people feel about the quality of their life. A key element of this is 'resilience', how people bounce back from adversity. Their work includes:

- Working with Lord Richard Layard from the London School of Economics and three leading local authorities, Hertfordshire, Manchester and South Tyneside, as the lead partner in the Local Wellbeing Project to look at the different ways in which local government and its local partners can promote wellbeing. The State of Happiness, the final Local Wellbeing Project report, brings together three years of groundbreaking work in the three partner local authority areas as well as other national and international developments in this field.

- Emotional Resilience for Gangs - commissioned by Harrow Metropolitan Police to develop and pilot an emotional resilience programme targeting 14-19 year olds who are offending or at risk of offending, and are associated with gang activity. The Young Foundation is working in collaboration with Dr Ilona Boniwell, one of Europe's leading positive psychologists, to develop this new programme, training professionals in Harrow from Youth Services, the Anti-social Behavior Unit, Safer Neighborhoods' Team and the Wealdstone Anti-social Behavior Partnership. Training of professionals and the delivery of the pilot will take place in early 2011 with a report to follow.

What about Resilience and social programs these are all part of Resilience and social programs.

Children and resilience:

Resilience in children refers to individuals who are doing better than expected, given a history that includes risk or adverse experience. Simply put, resilience requires two conditions to be met: (1) the child must have experienced some sort of risk or adversity that has been linked with poor outcomes, and (2) the child is generally doing okay despite being exposed to that risk or adversity; they are not showing that poor outcome.

One view is that resilience is a description of a group of children. It is not a trait or something that some children 'just

have.' There is no such thing as an 'invulnerable child' who can overcome any obstacle that life throws at her (although some children may seem that way!).
Resilience is not a rare and magical quality. In fact, it is quite common. Resilience is the product of a large number of developmental processes over time that has allowed children who experience some sort of risk to continue to develop competently (while other children have not).
Research on 'protective factors' has helped developmental scientists to understand what matters most for resilient children. Protective factors are characteristics of children or situations that particularly help children in the context of risk. There are many different protective factors that are important for resilient children.

Two that have emerged time and again in studies of resilient children are good cognitive functioning (like cognitive self-regulation and IQ) and positive relationships (especially with competent adults, like parents). Children who have protective factors in their lives tend to do better in some risky contexts when compared to children without protective factors in the same contexts. However, this is not a justification to expose any child to risk. Children do better when not exposed to high levels of risk or adversity.
A separate view is that certain children survive extremely high risk environments, such as a schizophrenic parent, through personal invulnerability—a stubborn resistance to being drawn into a maelstrom of mental illness due to a profound attachment to reality.

When it comes to children, there are still many scientific debates with respect to resilience. One debate involves differing opinions about what constitutes 'doing okay.' There is considerable agreement that child competence can be defined and measured in a way that can indicate whether or not the child is doing well. Called 'age-salient developmental tasks,' these are things that are generally expected of children of a certain age, in a certain culture, of a certain time or point in history.

Developmental tasks can span all areas or domains of a person's life. For example, in many cultures (but certainly not all) 14 month old children are expected to be able to show the beginnings of spoken language, early motor coordination that allows them to start walking, able to form an attachment relationship with a primary caregiver, etc.

These tasks certainly change with age; generally children are expected to show increasingly sophisticated cognitive and social abilities as they grow older: 5 year olds are expected to show a higher degree of independence and self-regulation skills (for example), compared to a 2 year old.
Resilient children can be thought of as those who show competence in age-salient developmental tasks even though they have experienced some risk or adversity that threatened that competence. Others have focused on different criteria for 'doing okay', such as the absence of mental health problems like depression or conduct problems. Still others have focused on happiness or the experience of positive emotions.

Resilience in Transgender Youths:

Transgender youth experience a wide-range of abuse and lack of understanding from the people in their environment and are better off with a high resilience to deal with their lives. A study was done looking at 55 transgender youths studying their sense of personal mastery, perceived social support, emotion-oriented coping and self-esteem.
It was seen that around 50% of the variation in the resilience aspects accounted for the problematic issues of the teens. This means that transgender youths with lower resilience were more prone to mental health issues, including depression and trauma symptoms. Emotion-oriented coping was a strong aspect of resilience in determining how depressed the individuals were.

Building resilience in the classroom:

Resilient children as described by Garmezy as working and playing well and holding high expectations, have often been characterized using constructs such as locus of control, self-esteem, self-efficacy, and autonomy.
Benard concluded that resilient children have high expectations, a meaning for life, goals, personal agency, and inter-personal problem-solving skills. All of these things work together to prevent the debilitating behaviors that are associated with learned helplessness.
Chess identified 'adaptive distancing' as the psychological process whereby an individual can stand apart from distressed family members and friends in order to accomplish constructive goals and advance his or her psychological development.
Moving away to college after high school is a way of practicing adaptive distancing. Classrooms in which students are given an opportunity to respond, an engaging cooperative learning environment, a participating role in setting goals, and a high expectation for. student achievement.

All of these characteristics help students develop a sense of belonging and involvement. These two characteristics help to reduce the feelings of alienation and disengagement. With that kind of connection in the school, students will have more of a protective shield against the adverse circumstances that life throws at them.

The role a community has in fostering resilience in a child:
Communities play a huge role in fostering resilience. Benard identifies three characteristics of those types of communities

(1) availability of social organizations that provide an array of resources to residents, (2) consistent expression of social norms so that community members understand what constitutes desirable behavior, (3) and opportunities for children and youth to participate in the life of the community as valued members.

The clearest sign of a cohesive and supportive community is the presence of social organizations that provide healthy human development. Services are unlikely to be used unless there is good communication concerning them. Community-school relationships are very important to give extra resources to meet even basic psychological needs of students and families.

The role a family has in fostering resilience in a child:

Fostering resilience in children requires family environments that are caring and structured, hold high expectations for children's behavior, and encourage participation in the life of the family. Most resilient children have a strong relationship with at least one adult, not always a parent, and this relationship helps to diminish risk associated with family discord.

Benard found that even though divorce produces stress, the availability of social support from family and community can reduce stress and yield positive outcomes. Any family that emphasizes the value of assigned chores, caring for brothers or sisters, and the contribution of part-time work in supporting the family helps to foster resilience.

The role religion plays in fostering resilience:

The Main Street Missionary Baptist Church prepares to hold service out on Main Street in Biloxi, Miss. Hurricane Katrina caused extensive damage to buildings all along the Mississippi gulf coast and caused the evacuation of New Orleans.

When youths from problem neighborhoods join a church their academic performance improves. The poorer a neighborhoods is, the more church attendance helps kids academically. Improving academic performance seems to flow more from attending church than from merely believing. The church's social life influences youth from poor communities more than doctrine does.

Church attendance also improves the physical, social, and emotional health of students. According to Glen Elder: 'What you have in the role of the religious community is a selected group of people who share values and are committed to the success of the child' this pattern is likely the result of many protective processes that take place inside a religious institution, Ungar and his colleagues identified seven aspects of resilience across many different cultures. Each depends on the other. These seven aspects include:

1. Access to material resources	Availability of financial, educational, medical and employment assistance and/or opportunities, as well as access to food, clothing and shelter
2. Access to supportive relationships	Relationships with significant others, peers and adults within one's family and community
3. Development of a desirable personal identity	Desirable sense of one's self as having a personal and collective sense of purpose, ability for self-appraisal of strengths and weaknesses, aspirations, beliefs and values, including spiritual and religious identification
4. Experiences of power and control	Experiences of caring for one's self and others, the ability to effect change in one's social and physical environment in order to access health resources
5. Adherence to cultural traditions	Adherence to, or knowledge of, one's local and/or global cultural practices, values and beliefs
6. Experiences of social justice	Experiences related to finding a meaningful role in one's community that brings with it acceptance and social equality
7. Experiences of a sense of cohesion with others	Balancing one's personal interests with a sense of responsibility to the greater good; feeling a part of something larger than one's self socially and spiritually.

For example, attending a church has been shown to increase a child's social network, provide a feeling of cohesion and belonging in her community, even promote a sense of personal control and sense of social justice when threatened. It is this complexity and multilevel nature of resilience that explains how people use the internal and external resources (assets) that are both available and accessible to overcome adversity.

Resilience and emotion

Some studies confirmed the association between resilience and positive emotion (e.g., Ong, Bergeman, Bisconti, & Wallace, 2006; Tugade et al., 2004).

Examining the role positive emotion plays in resilience, Ong et al. (2006) found that widows with high levels of resilience experience more positive (e.g., peaceful) and negative (e.g., anxious) emotions than those with low levels. The former group shows high emotional complexity which is the capacity to maintain the differentiation of positive and negative emotional states while underlying stress.

Ong et al. (2006) further suggest that the adaptive consequence of resilience is a function of an increase in emotional complexity while stress is present.

Moreover, high resilient widows showed the likelihood of controlling their positive emotional experiences to recover and bounce back from daily stress. Indeed, positive emotions were found to disrupt the experience of stress and help high resilient individuals to recover efficiently from daily stress (Fredrickson et al., 2003).

In this case, some studies argue (e.g., Fredrickson et al., 2003; Tugade et al., 2004) that positive emotion helps resilient people to construct psychological resources that are necessary for coping successfully with significant catastrophe, such as the September 11th attacks. As a result, positive emotion experienced by resilient people functions as a protective factor to moderate the magnitude of adversity to individuals and assists them to cope well in the future (Tugade et al., 2004).

In addition to the above findings, a study (Fredrickson et al., 2003) further suggests that positive emotions are active elements within resilience.

By examining people's emotional responses to the September 11th, Fredrickson et al. (2003) suggests that positive emotions are critical elements in resilience and as a mediator that buffer people from depression after the crises.
Moreover, high resilient people were more likely to notice positive meanings within the problems they faced (e.g., felt grateful to be alive), endured fewer depressive symptoms, and experienced more positive emotions than low resilient people after terrorism attacks (Fredrickson et al., 2003). Similar results were obtained in another study regarding the effects of 911 attacks on resilient individuals' healthy adjustment (Bonanno et al., 2007).
People with high levels of resilience are likely to show low levels of depression, and less likely to smoke cigarettes or use marijuana (Bonanno et al., 2007). Moreover, low resilient people exhibit the difficulties of regulating negative emotions and demonstrate sensitive reaction to daily stressful life events (e.g., the loss of loved one) (Ong et al., 2006).
They are likely to believe there is no end for the unpleasant experience of daily stressors and may have higher levels of stress. In general, resilient people are believed to possess positive emotions, and such emotions in turn influence their responses to adversity.

Resilient groups:

Psychological Resilience has been studied in a number of groups. Among those are the children of European Jews in the United States, the children of the Vietnamese boat people in the United States. Middle class families in times of the great depression, children of farmers in times of economic crisis, children of Spanish and Vietnamese immigrants in Germany, adoptive children, who went through trauma and malnutrition.

The children of poor Vietnamese parents in the U.S.A. and Germany:

Nathan Caplan studied the children of poor Vietnamese parents in the US. Most of these parents were refugees. In many cases they did not own anything but the clothes they were wearing when they arrived. Most did not speak English. Half of the parents had less than five years of formal schooling. The refugees studied by Caplan lived in the worst neighborhoods of big cities. Yet their children turned out to be academically more successful than American middle class children.

Why?

Caplan *et al.* found out the Vietnamese stress the value of education. Parents wanted their children to enjoy a better education than they did themselves. The Vietnamese children spend an average of 3 hours and 10 minutes per day doing their homework and reading for school, while American middle class students just spend an average of 1 hour and 30 minutes per day with these activities.
Nathan Caplan also found out the older siblings were supposed to help their younger siblings. That way the younger ones did not only learn facts but also attitudes towards school and learning from their older siblings. The more siblings a child of Vietnamese parentage has, the more likely is he or she to achieve in school.
Germany is a multi-ethnic society. 8% of the population and 25% of the 15 year olds are born abroad themselves or have as least one parent born abroad.
In Germany Vietnamese families started arriving as foreign workers during the 1980s and they are still coming in great numbers to search for a better life. As a rule children of immigrants are not as successful academically as children of native Germans.
However it is not true for children of Asian parentage. The Vietnamese are the biggest Asian group in Germany and also one of the poorest ethnic groups. It has been found that Vietnamese parents value education and that Vietnamese students spend a lot more time learning than their German counterparts.

Children of American farmers:

Elder and Conger examined data from several Iowa counties to see how the farm crisis of the 1980s and 1990s affected children growing up in rural parts of the state. They found that a large number of those young people were on paths to successful development and life achievement. Most children of those children grew up to be academically successful and law-abiding.

Elder was able to identify five resource mechanisms:

1. strong intergenerational bonds, joint activity between parents and children
2. being socialized into productive roles in work and social leadership; stressing non-material goals
3. a network of positive engagement in church, school, and community life
4. close ties with grandparents, support from grandparents
5. strong family connections with the community

Children in times of the Great Depression:

Elder studied the life of men who were children during the Great Depression of 1929-1939 and came to maturity at the outset of World War II. When the children came of age Elder found them to be healthy, law abiding, well adapted and bright.
One stunning finding was that poverty had slight positive effects on children from the middle classes, once they reached adulthood those men earned a college degree as often as men from non-deprived middle class homes. In later life they did a little better in terms of economic success than their non-deprived middle class peers.
Men of working class background did not do as well as men from middle class homes. However many of them were upwardly mobile and on most measures they did do just as well as men from never-deprived working class backgrounds.

Depressive Symptoms and Resilience among Pregnant Adolescents:

Pregnancies among adolescents are considered as a complication, as they favor education interruption, poor present and future health, higher rates of poverty, problems for present and future children, among other negative outcomes.

Investigators from the Ecuadorian Catholic University (Universidad Católica de Santiago de Guayaquil) (Guayaquil) and the Spanish University of Zaragoza (Zaragoza), performed a comparative study at the Enrique C. Sotomayor Obstetric and Gynecology Hospital (Guayaquil) assessing resilience differences between pregnant adolescents and adults.

A 56.6% of gravids presented total CESD-10 scores 10 or more indicating depressed mood. Despite this, total CESD-10 scores and depressed mood rate did not differ among studied groups. Adolescents did however display lower resilience reflected by lower total resilience scores and a higher rate of scores below the calculated median. Logistic regression analysis could not establish any risk factor for depressed mood among studied subjects; however, having an adolescent partner and a preterm delivery related to a higher risk for lower resilience.

Spaniards in Germany:

In the 1970s, Spain was a dictatorship under the rule of Francisco Franco. Many Spaniards fled to Germany in search of a better life. Most of those immigrants were poor and only few were able to speak proper German. Today their children do as well as German children when it comes to educational success and Spaniard adults do as well as German adults when it comes to occupational success.
If these are the case there should always be a level and, need to understand and to make reason out not only the need for positive impulses but also positive outcomes.

All these should readily come in mind if am in such a position of drinking or smoking excessively for example making people who care for us understand us. As a care knowing and, understanding what we go through is very important because for some of us, the situation we are in is a dilemma for us we know it and we just need help and encouragement.

My case was so serious a dilemma for me that it was when I had written my books I had to confront myself with what I have written in other to help myself to move on. If cares make patient understand to some extent trying to understand what they are going through they can help them in positive ways to move on further.

It could give some of them the feeling to take up positive initiatives by just simple impulse. It's always a good feeling and comes as a reward for positivity when other people give you the feeling they understand certain things about you it can be touchy to a level that can easily lead to change in positive direction.

It could be worthwhile and can be very helpful another aspect is its good for me to understand my own feelings as well. Some people carry cancer about yet they do not smoke, why should I easily let myself get hold of something that could give me cancer I mean why should I smoke to get myself infested with cancer by smoking or suffer from pancreatic cancer through excessive drinking of alcohol I do not have to wait until I began going through an experience that it is eating through my life before I give them up.

I was going through all these yet I was still a smoker and I drank alcohol excessively. It was when I began writing about my experience on smoking I had what it takes to reduce the amount of tobacco I smoked. There are myths behind smoking.

When you give up smoking you realize you do not go through dizzy spells or swaying which you had sometimes been going through while you were smoking luck could be on your side to give it up completely you might just have to get a grip on yourself and live by our star.

When you are a smoker or an alcoholic you are living through your emotions not your star the alcohol or cigarettes is your star which at the same time eats through you. I put myself through different experiments to see if I can quit smoking e.g. buy my brand of tobacco and keeping it saying to myself am not going to smoke it I mean to see if I can stay without smoking if tobacco is nearby.

And then I adjust myself with the voices I hear based on what they say not all voices are bad you can agree with some of them you can make friends with hearing voices in certain ways, you are going to use it wisely that's if, you are a voice hearer.

I have been hearing voices before 2005 and I still do it won't just go away and I do not know how to stop it. It just comes to me sometimes I had to do what the voices say even if it's to go out and buy tobacco. I have been going through the process in learning how to live with it.

E.g. hoping hearing voice can take the place of smoking or drinking alcohol all three put together might be the causes of my swaying or having dizzy spells there must be ways I can use hearing voices spiritually to stop both smoking and taking alcohol by just listening to voices. It comes easily if you have been putting yourself in perspectives over the years.

For example money you would have used on buying alcohol, tobacco or hard drugs use it in buying yourself a computer or buy yourself a wide screen TV at least showing some interest in it in such perspectives might get you started.

Once in a while cook yourself a nice meal try to dress well we all have our dignity to protect portray yourself as such. Humans are in some ways left to play with their lives we are therefore compelled through impulse or outcomes to make remedies, set goals, achieve goals or to, compromise.

Try to eat well hard drugs, smoking, alcohol prevents one from eating well or sometimes feel good about eating except one is a glutton on the other hand it could make one become a glutton. When it comes to drinking alcohol, smoking or on hard drugs in such case it has been taken for granted and you hardly know, take or consider the prose and cones of using them. It's good to be wise at every step.

Gluttony meaning 'to gulp down or swallow' means over-indulgence and over-consumption of food, drink, or wealth items. In Christianity, it is considered a sin if the excessive desire for food causes it to be withheld from the needy. Some Christian denominations consider gluttony one of the seven deadly sins.

Eat well and try to adjust regardless of the negative outcomes and you might discover a new you by balancing your equation. It's good to do things that make us feel positive.

Callimachus the famous Greek poet states, 'All that I have given to my stomach has disappeared, and I have retained all the fodder that I gave to my spirit.' Popular quote 'Eat to live, not live to eat' is commonly attributed to Socrates.

Consider there are times you do not know what to eat, you do not know how you feel in the future, you could see yourself passing time with your new computer or being able to seat down and watch TV comfortably with full attention.

With simple moves like these, you might find yourself noticing other things around you, you have not given or paid attention to which need, to have been considered e.g. the bathroom, toilet, kitchen, living room. You suddenly find yourself finding time to keep them tidy then you might find time taking a look inside you e.g. your mood, emotion, thoughts and feeling's knowing when they are in disarray and knowing or making details of the best things to do at the right time when it turns up. Recognizing your **emotions**, rather than ignoring them, can help you learn a lot about yourself, we need to pay attention in other to grow positively.

It's true there is nothing left to play around with whiles on welfare payment not eating well and smoking, or drinking alcohol excessively or on hard drug can be dangerous doctors and cares do not need to tell me because I know certain things it dose to me e.g. the way it makes me feel which can be negative.

If you are on the dole your realize those who are working are at an advantage more than you they can buy certain things for themselves or for their children you cannot afford even more expensive things like food, clothing while on welfare payment you have to struggle, worry or become impatient for money you are not working for to come in. You might find yourself waiting for it to come in. This can put some of us in a mood coupled with the hurt of not being able to work. What would it mean if we have bought something we later regret buying?

These explain cares should know what this dose to some of us if, we were to find ways of living positive life regardless of the symptoms we go through. It's all about basically using our initiatives' if we have the mind which we should have and realize we have the mind but coming to such terms might not be easy therefore, what is it cares need to do when it comes to such related topic, probably because there are other things distracting us.

Mind you each day something might turn up that will distract us what should we always do if not to be prepared and to be considerate towards whatever lies before us. These are slightly what cares are there to do because we need help and consideration in such related issues'.

When we go through such experience or undertakings once or twice and we realize what it means to have burnt our carpet or shirt we should know what to think of about our smoking for example it's through such experience positive feelings give rise putting effort on how we rightly feel about what we do. In this case for the better at the end of the day, we would either like or dislike ourselves. The only person you should try to be better than is, the person you were yesterday.

This brings us to a level of spanking ourselves nothing can bring you peace but yourself how do most sufferers feel about their paranoias how do they coup taking note of displaying positive mental attitudes in other to come out of it with positive attributes if you do your homework today it might help you to live well tomorrow, prolong your life, escape hardship and un-necessary hurt.

We are being confronted by this every day of our life using hard drug, smoking and alcohol intake to cover them up yet inside we want to do the right things and live honorably some of us go far as hating ourselves.

It still burgs me like an ancient or medieval fortress or walled town. Why had on my 21st birthday my late father slaughtered a sheep for me with plenty of food, drink to celebrate the occasion before the sheep was slaughtered, he instructed me to place my forehead on top of the live sheep three times?
It's good to go places, meet with other people from different background or culture for what you might expect or experience could mean something to you in the present or in the future. Something relevant to your past experience in a way that would make you move on in life or become stranded in your life's journey.
In the Western part of the world they talk of child abuse, pornography, incest. The meaning to this in relation to my 21st birthday might mean an admonishment 'we do not do such things in Nigeria' There is always something to learn from life's experience considering the experience later on in life it came to me that it was a ritual this, was after my appendicitis was removed.
I go through hallucination sheep's telling me indeed they do not like such occurrence's as incest within the Western hemisphere what did my late father got out of it having to do with sheep's within our African culture if not a chief whip made from sheep's tail which is common within Nigerian chieftaincy title holders.

On the day of my father's chieftaincy title ceremony while he left his private keys with me during the ceremony I remembered going into his living room and bedroom where I had lots of alcohol to drink I notice about two or three of such sheep's whip.

- Why do paranoias occur does it make anyone or a sufferer happy, confused, thoughtless or ignorant?
- Do paranoias have meaning?
- God no longer delight in sacrifice till this very day, why are sacrifice and rituals still relevant to humans.
- Are rituals and sacrifice taking a new form?

My late fathers origin Mid-Western region of Nigeria eat more varieties of fish, prawns, crabs than anywhere else in Nigeria just like the Riverine areas of Okrika, Calabari, and the Ijews few varieties of these e.g. Mackerel fish known as Eja Alarun is transported to my late mothers origin who feed more one sheep's, caws, goats, fowls or snails. All regions prepare their soup in different ways a question that would strike me if am new to rituals is to ask myself if it's through such acts rituals are formed or read.

Mackerel is a common name applied to a number of different species of pelagic fish, mostly, but not exclusively, from the family Scombridae. They are found in both temperate and tropical seas, mostly living along the coast or offshore in the oceanic environment.
Mackerel typically have vertical stripes on their backs and deeply forked tails. Many species are restricted in their distribution ranges, and live in separate populations or fish stocks based on geography. Some stocks migrate in large schools along the coast to suitable spawning grounds, where they spawn in fairly shallow waters. After spawning they return the way they came, in smaller schools, to suitable feeding grounds often near an area of upwelling. From there they may move offshore into deeper waters and spend the winter in relative inactivity. Other stocks migrate across oceans.
Smaller mackerel are forage fish for larger predators, including larger mackerel and Atlantic cod. Flocks of seabirds, as well as whales, dolphins, sharks and schools of larger fish such as tuna and marlin follow mackerel schools and attack them in sophisticated and cooperative ways. Mackerel is high in omega-3 oils and is intensively harvested by humans. In 2009, over five million tons were landed by commercial fishermen. Sport fishermen value the fighting abilities of the king mackerel.

Over 30 different species, principally belonging to the family Scombridae, are commonly referred to as mackerel. The term 'mackerel' means 'marked' or 'spotted', and derives from the Old French maquerel, around 1300, meaning a pimp or procurer. The connection is not altogether clear, but

mackerel spawn enthusiastically in shoals near the coast, and medieval ideas on animal procreation were creative.
I mostly feed on mackerel.

A documentary I watched depicted in France a creature which I would describe looks like a e-goat which climbs and live off a mountain by licking the rocks for mineral salt reminds me of Olumo rock at Abeokuta in Ogun state leading me all the way from within the city of Ibadan to Ori Oke situated on my way to Ile-Ife in Oyo state Nigeria I go through phase both of this mountains derives or sprang a female and a male having something in common.
The Mid-Western Region was a division of Nigeria from 1963 to 1991, from 1976 being known as the Bendel state. It was formed in June 1963 from Benin and Delta provinces of the Western Region, and its capital was Benin City. It was renamed a province in 1966, and in 1967 when the other provinces were split up into several states, it remained territorially intact, becoming a state.
During the Nigerian Civil War, the Biafran forces invaded the new Mid-Western state, en route to Lagos, in an attempt to force a quick end to the war. While under Biafran occupation, the state was declared the 'Republic of Benin'. As Nigerian forces retook the region, the republic collapsed only a day after the declaration when Nigerian troops captured Benin City. In 1976 the state was renamed Bendel. Bendel State was divided into Delta State and Edo State in 1991.

I have been told through hearing voices I should not take to my late fathers ways what strikes me is it's when I do my shaving I feel more like him the same lather in a container, same shaving lather stick to rub the lather on my chin, the same shaving stick and blade I mean the old type I even used Old Spice as he used to do right from when I was a young lad now in some chemist or stores the shaving stick and blade are no longer on sale except one I find the same but still different. I realize, I have been switching from using the old and modern shaving stick or not shave at all.
Whatever triggers this am yet to understand its full meaning or relevance so I kept the old method as a souvenir?

Later going through paranoias my star is above my head I began using electric shaver, as for scissors I told myself it's too risky since I do not want to loose any of my ear lobes or dent any of them claiming it's a mistake I thought precaution is better than cure. So I felt it was best if I use electric shaver but what electric shaver would do a better job than a shaving stick?

Why do humans go through such emotions or tendencies we all have it I suppose but what does it always mean is it part of growing up or understanding something about ourselves and the choice we make out of life's journey.
I later realized electric shaver's makes me smoke more with less temperament to give up smoking why do I have or go through such experience. I ask myself does it have anything to do with climate change while all kinds of shaving forms, gels frequently pops out for sale.

What creates preference in humans is basically to meet with our taste, requirements' but sometimes even trees bend for certain reasons. The old type of shaving stick used by my late father is used for shaving the skin of sheep's to remove its fleece in Nigeria when they are sometimes being slaughtered. I have never seen it done to a cow sometime after I arrived back to the UK my skin which was looking fresh with cluster, shiny, dazzling become less what it was.

- How do we unveil a course or ritual?
- How do we unveil a gifting
- How do we unveil a blessing
- How do we unveil dreams or visions
- How do we customarily become our true self and stop procrastinating.
-

When people hold a post of responsibility they would normally try to be nice or do well in life it shapes their life style, it unveils their true worth it means they hold a commitment to themselves or to other people. It's all part of social care, psychology of caring, hating or liking yourself, showing how good or bad you can be, demonstrating your limits and weak points.

During difficult times we are trying to overcome something do we often call upon our supernatural self it can be simply put down as consulting our conscience or consciousness as we meditate along such line we discover or address a new part of us that we never thought of as part of us and later on consider if, it co-exist or not with it.
Do you find yourself meditating why is it, it's your own situation or predicaments other people use in driving cars no different from when you go out on the street do you notice it's your body language, some car drivers use in driving their cars you notice this when you get to a junction or crossing the road. How do we these days see ourselves as a driving force in saving lives? How do we see ourselves as not putting ourselves in a position to be used customary we all go through endeavors covering various paradigms religion teaches us to go into heaven instead of going into hell?
There is no doubt this will steer us in the face till the end of time no matter how our world continue to being complex if science, technology or engineering can prove anything as to why our world continue to be a troubled place since they produce an advantage to some of the things which prevents we humans from crying and some of the things we fall in love with. Religion is not as simple as it looks it needs your full spiritual attention. I did not began to do well at school in my youth until, I really became religious.

Religion should come up with more ways on how we have or can use the past to shape the present it will produce clear vision as well as insight. Holding on to our past is a good thing how would it seem if we tend to behave foolishly or confuse our past with our future. How would we know what direction to head towards its good to show infarct demonstrate our gifting's in a way that would make us thick. Whatever direction we have been heading a time will always come knowing if we are right or wrong this is as long as truth prevails.

In which ever predicament you are in put your faith in God religion is now being used as an excuse for us to do our own thing ironically it's more a time when each of us feel we should not be misunderstood it's a good sign! No matter how

foolish, hypocritical a situation seems we are meant to learn something from it that's if we are not more in the line of being judgmental.
Foolishness and wisdom need to co-exist that a deduction be made put meaning into our journey of life. Believing in God puts us in a position of being open minded is this true or false, should I stick to my own religion and not listen to other religion, make them look foolish what role is science playing or holds on this matter.

We should join hands and be united not disenfranchise each other we are all in a journey to know and understand God and to be accepted by God. We should be pleasing each other at the same time be pleasing God or have we since time began just been splitting ourselves these are questions we should at this present time be asking ourselves.
How can some people believe in God they cannot tell you anything good about yourself? It's good to be complimented what does this mean in the business world of today, what does it mean in science how do we compliment ourselves on behalf of our spiritual life I guess we don't we look towards God for compliments.

We all wrestle with the difficult age-old questions, 'Why do the wicked prosper?' and 'Why do the righteous suffer?' It is especially hard when you have done right and you get penalized, while the guy who did wrong got ahead. You were praying and counting on God's promises, but things did not turn out the way you had expected. It seems as if God did not even hear your prayers. But the guy who scoffs at God is doing great. You begin to wonder, 'Why follow God when all I get is trials? If there is a God of justice in heaven, why doesn't He do something about all the injustice in the world? Is it worth it to follow the Lord?'

- Why doesn't truth prevails it prevails as far as we have pursued it
- Bear it in mind that you did not create yourself or your life
- Why do some of us have an opinion having too much respect for other people is not all that good

- Probably because we realize that we sometimes get hurt doing so
- Why could some people make you feel, you are good for nothing
- Then it's worth it to follow the Lord?'

Experience is an important aspect in every life we are all different, we think differently no one person is the same as the other why did God made us this way and what are we meant to learn from it?
When other people treat you wrongly or badly I mean very badly it is said we should not over react or be offended instead still treat them rightly or turn the other cheek this makes more sense, if we have given thought into considering and understanding the difference between Gods own leadership and human leadership, and the difference of looking for your own in heaven or looking for your own on this earth.

When other people treat you wrongly do not over react in ways that lessen your morals treat them rightly instead in reality, they are the once loosing their morals there must be something you will understand more about life through the experience if you live to see the next day or more years to come then you might likely understand masquerade's e.g. Okumagba juju at Warri Delta state and Eyo Masquerade held in Lagos state.

- Masquerades reflect omens all masquerades do
- Rituals and their omens
- Why do we have different sense of smell?
- It's when some of us notice odors in cloths that's when we feel it's dirty for other people its stains.
- Why do we have different opinions what sort of nature or circumstance brings this about.

Some juju, voodoo or magic caries smells or odors they will all do till the end of time magic caries stains what gives rise to social consciousness what could give the human souls uplifting, What can vibrate the human soul, what can really

keep it alive, define and true to itself or purpose, what is the human soul in relation to humility.
In religious, philosophical, and mythological traditions, there is a belief in the incorporeal essence of a living being called the soul.

Soul or psyche (Ancient Greek: 'to breathe') are the mental abilities of a living being: reason, character, feeling, consciousness, memory, perception, thinking, etc.
Depending on the philosophical system, a soul can either be mortal or immortal. In Judeo-Christianity, only human beings have immortal souls (although immortality is disputed within Judaism and may have been influenced by Plato). For example, the Catholic theologian Thomas Aquinas attributed 'soul' to all organisms but argued that only human souls are immortal.

Other religions (most notably Hinduism and Jainism) hold that all living things from the smallest bacterium to the largest of mammals are the souls themselves and have their physical representative (the body) in the world. The actual self is the soul, while the body is only a mechanism to experience the karma of that life i.e. if we see a tiger then there is a self-conscious identity residing in it (the soul), and a physical representative (the whole body of tiger which is observable) in the world.

Some teach that even non-biological entities (such as rivers and mountains) possess souls. This belief is called animism.
Greek philosophers, such as Socrates, Plato, and Aristotle, understood that the soul must have a logical faculty, the exercise of which was the most divine of human actions. At his defense trial, Socrates even summarized his teaching as nothing other than an exhortation for his fellow Athenians to excel in matters of the psyche since all bodily goods are dependent on such excellence.
God is the concept of a 'world soul' connecting all living organisms on planet Earth.

What can captivate the human soul, consciousness more in our world of today when so much have been centered to captivate the body all this while. What is elegance if not for portraying charismas' how can one divulge into the charisma's of his or her own soul?

- By being creative is one
- Not being too sensitive if we can help it
- Taking life easy at our own pace
-

While it's good to learn how to let go sometimes it might unveil more pressing matters on how over time, our world has become more complex behind which, there will always be new revelations based on this what is deceit when there is my lord said to my lord and there is hanger, there is pain and there is suffering. Who can see food and not eat.

What does it now mean when it seems we are looking for the world meanest rulers based on the way things are moving. When it comes to governance I hope, our world would not turn into a place for a group of people who want to rule the world heaven, I hope will intercede now, no leader should want to carry such blame. We should also contribute to not leaving our world in the hands of the world meanest leader another sorts of Adolf Hitler. This is the road it could head to if care is not taken.

Because of airplanes people all around the world could move around the world at its onset the effect is, it has done much good, created a sense of awareness within humans, enlightenment. We understand each other more through air travels within continents we have also educated each other more now our world is in a complex state so much talk and business are falling apart some business want to dominate other business through rivalries and rule the world through a notorious leader. It seems some parts of the world want to regroup themselves for such reason.

Some of us still find ourselves smoking our lives away, drinking excessive alcohol either on hard drugs or we are being put on E-pipes or E-cigarettes to generate fiber optics in the past its landlines but we now we use mobile phone instead of telephone connected to landline. Landline causes excessive drinking of alcohol. Air liners are creating a fix; internet providers are charging those on low income more they fill the pinch.

It's a difficult time for the poor yet the right time to test their faith to observe how they behave and interact within each other and for what good if we are no good to God who else can we be good to. The Holy Bible did not waver it says serve your master it's when you serve them it would contribute for you to serve him and appreciate him more.
Human development and advancement which has brought huge and positive impact in human lives should not be used against themselves while some people still want to depend on class or to set up a class so much evil, is surfacing the world needs considerate people at this hour. Am not born with hatred or wickedness in me it's what life has done to me and has turned me into that's what is wrong with me.
What if Britain remains or leaves the EU what are the correlations of what would be coming for us. For other groups its earth wind and fire 'Ain't no stopping us now'.
'Ain't No Stoppin' Us Now' is a 1979 disco song performed by R&B duo McFadden & Whitehead, from their debut album *McFadden & Whitehead*. They wrote and produced the song along with keyboard player Jerry Cohen. Released as the lead single from the album, the song spent a week at number one on the R&B singles chart.

It also proved to be a successful crossover hit, peaking at number 13 on the *Billboard* Hot 100, and reached number 5 in the UK. The single also made it to number 10 on the disco charts. It eventually went double platinum, selling over 2 million copies.

'Ain't No Stopping' Us Now' is about succeeding despite having faced previous disadvantages ('so many things that held us down'). It was widely interpreted to be about the experience of the African American community, and after attaining popularity, became referred to as 'the new black national anthem

Ain't No Stoppin' Us Now' was played at the 2008 Democratic National Convention on the night Barack Obama accepted the Democratic Party nomination for President of the United States.

Thieves flown into UK from Chile for burglaries 2018
A criminal gang which was flying burglars from Chile into the UK to target wealthy homes in the South East has been dismantled, police have said.
Luxury items worth more than £1m were stolen by the thieves, who targeted hundreds of homes, then shipped some of the goods out of the country.

Police disrupted the gang by tracking vehicles used in several burglaries.
The Met has arrested 36 men in the past eight months, while another 39 have been held by other forces.
The investigation, known as Operation Genie, started following a spate of burglaries in south-west London and Surrey in 2017.

Handbags, jewellery and watches

Detectives tracked vehicles used by the suspects and found burglars would normally commit offences within a week of flying into the country.
The gang carefully selected the homes they targeted, picking properties which were often empty and on the edges of parks or golf courses.
The burglars would climb into the first floor using low roofs or garden furniture, avoiding alarms on the ground floor and then take items including designer clothes, handbags, jewellery and watches.
Of the men held in London, 16 have been convicted of burglary-related offences, and of the remaining 20, eight have been deported.
Twelve of the others left the UK after being released under investigation.
Other suspects were also held in Hertfordshire, Surrey and Sussex.
Det Insp Tim Court, who co-ordinated the investigation, said offenders had ‘come to London with the intention of carrying out burglaries’.

'I would like to thank the Chilean Embassy, which has provided a great deal of support in helping to identify the people responsible for these crimes,' he added.

But this shouldn't be happening Scallop row: French police pledge more boats to keep peace 29th September 2018.

France has said it is ready to send more police boats to its north coast to prevent further clashes between French and British fishermen over scallops.

Authorities said they would increase the police presence 'if necessary' to prevent a repeat of clashes in which boats collided and stones were thrown.

French fishermen sent nearly 40 boats to confront UK rivals they accuse of depleting scallop stocks off Normandy.

But Environment Secretary Michael Gove said UK boats were fishing legally.

Local official Ingrid Parrot said the situation had been 'extremely tense' and both sides had thrown objects at each other.

She defended sending just one boat to police the incident overnight on Monday, saying: 'The aim was to stop the tensions from increasing. We sent only one ship that day, but we will send more if it's necessary.'

Mike Park, chief executive of the Scottish White Fish Producers Association, said the incident was 'high seas piracy' but said the French had agreed to a request for talks.

'We need to decrease tensions in the whole area,' he told the BBC's Victoria Derbyshire programme.

The European Commission urged France and Britain to find an 'amicable' solution.

What exactly happened?

The French boats gathered overnight on Monday in protest against so-called 'pillaging' by five larger British vessels.

The British were chased away with two boats, Golden Promise and Joanna C, returning to Brixham harbour with damaged windows.

The crews alleged they had been surrounded and had rocks and metal shackles thrown at them, but French police said UK boats responded in kind.

A video published by French media shows a Scottish scallop dredger, the Honeybourne 3, colliding with French vessels.
Why has it all blown up now?
Tension has rumbled for 15 years, but in the past five a deal has prevailed - larger British boats stayed out of the area in exchange for more fishing rights.
British boats can gather scallops year-round, but French law restricts the scallop fishing season to between 1 October and 15 May.

Marc Delahaye from the Normandy fishing committee said they also objected to the British using 'great dredgers' in the area, while the French used smaller boats.
The UK scallop industry is worth £120m and supports 1,350 jobs. About 60% of the catch is exported - with much of it being bought by the French.

But a 2016 report by the International Council for the Exploration of the Sea (ICES) warned that the fishing effort by France, the UK, Belgium and Ireland in the Bay of Seine was 'too high'.

How have the British responded?

Environment Secretary Michael Gove said the government was talking to French authorities to ensure there was 'no repeat' of the clashes.
He told the BBC his heart went out to the British fishermen involved, who had 'absolutely every right to be fishing in those waters'.
The French had a 'legal responsibility' to ensure their territorial waters were 'appropriately policed' to allow legal fishing to continue, he added.
Prime Minister Theresa May called for an 'amicable solution' to the row.
'It's what we want and it's what France wants and we will be working on that,' she said.
Mr Park rejected suggestions that British boats were overfishing the area.

They catch just 6% of the scallops in the area, he said, so 'if there's any accusation of over fishing it's not on the UK fishermen, it's on the French fishermen.'
'Scallops are plentiful and they're expensive,' he said. 'We're doing nothing wrong and what we can't do is be bullied.'
Sheryll Murray, MP for South East Cornwall, said environment secretary Michael Gove has assured her 'appropriate measures' are in place to enable UK fishermen to keep working.
But she questioned whether French authorities were 'turning a blind eye' while their fishermen 'took the law into their own hands'.

Local French officials said they could not intervene directly because the conflict took place in international waters.
How is it being reported in France?

By BBC Monitoring

French media have framed the scallop showdown as a 'battle' between two nations, with some outlets highlighting the future impact of Brexit.
Under the headline 'The battle for Saint-Jacques scallops off Normandy', left-wing daily Le Monde cited fishing chief Dimitri Rogoff who said that the UK would normally 'be considered a third country and will not have access to these [fishing] zones' after it leaves the European Union.
French fishermen are nevertheless worried by Brexit 'as Britain plans to pursue its own fishing policy starting from the end of March 2019, particularly regarding access to its territorial waters of boats from EU countries' noted weekly magazine L'Usine Nouvelle.
Popular regional newspaper Ouest-France said that sailors from Normandy 'insist that they respect the [fish] resources' and had gone to sea 'to explain this to the English'.
'We have won a battle, but we haven't won the war,' concluded one French fisherman in a report by public TV channel France 3.

In view of all these and Britain leaving the EU I do not know which of it will put a smile on us upon all these years of tackling illegal cigarettes and alcoholic drinks entering the

UK. In my opinion you can only get along with a true Irish man if you have not eaten from the devils seed or taken an oat from the devil though I have not been to Northern Ireland I observe Northern Ireland and its people as a religious site.
A vote has been carried out to either stay or leave the EU the people have made their vote to leave it is obvious the nature of the outcome of the vote would have demonstrate certain outcome mostly pleasing by the majority of the people if we remain in the EU or leave from what is happening in my own experience now is money given to me as a gift I find it difficult to spend. Hoping to live only on my welfare payments at the same time demonstrating the will of going back to work so that, I can spend my own earned money.

This might be considered as paranoia but sometimes we do things to believe in our self or our beliefs lots of people might think of things they would do with lottery money if they win. I hope to win £10.000 or £15.000 so that I can publish my books at the same time promote them believing if this becomes possible it's through the grace of God that, God called me into it for a special reason as I have said, at certain times in our lives we do things to believe not only in ourselves but also in God. A child might do this to believe in their parents, brothers or sisters or a friend.
Belief is the state of mind in which a person thinks something to be the case with or without there being empirical evidence to prove that something is the case with factual certainty. Another way of defining belief sees it as a mental representation of an attitude positively oriented towards the likelihood of something being true. In the context of Ancient Greek thought, two related concepts were identified with regards to the concept of belief: pistis and doxa. Simplified, we may say that pistis refers to 'trust' and 'confidence', while doxa refers to 'opinion' and 'acceptance'. The English word 'orthodoxy' derives from doxa. Jonathan Leicester suggests that belief has the purpose of guiding action rather than indicating truth.

For some of us we would want everything to go on well with whatever business leaders say e.g. if we are not working

probably for a long time at the same time claiming welfare benefit.
But an outcome in the future is what we have seen above that's not only all business leaders would have or want more power to control the government or even threaten the government and make a disgraces of themselves in Brussels. Our chance is to demonstrate how sufficient the United Kingdom is. This is the best chance we can have if Britain leaves the EU to be more self-sufficient and less dependent. Businesses would have more control over consumers you can't sue them within the UK you are going to Brussels.

From what I imagine cases we listen to in the radio or TV about lawsuits. Some of us need to understand the measures and difficulties people go through in some case with a loss at the same time un-wellness to bring them forward. Theresa May is conservative what would a conservative in the peoples interest after casting such a vote do?
And here is a labour leader how many employees do we have in the UK and how many business leaders do we, have. From the look of the applications it should not lead to political and social fragmentation. We have been going on, on how, the government should assist those who are working it might even push some of us who are unwell back to work. How satisfied are consumers recently with the goods and service provided by businesses, how happy and enjoyable has it been for those who have been working now it's about business leaders.

To me one of the key interests of the European Union is how it would lead to third world leaders, nations and its people to see themselves in the real view. We need some very solid diplomacy to demonstrate what a leader should be a capacity, to safeguard its people interest hold it dear to their heart and implement.
If businesses have more say than the government what would be the predicaments of the consumers? It seem the world might be going into chaos more small business are springing up they feel they need to receive more from big businesses or are trying to take over from big business it

might all seem a documentation for them if chaos broke out or they have money to find their way out may be to the moon.

We all have at one point heard about keeping our head straight a lot has been said about schizophrenia it seems to have died down recently we are behind sucking our tombs based on what is going on. For those of us who can hardly manage the illness it's about keeping our head straight from a point of losing it. Our worst nightmare is a dilemma of being unable to keep our head straight.

Through the outcome of the peoples vote they might have perceived certain negative outcome if the UK remains within the EU through the Brexit negotiation businesses, politicians would not much talk about them. Since entering the 21st century our world has been much pressurized mistakes should not be made in addressing our predicaments. All of us wants to be problem solvers is what, I would expect, some of us or groups would not like to be left behind or to be taken for granted or lose out whether the UK leaves or join the EU. There are fears a war might broke out the only excuse now is businesses, trade through which we might in the future be dividing ourselves going back to what can be complicated. We have put up much effort to arrest or adjust in the favor of what we believe in or stand for.

From where I stand and could make out of it, it seems likely am being made to be aware of much into what had caused the second world war that people like me would have been unware of as if, I have not been given the real facts.

Efforts have been made in advancement in trade, businesses, science, technology and engineering it would be more of the delicate parts fitting together that would make things, our life more rewarding. From what it seems we are not yet appreciative of what we have achieved or we would know exactly where we stand, where to put further efforts to justify human existence this also applies to our mind, soul, thoughts, feeling and emotions. For example if you are living off welfare benefit in this present time what are the reaction you get from other people especially dose who are working this will also shape the future.

Abortion pill can be taken at home in England, under new plan. 25 August 2018 Women in England will be allowed to take an early abortion pill at home, under a government plan due to take effect by the end of the year.

Currently, women ending a pregnancy in its first 10 weeks must take two pills at a clinic, 24 to 48 hours apart.
Under the new plans, which will bring England into line with Scotland and Wales, the second pill can be taken at home.
This avoids the risk of women miscarrying while on the journey home.
The chief medical officer said the move would increase choice for women, and ensures they received 'safe and dignified care'.
Legalising the home use of misoprostol was also welcomed by leading gynaecologists.
What is a medical abortion?
Official government figures show that each year around 180,000 abortions are carried out in England, with medical abortions the most common way of ending an unwanted pregnancy.
Medical abortion involves taking two types of tablet.
The first, mifepristone, stops the hormone that allows the pregnancy to continue working.
The second, misoprostol, is normally taken 24 to 48 hours later, and encourages the womb to contract to pass the pregnancy.

After four to six hours, the lining of the womb breaks down, causing bleeding and loss of the pregnancy.
The Department of Health said the change would come into force by the end of 2018.
It said it would work closely with doctors to develop clinical guidance for all professionals to follow when providing the abortion pill to patients.
Four in five terminations are early medical abortions, carried out before 10 weeks gestation, so the majority of women seeking abortions will now have the option for home-use.
They will still be free to choose to take the second abortion pill in a clinic if they wish.
Women wanting an early abortion will be given the usual checks under the Abortion Act - although this does not apply

in Northern Ireland where the law is much stricter than the rest of the UK and terminations are all but outlawed.
Abortion pill online sales 'increasing in Britain'.

By Chi Chi Izundu Victoria Derbyshire programme reporter
15 February 2017 the number of abortion pills being bought online in Britain is increasing, data shown to the Victoria Derbyshire programme suggests.
Government figures show 375 doses, sent to addresses in England, Wales, and Scotland, were seized in 2016, compared with just five in 2013.
Taking the pills while pregnant without medical approval is illegal in the UK.

The British Pregnancy Advisory Service said as awareness of the online pills increased, more women were using them.
The figures, from the Medicines and Healthcare products Regulatory Agency (MHRA) - which regulates medicines in the UK - show there were 375 pills seized last year, up from 270 in 2015 and 180 in 2014.
The seizures were made during the MHRA's annual week-long raids, known as Operation Pangea, at places like postal hubs where foreign post is kept before being distributed to local post offices.

Prison punishments

NHS abortion treatment is free and widely available in Britain, but remains mostly illegal in Northern Ireland.
However, the UK currently has the harshest punishment for self-induced abortion of any country in Europe, bar the Republic of Ireland.
Under the Offences Against the Person Act 1861, anyone taking the pills could, in theory, be punished with a life sentence - no matter what the gestational period.
Goats 'drawn to happy human faces'29 August 2018:
Scientists have found that goats are drawn to humans with happy facial expressions.
The result suggests a wider range of animals can read people's moods than was previously thought.

The team showed goats pairs of photos of the same person, one of them featuring an angry expression, and the other a happy demeanour.

The goats in the study made a beeline for the happy faces, the researchers report in the journal Open Science.
The result implies that the ability of animals to perceive human facial cues is not limited to those with a long history of working as human companions, such as dogs and horses.
Instead, it seems, animals domesticated for food production, such as goats, can also decipher human facial cues.
The study was carried out at the Buttercups Sanctuary for Goats in Kent, UK.
Co-author Dr Alan McElligott, from Queen Mary, University of London, and colleagues set up pairs of black-and-white photos about 1.3m apart on one wall in their test area.
Then, a goat would be let loose to explore the set-up.
Doe eyes

The researchers found that the goats strongly preferred the smiling faces, approaching the happy faces before acknowledging the angry photos. They also spent more time examining the smiling faces with their snouts.
But the effect was only significant when the happy-faced photo was placed on the right-hand side.
When the happy photos were placed on the left, the goats showed no significant preference either way.
The researchers think this is because the goats are using one side of their brain to process the information - something that's seen in other animals.
It could either be that the left side of the brain processes positive emotions, or that the right side of the brain is involved in avoidance of angry faces.
Dr McElligott, who is now based at the University of Roehampton, said: 'The study has important implications for how we interact with livestock and other species, because the abilities of animals to perceive human emotions might be widespread and not just limited to pets.'
Co-author Natalia Albuquerque, from the University of Sao Paulo, Brazil, said: 'The study of emotion perception has already shown very complex abilities in dogs and horses.

'However, to date, there was no evidence that animals such as goats were capable of reading human facial expressions. Our results open new paths to understanding the emotional lives of all domestic animals.'
The study could also have implications for animal welfare, helping change perceptions of these livestock animals by highlighting their sentience.
Dinosaur DNA clues unpicked by researchers at University of Kent 26 August 2018
British scientists say they have pieced together what dinosaur DNA looks like.

Researchers at the University of Kent say their work uncovers the genetic secret behind why dinosaurs came in such a variety of shapes and sizes.
This variation helped the creatures evolve quickly in response to a changing environment - helping them to dominate Earth for 180 million years.
But the researchers behind the DNA work say they have no plans to recreate dinosaurs, Jurassic Park style.
Of course, there was one final challenge the dinosaurs could not overcome - a massive asteroid impact 66 million years ago that wiped out all dinosaur groups.

Recently, Prof Darren Griffin's team used mathematical techniques to identify the possible genetic characteristics of the very first dinosaurs. They did this by working backwards from their closest modern-day relatives - birds and turtles.
Their results suggest that dinosaur DNA was probably organised into many chunks - called chromosomes. Birds usually have about 80 chromosomes - about three times the number humans possess.
It is notable that birds are among the most varied animal groups on Earth. If, as Prof Griffin thinks, dinosaurs also had a large number of chromosomes it might explain why they too came in such a range of shapes and sizes.

'We think it generates variation. Having a lot of chromosomes enables dinosaurs to shuffle their genes around much more than other types of animals. This shuffling means that dinosaurs can evolve more quickly and so help them survive so long as the planet changed,' Prof Griffin said.

Dr Rebecca O'Connor, from the University of Kent, said: 'The fossil evidence and now our evidence reinforce the idea that rather than birds and dinosaurs being distant relatives, they are one in the same. The birds around us today are dinosaurs.'

As for hopes that we might be able capture ancient dinosaur DNA from fossils, that looks doubtful.

Genetic material degrades over time, and the world record for the survival of ancient DNA is one million years. Dinosaurs lived between 66 and 245 million years ago.

However, the techniques being used by Prof Griffin and his colleagues may lead to an even more detailed understanding of what dinosaur DNA was like.

But this won't in itself allow us to recreate dinosaurs.

'We are not going to have Jurassic Park anytime soon,' according to Prof Griffin.

'If you take the DNA of a chicken and put it into an ostrich egg you won't end up with a chicken or an ostrich. You will end up with nothing. The same would be true of a velociraptor or a *T. rex*. It just wouldn't work'.

Galileo: Brexit funds released for sat-nav study 28 August 2018

UK ministers are setting aside £92m to study the feasibility of building a sovereign satellite-navigation system.

The new network would be an alternative to the Europe Union's Galileo project, in which Britain looks set to lose key roles as a result of Brexit.

The UK Space Agency will lead the technical assessment.

Officials will engage British industry to spec a potential design, its engineering requirements, schedule and likely cost.

The first contracts for this study work could be issued as early as October.

The UKSA expects the assessment to take about a year and a half.

Ministers could then decide if they really want to proceed with a venture that will have a price tag in the billions.

- Why is there a row about Galileo?
- Brexit: Key dates and potential hurdles
- EC seeks to boost space spending

Seeking a deal

London and Brussels are still negotiating Britain's future participation in Galileo.

The parties are currently in dispute over the UK's access, and industrial contribution, to the system's Public Regulated Service (PRS) beyond March of next year.
PRS is a special navigation and timing signal intended for use by government agencies, the armed forces and emergency responders. Expected to come online in 2020, it is designed to be available and robust even in times of crisis. Brussels says London cannot immediately have access to PRS when the UK leaves the European bloc because it will become a foreign entity. London says PRS is vital to its military and security interests and warns that if it cannot use and work on the signal then it will walk away from Galileo in its entirety.
The Prime Minister Theresa May, presently on a tour of Africa, told the BBC it was, 'not an idle threat to achieve our negotiating objectives'. The UK did not want to be simply an 'end user' and needed full access to Galileo if it was to continue to contribute to the system, she added.

- A project of the European Commission and the European Space Agency
- 24 satellites constitute a full system but it will have six spares in orbit also
- 26 spacecraft are in orbit today; the figure of 30 is likely to be reached in 2021
- Original budget was 3bn euros but will now cost more than three times that
- Works alongside the US GPS, Chinese Beidou and Russian Glonass systems
- Promises eventual real-time positioning down to a metre or less

'Best of British'

The UK as an EU member state has so far invested £1.2bn in Galileo, helping to build the satellites, to operate them in orbit, and to define important aspects of the system's encryption, including for PRS itself.
'Due to the European Commission post-Brexit rules imposed on UK companies, Airbus Defence and Space Ltd was not able to compete for the Galileo work we had undertaken for over the last decade,' Colin Paynter, MD of Airbus DS in the UK, said.
'We therefore very much welcome the UK Space Agency's announcement today which we believe will allow Airbus along with other affected UK companies to bring together an alliance of the Best of British to produce innovative solutions for a possible future UK navigation system.'
Analysis - Could the UK go it alone?
Few people doubt Britain is capable of developing its own satellite-navigation system. But the task would not be straight-forward.

Here are just four issues that will need to be addressed before ministers can sign off on such a major project:

COST: The initial estimate given for a sovereign system when first mooted was put in the region of £3bn-5bn. But major space infrastructure projects have a history of under-estimating complexities. Both GPS and Galileo cost far more - and took much longer - to build than anyone expected. In addition to the set-up cost, there are the annual running costs, which in the case of Galileo and GPS run into the hundreds of millions of euros/dollars. A sat-nav system needs long-term commitment from successive governments.
BENEFIT: Just the year-to-year financing for a sat-nav system would likely dwarf what the UK government currently spends on all other civil space activity - roughly £400m per year. The question is whether investments elsewhere, in either the space or military sectors, would bring greater returns, says Leicester University space and international relations expert Bleddyn Bowen: 'We could spend this £100m [feasibility money] doubling what the government is giving to develop launcher capability in the UK, which is only

£50m - it could make a real difference. You could also spend that money buying some imagery satellites for the MoD, which would transform their capabilities overnight.'

SKILLS: Britain has a vibrant space sector. It has many of the necessary skills and technologies to build its own sat-nav system, but it does not have them all. Many of the components for Galileo satellites, for example, have single suppliers in Europe. If Britain cannot develop domestic supply chains for the parts it needs, there may be no alternative but to bring them in from the continent. Spending the project's budget in the EU-27 may not be politically acceptable given the state of current relations on Galileo.

FREQUENCIES: The UKSA says a British system would be compatible with America's GPS - and by extension with Galileo - because both these systems transmit their timing and navigation signals in the same part of the radio spectrum. This simplifies receivers and allows manufacturers to produce equipment that works with all available systems. This is the case for the chips in the latest smartphones, for instance. But America and the EU had a huge row in 2003 over frequency compatibility and the potential for interference. It was British engineers who eventually showed the two systems could very happily co-exist. They would have to do the same again for a UK sovereign network. Without international acceptance on the frequencies in use, no project could proceed.

Some analysts believe the most fruitful approach now for the UK would be to extend its space expertise and capabilities in areas not already covered by others - in space surveillance, or in secure space communications, for example. This would make Britain an even more compelling partner for all manner of projects, including Galileo.

Alexandra Stickings from the Royal United Services Institute for Defence and Security Studies said: 'Working its way to a negotiated agreement on Galileo would allow the the UK to then focus its space budget and strategy to build UK capabilities and grow the things we're able to offer as an international partner.'

Theresa May visits Nigeria as Brexit trade mission continues in early September 2018
Theresa May is visiting Nigeria on the second day of her trade mission to boost ties with Africa after Brexit.
Mrs. May will discuss security, trade and people trafficking with President Muhammadu Buhari before meeting victims of modern slavery in Lagos.
The prime minister already announced £4bn of extra British support for African economies during the first leg of her trip on Tuesday.

She also insisted her 'sensible' Brexit plans will deliver a 'good' deal.

Mrs. May is travelling to Abuja, the capital of Nigeria - Britain's second largest trading partner in Africa - for talks with President Buhari.
She is expected to announce a new UK and French project to help Nigeria and Niger strengthen their borders to crack down on trafficking.
The prime minister will also pledge to support victims of modern slavery who have suffered 'enormous trauma'.
Speaking ahead of her visit, she said the UK was a 'world leader' in trying to end modern slavery.
Labour's Shadow Home Secretary Diane Abbott said Mrs. May's 'warm words' rang hollow as her government had cut Border Force staff and police officers, who were 'the frontline in the fight against modern slavery'.
Mrs May's three-day trip to Africa is aimed at deepen economic and trade ties with growing African economies ahead of Britain leaving the EU in 2019.
Arriving in South Africa on Tuesday, Mrs. May - who is accompanied by a team of business delegates - said she wanted the UK to overtake the US to become the G7's biggest investor in Africa by 2022.

She struck Britain's first post-Brexit trade pact with Mozambique and the Southern African Customs Union, made up of six African nations. The EU currently has an economic partnership with this union, and the UK will now continue working with it after Brexit.

And Mrs May also pledged a 'fundamental shift' in aid spending to focus on long-term economic and security challenges rather than short-term poverty reduction.
On Thursday, she will finish her tour in Kenya, where she will hold talks with President Uhuru Kenyatta and attend a state dinner, visit a business school and meet British troops.
While in South Africa, the prime minster also faced questions from journalists on Brexit.

She told the BBC's Ben Wright that the UK is 'still operating to the timetable' as it is originally set out in the Brexit negotiations.
It comes after the EU's chief negotiator Michel Barnier indicated last week that a deal may be pushed back to early November.
She played down warnings from Chancellor Philip Hammond - who said last week that a no-deal Brexit could damage the economy.

She said the comments were based on analysis first released in January that were, at the time, a 'work in progress'.

Mrs May then cited comments by the head of the World Trade Organisation, who said Brexit 'won't be a walk in the park, but won't be end of the world either'.
'We are working for a good deal, we have put forward our proposal for a good deal,' she said. 'I believe that deal is to the benefit, not only of the UK, but the EU.

'What the government is doing is putting in place the preparations to make sure we can make a success whatever our future relationship is with the EU and whatever the outcome of the negotiations.'

Talking to journalists on board RAF Voyager on Tuesday morning, Mrs. May reiterated that she believed a no-deal Brexit was still better than a bad deal.

Nigeria: May's trade mission

Nigeria is Britain's second largest trading partner in Africa, but should the country be so focused on the UK?
Tunji Andrews, an economist based in Nigeria's commercial hub Lagos, believes Nigeria should concentrate more on its relationship with the European Union.
'The diversity of demand of the EU market makes it slightly more attractive.

'I think it's impossible not to look at the British market at this point, but I'll also say that while Britain remains a viable trade partner, it just doesn't hold the same value to Africa as China and to a lesser extent, the US.'
Nigeria's top export to the UK is crude oil and its largest import is refined oil, a structural inefficiency that leads to regular fuel shortages as the populous West African nation lacks a properly functioning refinery.
Why President Emmanuel Macron of France is in Nigeria – Onyeama On July 3, 2018 President Emmanuel Macron of France, on Tuesday, arrived in Nigeria on official visit aboard French Presidential Jet A330 and landed at the Presidential wing of Nnamdi Azikiwe International Airport at about 3:10 p.m.

President Emmanuel Macron of France, inspecting a Guard of honour during his arrival at the Nnamdi Azikiwe International Airport in Abuja President Macron on arrival was received by the Nigeria's Minister of Foreign Affairs, Mr. Geoffrey Onyeama before he inspected the Presidential Guard of Honour.

He was also presented with a plaque by the Minister of Federal Capital Territory (FCT), Malam Muhammad Bello before leaving for the Presidential villa at about 3:40 p.m. The Minister of Foreign Affairs, in an interview with newsmen, said the visit would support improved ties and trade relations between the two countries. He said it would also be the first formal meeting between President Muhammadu Buhari and the French President since assumption of office.

Onyeama added that the visit would further help to reinforce the French support to Nigeria in the areas of security, trade and cultural ties. According to him, French is involved in the five Sahel countries in what they called the G5 Sahel and which is sorted around Mali and dealing with the Al-Qaida in the Sahel and also the other terrorist groups in the Sahel region. 'We are also going to be looking complementarily at the two security groupings, that is the G5 Sahel and of course the multinational joint task force that we have in fighting Boko Haram, so we can work together sharing intelligence.

'Also very importantly, there is the issue of funding for the fight against terrorism in the African countries and France has been supporting us in this and looking for greater United Nations involvement financially in the process.' So we are looking forward for the support of the French in engaging the UN to help. 'We have a stronger ally in the demand for the UN financial investment and involvement in fighting terrorism in the West African Sahel region,' he said. In the area of economy, Onyeama said that France had been one of the big investors in the country, adding that more investment was expected with the visit of Mr. Macron.

He said that President Buhari would let the French president know that Nigeria was very much ready for business notwithstanding the security challenges that the nation is facing. He also disclosed that a Memorandum of Understanding (MoU) would be signed for French Energy and Environmental companies for an environmental project in Ogun State during the visit.

According to him, this project is looking at reforestation and also brings in investments there in developing timber and other agricultural products that will now in turn create about 150,000 jobs. 'President Macron is a young president and he is a president that believes so much in the youth. 'So after meeting with Mr. President here and signing the MoU, he will be going to African shrine, Lagos, and also engage with the youth in Nigeria. 'He will also be meeting with some of our creative industry proprietors to promote greater cultural ties, and we are hoping that his engagement with the creative sector of our country will further enhance French-Nigeria cooperation,' he said.

I came to realize at certain times there isn't a day I do not eat without losing something but it so occurs that I do not eat at certain times because I do not want to be involved in something this might be physically, emotionally or spiritually do science have time for all this kind of stuffs I have been writing about it does have social impacts you know!
Without a fag for some time some smokers could feel faint, loose control, become imbalance to a point they feel they are losing their life or about to lose their lives if they do not have a fag the best way to handle such a situation is to seek for the spirituality involve it might even have or reveal philosophical meaning and then a revelation some people are clever, intelligent or become wise how do we come about spiritual revelations for example. The same thing applies to drinking excessive alcohol.

- Why do some people like keeping pets and some do not what can this mean to someone who likes pet but cannot keep pets.
- What kind of things leads to gang culture?
- Why do some of us sign secrete pacts?
- What kind of rituals and masquerade unfold or create such feelings?

Strange and complex things do occur in our world we are meant to unfold the mysteries behind them e.g. what sets a demarcation within science and religion we ought to really understand both if we understand our life experience though sometimes they could be very delicate but at the same time opens a floodgate within science and religion if we care to understand the psychology behind them.

What makes some of us sleep like a log during the night and what makes other people have sleepless nights? I mean this is different from e.g.

- Doing some serious thinking about an engineering work
- On spiritual meditation reflecting dreams or visions
- Partying or because there is a party going on next door
- Studying

What is positive thinking? **Positive thinking** is a mental and emotional attitude that focuses on the bright side of life and expects **positive** results. A **positive** person anticipates happiness, health and success, and believes he or she can overcome any obstacle or difficulty. **Positive thinking** is not a concept that everyone believes and follows. So what exactly is positive thinking? You might be tempted to assume that it implies seeing the world through rose-colored lenses by ignoring or glossing over the negative aspects of life. However, positive thinking actually means approaching life's challenges with a positive outlook.

How to think positive thoughts:

- Take responsibility for your attitude....
- Understand the benefits of being a positive thinker....
- Keep a diary to reflect your thoughts....

Benefits of positive thinking:

Researchers continue to explore the effects of positive thinking and its health benefits positive thinking may provide:

- Increase life span
- Lower rates of depression
- Lower levels of distress
- psychological and physical well-being
- Better coping skills during hardships or times of stress

Why do people who engage in positive thinking experience these health benefits one theory is that it reflects a positive outlook which enables us to cope better with stressful situations, which reduces the harmful health effects of stress on our body.

'Thousands upon thousands of people who I believe are like me are those who have never found the professional skin to fit the riot in their souls.' This reflects a description of somebody whose life is filled with the temptations of talent dose this in any way describes or reflects a promiscuous mind?

If you are creative at something later on, through your creative project become wealthy it's naturally good to believe God gave it to you and made it all possible for you. If this should be the case, you would not wish to rule e.g. your fellow human being if you have the opportunity to do so with drastic measures you will always want to collaborate make other people feel God is their helper e.g. probably through you.

- Your opinion of life will be made meaningful to other people
- Your opinions about life might be different but you will hope to create unions of harmony
- You will be happier in whatever you do
- Other people will see light in you and not darkness
- You will still find happiness in time of distress
- It would not be that easy for you to lose control of yourself
- You will learn rightly and do perfectly from other people's mistake
- You will live by making better sense and meaning out of life
- You will be good at making reason count towards experience
- And to acknowledge the true worth of life.
-

Two different groups have a defect one party, used his or hers in a more horrendous way or form while the other party tried to establish his or her defect to a more normal procedure and outcome one party is making or showing reason in an understandable way than the other party these are examples of what goes on in our everyday life. Such a given situation will spell more into the kind of person we are individually at the same time who we are as a group.

Constantly hearing voices I realize some voices wants to do just one thing that is to rule me is it therefore plausible to assume that some people can't help being good while some people can't help being a bad person?

Christian conceptions:

Instead of simply a sentimental feeling, Christian gratitude is regarded as a virtue that shapes not only emotions and thoughts but actions and deeds as well. According to Jonathan Edwards (theologian), in his A Treatise Concerning Religious Affections Love, Gratitude, and thankfulness toward God are among the signs of true religion. Because of this interpretation, modern measures of religious spirituality include assessments of thankfulness and gratitude towards God.
Allport (1950) suggested that mature religious intentions come from feelings of profound gratitude and Edwards (1746/1959) claimed that the 'affection' of gratitude is one of the most accurate ways of finding the presence of God in a person's life. In a study done by Samuels and Lester (1985) it was contended that in a small sample of Catholic nuns and priests, out of 50 emotions, love and gratitude was the most experienced emotion towards God.

Islamic conceptions:

The Islamic sacred text, The Quran, is filled with the idea of gratitude. Islam encourages its followers to be grateful and express thanks to God in all circumstances. Islamic teaching emphasizes the idea that those who are grateful will be rewarded with more. A traditional Islamic saying states that, 'The first who will be summoned to paradise are those who have praised God in every circumstance' In the Quran it is also stated in Sura 14 that those who are grateful will be given more by God.

The prophet Muhammad also said, 'Gratitude for the abundance you have received is the best insurance that the abundance will continue.' Many practices of the Islamic faith also encourage gratitude. The Pillar of Islam calling for daily prayer encourages believers to pray to God five times a day in order to thank him for his goodness. The pillar of fasting during the month of Ramadan is for the purpose of putting the believer in a state of gratitude.

Individual differences:

Much of the recent work psychological research into gratitude has focused on the nature of individual difference in gratitude, and the consequences of being a more or less grateful person. Three scales have been developed to measure individual differences in gratitude, each of which assesses somewhat different conceptions The GQ6 measures individual differences in how frequently and intensely people feel gratitude.

The Appreciation Scale measures 8 different aspects of gratitude: appreciation of people, possessions, the present moment, rituals, feeling of awe, social comparisons, existential concerns, and behavior which express gratitude. The GRAT assesses gratitude towards other people, gratitude towards the world in general, and a lack of resentment for what you do not have. A recent study showed that each of these scales are actually all measuring the same way of approaching life; this suggests that individual differences in gratitude include all of these components.

Empirical findings, Association with well-being:

A large body of recent work has suggested that people who are more grateful have higher levels of subjective well-being. Grateful people are happier, less depressed, less stressed, and more satisfied with their lives and social relationships grateful people also have higher levels of control of their environments, personal growth, purpose in life, and self-acceptance.

Grateful people have more positive ways of coping with the difficulties they experience in life, being more likely to seek support from other people, reinterpreted and grow from the experience, and spend more time planning how to deal with the problem. Grateful people also have less negative coping strategies, being less likely to try to avoid the problem, deny there is a problem, blame themselves, or cope through substance use. Grateful people sleep better, and this seems to be because they think less negative and more positive thoughts just before going to sleep.

Gratitude has been said to have one of the strongest links with mental health of any character trait. Numerous studies suggest that grateful people are more likely to have higher levels of happiness and lower levels of stress and depression. In one study concerning gratitude, participants were randomly assigned to one of six therapeutic intervention conditions designed to improve the participant's overall quality of life (Seligman et. all., 2005).

Out of these conditions, it was found that the biggest short-term effects came from a 'gratitude visit' where participants wrote and delivered a letter of gratitude to someone in their life. This condition showed a rise in happiness scores by 10 percent and a significant fall in depression scores, results which lasted up to one month after the visit. Out of the six conditions, the longest lasting effects were caused by the act of writing 'gratitude journals' where participants were asked to write down three things they were grateful for every day. These participants' happiness scores also increased and continued to increase each time they were tested periodically after the experiment. In fact, the greatest benefits were usually found to occur around six months after treatment began. This exercise was so successful that although participants were only asked to continue the journal for a week, many participants continued to keep the journal long after the study was over. Similar results have been found from studies conducted by Emmons and McCullough (2003) and Lyubomirsky et. all. (2005).

While many emotions and personality traits are important to well-being, there is evidence that gratitude may be uniquely important. First, a longitudinal study showed that people who were more grateful coped better with a life transition. Specifically, people who were more grateful before the transition were less stressed, less depressed, and more satisfied with their relationships three months later. Second, two recent studies have suggested that gratitude may have a unique relationship with well-being, and can explain aspects of well-being that other personality traits cannot. Both studies showed that gratitude was able to explain more well-being than the Big Five and 30 of the most commonly studied personality traits.

It's something we might all need to consider or reconsider rather than leaving some people in the open pretending they are good while they are not we are all partly hear to reconsider at the same time understand what is in the closet which we must do due to the problem of evil, pain and suffering it's all about giving and taking it had always been a matter of giving and taking it's just that we all do not do the same e.g. give. We rather tend to take rather than give if, it's for good use with a way of giving in return in the future it would be most considerate but if we had always give and would have nothing in return we will feel hurt and so there goes gratitude.

We would almost want to believe everything about cloning of human, surrogacy, test tub babies is wrong when it comes to all that has been done in relation to what these matters concerns since past centuries and what they are now we might not have a change of heart yet we will all not admit it has a way in our lives people have different experience in life and how it relates to them confirms who they are in relation to such matters it might be creating problems for other people but something has always been causing problem for everybody let's make sense how many people admire you for the good things you do these days only a few with common sense.

Admiration is a social emotion elicited by people of competence, talent, or skill exceeding standards. Admiration facilitates social learning in groups and motivates self-improvement through learning from role-models.

Definition:

Sara Algoe and Jonathan Haidt include admiration in the category of other-praising emotions, alongside awe, elevation, and gratitude. They propose that admiration is the emotion we feel towards non-moral excellence (i.e., witnessing an act of excellent skill), while elevation is the emotion we feel towards moral excellence (i.e., witnessing someone perform an act of exceeding virtue). Other authors term both these emotions as *admiration*, distinguishing between *admiration for skill* and *admiration for virtue*.

Richard Smith categorizes admiration as an other-focused assimilative emotion, leading people to aspire to be like (assimilate to) those they admire. He contrasts admiration with envy (an other-focused contrastive emotion), proposing that envy leads us to feel frustrated about the competence of others, while admiration is uplifting and motivating.

Function:

Learning of skills has been so important to our evolution that we have come to feel positively about talented or skillful people, in order to approach them and copy their actions. Admiration is the emotion that facilitates learning in social groups.

Relation to attainability:

Following from the view that admiration's function is learning and self-improvement, some authors have proposed that admiration will only activate when we believe improvement is possible for us, however one empirical study has suggested the opposite, that admiration is akin to passive contemplation of an other's superiority, while envy is the motivating emotion which activates when a better performance is attainable to us.

Associated behaviors:

Behaviors' concerning the self:

Witnessing admirable acts has been shown to increase motivation for self-improvement in the domain of witnessed excellence (e.g., sporting performance), but also a more general motivation to work towards achieving one's own life goals. Using fMRI, admiration has been shown to be related with higher-level cognitive processes involved in motivation (e.g., planning, pursuit of goals), but also relates to lower-level activating mechanisms, demonstrating that admiration is a physically energizing emotion.

Behaviors' concerning the relationship:

Admiration is also associated with a tendency to praise the admired act to others, and a desire for contact and proximity with the admired.

Group-based:

Admiration has also been studied in an intergroup context by Susan Fiske and her colleagues. They propose that admiration is the emotion we feel towards those social groups we perceive as competent (or high-status) and warm (friendly and cooperative) (e.g., in studies involving students in the US, an example of a group perceived as competent and warm is *the British*). Admiration is related to intentions to associate, cooperate with, and help members from groups that are admired.

- I do not have admiration for negative things moreover some people will always want, what is in the inside why or would anyone wants to be cloned what is it in the inside that they want.
- Why should anyone wants to come into this world by such choice I understand everything happens for reason but one mistake I would make is to make a wrong choice for another person if am grateful or feel gratitude for what I am or have.
- But some mystery still lies before us e.g. why do some babies die before they are born now this is part of divulging into the supernatural, into nature into what should be and not be or couldn't be.
- We exist in a world some people can't just help you being yourself is this really the case?
- What does the supernatural holds about how we come into this world?
- We in this world mature to certain age to know why we are in this world or for what reasons we are born into the world.
- Do we actually make or have choices when we are born into this world how often, do we feel gratitude for being born in this world

- This could relate to how happy we are or how sad we are in this world
- How far have we been ritualizing ourselves on this planet while our heavenly father bluntly said I no longer delight in sacrifices the sacrifice acceptable to me is a broken and contrite heart
- There are some culture a partner could ritualize the grave of a partners parent
- There are rituals, cult groups or religious groups carry out in other to prevent its members from leaving
- While some religious groups we invites new members in, in certain cases to drive out some of its old members
- Could cloned, test tube babies or surrogacy be here as a protest from their own world
- It's those who feel they are all right who predominantly feel they have nothing to protest about
- May be its because probably all they know is about me, me, me instead of nothing in my hands I bring but simply to the cross I cling
- This reminds me of what Christ did by dyeing on the cross
- Could these cloned humans be trying to seek immunity from something
- What makes some men or women masturbate
- What makes some people smoke or drink excessively
- What is practically now inducing young star into hard drug use
- All these are enough to cause thunderstruck e.g. in the sky
- What actually causes obesity
- What phenomena's come within such related issues it's not all of them you see on a notice board
- Some people may soon have the chance of committing assisted suicide
- Snake swallowing snakes similar to what occurred during the time of the prophet Moses

- Evil dose not often make us understand evil infarct it prevents us from doing so but only from a good mind we can understand evil
- Could it be said it's partly the pain and suffering involve which makes us understand evil or is it its effects on our emotions
- Pain and suffering makes us understand the problem of evil while at the same time it might hurt our emotions. if we are good, if we are bad, we hardly care or do not care, it would rather contributes to what other mischief or good we can do
- Why is it so difficult to call evil by its name
- Evil also uses our philosophy e.g. evil marketing
- Time have passed when the wealthy easily uses' their wealth to sting others and get away with it which one of them cares for respect now how many of them can you take a look at and say I have so much respect and admiration for this wealthy man or woman
- Being who you are is of most importance evil should have no part of your life
- Evil does not like the probability of facing the probabilities of its evil
- So what then is evil what do most of us consider to be evil it comes in all shape and size all around the world
- Most people have over time learn to taking life as it comes it seems to be the most tiring, daunting and difficult time for those who have strings to tie
- Less room for self-satisfaction it's not even present in the world of today but can be found only in yourself no wonder we are more precluded and preoccupied with ourselves these day it has made some of us more self-centered, some of us not knowing which way to turn while others are too certain in what, they are doing or up to
- These are varied reason why humans have different responses to life.

Social emotions: are emotions that depend upon the thoughts, feelings or actions of other people, 'as experienced, recalled, anticipated or imagined at first hand'. Examples are embarrassment, guilt, shame, jealousy, envy, empathy, and pride. In contrast, basic emotions such as happiness and sadness only require the awareness of one's own physical state.

Therefore, the development of social emotions is tightly linked with the development of social cognition, the ability to imagine other people's mental states, which generally develops in adolescence. Studies have found that children as young as 2 to 3 years of age can express emotions resembling guilt and remorse. However, while five-year-old children are able to imagine situations in which basic emotions would be felt, the ability to describe situations in which social emotions might be experienced does not appear until seven years of age.

People may not only share emotions with others, but may also experience similar physiological arousal to others if they feel a sense of social connectedness to the other person. A laboratory-based study by Cwir, Car, Walton, and Spencer (2011) showed that, when a participant felt a sense of social connectedness to a stranger (research confederate), the participant experienced similar emotional states and physiological responses to that of the stranger while observing the stranger perform a stressful task.
Social emotions are sometimes called moral emotions, because they play an important role in morality and moral decision making. In neuroeconomics, the role social emotions play in game theory and economic decision-making is just starting to be investigated.

Social or moral aspect:

Some social emotions are also referred to as moral emotions because of the fundamental role they play in morality. For example, guilt is the discomfort and regret one feels over one's wrongdoing. It is a social emotion, because it requires the perception that another person is being hurt by this act; and it also has implication in morality, such that the guilty actor, in virtue of feeling distressed and guilty, accepts responsibility for the wrongdoing, which might cause desire to make amends or punish the self.

Not all social emotions are moral emotions. Pride, for instance, is a social emotion which involves the perceived admiration of other people, but research on the role it plays in moral behaviors yields problematic results.

Social intelligence: is the capacity to know oneself and to know others. Social scientist Ross Honeywill believes social intelligence is an aggregated measure of self- and social-awareness, evolved social beliefs and attitudes, and a capacity and appetite to manage complex social change. Psychologist, Nicholas Humphrey believes that it is social intelligence, rather than quantitative intelligence, that defines who we are as humans.

The original definition by Edward Thorndike in 1920 is 'the ability to understand and manage men and women and boys and girls, to act wisely in human relations'. It is equivalent to interpersonal intelligence, one of the types of intelligence identified in Howard Gardner's theory of multiple intelligences, and closely related to theory of mind.

Some authors have restricted the definition to deal only with knowledge of social situations, perhaps more properly called social cognition or social marketing intelligence, as it pertains to trending socio-psychological advertising and marketing strategies and tactics. According to Sean Foleno, social intelligence is a person's competence to optimally understand one's environment and react appropriately for socially successful conduct. It is important to note the multiple definitions listed above, as there is yet to be a complete consensus on the operational definition of social intelligence.

- Discover what makes you satisfied discover the sensation you create its people who makes other people run out of luck who now own the world
- Two or more people do not put their head together unless it's about making money
- What is anything that hasn't got anything to do about making money?
- So daunting

- Why are some people praying for you and the rest of the world every Sunday for example
- Some of us throw-up sometimes asking what kind of a world is this it's because you know or understand how it should be
- While some of us know how we could fix our place up for whatever we want this, is where the lies, cheating, hating and result of conflict comes from self-intent can so often pilgrimage our lives at any time
- it's one reason why some of us go on holy pilgrimage to sustain us spiritually in case of such times
- It's one who, would not fast during lent who would in life run into a difficulty of getting hold of a bracelet such as in Mammy Returns
- Is the business world of today for very religious person
- Some people employers put at work go about pushing other people about and aside that's what is partly causing the recession one thing is they are never good at their work
- They could do whatever going higher in rack, create red tape, bureaucracy, favoritisms and talk all day at work; they are only good at their work when the house god walks in but by the time the house god leaves the job he or she is knackered or leave the job as unwell.
-

The term emotional literacy has often been used in parallel to, and sometimes interchangeably with, the term emotional intelligence. However, there are important differences between the two. Emotional literacy was noted as part of a project advocating humanistic education in the early 1970s Definition:

The term was used extensively by Claude Steiner (1997) who says:

Emotional literacy is made up of 'the ability to understand your emotions, the ability to listen to others and empathise with their emotions, and the ability to express emotions productively. To be emotionally literate is to be able to handle emotions in a way that improves your personal power and improves the quality of life around you. Emotional literacy improves relationships, creates loving possibilities between people, makes co-operative work possible, and facilitates the feeling of community.

Steiner breaks emotional literacy into 5 parts:

1. Knowing your feelings.
2. Having a sense of empathy.
3. Learning to manage our emotions.
4. Repairing emotional problems.
5. Putting it all together: emotional interactivity.
6.

Having its roots in counseling, it is a social definition that has interactions between people at its heart. According to Steiner emotional literacy is about understanding your feelings and those of others to facilitate relationships, including using dialogue and self-control to avoid negative arguments. The ability to be aware and read other people's feelings enables one to interact with them effectively so that powerful emotional situations can be handled in a skillful way. Steiner calls this 'emotional interactivity'.
Steiner's model of emotional literacy is therefore primarily about dealing constructively with the emotional difficulties we experience to build a sound future. He believes that personal power can be increased and relationships transformed. The emphasis is on the individual, and as such encourages one to look inward rather than to the social setting in which an individual operates.

British context:

In Britain, the term 'emotional literacy' is often used and has developed, building on the work of Steiner and Goleman as a social construction – as opposed to the more individualistic 'emotional intelligence' with the attempts to measure it as if emotions were measurable in a relatively rational way. Educators did not like the way that 'emotional intelligence' focused so much on the individual and there were clear attempts to avoid the narrow EQ tests that were in use for two reasons:

1. The idea of an EQ test had resonance with discredited psychometric measures of intelligence such as IQ tests.
2. People were also concerned with the way that pupils could be subject to even more control through the introduction of emotional intelligence into the curriculum.
3.

The National Curriculum in England and Wales emphasized a range of cognitive skills that were controlled through exams. Educators saw the need to expand the range of skills that pupils required and were also concerned with social inclusion. The Labour Government provided an overarching rationale for this with its promotion of well-being. However, when the Department of Children, Schools and Families developed a scheme for schools – called the Social and Emotional Aspects of Learning (SEAL) – it was based on Goleman's definition of emotional intelligence.
Hence any distinctions between the terms emotional intelligence and emotional literacy were blurred. Even so, key educators in Britain continued to use the term emotional literacy. Emotional literacy took on an aspect that was concern with personal growth. For example, the importance of developing relationships is, to a degree, in Weare's definition:

The ability to understand ourselves and other people, and in particular to be aware of, understand, and use information about the emotional states of ourselves and others with competence it, includes the ability to understand, express and manage our own emotions, and respond to the emotions of others, in ways that are helpful to ourselves and others.

Similarly, the organization Antidote defined emotional literacy as:

The practice of interacting with others in ways that build understanding of our own and others' emotions then, using this understanding to inform our actions.

These definitions acknowledge both the individual and other people and so inter-personal relationships and the need for dialogue are included. Sharp has taken a broad approach to emotional literacy in a Local Education Authority (LEA) where he considers its development is important for teachers as well as pupils.

However, there was still an underlying assumption about the individual and how they develop as if they were culturally isolated and separate from factors such as religion and gender. Also, the development of emotional literacy was justified by arguing that its introduction would help to improve other factors such as behavior, attendance and academic achievement. Boler researched four of the emotional programs in America. She pointed out that the programs tended to view pupils as individuals who are in need of development through enabling them to control their impulses.

This can mean that pupils are to become responsible for their own control and that other social factor can be ignored. It is possible that these programs can open the way for greater control of pupils with even their emotions being assessed. On the one hand the development of emotional literacy programs can be seen as progressive, but on the other the focus seems quite inward, as there is little reference leading to any broader concept of social and political reform.

In the same way that Goleman discusses emotional intelligence educational programs, emotional literacy programs can also be more about coping with the social and political status quo in a caring, interactive and emotionally supportive environment than with any systematic attempt to move beyond it to social improvement.

Culturally situated:

Matthews (2006) argues against the concept of 'emotional intelligence' and for a developed definition of 'emotional literacy'. His starting point is that all social and emotional interactions take place in a cultural context and that generally all emotions are felt because of interactions with other people. He argues that a group may, for example, contain men and women and people from a range of ethnicities. One could judge a person's emotional literacy by observing what they brought to the situation, the way they interacted and the degree to which they showed empathy, and, the recognition of 'self' and 'others'.

The way that one can reliably gauge the emotional literacy of a person is to see them interacting in a group and see how they behave towards other people of different genders, sexuality and social class. Hence, it makes little sense to talk about emotional literacy of a person as if it were separate from such factors – someone may be able to empathize with people of their own sex, but not different sexualities or religions. Also, one may think that they can empathize with the other sex, or another religion, but the other person may not agree with them. Indeed, the views of other people are essential in deciding upon such factors.

There is always a social context and in any context power differentials operate. Any form of paper and pen test will only give access to what a person thinks, not to the important view of how others think. For example, many men (and women) would say that they were not sexist, yet a person from the opposite sex may not agree. A person cannot tell how well they, say, empathize; only other people tell them if they are. A manager may think they are self-confident, open and friendly, but others find him or her aggressive and bullying.

Hence, according to Matthews, emotional literacy is a social process that takes place in a social setting, is something that is never really achieved, and has to be seen in conjunction with others. This indicates that key components of emotional literacy, which is a continual process that includes dialogue, acceptance of ambiguity and the ability to reflect. Judgments are made on a person's individual-in-group emotional literacy. He argues:

Emotional literacy involves factors such as people understanding their own and others' emotional states; learning to manage their emotions and to empathize with others. It also includes the recognition that emotional literacy

is both an individual development and a collective activity and is both about self-development and the building of community so that one's own sense of emotional well-being grows along with that of others, and not at their expense.
Emotional literacy involves connections between people and working with their differences and similarities while being able to handle ambiguity and contradiction. It is a dynamic process through which the individual develops emotionally and involves culture and empowerment. For example, it includes understanding how the nature of social class, 'race' and gender (sexism and homophobia) impinge on peoples' emotional states to lead to an understanding of how society could change. Hence it incorporates an understanding of power exchanges between people and a challenging of power differentials.
On this view emotional literacy is developed to help people understand themselves, others and the power connections between them. Matthews links emotional literacy to equality and social justice. Emotional literacy is not just to be 'nice', but also to know when to stand up for viewpoints and fight for a case. It is not about more control over people, but less. As McIntosh and Style argue schools are always involved in social, emotional and power relations, yet 'power relations are a taboo subject in K-12 schooling and in the majority culture of the United States. Power relations are therefore little understood systemically. Students, however, learn about power by watching, by imitating, by avoidance of what they fear'.

In education:

In general, most of the criticisms of courses to promote pupils' emotional development have been directed at those that develop emotional intelligence. For example, there are the courses developed in the USA and Britain. The critiques of these courses include that:

1. Emotional intelligence/literacy courses can lead to more control over pupils with them being more defined in their behavior.
2. The assessment of emotional intelligence/literacy can lead to pupils being labeled as inadequate.

3. Emotional intelligence courses can locate problems in the individual that are also a function of how society is organized.
4. When courses are taught it is often assumed that pupils are emotionally ready to deal with what is on the curriculum, whereas they may not be.
5. The whole agenda of teaching emotional development can lead to pupils being seen as deficit in emotional control and so can depress their potential to have faith in future goals
6. Emotional intelligence courses have moral and ethical aspects that are not made explicit.

Matthews has tried to avoid some of the difficulties. For example, his strategies for the classroom mean that pupils only develop when, and in what areas, they are able. Emotional development between the genders has been the focus of research with a small reference to 'race'. But these are limited in strategies and do not tackle fully the critiques.

- What doors do we open that could create resemblance within you and your family and with people outside your family
- Why does the British not easily become irrational among other race, culture and ethnic background it's no irony they could live to have created a multi-cultural Britain made of people from different ethnic groups from all parts of the world
- No one should give you a flimsy excuse they are penniless in the UK no food, no cloth or shelter living on the street I do not see any reason for anyone portraying his or her self as a White Trash in the UK
- In this present time how religious really are those who say or portray themselves as religious
- Good for you if you are not observing the current state of the world as a masquerade. If, it comes to you as a sort of masquerade you understand better for you if not, you are in real trouble do not live in ignorance its one good achievement this country signifies

- It surprise me not much of hand shaking goes on within men these days
- How often do we wish ourselves luck in this present time everything now means go for it
- This are times when the most religious are feeling sulky they are more worried for the sake of the world than most of us pay attention to
- the human mind is always in need of guidance
- Could the present state of the world now be for playing solitaire based on its complexity if care is not taken it could make matters complicated
- Solitaire is any tabletop game which one can play by oneself. The term 'solitaire' is also used for single-player games of concentration and skill using a set layout of tiles, pegs or stones rather than cards. These games include peg solitaire and mahjong solitaire. Most solitaire games function as a puzzle which, due to a different starting position, may (or may not) be solved in a different fashion each time.
- How far has humans prevented themselves from being masquerades to each other
- How closely have we been shearing tolerance on our religious views
- Thank God we are not all going mad to make money
- But yes we can all go mad without food in our mouth
- The knowledge of knowing God is good we have been created in a way that we are confined to knowing him whether you like it or not it's good to understand and appreciate how we have been created in his own image then most of us can really see ourselves in the real view
- We are constantly aware or reminded we are bound to either live forever or die
- You can constantly be aware that you are immortal some of us are
- How could it be uncomfortable to talk about death?
-

Death is the cessation of all biological functions that sustain a living organism. Phenomena which commonly bring about death include aging, predation, malnutrition, disease, suicide, homicide, starvation, dehydration, and accidents or

trauma resulting in terminal injury. In most cases, bodies of living organisms begin to decompose shortly after death.
Death – particularly the death of humans – has commonly been considered a sad or unpleasant occasion, due to the affection for the being that has died and the termination of social and familial bonds with the deceased. Other concerns include fear of death, necrophobia, anxiety, sorrow, grief, emotional pain, depression, sympathy, compassion, solitude, or saudade. Many cultures and religions have the idea of an afterlife, and also hold the idea of reward or judgement and punishment for past sin.

The concept and symptoms of death, and varying degrees of delicacy used in discussion in public forums, have generated numerous scientific, legal, and socially acceptable terms or euphemisms for death. When a person has died, it is also said they have *passed away*, *passed on*, *expired*, or are *gone*, among numerous other socially accepted, religiously specific, slang, and irreverent terms.
Bereft of life, the dead person is then a *corpse*, *cadaver*, a *body*, a *set of remains*, and when all flesh has rotted away, a skeleton. The terms *carrion* and *carcass* can also be used, though these more often connote the remains of non-human animals. As a polite reference to a dead person, it has become common practice to use the participle form of 'decease', as in *the deceased*; another noun form is *decedent*. The ashes left after a cremation are sometimes referred to by the neologism *cremains*, a portmanteau of 'cremation' and 'remains'.
Senescence refers to a scenario when a living being is able to survive all calamities, but eventually dies due to causes relating to old age.

The concept of death is a key to human understanding of the phenomenon. There are many scientific approaches to the concept. For example, brain death, as practiced in medical science, defines death as a point in time at which brain activity ceases.
One of the challenges in defining death is in distinguishing it from life. As a point in time, death would seem to refer to the moment at which life ends.

Life extension refers to an increase in maximum or average lifespan, especially in humans, by slowing down or reversing the processes of aging. Average lifespan is determined by vulnerability to accidents and age or lifestyle-related afflictions such as cancer, or cardiovascular disease. Extension of average lifespan can be achieved by good diet, exercise and avoidance of hazards such as smoking.

Maximum lifespan is also determined by the rate of aging for a species inherent in its genes. Currently, the only widely recognized method of extending maximum lifespan is calorie restriction. Theoretically, extension of maximum lifespan can be achieved by reducing the rate of aging damage, by periodic replacement of damaged tissues, or by molecular repair or rejuvenation of deteriorated cells and tissues.

What about drinking blood in other to extend life it's found in some cult groups?

In society, the nature of death and humanity's awareness of its own mortality has for millennia been a concern of the world's religious traditions and of philosophical inquiry. This includes belief in resurrection or an afterlife (associated with Abrahamic religions), reincarnation or rebirth (associated with Dharmic religions), or that consciousness permanently ceases to exist, known as eternal oblivion (associated with atheism.

The Last Judgment, Final Judgment, Day of Judgment, Judgment Day, Doomsday, or The Day of the Lord is part of the eschatological world view of the Abrahamic religions and in the Frashokereti of Zoroastrianism.

Some Christian denominations consider the Second Coming of Christ to be the final and eternal judgment by God of the people in every nation resulting in the glorification of some and the punishment of others. The concept is found in all the Canonical gospels, particularly the Gospel of Matthew. Christian Futurists believe it will take place after the Resurrection of the Dead and the Second Coming of Christ while Full Preterists believe it has already occurred. The Last Judgment has inspired numerous artistic depictions.

In the law of evidence, a dying declaration is testimony that would normally be barred as hearsay but may in common law nonetheless be admitted as evidence in criminal law trials because it constituted the last words of a dying person.

The rationale, accurate or not, is that someone who is dying or believes death to be imminent would have less incentive to fabricate testimony, and as such, the hearsay statement carries with it some reliability.

- How often do we wish each other well recently?
- It could be part of being irrational recently
- Knowing how to express our true feeling is becoming difficult
- More and more people are letting go too easily could it not be its because they are fed-up or not knowing which way to turn
- To be honest why should some people want or really need assisted suicide or is it now just another way for some of us to make a show out of our lives
- What could amount to a word of such a dying man or woman
- What sort of human involvement's can turn our world into a place of chaos we see and experience them each day of our lives and they are mostly all part of the works of our own doing
- There is now a disparity on how we matriculate ourselves in life it would be nice to give credence to the strongest link it's not a time to give in to a weaker party among groups with flimsy excuse just to make its presence felt or have its own selfish wimp you will know them once you have given them a little chance they would want your own shear
- Is it an irony why the level of pain and suffering is increasing? We need to come across more people especially in high places, who have done some serious thinking
- In all parts of the world group talk is becoming more than ever before complex taking on a serious tone what disturbs most of us about this is that it leads to more serious outcomes e.g. trouble
- Most people who, we would expect to be happier are going through emotional pain.

Psychological pain, mental pain, or emotional pain is an unpleasant feeling (a suffering) of a psychological, nonphysical origin. It is mental suffering; mental torment.' There is no shortage in the many ways psychological pain is referred to, and using a different word usually reflects an emphasis on a particular aspect of mind life but it may also be called mental pain, emotional pain, psychic pain, social pain, spiritual or soul pain, or suffering.

While these clearly are not equivalent terms, one systematic comparison of theories and models of psychological pain, psychic pain, emotional pain, and suffering concluded that each describe the same profoundly unpleasant feeling. Psychological pain is believed to be an inescapable aspect of human existence.

Other descriptions of psychological pain are 'a wide range of subjective experiences characterized as an awareness of negative changes in the self and in its functions accompanied by negative feelings', 'a diffuse subjective experience ... differentiated from physical pain which is often localized and associated with noxious physical stimuli', and 'a lasting, unsustainable, and unpleasant feeling resulting from negative appraisal of an inability or deficiency of the self.

How far has psychology gone to ascertaining the sort of emotional pain one goes through when they drink alcohol or smoke excessively do they consider if there are any or they feel some people just like or enjoy smoking or drinking alcohol excessively? Why are they difficult to quite we know of the hazards they pose it does not stop some of us yet we feel the pain that these things are hazardous to our health.

Causes of emotional pain:

The adjective 'psychological' is thought to encompass the functions of beliefs, thoughts, feelings, and behaviors, which may be seen as an indication for the many sources of psychological pain. One way of grouping these different sources of pain was offered by Shneidman, who stated that psychological pain is caused by frustrated psychological needs for example the need for love, autonomy, affiliation, and achievement, or the need to avoid harm, shame, and embarrassment.

Psychological needs were originally described by Henry Murray in 1938 as needs that motivate human behavior.

Shneidman maintained that people rate the importance of each need differently, which explains why people's level of psychological pain differs when confronted with the same frustrated need. This needs perspective coincides with Patrick David Wall's description of physical pain that says that physical pain indicates a need state much more than a sensory experience.

In the fields of social psychology and personality psychology, the term social pain is used to denote psychological pain caused by harm or threat to social connection; bereavement, embarrassment, shame and hurt feelings are subtypes of social pain. From an evolutionary perspective, psychological pain forces the assessment of actual or potential social problems that might reduce the individual's fitness for survival. The way we display our psychological pain socially (for example, crying, shouting, moaning) serves the purpose of indicating that we are in need.

- Giving up smoking or excessive alcohol can be agony for some people as well as carrying out the act this is where care comes in and can be made relevant.

Emotional agony in borderline personality disorder:

Borderline personality disorder (BPD) has long been believed to be the one psychiatric disorder that produced the most intense emotional pain, agony, and distress in those who suffer with this condition. Studies have shown that borderline patients experience chronic and significant emotional suffering and mental agony. Borderline patients may feel overwhelmed by negative emotions, experiencing intense grief instead of sadness, shame and humiliation instead of mild embarrassment, rage instead of annoyance and panic instead of nervousness. People with BPD are especially sensitive to feelings of rejection, isolation and perceived failure.
Both clinicians and laymen alike have witnessed the desperate attempts to escape these subjective inner

experiences of these patients. Borderline patients are severely impulsive and their attempts to alleviate the agony are often very destructive or self-destructive. Suicidal ideation, suicide attempts, eating disorders (anorexia nervosa and bulimia nervosa), self-harm (cutting, overdosing, etc.), compulsive spending, gambling, sex addiction, violent and aggressive behavior, sexual promiscuity and deviant sexual behaviors, are desperate attempts to escape.

The intrapsychic pain experienced by those diagnosed with BPD has been studied and compared to normal healthy controls and to others suffering from major depression, bipolar disorder, substance use disorder, schizophrenia, other personality disorders, and a range of other conditions. The excruciatingly painful inner experience of the borderline patient is both unique and perplexing.

In clinical populations, the rate of suicide of patients with borderline personality disorder is estimated to be 10%, a rate far greater than that in the general population and still considerably greater than for patients with schizophrenia and bipolar disorder. However, since 60–70% of patients with borderline personality disorder make suicide attempts, unsuccessful suicide attempts are far more frequent than completed suicides in patients with borderline personality disorder.

We all want to hold the steering wheels of our lives don't we?

It's now time to take caution human involvement do not run into a frenzy and then to chaos.

It's why we have good people something reasonable and tangible will always pup up.

The impact of humans and their ways of life is on a course needing to be steered positively not negatively it has all turns to a situation of something to do about anything to make the world a better place it all reflects what had being going on in the past e.g. masquerades and they are not giving up.

All it amounts is that we basically have and need to consider and respect Gods position in our lives try it give it a thought you will observe that God himself in a miraculous way will enlighten you more on his position and the more you will realize what is actually happening.

Nevertheless now is a time some people would also blaspheme against God while on the other hand now is a time to realize God is democratic. We now know enough that our lives is what we make out of it, we have freewill isn't God democratic enough from what it has always been.
We should not put ourselves in a position we would kill or steal to get what we want God doesn't kill us to get what he wants he blesses us to get what he wants but if we sin, he turns away from us or we are shielded from his eyes which means he cannot see us in that particular moment.
You who believe in God will not kill or steal to get what you want, you will not want to tell lies or cheat you are always trying to be fair, honest, compassionate, loving this is what God looks out for in us that's when he actually sees us.
Now is a time if other people treat you wrongly do not retaliate look up to God who has placed the will to love, to be compassionate and caring in your heart for he has a more important need of you.

Whatever is going on or taking place we should not see them as a disadvantage but a means to move on the disadvantage had been there before it all began.
I heard two voices one saying to me that I should use my hands to wash my handkerchief while the other voice said no, I should use my washing machine saying its better it never came to my head at the time, if I should wash my handkerchief with my other cloths or not. What brought this about in the first place I had not the slightest idea. One of the voices was that of an Albino.

Knowing when other people are being nice to you, can be sometimes tricky.

And then I remembered when Godwin Emiko was crowned the Olu of Warri after his late father he made a visit with an entourage from Warri to Port Harcourt one of the entourage was late Chief Meneafejuku who was a very good friend to my father both of whom, are Freemasons and members of the reformed Ogboni fraternity. Meneafejuku was much older than my father and a very close family friend to his mother Awoma.

On the day the Olu made the visit to Port Harcourt both of my father's wives were present coming all the way from Warri to Port Harcourt I and my brother Mr. Omagbemi were dressed traditionally I remembered having my handkerchief with me I later realized something triggered me to have bought the handkerchief and later on realized I have to find out what will trigger other reaction which then, I was not aware of.

On the day Olu of Warri came to Port Harcourt, as we, myself our father his driver Mr. Vincent and my brother arrived and came out of the car to attend the ceremony we had to cross a two way motor way to where the ceremony will take place as we all came out of the car, we somehow, drifted apart as we were standing side by side by the motor way.

At that point I knew I heard a voice saying it's this one we would use that means 'me'. And all of a sudden a blathering wind come and blow my handkerchief away from my hand and left it on the road later on to the middle of the two way motor way.

I thought of getting it back but how, am I going to do that? Running within the midst of a crowd in such an occasion to retrieve just a handkerchief which had and been blown away from my hand to the middle of the road. I heard a voices saying do not take it back it's a motor way, it's an occasion then I hesitated back thinking should I try to retrieve my handkerchief from the middle of the road or leave it.

Then, I suddenly felt if, I do not retrieve it back something about my own personal life will banish from me. A feeling came through me am not just losing a handkerchief. If I lose the handkerchief in another stronger wind which was forthcoming the wind that was about to come shortly spelt an omen of something am yet, to understand.

All that while people and cars were bustling around with me far; away in my own thoughts and feeling several cars, had passed by to and fro from the two way motor way. I thought of what will leave me alone that might be crucial in my life if I do not retrieve the handkerchief no reason came to me at that point in time.

At that point something got hold of me as if it had something to do with death I can't explain what got hold of me probably then I should have realized I was born to understand and the same time to renounce evil I was about to understand evil and its ways.
I remembered taking in a deep breath looking both ways of the road if there was any cars coming I suddenly had a chance and went for the handkerchief which was still lying at the middle of the road infarct retrieving it took me to where the ceremony was being held. Which seems like taking few leaps from where laid the handkerchief I was beguiled by the handkerchief still laying at the middle of road e.g. with the wind and the cars going throw and fro it could have gone further than I could reach. I took my handkerchief back without being embarrassed saying to myself or was it someone else saying whatever this means I must get down to the bottom of it. It was the same handkerchief my grandfather wanted one night after his son had been conferred his chieftaincy tiled as the Agbueju of Warri by the Olu of Warri.

By the time I got to where the ceremony was being held my father was among those standing by the side of the Olu of Warri his two wives were there also, Chief Meneafejuku, some people whom am familiar with. At that point I remembered being steered by the experience but was not shaken I also joined the dancing group and made a few steps. As far as I can remember I wore my first Itsekiri traditional dress I guess it all took place because there was culture in me all these took place without knowing my father would be made a chief soon.

May be something similar did occurred when I went to the traditional funeral of Olu's father it all came too quickly with a whizzing effect and we all made our way home. It took place in a house at Big Warri it involves me, my bother Omagbemi, our father and his two wives Cordelier and Aya Megbele some relatives and friends this was before our father got married to Mama Gbawo infarct I and my immediate elder brother had left Nigeria for the UK before he got married to her.

I was aware my father was offered a bottle of Guinness he drank a little bit out of it from a glass it was poured into I heard, a voice saying the remaining of the Guinness should be offered to me I should have asked myself why me at the time I guess my attention was trying to understand our mission at Big Warri. I felt my father groaned at that point inwardly and said it should be offered to Omagbemi one reason I might later have accepted the turnout of event was that our mother was not present.

Meanwhile I and my brothershould not seem to be behaving indifferently within ourselves while working for our father at Port Harcourt his two wives where at Warri with the rest of the family. They might have thought I and Omagbemi were having the best out of our father behind their back good for our mother who was going to have that? So my father played a game I hope if you have read my previous books, you will understand why I behave to my late father the way I did in London even if it would be considered as uncalled for I guess I should have felt why not offer the remaining Guinness to either of his two wives present at the family gathering of some people I do not know or have not met before. It's good to make friends another thing is that it's good to be honest with friends.

I have always had this simplicity since my childhood a nature which implies do not brag on what you do not understand rather brace yourself up and wait until the right time comes which would make matters much clearer and simpler to understand even if it might hurt a little bit.

Probably if my father had offered it to any of his wives who were present it might mean he would need to have another child with either of them at which time, I was going out with a young lady my age group from Okrika in Rivers state. The person whose voice I heard suggesting to my father he offer me the Guinness was his wife Cordelier.

I got my Nigerian driving license but I never drove any of my late father's car he, never did any of his driving it's either done by his driver Mr. Vincent or my brother Omagbemi.
Big Warri is a village Journeys are made through paddling canoes or towboats taking a look at the effect of water hyacinth having a telephone connected in our dwelling at Warri GRA. I went on the errand as my father instructed to get our telephone line connected. How did I find my way to its office to handover a letter my father sent me with? I could have made a fool of myself saying I would not go because I do not know where the office was at Warri and am working for my father to ask for the connection to be made, or I could have got lost on my way there. And why did I cry at the living room where the telephone was connected in the evening on the day my father become a chief probably if it wasn't for this reaction he might not have lived longer than he did.

Within African culture, tradition or belief system when a spell is cast how do we, produce an antidote, how do we revoke the spell when it involves two different continents of the world things have never been like this before in history. Could it be right if I was being compelled to go back and stay with my mother at Ibadan or why should I have left my late mother at Ibadan with my step brother Mr. Sola Awe?
My mother had four children with my father within the two accommodations she dwelled in at Ibadan the first one was a ground floor three bedroom house owned by a landlord who makes and sells bread. The second house we moved to was a four bedroom ground floor house owned by a school principle by Name Mr. Osibowale from Ijebu origin. Mr. Vincent slept in the house on an occasion he, our father myself and Omagbemi went to Ibadan for an occasion he would have noticed how spacious and very accommodating it was even he, would have asked why did I move in with my father at Port Harcourt at all.

But in whichever case I was not the one who was squeezing my face. Wearing a suite my late father bought in the 1970s not particularly for me but intended for me. And my brother wearing a suite our father gave him did not make me squeeze face even when it boils down to issues like these I do not tend to squeeze face but in some given scenarios like these it borders me or could make me tend to withdraw. But that's how I managed to fly myself into the UK holding on to the aircraft to identify myself why should anyone including my father want to change this for me in my council block of flat. Having lived in several places e.g. three hostels, a hotel and with three private landlords before I got my council flat in Woolwich.

Why should I have been dwelling in it for over 24 years? How could I have managed to write my books? Concentrate, meditate, with my illness program myself for how many years would all these have been considered beforehand and what it means to me in this present time, I did not squeeze face but just try each day to be focused and remain the pillar I am.

And what induced Mrs. Cordelier Megbele to come and see me in 2018 in one of her visit to the UK in my council block of flat? She had eye problem looked frail but strong and determined she told me in the presence of my brother I have given her, her life back and with more years to live. Believe it or not prophesies do come true if prophesies are in you harder to them. Pepper soup ingredients, rice, traditional oil which might have been she who bought bottled and bagged for my late father now invariably it would had been Mama Gbawo's own when she and my father come to visit me and I would not let him into my flat.

If, I do not squeeze face on issues like these would it be a thing of squeezing face if I win or do not win the national lottery or if my books will sell or not? Nature has its way of taking and proving its tolls even, Mother Nature has its own way of doing the same thing. My books are for those who have had the mind to have explored life having a willingness to understand the world's problem.

Believing in yourself: Push, past your discomfort, out growing our discomfort methods put yourself, out there and be OK without knowing if people will accept you stick, to a habit not, listening to the negative self-talk that normally holds you back and stick to it some more, and learn to trust yourself.

Believing in yourself: Make a list of your past accomplishment writing out a list of your accomplishments will help you begin to believe in yourself sit down and make a list of all of the things you feel you have excelled at during some point in your life. Include even the most minor activities, like putting together furniture from Argos or how you organize yourself, make yourself fill free and relaxed talk, to people who love you if, you're having trouble seeing all the wonderful things about yourself.
It takes time to really know other people but I do not know, why employers give some people work for just to do as they please especially to certain people in certain given situations. Do not take me as being too skeptical negatively towards other people it's the kind of world we live in which could seem daunting at certain times. If it's about squeezing face, all the while, this are the wrong time to do so since entering the 21st century I rather believe in those, who are using practical reasoning and common sense in what they do.

I would like other people to see the best in me just as I would like to see the best in them it would not be right training mother and sons to fall in love or daughters and fathers to fall practically in love.

Humans are bound to feeling skeptical sometimes it's good when information on experience, emotions and feelings are well gathered but it would be wrong to be skeptical on what God wants out of us if we truly have a relationship with him. We would not need to procrastinate. Nevertheless it would be wrong being a critic or being judgmental or skeptical in a case like this if there is, it should be limited to certain areas e.g. life experience, information gathered, what is currently most needed, important or have a fall! I mean get 'twisted'.
I must emphasis that even those who put their faith in God do have certain questions to ask him every day of their lives God gave us life for reason in which lots of things can go wrong depending on how we intend to view or make out of

life how do we correlate such relationship with God and that of our family. What are purpose and outcomes when pressure is applied science has a lot to say about pressure but this one is not tricky but serious, delicate when it comes to human relationship with God.

Critic:

A critic is a professional who communicates an assessment and an opinion of various forms of creative works such as art, literature, music, cinema, theater, fashion, architecture, and food. Critics may also take as their subject social or government policy. Critical judgments, whether derived from critical thinking or not, weigh up a range of factors, including an assessment of the extent to which the item under review achieves its purpose and its creator's intention and a knowledge of its context. They may also include a positive or negative personal response.

Characteristics of a good critic are articulateness, preferably having the ability to use language with a high level of appeal and skill. Sympathy, sensitivity and insight are important too. Form, style and medium are all considered by the critic. In architecture and food criticism, the item's function, value and cost may be added components.
Critics are publicly accepted and, to a significant degree, followed because of the quality of their assessments or their reputation. Influential critics of art, music, theatre and architecture often present their arguments in complete books. One very famous example is John Ruskin's *Seven Lamps of Architecture* and *The Stones of Venice*. Critics may base their assessment on a range of theoretical positions. For instance, they may take a Feminist or Freudian perspective.

Unlike other individuals who may editorialize on subjects via websites or letters written to publications, professional critics are paid to produce their assessment and opinions for print, radio, magazine, television, or Internet companies. When their personal opinion outweighs considered judgment, people who give opinions, whether on current events, public affairs, sports, media or art are often referred to as 'pundits' instead of critics.

Critics are themselves subject to competing critics, since the final critical judgment always entails some subjectivity. An established critic can play a powerful role as a public arbiter of taste or opinion. Also, critics or a coordinated group of critics, may award symbols of recognition.
The word 'critic' comes from Greek meaning 'able to discern', which is a Greek derivation of a word, meaning a person who offers reasoned judgment or analysis, value judgment, interpretation or observation. Early English meaning of criticism was based mainly on the criticism of literature and it was in the 17th century that more general forms of criticism began.

Skeptical:

Skepticism (American English) or skepticism (British English, Australian English) is generally any questioning attitude or doubt towards one or more items of putative knowledge or belief. It is often directed at domains, such as the supernatural, morality (moral skepticism), religion (skepticism about the existence of God), or knowledge (skepticism about the possibility of knowledge, or of certainty). Formally, skepticism as a topic occurs in the context of philosophy, particularly epistemology, although it can be applied to any topic such as politics, religion, and pseudoscience.
Philosophical skepticism comes in various forms. Radical forms of skepticism deny that knowledge or rational belief is possible and urges us to suspend judgment on many or all controversial matters. More moderate forms of skepticism claim only that nothing can be known with certainty or that we can know little or nothing about the 'big questions' in life, such as whether God exists or whether there is an afterlife. Religious skepticism is 'doubt concerning basic religious principles (such as immortality, providence, and revelation)'. Scientific skepticism concerns testing beliefs for reliability, by subjecting them to systematic investigation using the scientific method, to discover empirical evidence for them.

Definition:

In ordinary usage, skepticism (US) or skepticism (UK) to search, to think about or look for; see also spelling differences) can refer to:

1. an attitude of doubt or a disposition to incredulity either in general or toward a particular object;
2. the doctrine that true knowledge or some particular knowledge is uncertain;
3. the method of suspended judgment, systematic doubt, or criticism that is characteristic of skeptics (Merriam–Webster).

In philosophy, skepticism can refer to:

1. a mode of inquiry that emphasizes critical scrutiny, caution, and intellectual rigor;
2. a method of obtaining knowledge through systematic doubt and continual testing;
3. a set of claims about the limitations of human knowledge and the proper response to such limitations.

Judgmental:

A value judgment (or value judgement) is a judgment of the rightness or wrongness of something or someone, or of the usefulness of something or someone, based on a comparison or other relativity. As a generalization, a value judgment can refer to a judgment based upon a particular set of values or on a particular value system. A related meaning of value judgment is an expedient evaluation based upon limited information at hand, an evaluation undertaken because a decision must be made on short notice.

Explanation:

The term *value judgment* can be used objectively to refer to any injunction that implies an obligation to carry out an act, implicitly involving the terms 'ought' or 'should'. It can be used either in a positive sense, signifying that a judgment must be made taking a value system into account or in a disparaging sense, signifying a judgment made by personal whim rather than objective thought or evidence.

In its positive sense, a recommendation to make a value judgment is an admonition to consider carefully, to avoid whim and impetuousness, and search for consonance with one's deeper convictions, and to search for an objective, verifiable, public, and consensual set of evidence for the opinion.

In its disparaging sense the term *value judgment* implies a conclusion is insular, one-sided, and not objective contrasting with judgments based upon deliberation, balance and public evidence.

Value judgment also can refer to a tentative judgment based on a considered appraisal of the information at hand, taken to be incomplete and evolving for example, a *value judgment* on whether to launch a military attack, or as to procedure in a medical emergency. In this case the quality of judgment suffers because the information available is incomplete as a result of exigency, rather than as a result of cultural or personal limitations.

Most commonly the term *value judgment* refers to an individual's opinion. Of course, the individual's opinion is formed to a degree by their belief system, and the culture to which they belong. So a natural extension of the term *value judgment* is to include declarations seen one way from one value system, but may be seen differently from another.

Conceptually this extension of definition is related both to the anthropological axiom 'cultural relativism' (that is, that cultural meaning derives from a context) and to the term 'moral relativism' (that is, that moral and ethical propositions are not universal truths, but stem from cultural context). A value judgment formed within a specific value system may be parochial, and may be subject to dispute in a wider audience.

As I have said humans are bound to be skeptical whenever skeptical it comes with experience or a need to use wisdom or discretion not all that based on foolishness for what we want basically the aim should be wisdom towards having result for a positive outcome or correctness. It comes with experience, emotions, and feelings when we become skeptical about God and our relationship with him or within we ourselves.

It has to do with life experience not being a critic or being judgmental our skepticism are then made sensibly with reason since it has to do about our life experience, feelings, emotions and thoughts for what is seen and unseen. Since our skepticism is limited to certain areas nevertheless we could still strongly have faith in God or whatever it is that lays before us as a given situation that needs conformity.
Since those who put their faith in God still have lots of questions for him that's why he is made unseen because of those questions that will be there and need answers in other to accredit himself. Being skeptical, a critic or judgmental about God or to my parents I rather chose redress or seek redress.

Rather than being too skeptical, a critic or being judgmental towards God why not seek redress to your questions e.g. Dose God exist if, he exist why dose he allow suffering in short why do we suffer.

Now wouldn't it be right to say if you feel God does not exist why not keep your feeling to yourself and not temper with other people's faith and relationship with God.

Immanent evaluation is a philosophical concept used by Gilles Deleuze in his essay 'Qu'est-ce qu'un dispositif ?' (1989), where it is seen as the opposite of transcendent judgment.

Deleuze writes about Michel Foucault: 'Foucault ... makes allusion to 'aesthetic' criteria, which are understood as criteria for life and replace on each occasion the claims of transcendental [*sic*] judgement [*jugement transcendant*] with an immanent evaluation [*évaluation immanente*]'.
In philosophy, transcendence conveys the basic ground concept from the word's literal meaning (from Latin), of climbing or going beyond, albeit with varying connotations in its different historical and cultural stages. It includes philosophies, systems, and approaches that describe the fundamental structures of being, not as an ontology (theory of being), but as the framework of emergence and validation of knowledge of being. 'Transcendental' is a word derived

from the scholastic, designating the extra-categorical attributes of beings.

Religious definition:

In religion, transcendence refers to the aspect of a god's nature and power which is wholly independent of the material universe, beyond all physical laws. This is contrasted with immanence, where a god is said to be fully present in the physical world and thus accessible to creatures in various ways. In religious experience transcendence is a state of being that has overcome the limitations of physical existence and by some definitions has also become independent of it. This is typically manifested in prayer, séance, meditation, psychedelics and paranormal 'visions'.
It is affirmed in various religious traditions' concept of the divine, which contrasts with the notion of a god (or, the Absolute) that exists exclusively in the physical order (immanentism), or indistinguishable from it (pantheism). Transcendence can be attributed to the divine not only in its being, but also in its knowledge. Thus, a god may transcend both the universe and knowledge (is beyond the grasp of the human mind).

Although transcendence is defined as the opposite of immanence, the two are not necessarily mutually exclusive. Some theologians and metaphysicians of various religious traditions affirm that a god is both within and beyond the universe (panentheism); in it, but not of it; simultaneously pervading it and surpassing it.

Modern philosophy:

In modern philosophy, Immanuel Kant introduced a new term *transcendental*, thus instituting a new, third meaning. In his theory of knowledge, this concept is concerned with the condition of possibility of knowledge itself. He also opposed the term *transcendental* to the term *transcendent*; the latter meaning 'that which goes beyond' (transcends) any possible knowledge of a human being.

For him *transcendental* meant knowledge about our cognitive faculty with regard to how objects are possible *a priori*. 'I call all knowledge *transcendental* if it is occupied, not with objects, but with the way that we can possibly know objects even before we experience them.' Therefore, metaphysics, as a fundamental and universal theory, turns out to be an epistemology. Transcendental philosophy, consequently, is not considered a traditional ontological form of metaphysics.

Kant also equated *transcendental* with that which is '...in respect of the subject's faculty of cognition.' Something is transcendental if it plays a role in the way in which the mind 'constitutes' objects and makes it possible for us to experience them as objects in the first place. Ordinary knowledge is knowledge of objects; transcendental knowledge is knowledge of how it is possible for us to experience those objects as objects.
This is based on Kant's acceptance of David Hume's argument that certain general features of objects (e.g. persistence, causal relationships) cannot be derived from the sense impressions we have of them. Kant argues that the mind must contribute those features and make it possible for us to experience objects as objects. In the central part of his *Critique of Pure Reason*, the 'Transcendental Deduction of the Categories', Kant argues for a deep interconnection between the ability to have self-consciousness and the ability to experience a world of objects. Through a process of synthesis, the mind generates both the structure of objects and its own unity.

A metaphilosophical question discussed by many Kantian scholars is how transcendental reflection is itself possible. Stephen Palmquist interprets Kant's appeal to faith as his most effective solution to this problem.

For Kant, the 'transcendent', as opposed to the 'transcendental', is that which lies beyond what our faculty of knowledge can legitimately know. Hegel's counter-argument to Kant was that to know a boundary is also to be aware of what it bounds and as such what lies beyond it – in other words, to have already transcended it.

Contemporary philosophy:

In phenomenology, the 'transcendent' is that which transcends our own consciousness: that which is objective rather than only a phenomenon of consciousness. Noema is employed in phenomenology to refer to the terminus of an intention as given for consciousness.
Jean-Paul Sartre also speaks of transcendence in his works. In *Being and Nothingness*, Sartre uses transcendence to describe the relation of the self to the object oriented world, as well as our concrete relations with others. For Sartre, the for-itself is sometimes called a transcendence. Additionally if the other is viewed strictly as an object, much like any other object, then the other is, for the for-itself, a transcendence-transcended. When the for-itself grasps the other in the others world, and grasps the subjectivity that the other has, it is referred to as transcending-transcendence. Thus, Sartre defines relations with others in terms of transcendence.
Contemporary transcendental philosophy is developed by German philosopher Harald Holz with a holistic approach. Holz liberated transcendental philosophy from the convergence of neo-Kantianism, he critically discussed transcendental pragmatism and the relation between transcendental philosophy, neo-empiricism and the so-called postmodernism.

Colloquial usage:

In everyday language, 'transcendence' means 'going beyond', and 'self-transcendence' means going beyond a prior form or state of oneself. Mystical experience is thought of as a particularly advanced state of self-transcendence, in which the sense of a separate self is abandoned. 'Self-transcendence' is believed to be psychometrically measurable, and (at least partially) inherited, and has been incorporated as a personality dimension in the Temperament and Character Inventory. The discovery of this is described in the book 'The God Gene' by Dean Hamer, although this has been criticized by commentators such as Carl Zimmer.
Gilles Deleuze (French:; 18 January 1925 – 4 November 1995) was a French philosopher who, from the early 1960s

until his death in 1995, wrote on philosophy, literature, film, and fine art. His most popular works were the two volumes of *Capitalism and Schizophrenia*: *Anti-Oedipus* (1972) and *A Thousand Plateaus* (1980), both co-written with psychoanalyst Félix Guattari. His metaphysical treatise *Difference and Repetition* (1968) is considered by many scholars to be his magnum opus. A. W. Moore, citing Bernard Williams's criteria for a great thinker, ranks Deleuze among the 'greatest philosophers'. His work has influenced a variety of disciplines across philosophy and art, including literary theory, post-structuralism and postmodernism.
Paul-Michel Foucault (15 October 1926 – 25 June 1984), generally known as Michel Foucault was a French philosopher, historian of ideas, social theorist, and literary critic.

Foucault's theories primarily address the relationship between power and knowledge, and how they are used as a form of social control through societal institutions. Though often cited as a post-structuralist and postmodernist, Foucault rejected these labels, preferring to present his thought as a critical history of modernity. His thought has influenced academics, especially those working in communication studies, sociology, cultural studies, literary theory, feminism, and critical theory. Activist groups have also found his theories compelling.
Born in Poitiers, France, into an upper-middle-class family, Foucault was educated at the Lycée Henri-IV, at the École Normale Supérieure, where he developed an interest in philosophy and came under the influence of his tutors Jean Hyppolite and Louis Althusser, and at the University of Paris (Sorbonne), where he earned degrees in philosophy and psychology.

After several years as a cultural diplomat abroad, he returned to France and published his first major book, *The History of Madness* (1961). After obtaining work between 1960 and 1966 at the University of Clermont-Ferrand, he produced *The Birth of the Clinic* (1963) and *The Order of Things* (1966), publications which displayed his increasing involvement with structuralism, from which he later distanced himself. These first three histories exemplified a historiographical technique Foucault was developing called 'archaeology'.

From 1966 to 1968, Foucault lectured at the University of Tunis before returning to France, where he became head of the philosophy department at the new experimental university of Paris VIII. Foucault subsequently published *The Archaeology of Knowledge* (1969). In 1970, Foucault was admitted to the Collège de France, a membership he retained until his death.

He also became active in a number of left-wing groups involved in campaigns against racism and human rights abuses and for penal reform. Foucault later published *Discipline and Punish* (1975) and *The History of Sexuality* (1976), in which he developed archaeological and genealogical methods which emphasized the role that power plays in society.

Foucault died in Paris of neurological problems compounded by HIV/AIDS; he became the first public figure in France to die from the disease. His partner Daniel Defert founded the AIDES charity in his memory.

Jean-Paul Charles Aymard Sartre 21 June 1905 – 15 April 1980 was a French philosopher, playwright, novelist, political activist, biographer, and literary critic. He was one of the key figures in the philosophy of existentialism and phenomenology, and one of the leading figures in 20th-century French philosophy and Marxism. His work has also influenced sociology, critical theory, post-colonial theory, and literary studies, and continues to influence these disciplines.

Sartre was also noted for his open relationship with prominent feminist and fellow existentialist philosopher and writer Simone de Beauvoir. Together, Sartre and de Beauvoir challenged the cultural and social assumptions and expectations of their upbringings, which they considered bourgeois, in both lifestyle and thought.

The conflict between oppressive, spiritually destructive conformity (*mauvaise foi*, literally, 'bad faith') and an 'authentic' way of 'being' became the dominant theme of Sartre's early work, a theme embodied in his principal

philosophical work Being and Nothingness (*L'Être et le Néant*, 1943). Sartre's introduction to his philosophy is his work *Existentialism and Humanism* (*L'existentialisme est un humanisme*, 1946), originally presented as a lecture.
He was awarded the 1964 Nobel Prize in Literature despite attempting to refuse it, saying that he always declined official honors and that 'a writer should not allow himself to be turned into an institution'.

Cultural relativism is the idea that a person's beliefs, values, and practices should be understood based on that person's own culture, rather than be judged against the criteria of another.

It was established as axiomatic in anthropological research by Franz Boas in the first few decades of the 20th century and later popularized by his students. Boas first articulated the idea in 1887: 'civilization is not something absolute, but ... is relative, and ... our ideas and conceptions are true only so far as our civilization goes'. However, Boas did not coin the term. Neither did the 21st century relativist James Lawrence Wray-Miller.

The first use of the term recorded in the *Oxford English Dictionary* was by philosopher and social theorist Alain Locke in 1924 to describe Robert Lowie's 'extreme cultural relativism', found in the latter's 1917 book *Culture and Ethnology*. The term became common among anthropologists after Boas' death in 1942, to express their synthesis of a number of ideas Boas had developed.
Boas believed that the sweep of cultures, to be found in connection with any sub species, is so vast and pervasive that there cannot be a relationship between culture and race. Cultural relativism involves specific epistemological and methodological claims. Whether or not these claims necessitate a specific ethical stance is a matter of debate. This principle should not be confused with moral relativism.
Moral relativism may be any of several philosophical positions concerned with the differences in moral judgments across different people and cultures. *Descriptive* moral relativism holds only that some people do in fact disagree about what is moral; *meta-ethical* moral relativism holds that

in such disagreements, nobody is objectively right or wrong; and *normative* moral relativism holds that because nobody is right or wrong, we ought to tolerate the behavior of others even when we disagree about the morality of it.

Not all descriptive relativists adopt meta-ethical relativism, and moreover, not all meta-ethical relativists adopt normative relativism. Richard Rorty, for example, argued that relativist philosophers believe 'that the grounds for choosing between such opinions is less algorithmic than had been thought', but not that any belief is as valid as any other. Moral relativism has been debated for thousands of years, from ancient Greece and India to the present day, in diverse fields including art, philosophy, science, and religion.

Variations:-

Descriptive:

Descriptive moral relativism is merely the positive or descriptive position that there exist, in fact, fundamental disagreements about the right course of action even when the same facts hold true and the same consequences seem likely to arise. It is the observation that different cultures have different moral standards.
Descriptive relativists do not necessarily advocate the tolerance of all behavior in light of such disagreement; that is to say, they are not necessarily normative relativists. Likewise, they do not necessarily make any commitments to the semantics, ontology, or epistemology of moral judgement; that is, not all descriptive relativists are meta-ethical relativists.
Descriptive relativism is a widespread position in academic fields such as anthropology and sociology, which simply admit that it is incorrect to assume that the same moral or ethical frameworks are always in play in all historical and cultural circumstances.

Meta-ethical:

Meta-ethical moral relativism is unpopular among philosophers; many are quite critical of it, though there are several contemporary philosophers who support it.
Meta-ethical moral relativists believe not only that people disagree about moral issues, but that terms such as 'good', 'bad', 'right' and 'wrong' do not stand subject to universal truth conditions at all; rather, they are relative to the traditions, convictions, or practices of an individual or a group of people. The American anthropologist William Graham Sumner was an influential advocate of this view. He argues in his 1906 work *Folkways* that what people consider right and wrong is shaped entirely - not primarily - by the traditions, customs, and practices of their culture. Moreover, since in his analysis of human understanding there cannot be any higher moral standard than that provided by the local morals of a culture, no trans-cultural judgement about the rightness or wrongness of a culture's morals could possibly be justified.

Meta-ethical relativists are, first, descriptive relativists: they believe that, given the same set of facts, some societies or individuals will have a fundamental disagreement about what a person *ought* to do or prefer (based on societal or individual norms). What's more, they argue that one cannot adjudicate these disagreements using any available independent standard of evaluation—any appeal to a relevant standard would always be merely personal or at best societal.

This view contrasts with moral universalism, which argues that, even though well-intentioned persons disagree, and some may even remain unpersuadable (e.g. someone who is closed-minded), there is still a meaningful sense in which an action could be more 'moral' (morally preferable) than another; that is, they believe there *are* objective standards of evaluation that seem worth calling 'moral facts' regardless of whether they are universally accepted.

Normative:

Normative moral relativists believe not only the meta-ethical thesis, but that it has normative implications on what we ought to do. They argue that meta-ethical relativism implies that we *ought* to tolerate the behavior of others even when it runs counter to our personal or cultural moral standards. Most philosophers do not agree, partially because of the challenges of arriving at an 'ought' from relativistic premises. Meta-ethical relativism seems to eliminate the normative relativist's ability to make prescriptive claims. In other words, normative relativism may find it difficult to make a statement like 'we think it is moral to tolerate behavior' without always adding 'other people think *intolerance* of certain behaviors is moral'.

Philosophers like Russell Blackford even argue that intolerance is, to some degree, important. As he puts it, 'we need not adopt quietism about moral traditions that cause hardship and suffering. Nor need we passively accept the moral norms of our own respective societies, to the extent that they are ineffective or counterproductive or simply unnecessary'. That is, it is perfectly reasonable (and practical) for a person or group to defend their subjective values against others, even if there is no universal prescription or morality. We can also criticize other cultures for failing to pursue even *their own goals* effectively.
The moral relativists may also still try to make sense of non-universal statements like 'in this country, it is wrong to do X' or even 'to me, it is right to do Y'.

Moral Universalists argue further that their system often *does* justify tolerance, and that disagreement with moral systems does not always demand interference, and certainly not aggressive interference. For example, the utilitarian might call another society's practice 'ignorant' or 'less moral', but there would still be much debate about courses of action (e.g. whether to focus on providing better education, or technology, etc.).

What is Universal Truth? Is there such a thing as absolute truth or universal truth?

In order to understand absolute or universal truth, we must begin by defining truth. Truth, according to the dictionary, is 'conformity to fact or actuality; a statement proven to be or accepted as true.' Some people would say that there is no true reality, only perceptions and opinions. Others would argue that there must be some absolute reality or truth.

One view says that there are no absolutes that define reality what about pain, suffering and the problem of evil in our world. Those who hold this view believe everything is relative to something else, and thus there can be no actual reality. Because of that, there are ultimately no moral absolutes, no authority for deciding if an action is positive or negative, right or wrong.

This view leads to 'situational ethics,' the belief that what is right or wrong is relative to the situation. There is no right or wrong; therefore, whatever feels or seems right at the time and in that situation is right. Of course, situational ethics leads to a subjective, 'whatever feels good' mentality and lifestyle, which has a devastating effect on society and individuals. This is postmodernism, creating a society that regards all values, beliefs, lifestyles, and truth claims as equally valid.

There is universal truth in you, in the things you do, how you do them because you are a living being. You exist so you can do those things what if you cannot do them then, there is no reality of you or of what you can do or can't do.

Therefore you are a reality of something there must be good or bad in you or there can be both you are here to understand and go through absolute truth of what would make you, universal something that would make you or pave the way for you, to exist for ever. How you will be able to do this is left for you to find out within good and bad of which you must make a choice.

To make this choice you must live within what is considered universally truthful does this make sense if you like you can say if you do not exist there is no universal truth. I am me you are you, you can be good or bad I can be good or bad in which we have to make a choice we do not need to make the same choice.

If there is a God one of us is universally right but if there is no God it means just one within both of us is right. But not universally since you still have me to reckon with. While I at the end of the day, I will not agree or accept to call you God so where does this leave us? So, rather than both of us just being, judgmental, in disagreement against each other of what is universally right or wrong what should we do? Go on arguing is death a good or a bad thing?

I must have been more reasonably, thoughtful and considerate within you and myself, to have brought the existence of God into it because if not, tomorrow you and I will be fighting of who should be called God now let us see who within both of us is putting himself in the place of God?
The other view holds that there are indeed absolute realities and standards that define what is true and what is not. Therefore, actions can be determined to be either right or wrong by how they measure up to those absolute standards. If there are no absolutes, no reality, chaos ensues. Take the law of gravity, for instance.
If it were not absolute, we could not be certain we could stand or sit in one place until we decided to move. Or if two plus two did not always equal four, the effects on civilization would be disastrous. Laws of science and physics would be irrelevant, and commerce would be impossible. What a mess that would be! Thankfully, two plus two does equal four. There is absolute truth, and it can be found and understood.
To make the statement that there is no absolute truth is illogical. Yet, today, lots of people are embracing a cultural relativism that denies any type of absolute truth. A good question to ask people is who say, 'There is no absolute truth' is this: 'Are you absolutely sure of that?' then you become skeptical looking for an answer.

You do not have to agree with me, I do not have to agree with you. Where does this leave us I say leave it in the hands of God. If they say 'yes,' they have not made an absolute statement which itself implies that everything in existence is absolutes but, if am saying God exist with this very fact there is absolute truth by which I define myself, my words and action I do not need to define motion since it's part of life what keeps me in motion I can feel it.

- I exist you exist who made us
- I did not make the trees you did not make them but God made them should we quarrel within our solves who made the trees
- We both end up in our grave but God exist forever our children after us will go on believing in him
- The more they will live in peace
- Another problem with the denial of absolute truth or universal truth is that it fails to live up to what we know to be true in our own consciences, our own experiences, and what we see in the real world. If there is no such thing as absolute truth, then there is nothing ultimately right or wrong about anything. What might be 'right' for you does not mean it is 'right' for me. If this should be the case one party is saying there should be no religious beliefs
- Is it one and absolute truth that we all should sin
- Those who have a relationship with God always have questions for him to answer throughout their daily lives the Holy Bible ends with the book of revelation and an Amen.
- If people always put the blame of something on you that is not wholly your fault what should you do? You will seek absolute truth
- Even in death some people seek for absolute truth
- What does the health care system think of people who want to commit assisted suicide?
- Is this what our health care system should stand for?
- And a Modern craze of why God allows suffering if he is God, if he exist why should he allow suffering therefore God does not exist what would they want me to believe in?

- Garlic now seems to have all sorts of cure because it's native, negative effect might likely come with an omen what it has is healing powers and will have to confirm to certain peoples genetic makeup. It might not be absolutely true but it makes some sense towards certain truth or reality more in line in a spiritual or scientific way
- It's when you seek to be spiritually whole, that's when garlic is very good for you. You will enjoy its flavor more and realize its spiritual essence.

One of the problems I find in those who care for we sufferers is they put the blame 70% on us some of the things they know they know it through us or through their experiments. for example if patient under their care wants to commit assisted suicide atheist would see them as taking us forward but not really in my opinion but to take them forward in their act of criticizing God and his creation.

We take things from each other to lean on and then start gradually in a new dimension to take over the world or making cover-ups, make amends, show our true feelings within ourselves. Sometimes I feel the most difficult thing I want them to know they, already know. Not just me but also other people might have problems they already know about. A difficult scenario's is when you take such issues to religious grounds the religious leaders do practically the same thing or it becomes their own cup of tea no wonder our faith and relationship with God is becoming more personal. How would you feel when you get to know you are being cheated on?

Why is it that everything you do as a schizophrenia sufferer or any other form of mental health un-wellness its criticism you will receive there is nothing left to play with when one is on welfare payment true or false? Just waiting for welfare benefit to come in through your post office of bank each week or every fortnight one is adding suffering to their lives our feelings or emotions should be on other positive things we can do or think about.

Yet try and place a computer in your dwelling, be on the internet, write a book, cloth yourself well, try and have your bath regularly regardless of the effect and symptoms of your illness do all this it's still criticism you might receive no wonder some of us don't even try they just leave their lives to get rotten if not out of being a spoilt egg in the community one is actually suffering by the time you could get hold of even a computer you will realize, you are skinning yourself positively against negative odds.

This you thought of doing through your own initiatives with difficulties I mean out of being considerate I was skinned for over £1,000.00 trying to get two of my book published. People are making a living out of mental health issues it should not all be the case we need to be encouraged.
For some of us it should not be at the end of the day it boils down to us going through it all positively all on our own we hear all kind of strange stories the more it will be for people like we putting things in perspective in just getting along but we feel the pain the strange stories also bears on us. It might make some of us get fed-up, angry, frustrated, disorientated. With those who of who might be managing our illness and the effect it does not make things go as planned e.g. our day becomes clouded which can go on for weeks before put our self together once again.

I realized if I hadn't taken or made an initiative or effort in writing my books I could have been suffering from a very serious and difficult form of paranoias or hallucination it gave me insight into what I had to do, what was happening to me rather than just going deeper into negative forms of paranoias or hallucination's I find myself pulling through it and making sense out of it each day through writing and word processing now this didn't come easy.

For example I was a smoker and an alcoholic at one point it did not made me go into taking more serious hard drugs. With a feeling hard drugs would easily and quickly send me to my grave and if I didn't care listening to my conscience where would it have left me and here I am having the thought of quitting smoking after dropping alcohol to a very low limit.

I came about realizing it's all about getting hold of once self these are issues we should be discussing to make the world a better place entering the 21st century but why bring in E-cigarettes or E-pipes into it when there were other harder drugs even if they had to we should be more certain of its positive impacts. What impacts dose this hold on hard drugs I have the feeling E-cigarettes will make one drink more alcohol daily.

If we were to continually make our world a better place this are issues of importance we should consider and not about God does not exist but how, we should say prayers for him to grant us the grace to pull through and move on. If he exist why dose he allow pain and suffering these are all evil in our lives why do we allow them could there be anything wrong if I make God my refuge no wonder we seems to be failing each other in a spiritual and emotional sense. I can understand we all individually have our own different opinion and experience about this it's simply because God is democratic.

When it comes to issues concerning money, being a successful business man or woman, a pronounced athletic, a writer, a singer, an artist, a politician you did not make all the move something must have triggered you into it. do you really know what it was if you actually know then, you will know your mission it will be straight forward and straight to the point, short if need be and concise. When you become successful you began having faith in yourself you wanted to make those around you, what you want them to be. Probably simply because there is much for you to believe in yourself e.g. you are very successful, popular, respected, dignified or feared.

Could there be so much going wrong because someone believes and has faith in God it makes us a better person it's sometimes true it's only at that point we are a better person but when we become successful we might become something else. Why do some people do not want to hear about God How do we come about losing the touch of God

in our existence when it's all practically what we are made up of.
Human tend to seek power in all sorts of ways much of this cause problem along the way but we never wonder about the amount of freewill we have and where it comes from and for what purpose really if we do, we would be more open we would not doubt too easily the existence of God for this reason certain expects of our lives and the way we go about them can be very daunting. Couldn't this be as a result of the amount of freewill we have to do and undo, to please ourselves as we like and careless for certain important issues about life. Something is always reminding me or asking me where I am going to. What is this journey for and then end up in my grave. It's likely asking or leading me to understand this life and then my after life or what else dose this emotional pain about suffering from a mental health issues called schizophrenia?

How do you live a life realizing other people use your spiritual motives before you do what kind of a game can one call it? The most exciting part of it is that we all need to have a winning ticket to identify ourselves with.

I can't be going mentally unwell or insane at the same time somebody expects me to be foolish it should be considered uncalled for at the same time demoting. The word *demotion* is not restricted to the world of employment; it can be used in a number of areas. When other people make you feel they are in control, there should be a positive side to it somewhat beneficial to you.
If some people could live to imply God doesn't exist why should some of us change our name should there be a need to change our name.

Could it be said or accepted that some of us just bring ourselves into this world to annoy other people which sometimes lead to grievous bodily or emotional harm.
If we know things like these and are very much in aware of the problems of evil in this world as we experience them probably each day what are we doing or have been doing to overcome them.

We are ever than before becoming aware of our pain and suffering. We are much aware of what we want from each other but find it difficult to communicate or is it because we are more than ever than before becoming closer to each other.

What would you want from the lives of those who believe in God I might want something in the life of a fellow believer in God e.g. they should not suffer, they should experience the beauty of God, if we believe God created all things do we need to be lectured on the issues of evil, pain and suffering?
If you want something out of those who believe in God or you have a problem with them or about them try to tell them specifically basically they will be willing and open to speak with you but you need not speak to them against what they believe in. What you are trying to imply mind you, is also your own belief. It ought to be on how to obey Gods commandments more in a way that express how it's beneficial to all and makes us unique in our ways, for example how we express love and understanding, how we let the light of God gives us guidance in everything we do.
If we are good, we would customarily encourage other people to be good it reflects other people would know us as a nice person and not when you have an appointment with the beast you give the beast an opportunity to abuse at the same time to give you what you want.
If you feel you are a slave somebody else is milking you while our world is part of suffering, pain and evil, you are making a big mistake you cannot be a slave and there is pain and suffering in the world you might infer to being a slave to material things or the flesh, a slave to being used but there is what is called not spiritual slavery but psychological slavery related to views, thoughts, negative emotions, paranoias. The master would be the first to know this before his son or you. Remorse I feel is somehow better off than paranoias it could wipe off paranoias induce positive reverie it, dose not all that calls for hate but pity.

A master always knows a stupide slave or a stupid son. It means lacking intelligence not that you are not human but inquire if you are truly human, you have a heart, a mind and a soul. It takes a lot to be human you should be happy for this in yourself your aim, would be, to be your own master while before you will be a master and a very good master for that matter you will really have to know God. You will have to be a master in three different things to understand that two wrong cannot make a right but the third wrong might.

I do not know God in fear I know him as wise how could our world become a place a wise person is never feared but reverend there are lots of reason why we cannot see God but can feel his presence why should we have kings or queens if there is God instead of fearing God reverend him so we are here to learn a lot about ourselves, our master e.g. teachers and God or there will be no pain, evil or suffering in our world.

Man does not live by bread alone but by every word of the commandments of God yet do not judge anyone or you be judged. Stupidity is quite different from ignorance you should not be ignorant at the same time lack knowledge, wisdom or reasoning or you are no different from a buffoon while a buffoon is not a good way to describe any human being a slave can never be a buffoon.

Naturally if you are a good person, very good indeed when you are down you might realize you understand your own weak points, capable of enhancing yourself as well as encouraging yourself to still move on for example pretending your feeling down is nothing you find out you have a great resilience to coup when things go wrong or can snap out of it with ease than most people so being good gives you strength. Because of your goodness you can get away from some nastier situation or impulses.

People who are good tend to have nice responses from other people this is a time they are very much at work in what they are good at if we all respond liking such people the world would be less troublesome.

It's daunting when you do something good and people turn a blind eye or response at it these days things happen so very quickly our world seems overpopulated we all need food but most people are interested in money we are more interested in retail goods and services.

Why does schizophrenia go through phase that other people are inside them are we all turning into a mass?

I understand the energy and mass can change back and forth according to Einstein. It is fluid; it can go from one to the other. So, what keeps mass from just turning into energy? Is there some force holding a subatomic particle together? What keeps mass in its state? I hope this is not a silly question but I am clueless.
You will know them by their works and the words from their mouth they are the once who are making the mess. They may turn it into a demonstration or a street protest in favour of a political or other cause. If its money they are after then its personal from the real issues at stake e.g. euthanasia. It's not all mostly about food to lots of people food is just sustenance, it test like food that's all I know it's the most important thing to me it's something I should not lose but consider dear.

The government is considering imposing stricter regulations on the sale of laxatives amid concerns they could be abused by people with eating disorders.
The Medicines and Healthcare products Regulatory Agency will examine measures such as age limits on purchasers and possibly ending over-the-counter sales.

24/9/2018:
Labour conference to debate option of fresh Brexit vote
Labour members are to vote on keeping 'all options on the table' on Brexit, including possibly campaigning for a new referendum, at their conference.
The party's leadership wants a general election allowing Labour to take control of negotiations if it won.
Labour conference: John McDonnell unveils shares plan for workers. Labour would force all large firms to give workers shares worth up to £500 a year each, John McDonnell has said.

In his main party conference speech, the shadow chancellor set out plans for 'inclusive ownership funds'.

He also announced that the water industry in England would be the first to be re-nationalised under Labour.
Brexit: No 10 says cabinet 'fully behind' PM's plan
The cabinet remains fully behind Theresa May's Brexit policy in the face of growing calls within her party to change direction, No 10 has insisted.

The prime minister is sticking by her Chequers plan for future co-operation despite European leaders attacking it.
Brexit: Pet travel warning in no-deal planning papers
Pet owners who want to take their animals to the EU face having to make plans at least four months in advance if there is no Brexit deal.

This worst-case scenario is set out in the latest batch of government papers about planning for leaving the EU without a deal in place.
Currently pets can travel with their owners throughout the EU thanks to the pet passport scheme.
But without a Brexit deal, the UK will become a 'third country'.

When you are brought up the godly way, believe in morals, principles and virtues you tend to have a dislike for hypocrisy.

Hypocrisy is the contrivance of a false appearance of virtue or goodness, while concealing real character or inclinations, especially with respect to religious and moral beliefs; hence, in a general sense, hypocrisy may involve dissimulation, pretense, or a sham. Hypocrisy is the practice of engaging in the same behavior or activity for which one criticizes another.

In moral psychology, it is the failure to follow one's own expressed moral rules and principles. According to British political philosopher David Runciman, 'Other kinds of hypocritical deception include claims to knowledge that one lacks, claims to a consistency that one cannot sustain, claims to a loyalty that one does not possess, claims to an identity that one does not hold'. American political journalist Michael Gerson says that political hypocrisy is 'the conscious use of a mask to fool the public and gain political benefit'.

Hypocrisy has been a subject of folk wisdom and wisdom literature from the beginnings of human history. Increasingly, since the 1980s, it has also become central to studies in behavioral economics, cognitive science, cultural psychology, decision making, ethics, evolutionary psychology, moral psychology, political sociology, positive psychology, social psychology and sociological social psychology.

David Walter Runciman FBA (born 1 March 1967) is an English academic who teaches politics and history at Cambridge University, where he is Head of the Department of Politics and International Studies, Professor of Politics, and a fellow of Trinity Hall, Cambridge.
Michael John Gerson (born May 15, 1964) is an op-ed columnist for *The Washington Post*, a Policy Fellow with the ONE Campaign, a visiting fellow with the Center for Public Justice, and a former senior fellow at the Council on Foreign Relations. He served as President George W. Bush's chief speechwriter from 2001 until June 2006, as a senior policy advisor from 2000 through June 2006, and was a member of the White House Iraq Group.

Naturally if people are good I mean very good if so whenever you are down they will seek to support you out of your misery because of their goodness to you or to other people at least there should be a way of paying them back for having being good. How do you support a dead person since they could leave good or bad memory can you forget the past or the dead?

This is a time to really consider and use adoptive memories! How often do other people come to you just to be nice or good to you why would other people want to be good to a person like me when all that is being said about schizophrenia? I should not be made to feel am all alone I should do as am told if I do not want to do as am told and

am not happy with what am given I could chose to end my life.
Why and how and for what reason should I give myself an honorable death can euthanasia be considered as an honorable death? An honorable death is the stated goal of many men, from warriors to firefighters. And, while sociologists across the world now study the phenomena of this idea, perhaps the best explanation for the quest of an honorable death is that such a way of dying cannot give the ultimate meaning to all life itself.

The honourable death is an important, albeit very frightening, tradition in almost every human culture that has ever existed, but its practice and style is amazingly varied. In no culture is it taken lightly, of course, and the emotions involved are as intense as any part of humanity. But cultures certainly do have differences in the idea of an honourable death.

These differences appear, perhaps, subtle – and even moot – to the casual observer, but understanding them can be of great value to all of humanity. From what is going on in our world today may be here is a brief look at the way several of the world's most important cultures of today have treated the idea of honourable death over the centuries.
Things, situation varies in sensitivity they all occur for different reasons sensitive they might be or difficult to come out with but there should be a way out in the most technical but pleasant way because it makes us more alive in what we believe in our life experience our pain and suffering is for us to be more watchful, carful and not being too care free, to do away with un-necessary attachment. Sometimes God has to cut the grass down in your life, so that you can see the snakes.

Life is all about exploring, chasing passion, and pursuing things that give us eternal happiness people, who set themselves free from unnecessary attachments and continue doing things their way can make the most of this opportunity called life. Here in this book are demonstrated signs of those carefree and light-hearted people who have a unique perspective towards life and make sure they are happy no matter what!

There are certain things we do or go through demonstrating we are more alive our pain, suffering can sometimes be our watchword in this case, and it's not a word or phrase but an act which requires response. How are we often reminded we are all here for the good of all mankind?
When someone is in a process of dying, in pain or in suffering, in jubilation, in need to be more powerful than others or to be at the top their mind, head, heart, body speaks to them secretly the same thing applies when one is in fear such times are not for hearing voices. This might have something to do with the state of the world, our lives, work and activity how do humans often reconsider their ways?

If you feel you are going to win the national lottery because you believe it's in your star to win with such a game as the national lottery how would you feel playing just £2.00 you hit the jackpot I have this feeling there is no way I can determine my own chance of being a winner.
With more players who are real gamers wining little or nothing it's quite discouraging. There are no personal technique open for me to win which I can enforce. If I win with my own techniques then it's a game because it makes it fun, educating and quite an experience for me. Yet some of us are going superstitious with such a game e.g. Am one of the pillars or tuned to one of the pillars of the Solar system. If that's the case it would not be to win even if you win the jackpot you will lose your balance.
No gambling game will let you leave the real players behind what kind of a star could make you win such a lottery.
Understanding the philosophy, psychology, religiosity or omens of wining and loosing that's what I call a game e.g. after winning a small amount keeping the ticket for a while as you play along, you might have experience something spiritual about the stars, climate, mood, sensation that a past ticket you have played will be a winning number in the coming draw.

It would be the gaming day that really spells out what's in the stars if I believe it's written in my stars am going to win the national lottery so that's the day I would often play the lottery. For me on the other hand the gaming day might come a day or two after or before the gaming day do you realize some of us are getting superstitious with such a game the machine should be named after other planets, the sun or moon.

How many of us go through feelings or emotions that everything going on in our lives are worth experiencing where would you place such feelings or emotions if you have probably been on welfare benefit for a long time.

- Or if you are:
- Suffering from obesity
- Alcoholism
- Drug addiction
- If you have too much money
- If you have mental health issues

These are issues we often hear about recently but what is it that is really in the closet how you can be alone and be more alive or dead. It's really good to know what's actually in the closet whether good or bad so we are more aware or in a position to brace ourselves up for whatever turns up. In some cases we might have been taken by the effect before due consideration is given which comes as surprise, surprise. Some people like surprise while some of us do not.

We all could listen to the regulars as they come through the news on our Radio or Television these days I wonder why you need to be in one group or the other while half of what goes on are augments I guess this is one issue that could be bringing Great Britain out of the EU now is not the time for augment now even things of small details can easily result to augments or conflict.

After living in my parental native land with step mothers, brothers and sisters based on all the experience I had been through over there living with them and here in the UK I happen to meet with a Rastafarian who has a very close resemblance in looks and physics just like one of my step brother living in Norther Island what is schizophrenia, what are its cases and related symptoms when it comes to such a mysterious perspective.

Samson wanted Delilah he was given the grace to put down a lion forth and killed many with its born. I have a strange feeling one of the reason for the call of Samson has something to do with crossing the River Nile. I have heard of folks stories while I was a young lad that e.g. people, Mermaid's live below the sea or how would those stones shout out and call God in praises if we seize to obey him. They were evacuated during the crossing of the Nile what awesome powers can do such a thing they might be no different from the dragons that were called into repentance.

Why do we Nigerians live the way we do when doors are open to changes when we were young, things or reasons for occurrences the adults know about better than us they, often kept secret to themselves.

How long are we going to continue living is such ways, we are not the only race within West Africa or even Africa not to include other parts of the world on the other hand I think God had always wanted us to take things gradually because we are on a great religious site.

It's time to come out of our being scotched by things we should now have an understanding of. We should no longer exist in neglect its either we now exist to have a heart or in the near future we exist to become heartless.
Port Moresby: The world's most dangerous city to be a woman?

Papua New Guinea is one of the most dangerous countries in the world for women. Some estimates say that 70% of women in PNG will be raped in their lifetime.
Ben Zand travels to the capital Port Moresby to meet the men who believe violence against women is acceptable - and those women who say enough is enough.
How do career dreams really work out?

When young people were asked in 2011 about the careers they wanted, the most popular ambitions were for jobs such as doctors, vets, firefighters, police officers, nurses, teachers and actors.

But the Office for National Statistics has gone back and found a reality gap with what really happened to their lives six years later.

Apart from those who aimed to go into teaching, less than one in 50 were in the career they had wanted - with most working as sales assistants, carers or in sales and marketing.

They were also earning less than they had expected and fewer of them had gone to university than they had hoped.

When a child won't see one parent 12 September 2018

When parents separate, where the children live, how much time they spend with mum or dad, can be hard to agree.

Sometimes a child starts refusing to see their other parent.

This autumn, social workers who look after a child's interests in the family courts are being given new guidelines to help with these cases.

For the first time this will consider the possibility a child has been deliberately turned against one parent, by the other.

Parental alienation, as it's called, will be just one of the options a social worker might consider.

It's a controversial concept which the courts have been trying to grapple with for years in cases where the parents are locked into entrenched legal action over contact.

There is no consensus and not a great deal of research, so how might it be considered by courts here?

The intensity or frequency of behavior might be one of the ways this is set apart from the disagreements that are often part of separation.

'Think of a child experiencing a separation, the mother or father bad mouthing, or withholding warmth and affection unless they agree with an argument,' says Sarah Parsons of the Children and Families Court Advisory Service.

'If it's repeated it can have an invasive, intrusive effect on wellbeing. A child can think the only way to stay safe is to side with one parent and reject the other.'

The recognition in the advice to social workers does not mean other possibilities won't be considered.

Children might refuse to see a parent because of authoritarian or abusive behaviour, or because they feel naturally emotionally very attached to one parent.

High level of conflict:

So how common might parental alienation be?
Around 10% of separated parents have contact agreements made through the courts.
Each year around 1,400 cases return to court in England seeking enforcement of contact orders, according to research published by the Nuffield Foundation in 2013.
Professor Liz Trinder, from the University of Exeter, has studied cases where there is a high level of conflict between the parents.

She thinks the idea of parental alienation as a pattern of behaviors needs to be treated carefully, because the courts have a duty to consider the child's best interests.
Part of that is listening carefully to what children say themselves about their feelings.
'The problem with the alienation concept is that if your premise is the child has been brainwashed, it means you can't trust what the child is saying to the court. So if you make an accusation of alienation it almost automatically casts suspicion on anything the child might say.'
Professor Trinder believes England could learn from Canada, where concerns emerged of counsellors and expert advisors to the courts whose careers were invested in a strong belief in parental alienation.
The consequences of a diagnosis of alienation can have a huge impact on a child, she argues, with some supporters of the concept arguing it should lead to a transfer of care and residency.

'Supporters of alienation will generally insist that should be done literally overnight. So the child is removed from the alienating parent and placed with the so called innocent parent, and the child won't have any contact with the first parent. For me that feels like child abuse'

The charity Women's Aid has also expressed concern this year that accusations of parental alienation may lead to a history of an abusive relationship not being given enough weight.

While some campaigners have tried to press for its recognition as a syndrome the charity warned the development of the theory in the US has been highly disputed.

All of this is very challenging for the family courts to manage.

In one case in 2010 which provoked debate a family court ordered a 12-year-old boy should be transferred from living with his mum, to his dad.

Contact with his father had broken down four years previously, but the court battles had lasted most of his life.

An appeal by his mother was turned down.

Then an appeal on behalf of the boy led to him being put into foster care with the aim of building contact with his father before a move.

In contact sessions with his father, the boy was described as sitting with his head in his lap, hands over his ears.

The court eventually accepted the order could not be enforced.

The judge was told the father, described as 'wholly deserving', was heard sobbing as he left the final contact meeting.

CAFCASS said it hopes its guidelines will help form a basis for social workers to explore what is happening with both parents, rather than attributing blame.

But Sarah Parsons also said it is important not to overlook the lifelong impact where a child is alienated.

'It can be devastating, an adult can look back on childhood and feel misled by trusted parents, adults can have mental health issues, just like any other abuse would.

Infanticide in Kenya: 'I was told to kill my disabled baby'

Lydia Njoki's youngest child Samwell, who has epilepsy and physical disabilities, would not be here if some of her family had their way. 27th September 2018:

Her own grandmother went as far as suggesting how she could kill her baby.

'She told me to insert needles into Samwell's veins - that they would kill him slowly and no-one would know what had happened,' she said.
The 56-year-old mother-of-four lives in Narok County, Kenya.

'People said I was cursed, that's why I got a child with a disability,' Ms. Njoki said.
Many a night, she cried herself to sleep: 'I hated myself and asked God, why me?'
Florence Kipchumba faced similar pressure - her family told her that her baby should be sacrificed.
'As an infant, Meshack used to cry a lot, and when my family couldn't take it anymore, I was kicked out of home,' she said.
A friend then took her in, only to also suggest she kill the baby a month later. 'She asked me to put acid in his food so that he could die, but I refused to do so and left her house.'
The decision to resist the pressure to kill has had lifelong consequences for Ms Kipchumba. She was forced to flee her community, and now lives with her son in a tin shack, doing odd jobs to survive.
When Meshack was younger, his backbone was weak and he had no head control. 'I would dig a hole in the ground, lay him in it and use the soil to form a cushion around him,' his mother said.
She tells me she doesn't regret her decision to keep her child for a moment. The boy is now eight years old and can sit and walk short distances, albeit with some difficulty.
Ms. Njoki and Ms. Kipchumba are not alone. A new study in Kenya has found that 45% of mothers interviewed by a leading charity faced pressure to kill their babies born with disabilities.
The survey found that the situation was worse in rural areas - where the figure could be as high as two in every three mothers.

Cultural roots:

Most of the women interviewed by Disability Rights International said their children were considered 'cursed, bewitched and possessed' and that a belief prevailed that

the mothers were being punished for their sins, including being 'unfaithful to their husbands'.
Infanticide is rooted in old traditions and beliefs. An elderly traditional birth attendant in Narok - south-west of the capital Nairobi - told the BBC that according to her culture, babies with disabilities were killed out of love.
'What used to push people to do that was the helplessness,' said Timpiyan enole Koipa, seated inside her mud-walled one-roomed house dressed in a bright chequered red and white shawl and rows of traditional beaded necklaces.
'The child would otherwise suffer if it was allowed to live,' she adds.

While infanticide was the most shocking part of the Disability Rights International's report, it is not its only finding. The researchers initially set out to assess conditions in orphanages and care homes, where nearly 3,500 children in Kenya live.
The author of the report, Priscila Rodriguez, told the BBC: 'What is outrageous is that the government is passing the responsibility for these children to orphanages... Out of sight, out of mind; the government does not need to care for them anymore, does not need to provide for them, and does not need to ensure the supports they need are there.'
They took us to see one, Compassionate Hands for the Disabled, in Nairobi. The story of the home, and its owner, in some ways encapsulates the problems this society has with disability.

Anne Njeri was born disabled and decided to start a day-care centre for children with mental and physical conditions. She never intended it to be a residential home.
'But in a week, we had 11 abandoned children, and in a month we had 30,' she said.
She tried to look for the parents who had abandoned the children, but to no avail - they dropped the children off in the morning and simply never picked them up again.
She now has 86 children in her care. Watching her interact with them, it's clear they love her, and are loved in return, but she admits the home needs to do more. Researchers agree, and told us the way they are looked after, kept

indoors and often restrained, will make their conditions worse.

Government criticism:

But it is the government of Kenya they are most critical of.
The Kenyan government did not respond to our request for a response, although it is understood they admit more needs to be done.
While the idea that half of women with disabled children faced pressure to kill them as babies is truly shocking, it only reflects those whose babies made it to childhood. We have no idea how many others gave in to that terrible pressure.
Infanticide of children with disabilities is not unique to Kenya, but data is hard to come by across the world.
Studies recognize that it has history back to ancient times, remaining a significant problem during the 20th and 21st Centuries.
Research says children under one are at four time's greater risk of being murdered than any other age group.
Cases often go unrecorded or combined with other offences, and most countries lack institutions that track such deaths, so the true magnitude of infanticide remains unknown across the world.
'They are done underground,' says Veronica Sialo, a mother of a child with cerebral palsy and a community leader in Narok.
'Because any child can die at birth or when they go home [from hospital] you just hear the child has died. But when you follow the background, that child was disabled and that's why the family killed that child,' she adds.
'Some of us in our culture believe it's a curse, that you've been bewitched, so you're not wanted in the community.'
Her views correspond to the findings of a report titled Children accused of Witchcraft, by the UN Children's Agency, Unicef.

The report, which focused on the African continent, says 'abnormal births' would often led to the killing or abandonment of babies.

But in some countries, practices and beliefs changed because of the influence of colonial missionaries. Other communities have seen the introduction of alternative practices such as paying fines in the form of dances and ceremonies instead of sentencing the child to death, helping to erase suspicions.

New laws and the actions of organizations defending children's rights have also seen cases of infanticide reduce.

Back in Narok, Veronica is doing her best to improve the lives of mothers like her and their children. She has formed a support group that now has 43 members, including Florence Chebet and Lydia Njoki.

These mothers say they have found solace in knowing others like them. They want their children to be accepted by society. They meet once a month to share experiences and to encourage one another. Veronica's mission is to see her community overcome one of the oldest and most cruel beliefs.

'We need to do awareness so that they know that these are children like any other,' she concludes.

Situated on the equator on Africa's east coast, Kenya has been described as 'the cradle of humanity'.

In the Great Rift Valley palaeontologists have discovered some of the earliest evidence of man's ancestors.

In the present day, Kenya's ethnic diversity has produced a vibrant culture but is also a source of conflict.

Why do some of us grow-up with disfigured teeth in our mouth could it be due to certain harassment e.g. sexual.

God could nominate leaders; leaders in certain cases might nominate themselves to be leaders while nature, beliefs of the citizens can bring about who should be a leader.

Why do thunderstruck or storms occur we have come very far for centuries through sociology, psychology, philosophy, religion and much more through our life experiences but not much is given in consideration that God is within us and all things except for those who really still have a relationship with him.

An experience I went through in the land I was born in while going to Church to take Holy Communion in an environment and life style quite different from that of my parental native land Nigeria where I grow-up. What would I and the priest or curate expect from each other?

I have in the past eaten food prepared by my mother and step mothers who came from three different ethnic background in Nigeria how some people feel you ought to know them better we all feel the same way at certain times its why we have commitments, feelings, emotions and thoughts to shear. Since its part of what makes us humans who among us, is always ready to give support how ready are we prepared to give the support for less personal reasons?

I mean put aside the hat, the greed, lies, difference in gender, religion, race, color of a person skin. God did not created us this way rather, all things around us in a way we should not hat each other including things we do for personal reason as part of being ourselves should enrich us. Life should not reach a stage, where people can make you feel it doesn't pay to be good to other people.

A problem is some people you could do them lots of good an annoying thing, is they might want more and more out of you and if they get to know where and how it came about they would likely invade it or you privacy.

Being good:

1. What is the advocacy of being good
2. What are the psychology of being good
3. Part of being good is to help yourself psychologically or spiritually
4. Would you rather give or take
5. Its God who, is our mediator in things like these therefore its good having a relationship with him
6. I can trap myself when it comes to such issues others can trap me but the position of God in my life, would not

7. These are important issues to consider towards understanding and making choice humans are now found to dramatize themselves we need leaders who would set the ultimate goals.

A goal is an idea of the future or desired result that a person or a group of people envisions, plans and commits to achieve. People endeavor to reach goals within a finite time by setting deadlines.
A goal is roughly similar to a purpose or aim, the anticipated result which guides reaction, or an end, which is an object, either a physical object or an abstract object, that has intrinsic value.
This book may seem emotional in some ways but when you relate them to the emotions, feelings, thoughts and the consequence, effects or results you tend to realize the relationship with melodrama to realism is not all that too complex because of its distinct nature.
Now is a time for children of God to show their worthiness regardless of the circumstances in due effect, God's blessing on them remains as he reveals to them what has been and would be.

Some of us might have been taken over by segregation, racism, gender bias, unhealthy life style at this times who can be on welfare benefit at the same time be happy the stance of who we are is being tested. At this hour our faith, tendencies, perceptions, tolerance are being called upon to justify who we are. How we poise ourselves should justify who we are, our stance and our will to exist we might seem or sound ambiguous but it should be on a positive stance which reflects meaning to what we are and what lies before us.

Since life has different meaning related to what might have always been complicated to understand except where a situation or condition is well experiences it brings to mind the problem of evil, pain and suffering which should bring about efficacy for reasons, we should not always go into conflicts. Conflict of any kind should be avoided or dealt with.
Ambiguity is a type of meaning in which several interpretations are plausible. A common aspect of ambiguity

is uncertainty. It is thus an attribute of any idea or statement whose intended meaning cannot be definitively resolved according to a rule or process with a finite number of steps. (The part of the term reflects an idea of 'two', as in 'two meanings'.)
The concept of ambiguity is generally contrasted with vagueness. In ambiguity, specific and distinct interpretations are permitted (although some may not be immediately obvious), whereas with information that is vague, it is difficult to form any interpretation at the desired level of specificity.
Context may play a role in resolving ambiguity. For example, the same piece of information may be ambiguous in one context and unambiguous in another.
Our world, life have always been complex and ambiguous this, is where God have always had the higher score and would have given us leaders while he had more than cleverly given us parents in the first place. It's when we have a relationship with God we tend to realize such things on the other hand the basis for these could have been for us to trash things out in so doing to be ourselves. We have always been making a difference since all these while for God had always given us the will not to underestimate ourselves in what has always been an ambiguous world, self with complicacies to define himself which best defines us and our taste for food, culture, religion, tradition, sex, intelligence, knowledge, wisdom, craft etc.

Is throwing a long face a good or a bad thing? E.g. within a polygamous home, parent go out to work, meet with friends, relatives. Within their children it seems it's the one who sometimes throw a long face within such family is the one in the family, who really draw the attention of their parents to what goes on in the family some of which nobody might notice inside or outside the family.

If you are like such a child, and you do not take to your own way irrationally on how you do things you might realize later in life you understand lots of things because for example while it was all going on you had always kept an open mind, you were considerate, thoughtful, caring etc. You might find out, you naturally understand people or notice things.

People who do not pray to receive what they get or wants and always get or receive what they want might involve the nature of the beast why do we give each other encouragement, why is this necessary.

When people give you encouragement if means they are praying for you the more you hope, put in more effort for your hopes, aspiration or what lies before you to turn out right. The fulfilment of this might be or seem ambiguous since the nature of the beast do not pray for us therefore what our mouth say should also come out from our mind.

Certain words or phrase are often used dealing with ambiguity, emphasis are made the word that, this, and, how, who but etc. are often used opinions, suggestion, explanations, conclusions, attention and the use of repeated words often occur to make the ambiguity clearer simply because the ambiguity could probably be, beyond beliefs.

Now people who always want what they want would not know or realize it when they are told that our world is now partly a terrible place the issues that lies before us is beyond food, shelter and clothing to make things stick we are being moved to go beyond to face consequence of realities.

A businesses or politicians seems to be on a dialogue on what matters more to consumers some of us want to go back to our ways and life of simplicity it's not everybody who owns a car or wants to drive a car, it's not everybody own owns a house or a business and not everybody would want to be a politician culture, tradition, beliefs, ideology, temperament's are at stack some of us would which to remain who we are rather than enter into a crisis for what we do not want it's the hesitation psychologies need to study or analyze. It seems all good and rosy but people hesitated.

In psychology, a drive theory or drive doctrine is a theory that attempts to define, analyze, or classify the psychological drives. A drive is an 'excitatory state produced by a homeostatic disturbance', an instinctual need that has the power of driving the behavior of an individual.

Drive theory is based on the principle that organisms are born with certain psychological needs and that a negative state of tension is created when these needs are not satisfied. When a need is satisfied, drive is reduced and the organism returns to a state of homeostasis and relaxation. According to the theory, drive tends to increase over time and operates on a feedback control system, much like a thermostat.

In psychology, genetic memory is a memory present at birth that exists in the absence of sensory experience, and is incorporated into the genome over long spans of time. It is based on the idea that common experiences of a species become incorporated into its genetic code, not by a Lamarckian process that encodes specific memories but by a much vaguer tendency to encode a readiness to respond in certain ways to certain stimuli.

Adaptive memory is the study of memory systems that have evolved to help retain survival- and fitness-related information, i.e., that are geared toward helping an organism enhance its reproductive fitness and chances of surviving. One key element of adaptive memory research is the notion that memory evolved to help survival by better retaining information that is fitness-relevant.

One of the foundations of this method of studying memory is the relatively little adaptive value of a memory system that evolved merely to remember past events. Memory systems, it is argued, must use the past in some service of the present or the planning of the future. Another assumption under this model is that the evolved memory mechanisms are likely to be domain-specific, or sensitive to certain types of information.

Human ethology is the study of behavior. Ethology as a discipline is generally thought of as a sub-category of biology, though psychological theories have sprung up based on ethological ideas (e.g. sociobiology, evolutionary psychology, attachment theory, and theories about human universals such as gender differences, incest avoidance, mourning, hierarchy and pursuit of possession).

Usage of distinct: A thing is *distinct* if it is sharply distinguished from other things; a property or attribute is *distinctive* if it enables us to distinguish one thing from another. *There are two distinct colors on the face of the Canada goose* means that the two colors are clearly different from each other, while *There are two distinctive colors on the face of the Canada goose* means that the two colors are different from colors found on the faces of other birds, and the Canada goose may be identified by these two colors.

Based on the content of this book and any other of the authors books is to address distinctions on certain issues or basis on how for example do we come about living in a world where we ought to realize there are certain things we should not do or there are certain ways or things we ought to live by it could be by certain laws, condition, thing which constitute our world and heaven that is to come that would makes us who we are. It's all part of searching for life after death or what heaven would be after a world of beauty, ugliness and death like ours. What is everlasting life? Is there anything such as everlasting love? If there is then there could be everlasting life.

Trademark distinctiveness is an important concept in the law governing trademarks and service marks. A trademark may be eligible for registration, or registrable, if it performs the essential trademark function, and has distinctive character. Registrability can be understood as a continuum, with 'inherently distinctive' marks at one end, 'generic' and 'descriptive' marks with no distinctive character at the other end, and 'suggestive' and 'arbitrary' marks lying between these two points. 'Descriptive' marks must acquire distinctiveness through secondary meaning - consumers have come to recognize the mark as a source indicator - to be protectable.

'Generic' terms are used to refer to the product or service itself and cannot be used as trademarks. This book also has a descriptive trade mark like no other when it comes to religion, psychology, life experience therefore it is distinct. It's also exclusive. It's not all that complex in its ambiguity in relation to religion or psychology life needs some interpretation to meet this current age. This is something the author feels strongly about which had brought him forward with resilience regardless of his illness to have written his books. With his books psychology would have more meaning, culturally situated, become more easily descriptive if researches are true or false to their findings in this present age.

He expound on beliefs, culture, sermons, the manifold wisdom of God and psychology in view of research that has been made not only by psychologist but also by philosophers.

We are all basically trying to exist directly and not indirectly we all have roles, a destiny to face in such a world an individual can push a next person into a state of confusion it can involve politics, religion, the law itself, about God the architect of the universe. Some people can make you look foolish even when you want to play a decent role. In certain cases humans can throw taboos at themselves what dose science know about taboos they feel they have no part to play in such matters but it's everywhere even around them.

It should not seem we are trying to blame each other as the course of the world's problem unfolds we should be making ends meet in understandable ways. Such a situation should not likely occur it should be for certain. We should at the same time try to make reason our amour. Life does not boil down into something or a situation we cannot handle or find difficult to bear. For example what does it mean for Britain if they leave the EU are we being told its sugar coated if we leave the EU. What has the situation been or left for us if Britain Leaves the EU? It's not even over with there are huge consequences to correlate.

It reminds me the British are moving at a pace they can handle themselves, contain themselves I do not really know what lies in the closet when it comes to such matters but in it, I have a predicament or a consequence to face I have been on the dole since 2008.

Am unwell with an illness of diagnosed paranoid schizophrenia sometimes I cannot eat, sleep well, write my books by hand talk less of word process how have come so far doing this to some level should be given a second thought if it is good.

It's good to be grateful to all those out there who are resuscitating the world bringing hidden issues to the surface it's who the poor and needy gives support to from their hearts and mind are the once God's grace is with.

It's not only in this present age people, culture, race have been doing things with an intention as when they had been doing it in heaven before it all began. Here we move towards heaven or hell. Here we know better of what it would later be in heaven or in hell. What cause conflict, pain and suffering are not new to humans we have been made sufficient in our own way by the architect of the Universe.

When our spirit level isn't poor we set ourselves goals easily from most of our hardship not that we prefer not having things we should have it's because we choose to dwell on the brilliancy, intellect, wisdom of our heart, mind and soul. God calls some of us through how we use such intellects to outwit evil, pain and suffering since we have been created to use our intellect not only as a means of survival but also going about our life and do the things we love.

Certain wizards or witches do not lie down on their back while sleeping the sleep sideways if it happens they die it's the things or issues behind other peoples they know they wake up to especially those they had dwelled on negatively to be who, they were. A defect is sometimes we might use negative things for better result it might become their amour with which they move on from strength to strength. It depends if they can use negative things for good then its ok but, if they would use it selfishly then, it's a problem.

It brings to mind the advantages of civilization how it has helped humans in making our world a better place. Humans have over time become tolerant through work and activities. Put up immense effort towards positivity by choosing bearings on how to achieve goals. Out of certain decency, tendencies, requirements, needs they tend to do things. But in today's times, I hope human tendency for **respect** and **common decency** is not losing its grip.

If you have read this book or any other of my books, how would you describe their content as a trademark or as a philosophical theology?

Philosophical theology is both a branch and form of theology in which philosophical methods are used in developing or analyzing theological concepts. It therefore includes natural theology as well as philosophical treatments of orthodox and heterodox theology. Philosophical theology is also closely related to the philosophy of religion.

Mortimer J. Adler distinguishes philosophical theology from natural theology. While the former is, according to him, theology done by non-Christian philosophers, the latter is done by those who are already Christians and are actually trying to find rational proofs for their faith. Adler thinks that the term 'natural theology' is a misnomer and is actually apologetics, and cites as an example Thomas Aquinas' *Summa Contra Gentiles*, addressed to the Jews and Moors in Spain, which though written as if it were philosophical theology, was in fact, apologetics and not philosophical theology, as it was written by a Christian and not by a pagan. In Adler's view, few if any of the books on natural theology, are sound as works in philosophical theology, because they are not written by pagans. An example of philosophical theology, according to Adler, is Aristotle's theology as found in his *Metaphysics*.
Contrary to Adler's view, Charles Taliaferro and Chad Meister think that doing philosophical theology may not be restricted by whether the doer is an insider to faith or not, for anyone doing philosophical theology only tries to consider whether a theological doctrine can make philosophical sense

or not. But, as Adler points it out, a pagan doing philosophical theology and coming to a theological conclusion has a different route than an insider using philosophy to examine or seek to understand his faith.

Mortimer Jerome Adler (December 28, 1902 – June 28, 2001) was an American philosopher, educator, and popular author. As a philosopher he worked within the Aristotelian and Thomistic traditions. He lived for long stretches in New York City, Chicago, San Francisco, and San Mateo, California. He worked for Columbia University, the University of Chicago, *Encyclopædia Britannica*, and Adler's own Institute for Philosophical Research.

The relationship between theology and philosophy has been long-debated and discussed with the Christian tradition. Tertullian, an influential early Christian theologian and apologist, believed that philosophy has little to do with theology, arguing that the use of philosophy often corrupted theology, leading to unorthodox beliefs that were not grounded in the early Christian tradition. He famously asked the question 'What has Athens to do with Jerusalem?'.

(Athens symbolized the philosophical approach because of its role as a leading center of Hellenistic philosophy, while Jerusalem represented Christianity because of its role as an important location and intellectual centre in the early church.)

Other leaders, however, saw a closer relationship between philosophy and theology. Justin Martyr looked at people like Heraclitus and Socrates as possessing the divine light of revelation and believed them to be true philosophers. Justin saw Christianity as the True Philosophy and argued for Christianity using philosophical methods and terminology.

St. Augustine, who became one of the most influential theologians in history and whose works laid the foundation for much of Western philosophy (as well as much of Western theology), espoused a more middle-of-the-road, moderate approach, arguing that philosophy and theology often complement each other while at the same time cautioning that philosophy should not always be used in theological discourse. Instead, he argued, one should make sure that a philosophical approach toward a particular issue was grounded in prior Christian commitments.The disciplines of Philosophy and Theology have often been connected, with

theologians and philosophers interacting and debating similar and sometimes overlapping issues.
Philosophy played a key role in the formation of Western theology. Thomas Aquinas, one of the most influential philosophers and theologians in history, for instance, borrowed much of his concepts from Aristotle. Scholasticism dominated both the philosophical and theological landscape in the Middle Ages, with theologians such as Aquinas, Anselm of Canterbury, Duns Scotus, William of Ockham, Peter Abelard, Bonaventure, and Albertus Magnus playing key role in both philosophy and theology.

In modern times, Anthony Thiselton has shown in his *Fusion of Horizons* the role that philosophy has played in the interpretation of scriptures, i.e., in the field of hermeneutics. Philosophy provides interpretive grids for apprehension of revelation. There are others, like Sadhu Sundar Singh, for instance, who believed that it is the illumination of the Holy Spirit that gives the truest meaning of revelation. Yet, one can't fail to see that cultural grids play an important role in the development of theology.
Many contemporary philosophers continue to write and argue from a Christian perspective, with Christian concepts undergirding their philosophical work. In recent decades some of the most well-known philosophers who have written from a Christian perspective are Alvin Plantinga, Alasdair MacIntyre, William Lane Craig, Jean-Luc Marion, Paul Tillich, Charles Taylor, Richard Swinburne, and James K. A. Smith.

During the 18th, 19th centuries, and 20th centuries many theologians reacted against the modernist, Enlightenment, and positivist attacks on Christian theology. Some existentialistic or neo-orthodox Protestant intellectuals like the Swiss Reformed theologian Karl Barth turned away from philosophy (called fideism) and argued that faith should be based strictly upon divine revelation.
A popular approach in some circles is the approach of Reformed epistemologists, such as Alvin Plantinga and Nicholas Wolterstorff, who assert that belief in God might be foundational (or, properly 'basic') and warranted without the

need for logical or evidential justification, like belief in other minds or the external world, rather than inferentially derived from other beliefs; it can, however, be subject to defeaters, rationally requiring that one give up the belief.

Many other philosophers and theologians, however, disagree with this perspective and provide alternative views. Many other theologians have turned to continental philosophy, analytic philosophy, and postmodern philosophy in attempts to analyze and reframe the Christian theology in contemporary contexts.

While philosophical theology can denote an approach to theology which is philosophical in nature, it can also denote a specific area of theology in which philosophical methods and terminology are used to analyze theological concepts. One task of philosophical theologians is to attempt to reconcile certain aspects of Christian doctrine with developments in philosophy. One question concerns how to prove the existence and nature of God.

The knowledge of God is dealt with in the epistemology of religion. There are many different perspectives with philosophical theology on such questions. In modern times process theology, open theism and Christian panentheism have tried to look at God as the Being who is not only the Source and Ground of all being but also influenced by the people and processes of the world which he created and to which he belongs—rejecting or at least amending the classical medieval doctrine of impassibility.

Within Christology, a number of philosophical questions have been raised, such as how the divine can incarnate as a human, how the eternal can enter the temporal, and how the divine and the human can be united in one yet remain distinct. Such questions led to earlier heresies like Arianism, Sabellianism, Docetism, etc.

Often, one's epistemic theory can play an important role in how one answers such questions. There is, for instance, sometimes a clash between those who want to emphasize the rational foundation for theology and those who want to emphasize the empirical foundation for theology. There has also been a contrast made between Christology from above and Christology from below.

The former emphasizes the divine side of Christ; the latter, the human side. The human side obviously tends to look at it more empirically. The Scriptures call the Incarnation as a mystery of godliness. It baffles human imagination, leading many to call it a divine mystery. Yet, philosophical theologians argue that it is also important to find a philosophical ground for asserting both the divinity and humanity of Christ. Others theologians, however, like Rudolph Bultmann, ventured to remove any myths from the Bible, a hermeneutical approach they called demythology.
They have therefore looked at the New Testament Christology as greatly tampered with and in need of being demythologized. There has been a separation made between the Jesus of history and the Christ of faith.
Religious epistemology as a broad label covers any approach to epistemological questions from a religious perspective, or attempts to understand the epistemological issues that come from religious belief. The questions which epistemologists may ask about any particular belief also apply to religious beliefs and propositions: whether they seem rational, justified, warranted, reasonable, based on evidence and so on. Religious views also influence epistemological theories, such as in the case of Reformed epistemology.

Faith and rationality are two ideologies that exist in varying degrees of conflict or compatibility. Rationality is based on reason or facts. Faith is belief in inspiration, revelation, or authority. The word *faith* sometimes refers to a belief that is held with lack of reason or evidence, a belief that is held in spite of or against reason or evidence, or it can refer to belief based upon a degree of evidential warrant.
Although the words *faith* and *belief* are sometimes erroneously conflated and used as synonyms, *faith* properly refers to a particular type (or subset) of *belief*, as defined above.

Broadly speaking, there are two categories of views regarding the relationship between faith and rationality:

1. Rationalism holds that truth should be determined by reason and factual analysis, rather than faith, dogma, tradition or religious teaching.
2. Fideism holds that faith is necessary, and that beliefs may be held without any evidence or reason and even in conflict with evidence and reason.

The Catholic Church also has taught that true faith and correct reason can and must work together, and, viewed properly, can never be in conflict with one another, as both have their origin in God, as stated in the Papal encyclical letter issued by Pope John Paul II, *Fides et Ratio* ('[On] Faith and Reason').

An evil fume to bring out truth, reality with little or no concepts doesn't justify much. Such fumes are often revealed through wisdom, knowledge of secrets through which evil is overcome.

In some culture parents would kill children slowly for their own goals or aims until after, their death the once who want to carry them forward for their own personal aims simply put, would it be called a family can this be the meaning of a family relationship. They easily flaunt themselves what it brings about is pain, evil and suffering. Knowing about such things or issues will help us understand psychology, religion and our ways of life. Would we make a mistake without realizing it? When we fail to realize our mistake we want something personal which overrides apologizing for our mistake what, if it's not for the good of someone else the whole of mankind.

We observe such related issues steering at us in the face each day what do we do about it every man cannot live for himself while we are all here to make a difference we should not let it be our ways of life and should not take life for granted.

How do we get to know things which fails religion and rituals in practical terms consider now what we all seems to know about is 'money talks' money seems to be talking louder than our voice, action putting us into disposition which somewhat overrides knowledge or our being. Since for example some people in certain part of the world claim welfare benefit leads to rituals in which they have little or no voice.

Yet there is a lot going on about poverty, suffering and pain even if am on welfare payment I cannot go out buying something I regret buying with little or no voice in the matter. Yet we know our world is becoming the more unequal how dose our world become more violent why do people claim our **world is becoming** more secular? And how do we create a crucifix is it by implying or stressing that our world is becoming finite?

Ok I and lots of people are on welfare payment because we can't work for one reason or the other the strongest link some of us have for remaining in the EU that businesses would flourish, welfare payment will be made possible to help those out of work and in need financially what about the market situation? What does it mean if I can buy a tin of powdered milk for £3.99p and I can also buy the same product somewhere else within the UK for £1.00 or £2.00p? Welfare payment might be coming in how do we describe such an embarrassing marketing situation and why are more people becoming unwell and out of work are some goods and service at the moment worth having in relation to upgrading our quality of life.

Considering it might be a bid to make quick money for some of us how more ritualistic can it become in a way that it might lead to a direction we might someday regret where are the strategies in business and politics what have we learnt most from the past that could have led to a majority of Great Britain leaving the European Union. I hope it's all not going to be on a gamble if we leave then we become more certain of ourselves and where we stand that's all that matters now.

It's always good when there is certainty when we think of the immense effort we have put in and the progress we have made all these years. As a matter of fact in the present stance things should not get more complicated at this hour. If the going was good to have got somewhere we should not be asking ourselves why and how do birds fly. When we already know what makes a bird fly.

Why do birds fly? Where birds nest is a by-product of getting to their food source. Flight is also very useful for evading predators. Birds fly to get to their food source, whether that means foraging locally or migrating hundreds of miles to get to feeding grounds.
Bird flight is the primary mode of locomotion used by most bird species in which birds take off and fly. Flight assists birds while feeding, breeding, avoiding predators, and migrating.
Bird flight is one of the most complex forms of locomotion in the animal kingdom. Each facet of this type of motion, including hovering, taking off, and landing, involves many complex movements. As different bird species have adapted to specific environments, prey, predators, and other needs, they have developed varied forms of wings and varied forms of flight.

Research into how birds fly has yielded various theories as to the evolution of bird flight, a topic that is still hotly debated among scholars. Some suggest that flight originated from falling/gliding behaviors (the *trees down* hypothesis); some suggest that flight originated from running/leaping behaviors (the *ground up* hypothesis); and yet others suggest variations on these theories such as the *wing-assisted incline running* theory and the *pouncing proavis* theory.
All the while, it probably seems the case but within May to September 2018 I realized I wasn't addicted to smoking because I did not smoke or drank any alcohol which I hadn't had for a very long time. I was reassured but was troubled why I had to return to smoking once again infarct; I thought I had given up smoking completely. Whatever triggers such an event was out of my control for which, I was deeply concerned I was referred by my GP Georgina Deighton for support I said no because I felt it was something I had to come in terms with by myself to give up smoking.

Ways in which, I have come about in my ability to coup in relation to my illness at the same time writing my books are through knowledge gained by my own personal experience of myself when it comes to matters relating to the sea and dry land leads to how the cloud determines other factors which bears on the people in the area and how they live their lives. An old and rusty boat could hold a mystic quite different from that of an old rusty car. In this case instead of a mystic I would consider it as an aura with an effect seen distinctly in the rugged shaped hands of a village boat owner. A mystic which might come to mind in such a case is the effect of a crucifix how effective of it to do squirt.

The human aura, also known as the spiritual aura, is **energy emanating from the spinal column**. The energy comes from the combination of body, soul and mind working together in a person. Everything that you are, you have done, have been, you could do is all beamed out in your spiritual force-field.

Can the formation of the clouds have anything to do with children at birth e.g. how they take form?

If you understand issues such as this it means you are being inspired or it could lead to inspiration.

How could humans sip power, knowledge, and wisdom from the cloud if not by gaining divinity?

Below the stomach where lies the abdomen entwined with the soul becomes a center of strength.

Tranquility would contribute to your strength, bodily purpose; impulses would co-ordinate positively based on the heritage and aristocracy of your background or culture.

A question is if I can go through all these or have insight or knowledge to them why do I continue to smoke.

I guess it's a matrix in which am in, born into or found myself in.

An interesting part of it is when I go through such experience it makes me more human something natural I would call it quit uniquely me my suffering and confusion are put behind me. These are not easy self-explanatory but not contradictory to who I am or to what the experience is it implies nature contributes to who we are in a way we are left to explain things.

Having lots of good times right from when we are young, brings good memories it's good to have what brings back good memories, it's good to have the good things in life since it makes us happy, brings us good and healthy memories.

Some of us pray for peace of mind rather than prosperity I guess they want to be entitled to it in a spiritual way they should be entitled to it if it will brings them happiness this depends on lots of things e.g. past experience and the situation in which they are or have been in. It might be simply because they know what it means to them or they have taken time examining life and what it means to them. It might have anything to do with having gone through a broken heart through a relationship. On the other hand it might have to do with running away from the turmoil's of our time depending on their position in life.

How far do humans encourage themselves not to feel defeated. The thing about feeling defeated is that it results in you carrying around a heavy burden. You feel like you are not enough and that you do not have the ability to achieve what you desire. This is a terrible mindset to be in because it keeps you tied down and it limits once potential to move on.

If you are a smoker or an alcoholic how self-explanatory it is to come out with the experience if you try to give it up in some ways you go into phase you are leaving yourself to be dehumanized. Would this make sense to other people that you, just can't give it up even if it's just a case for simplicity.

Demons, fallen angels exist they read the contents of human mind, the coming of the Lord they also contribute to holding back revelations of the coming of Christ. Even in his return, going through such an experience enables one to understand the effects of demons or fallen angles they go through what most people will call a spiritual contest. Why do we have evil in the world what can be learnt from evil, its considered now is a time for humans to be very well self-contained in what they do? People say things about hearing voices I mean lots of things so they do about religion.

I do like to know other people's opinions about hearing voices but then it comes to how the brain functions, how it has to do with the shape of a humans head or how it works that part has gone past me. I try to imagine it but it goes into thin air it does not come self-explanatory to me even if I try it doesn't mean I have no interest in science. But from a social, religious and spiritual concept or perspectives I can at least make sense out of it. It comes to mind that it is good to be educated. I was good at biology in my secondary school years but not in chemistry or physics regardless at one point in my final year, they were part of my GCE.

The West African Examinations Council (WAEC) is an examination board that conducts the West African Senior School Certificate Examination, for University and Jamb entry examination in West African countries. Established in 1952, the council has contributed to education in Anglophonic countries of West Africa (Ghana, Nigeria, Sierra Leone, Liberia, and the Gambia), with the number of examinations they have coordinated, and certificates they have issued. They also formed an endowment fund, to contribute to the education in West Africa, through lectures, and aid to those who cannot afford education.

Who says crucifix no longer do squirt putting my crucifix somewhere I experience enigmas about something I began hearing a voice say I should take it off from the place meanwhile some other voices I have been hearing subsided.

What is this tobacco and cigarette leaves most of us smoke but we do not know do they have any cultural concurrences to us. Why are we taken by them, what intrigues us to smoke while some of its effect can be devastating? Most of us would like to give them up what is really particular about these leaves.

Tobacco is a product prepared from the leaves of the tobacco plant by curing them. The plant is part of the genus *Nicotiana* and of the Solanaceae (nightshade) family. While more than 70 species of tobacco are known, the chief commercial crop is *N. tabacum*. The more potent variant *N. rustica* is also used around the world.
Tobacco contains the alkaloid nicotine, which is a stimulant, and harmala alkaloids. Dried tobacco leaves are mainly used for smoking in cigarettes, cigars, pipe tobacco, and flavored shisha tobacco. They can also be consumed as snuff, chewing tobacco, dipping tobacco and snus.
Tobacco use is a risk factor for many diseases, especially those affecting the heart, liver, and lungs, as well as many cancers. In 2008, the World Health Organization named tobacco as the world's single greatest preventable cause of death.

Tobacco has long been used in the Americas, with some cultivation sites in Mexico dating back to 1400–1000 BC. Many Native American tribes have traditionally grown and used tobacco. Eastern North American tribes historically carried tobacco in pouches as a readily accepted trade item, as well as smoking it, both socially and ceremonially, such as to seal a peace treaty or trade agreement. In some populations, tobacco is seen as a gift from the Creator, with the ceremonial tobacco smoke carrying one's thoughts and prayers to the Creator.
Doctors can prescribe medical cannabis from November in UK 11 October 2018. Doctors will be able to prescribe cannabis products to patients from 1 November, the Home Secretary Sajid Javid says.
The new regulations apply to England, Wales, Scotland and Northern Ireland.

Mr Javid decided to relax the rules on when cannabis products could be given to patients after a review into medicinal cannabis earlier that year.
God so created our world in a way that no matter how things go wrong or difficult we would always have hope if we do have hope or cannot continue in hope we might be bound to do something drastic or let go.
The Art of Letting Go:

It is human nature to become too attached to things or people. Learn how to let go with grace.

It is human nature to become too attached to things or people. While it can be difficult to find out how to let go from certain attachments even if we know that they are not good for us. The Buddha even went so far as saying that our addictive behavior is the root of all suffering.
I had been a heavy drinker for some time I smoked heavily at the same time giving up drinking alcohol I resort to giving up smoking which came with varied experience. Recently I realize I was not addicted to smoking I can give it up if I want to. I continued going back to it because if I stopped smoking within some period I go sick. I hear voices telling me I should go back to it that it's like a life support machine for me. I continue the struggle of giving it up it came, with a pleasant feeling and I having positive thoughts of giving it up. Wondering why I go back to it and continually hear the voices that I should if I felt like having it. I later felt like it was a pact I had taken which gears me to smoke.

As for alcohol I knew I went through certain experiences which made me feel within myself alcohol was no longer part of me. I felt this same experience would have to come before I can have what it takes to give up smoking. But I never signed a pact giving thought to why I smoke when I felt It should be done with. I went through certain experience call it hallucination if you like such as asking myself what is a tree it's something we know much about trees do not speak but mysteriously, strangely they do.

Some trees grow fruits we know how useful they are to us when we eat them some trees grow fruits which we do not eat how do we know if they might be useful to us or if they are unhealthy to us. Humans perform rituals in all sorts of ways to understand mystics behind nature may be, am yet to understand certain things that's why am concerned about my continued smoking. I do the necessaries e.g. wash my hands, not smoking when lying down on my bed, keep fresh air coming in I mean anything I deem necessary for me to do in other to avoid danger.

I do not feel it in my mouth infarct I detest certain aspects of smoking or drinking alcohol that's what am worried about. I know sometimes I go through inspiration but the capacity to go on worrying is not good for me. Hoping when I have grasp the true meaning of the inspiration I might be looking for as the philosopher stone to do it all without smoking and then later consider I might have to reach certain age before I can quit smoking.

A chunk of the moon that fell to Earth as a lunar meteorite has fetched more than $600,000 (£458,997) at auction.

The 5.5kg (12lb) lump, affectionately known as The Moon Puzzle, is comprised of six fragments that fit together.

RR Auction in Boston, Massachusetts, announced on Friday that the set had sold for $612,500 (£468,559).

What is the difference within a dog poo and a moon rock things always turn out in meaningful different isn't God wonderful in his creation?

When I observed the moon rock on my computer it gave me, a strange and strange feeling which I would not recount but for a year I have not drank any alcohol to my dismay, I realise I was having dry cider something mild I then considered it's a matter of live and let die of which, I have to be careful.

21st October 2018 which was a Sunday I bought myself a blender and grinder from Simons store at Powis Street Woolwich I thought of buying it at Argos or Sainsbury's infarct I attempted it but though otherwise for me to grind my Pepper, Tomatoes, Onions, Egusi and Crayfish. I did not feel like having Ogbono and Okro soup as I used to because I felt Ogbono and Okro is too harsh for more me so, until recently I tend to prepare them very simple and light in texture.

It means more hard work for me preparing my meals but how do I explain the effects why, should I take such measures when it has been made much easier if I can have Egusi or Ogbono already ground in my African Asian food

store. I have to determine the effects with my smoking through which I have the feeling it could stop me from smoking or reduce it drastically because I would prefer if I would not smoke at all. The question now is am I procrastinating am I leaving myself to be taken by procrastination when one issue triggers the other. Do these factors form a basis for action on a justification for a belief?
Would we mange getting to a point we would use electricity in the new world, would cars, trains, tramps, TV radios, computers be functional through electricity or solar energy what if these things would be no more how, would we live our lives?

Going back taking dry fish, prawns, snails, stock fish, gbegiri back from the Ogboni's after years of living under them means you have taken the blue pill. Taking the red pills by abstaining from them means you do not live in a dream world but that of reality that of the blue pill is a dreams world. The culture of the Ogboni's and their ways is already engraved in it there are no ways of replicating it.
While taking the red ill I am replicating myself on the other hand if they come back to life it's through their acts, ways in which they replicate themselves. Or the more I might suffer from mental fragmentation now in the real sense am avoiding fragmentation on the other hand the blue pill will not do all this e.g. for me to have come about writing this book.
Any power gained or attributes articulated by Ogboni members' remains with them even after their death it's something, they strive for. What then, is left for the deities on which to articulate themselves when there is pain, suffering and evil they know it all if not that the power , enigmas of the supernatural speaks for them on their behalf things might have been different. How many of us often, do as we are told in the right perspectives for some of us wishes are horse we will always raise because we know how to go about it or because there is something behind us taking us to our destination. They reincarnate greater suffering comes into the world they manage and they are gone to hold the pillars from where it all started or where it will begin and returned once more to where it's more meaningful.

I am existing within two different continent one, two I originate from two different background three I have lived with step mothers four I have lived within this two different continent at different dwelling it should be right, considerate for me grinding my egusi, ogbono and crayfish within my present dwelling. I am not here to listen to other people's body language for my GP a study would be to determine the cause or reason for skin cancer if it's likely to occur to me or other people one thing is for sure its food it depends on how much people know about themselves or their culture. Can food cause boil or skin cancer? They are the result and effects of the horrors we cause during our livelihood here on this planet.

Schizophrenia is a condition from my experience when someone suffers from something fragmented sort of fragmented disorder I would not leave myself to be replicated while am not going through habitual fragmentation even in some ways if its detected I have course to have written this book. May be my readers or through psychological studies it might be determined if it has anything to do with erosion and habitual conservation. Another thing is for sure it can determine my centre of origin biological conservation and the struggle and will to move on. I might in some ways be suffering from mental fragmentation but writing my books makes it different while I wait for multiple unfinished businesses.

Mental fragmentation is a phrase used to describe the mental state of someone who has memories written into their brain from multiple sources over time, especially those who are heavy multitaskers. When multitasking, the brain does not store related memories in one place, but in small pieces. This causes performance and recall to suffer.

One can easily see this when installing software while leaving other programs running, or downloading a bunch of images and storing them in different places all over the hard drive. The computer's memory gets fragmented, much like a brain becomes fragmented.

Mental hygiene becomes difficult, but important, in environments like these. Simultaneous time also causes social punctuation, as techno-social connectivity seeps into every part of social relations. In addition, memories written to

the brain during these data binges are generally forgotten during REM sleep and not written to permanent or embodied memory. Conversely, one who spends physical time in the practice of study or experience of a subject will be more likely to write it into physical memory.
Thomas Eriksen wrote that '...the surplus of information has a powerful democratizing effect since it makes it impossible for the State or self-appointed elites to dictate which knowledge each of us should appropriate; at the same time, it has – for the exact same reason – fragmenting effects. A new scarce resource is coherence.' Thus, 'whoever is able to filter and sort the information at his or her disposal, and is thereby able to discard ninety-nine per cent as irrelevant, wins this game – not whoever is able to remember the names of Russian rivers or African heads of state'.
A self-replicating machine is a type of autonomous robot that is capable of reproducing itself autonomously using raw materials found in the environment, thus exhibiting self-replication in a way analogous to that found in nature.
The concept of self-replicating machines has been advanced and examined by Homer Jacobsen, Edward F. Moore, Freeman Dyson, John von Neumann and in more recent times by K. Eric Drexler in his book on nanotechnology, *Engines of Creation* (coining the term clanking replicator for such machines) and by Robert Freitas and Ralph Merkle in their review *Kinematic Self-Replicating Machines* which provided the first comprehensive analysis of the entire replicator design space.

The future development of such technology is an integral part of several plans involving the mining of moons and asteroid belts for ore and other materials, the creation of lunar factories, and even the construction of solar power satellites in space. The possibly misnamed von Neumann probe is one theoretical example of such a machine. Von Neumann also worked on what he called the universal constructor, a self-replicating machine that would operate in a cellular automata environment.

A self-replicating machine is an artificial self-replicating system that relies on conventional large-scale technology

and automation. Certain idiosyncratic terms are occasionally found in the literature. For example, the term clanking replicator was once used by Drexler to distinguish macroscale replicating systems from the microscopic nanorobots or 'assemblers' that nanotechnology may make possible, but the term is informal and is rarely used by others in popular or technical discussions.
Replicators have also been called 'von Neumann machines' after John von Neumann, who first rigorously studied the idea. However, the term 'von Neumann machine' is less specific and also refers to a completely unrelated computer architecture that von Neumann proposed and so its use is discouraged where accuracy is important. Von Neumann himself used the term universal constructor to describe such self-replicating machines.

Historians of machine tools, even before the numerical control era, sometimes figuratively said that machine tools were a unique class of machines because they have the ability to 'reproduce themselves' by copying all of their parts. Implicit in these discussions is that a human would direct the cutting processes (later planning and programming the machines), and would then be assembling the parts. The same is true for RepRaps, which are another class of machines sometimes mentioned in reference to such non-autonomous 'self-replication'. In contrast, machines that are *truly autonomously* self-replicating (like biological machines) are the main subject.
How can I use my experience writing my books at the same time not replicating my experience?
A replication study involves repeating a study using the same methods but with different subjects and experimenters.

Suppose you are part of a healthcare team facing a problem, for instance, regarding use and efficacy of certain 'pain killer medicine' in patients before surgery. You search the literature for same problem and identify an article exactly addressing 'this' problem.
Now questions arise on how can you be sure the results of this study at hand is applicable and transferable into 'your' clinical setting? Therefore you decide to focus on

preparation and implementation of a replication study. You will perform the deliberate repetition of previous research procedures in your clinical setting and thus will be able to strengthen the evidence of previous research finding, and correct limitations, and thus overall results may be in favour of the results of previous study or you may find completely different results.

I would not have or shear an opinion you can replicate the human body it replicate itself if, it's the case, then am living in line to what I am. I am not implying replication cannot take place growing much older or unwell one changes facially looking more like a close relative or friend it might be replication taking place or after a close relatives death. My taking up smoking might be due to an effect for me not to be replicated.

Times I would have used in ironing my cloths I use it smoking.

Before 2018 if I do not smoke for a long time I suffer from irritation involuntary, jerky movement, feeling uncomfortable, un at ease, remorse I have gone all past this except only on occasion. I realize I no longer felt all these but calmness and tranquility each week I do not smoke. At certain point I had to fuss because I had not the finance to smoke and how I would reduce my smoking drastically to improve or better manage my finances. That part of the finance can sometimes be difficult because when the urge really hits one thing can be very difficult the money better be there because if you do not go out begging one might steal. It leaves questions why does it lead to such an experience. It is partly left for the philosophers to find out as far, as it continues this way.

In my endeavors to quit smoking I had stayed for more than two months without smoking 2018 as at October I had stayed without taking any alcohol. Regardless of my taking precaution it just comes all of a sudden and swept me back into smoking. What is in this leave what is it about it that makes it trigger me into such experience and phenomena's leading to some extent mysteries into the paranormal.

On the other hand it could relate to rituals, if certain wishes can be made through a particular tree ceremonies or rituals is carried out through an effect of putting one to a subjugation to smoking making the wish comes trues e.g. after a person's death a wife should not have sexual relationship with someone else, or through a reincarnation process a person comes back holding insignias to what they want out of life through the inducement.

Identifying the tree one, having someone in a family who holds an affinity to the tree, a slaughter is made, they could shed their blood deliberately through a cut and then triggers the rituals. It could leave a person hopeless or helpless while there is this tobacco leave to further get hold of the person. Or the person feels helpless left at the mercy of the tobacco leave. It might be a continued process due to further inducements from bruises or cuts on the part of a smoker.

Smoking can demonstrate willingness or a withdrawal to something e.g. an act, a ritual, a group or a particular person in one case you might be refuting smoking on another level voices or certain experience calls one into it again. Something you completely do not want to do what is that thing that is so stubborn inside a smoker that induces them going back to smoking when they have considered giving it up. Are there any spiritual interpretation for it or else what is this tobacco leaves? Can it be as an effect of a spiritual bruising?

At some point of smoking excessively one realize they are grassing themselves up its time to think of giving it up or your heart, lounges begins to say 'Pechesh' meaning buy, buy. Grassing one-self up you start experience a tingling effect or sensation in once heart sort, of squashing, seizing, quizzing or grinding effect. I wonder how one can go through such experience without considering lowering its intake or giving it up. Word processing these down I realized I am talking at the same time advising myself. At one point I asked myself why should it be so difficult why isn't it something I can just make a decision listen to my heart and mind and take to my decision 'for what'? I think it's right for me to apply reason its good and simple but not easy sometimes getting down to it and do as you want can be really difficult.

Cognitive ability and reasoning are **essential to work and performance**. The Applied Reasoning Test – Managerial & Professional (ART – M/P) is an ability test that measures an individual's ability to reason, problem solve, learn new concepts, and understand complex relationships.
How far dose this applies to Inductive reasoning. A causal inference draws a conclusion about a causal connection based on the conditions of the occurrence of an effect. Premises about the correlation of two things can indicate a causal relationship between them, but additional factors must be confirmed to establish the exact form of the causal relationship.
Deductive reasoning, also deductive logic, logical deduction is the process of reasoning from one or more statements (premises) to reach a logically certain conclusion.
Deductive reasoning goes in the same direction as that of the conditionals, and links premises with conclusions. If all premises are true, the terms are clear, and the rules of deductive logic are followed, then the conclusion reached is necessarily true.
Deductive reasoning (*'top-down logic'*) contrasts with inductive reasoning (*'bottom-up logic'*) in the following way; in deductive reasoning, a conclusion is reached reductively by applying general rules which hold over the entirety of a closed domain of discourse, narrowing the range under consideration until *only* the conclusion(s) is left. In inductive reasoning, the conclusion is reached by generalizing or extrapolating from specific cases to general rules, i.e., there is epistemic uncertainty. However, the inductive reasoning mentioned here is not the same as induction used in mathematical proofs – mathematical induction is actually a form of deductive reasoning.
Deductive reasoning differs from abductive reasoning by the direction of the reasoning relative to the conditionals. Deductive reasoning goes in the *same direction as that of the conditionals, whereas* abductive reasoning *goes in the opposite direction to that of the conditionals.*

Reasoning with modus ponens, modus tollens, and syllogism is my points here far from fallacy I have made up my mind why do I not just give it up. It's not a material thing rather than some of us buying a new pair of shoes we would rather buy a packet of tobacco or cigarette and smoke. If money means nothing to me I can still loose my mind on other things.

Money is something to generate the human mind the body needs it so dose my emotional health if I really know myself, the right things around me can the human mind alone always solve its innermost feeling when it comes to emotions. It cannot be a complete, inheritance in a world of the good the bad and the ugly in itself? Can money mean anything to me without the human mind is it not then obvious when someone says cross my mind I have told you the truth in a world of different beliefs, culture, tradition and creed they mean the truth.

What does someone mean when they demonstrate something if not to create accuracy coming from the mind when there is mouth, cloth and shelter to be sort for in the human ways of life? Why so many Sherlock's in William Shakespeare book in our life are there now and what diabolic inference do they bear on dose of us who have mental health issues?

A fallacy is the use of invalid or otherwise faulty reasoning, or 'wrong moves' in the construction of an argument. A fallacious argument may be deceptive by appearing to be better than it really is. Some fallacies are committed intentionally to manipulate or persuade by deception, while others are committed unintentionally due to carelessness or ignorance. The soundness of legal arguments depends on the context in which the arguments are made.

Fallacies are commonly divided into 'formal' and 'informal'. A formal fallacy can be expressed neatly in a standard system of logic, such as propositional logic, while an informal fallacy originates in an error in reasoning other than an improper logical form. Arguments containing informal fallacies may be formally valid, but still fallacious.

A special case is a mathematical fallacy, an intentionally invalid mathematical proof, often with the error subtle and

somehow concealed. Mathematical fallacies are typically crafted and exhibited for educational purposes, usually taking the form of spurious proofs of obvious contradictions.
One hasn't wash his or her mouth early in the morning, or had tooth gum problem regardless of things one smokes sounds far from neuroticism but slightly seems the case giving up smoking with my effort, inquiry, writing this book should not be put down simply as neuroticism.
Neuroticism is one of the Big Five higher-order personality traits in the study of psychology. Individuals who score high on neuroticism are more likely than average to be moody and to experience such feelings as anxiety, worry, fear, anger, frustration, envy, jealousy, guilt, depressed mood, and loneliness. It is said people who are neurotic respond worse to stressors and are more likely to interpret ordinary situations as threatening and minor frustrations as hopelessly difficult. They are often self-conscious and shy, and they may have trouble controlling urges and delaying gratification.
People with high neuroticism indexes are at risk for the development and onset of common mental disorders, such as mood disorders, anxiety disorders, and substance use disorder, symptoms of which had traditionally been called neuroses.
Having written this book I might consider a deductive reasoning as to why I am a smoker it's also an inquiry.

An inquiry is any process that has the aim of augmenting knowledge, resolving doubt, or solving a problem. A theory of inquiry is an account of the various types of inquiry and a treatment of the ways that each type of inquiry achieves its aim.

It's likely it's a 'Gibiti or Eshu leaf' because it makes one play truant, deceit, betrayal to true course of life with greed for the human heart, lounges or soul.

The Yoruba treat their ancestors with great respect, as might be expected in a culture with only oral records of the past, but anthropologist's debate as to whether the rituals dealing with ancestry are religious in nature, or simply respectful. At least a few groups believe ancestors, after death, become demigods, but only once they have assumed the persona of a true deity. This resembles another facet of the Yoruba faith, the phenomenon of possession, in which mediums take on the characteristics of one or another of the gods. The characteristics of each god are so well stereotyped that mediums as far off as Haiti loll back their heads and cross their legs in the same way when possessed by the lightning god.

The Yoruba pantheon, however, has no evil gods; a more accurate comparison would be between Eshu and the Satan of the Book of Job, to whom God assigns the task of trying men's faith one myth dealing with Eshu illustrates his mischievousness.

Eshu, posing as a merchant, alternately sold increasingly magnificent gifts to each of a man's two wives; the ensuing battle for the husband's favor tore the family apart. Surprisingly, Eshu also serves as the guardian of houses and villages. When worshipped in this tutelary position, his followers call him Baba ('father'). Eshu also serves as the god of Ifa, a sophisticated and complex geomantic divinatory tool which uses nuts, signs, and increasing squares of the number four to predict all facets of the future.

It is said that Shango, the god Wole Soyinka refers to in his poem 'Hunt of the Stone', occupies a major position in the pantheon of the Yoruba, although he holds a less important position in neighbouring ethnic groups. Shango (also spelled Sango and Sagoe) creates thunder and lightning by casting 'thunderstones' down to earth; wherever lightning strikes, priests search the surrounding area for the thrown stone.

The Yoruba believe these stones have special powers, and they enshrine the stones in temples to the god. Shango has four wives, each personified by a major Nigerian river; his chief wife, Oya, is represented by the River Niger. One myth about Shango tells of when he was human and ruled as the fourth king of the ancient Yoruba capital of Oyo. He had a charm that could cause lightning, with which he inadvertently killed his entire family.

In remorse he hanged himself, and upon his death he became deified. Although the 'foremost national deity', according to some, the Yoruba do not consider him the most powerful or even the most important god; rather, his popularity may have resulted from attempts to ward off the frequent tornadoes that strike western Africa.

When a sufferer walks with quick steps his or her muscles works harder probably because they are likely agitated, anxious because of an effect of their illness so I do not go out to the gym but do my exercise indoors little steps that I can manage to do, to keep me fit with some meditation and breathing in and out to loosen-up.

The little good things we do or grow up with sometimes even the difficult once might prove to be worthy or helpful to us in the future. Some of which when we get much older, we might not enjoy doing but use two and two in relation to other variables attached to our present experience to manage a much difficult scenario either because we have become more mature or due to changes in our life.
Putting two and two might come in much handy as we move on nothing is ever too late to accomplish as far as there is life you might have to lose some of your own ways because of other peoples influence but your willingness taking such a stand proves you very mature and an understandable person. Guided by reason and good intention or because you are rich in spirit not daunting every day is a struggle to make life worth living it depicts what is known as our living planet.

Psychology of human behaviors still remains to be better understand also is the psychology of creation in my opinion, in the 21st century chicken boiler in the market place in London knows who owns them for food before they give themselves up to be taken they always hope, they would not get to the wrong hands. I mean they destine themselves for those they actually want who would have them. Are must of us aware this it now has relation to hearing voices.
I dear not say it out loud because I know what it would mean e.g. I might be sectioned. How many of us are aware there are new dimensions to our lives spiritually, psychologically, biologically as for science I do not know much and am not a

biological waste. Certain hard drug intake is as a result of poor housing, industrial waste and manufacturing, self-neglect or a confused state of life.
It's good to have the good things in life some of us are experiencing dimensions to it if am not the only one how do I walk into my African Asian food store and say I want this boiler not that one this one in particular pointing at it. What creates such an affinity while at that point of sale I can hear a voice inside say to me yes that one? Meanwhile before I went out of my flat, I heard a voice saying I should go out of my flat and buy chicken boiler. What is choice what is the meaning of hearing voices and making a choice. This would have been after we have had a little interrogation within ourselves as voice bearer and voice hearer e.g. I have no money, I have not enough money to buy the chicken boiler; I want to use the money to buy something else.
It is said in religion do not think of what you have live by but by every word and commandments of God this may have occurred because I deserve something or someone wants me to eat well or feel the boiler chicken is good for me. It's not like a rationing taking place. How do we understand expressions of creation? If it's the boiler chicken telling me all this in my flat or in a store what would a life chicken do?
Dale Winton wants me to win the national lottery, Verne Troyer Mini-Me also wants me to win the lottery before he passed away. A Scottish Anerupupo I met with at Lancelot Andrews hostel in South East London wants me to win Anerupupo on a wheelchair Abdul Rahman at GLLaB Greenwich Local Labour and Business at Woolwich also wants me to win the national lottery. Can you or other people who wants you to win the national lottery make a wish with such a machine ball set and they win the national lottery? Can it easily or adaptably induce one to play the lottery rather than using the money to have a fag most smokers are looking for ways to give it up playing the national lottery in chance might help?

Dale Jonathan Winton (22 May 1955 – 18 April 2018) was an English radio DJ and television presenter. He presented the shows *Dale's Supermarket Sweep* from 1993 until 2001 and again in 2007, the National Lottery game show *In It to Win It* between 2002 and 2016 and the 2008 series of *Hole*

in the Wall. Winton also presented *Pets Win Prizes* (1995–96) and *The Other Half* (1997–2002).
Mini-Me is a character played by Verne Troyer in the second and third Austin Powers movies: *Austin Powers: The Spy Who Shagged Me* and *Austin Powers in Goldmember*.

We have been making for ourselves a conditional life instead of making it less conditional so we can more abide by Gods own condition which are basis of addressing life issues in a spiritual path that which should make our live less but appropriately conditioned. Then we can co-easily exist in a conditional order in a world of beauty, ugliness and death in relation to our conditional expectations identifying conditions we need to abide by orders and the rules if and when we are to solve problems, make our life more bearable or pragmatic.
Programing are due to occur assisting us to co-existing because of this, we must all abide by the rules to exist in an orderly way the happiness would be ours. We would see ourselves as having something in common loyalty would be our best mat how do we create loyalty through the things we do and how we do them. One way to do this is to apply logic in things we do on the basis that we understand the good the bad and the ugly also what is really expected of us.
Religious people talk a lot about God they try to demonstrate what God wants out of them e.g. they can shear the good news with you, pray, give advice and try as much as they can to draw you closer to God. In some case people think when they go about doing such things they call other people or sects name e.g. sinners.
It's the joy of knowing God they are calling you into because they understand what it means to them. They feel it is right having such a relationship with the creator at least; this is what it should be it is part of the joy of creation and knowing God.

Crimes committed against someone because of their disability, transgender-identity, race, religion or belief, or sexual orientation are hate crimes and should be reported to the police.

Hate crimes can include:

- threatening behavior
- assault
- robbery
- damage to property
- inciting others to commit hate crimes
- harassment
- and if I may add negative prejudice against people with mental health issues.

Prejudice or bigotry: is an affective feeling towards a person or group member based solely on that person's group membership. The word is often used to refer to preconceived, usually unfavorable, feelings towards people or a person because of their sex, gender, beliefs, values, social class, age, disability, religion, sexuality, race/ethnicity, language, nationality, beauty, occupation, education, criminality, sport team affiliation or other personal characteristics. In this case, it refers to a positive or negative evaluation of another person based on that person's perceived group membership.
Prejudice can also refer to unfounded or pigeonholed beliefs and it may include 'any unreasonable attitude that is unusually resistant to rational influence'. Gordon Allport defined prejudice as a 'feeling, favorable or unfavorable, toward a person or thing, prior to, or not based on, actual experience'. For the evolutionary psychology perspective, see Prejudice from an evolutionary perspective. Auestad (2015) defines prejudice as characterized by 'symbolic transfer', transfer of a value-laden meaning content onto a socially formed category and then on to individuals who are taken to belong to that category, resistance to change, and overgeneralization.

Prejudice: can be considered from an evolutionary perspective. Evolutionary psychologists posit that our psychology, e.g. emotion and cognition, has not been uniquely isolated from the forces of evolution. Although there is psychological variation among individuals, the majority of our psychological mechanisms should be adaptations designed specifically to solve recurrent problems, many of which were social in nature, in our evolutionary history. To balance the costs and benefits of sociality we must be able to recognize and functionally respond to threats and opportunities (see James J. Gibson), and our errors in judgment should be biased toward minimizing costs to reproductive fitness.

Our implicit responses to others result from the activation of functionally specific adaptations to motivate action, either to take advantage of opportunities, avoid or confront threats. The valence positive or negative of those responses can be measured using implicit association tests. Unconscious, negative reactions are often referred to as prejudice, but these prejudices are much more contextually rich than simple, positive or negative affect, and often involve discrete emotions, which likely represent unique adaptations to motivate functionally distinct actions. Our evolved biases toward minimizing fitness costs may have implications for the function and/or malfunction of stigma, prejudice, and discriminatory behavior in post-industrial societies. Some common biases (sex, age, race) are discussed.
James Jerome Gibson: January 27, 1904 – December 11, 1979), was an American psychologist and one of the most important contributors to the field of visual perception. Gibson challenged the idea that the nervous system actively constructs conscious visual perception, and instead promoted ecological psychology, in which the mind directly perceives environmental stimuli without additional cognitive construction or processing. A *Review of General Psychology* survey, published in 2002, ranked him as the 88th most cited psychologist of the 20th century, tied with John Garcia, David Rumelhart, Louis Leon Thurstone, Margaret Floy Washburn, and Robert S. Woodworth.

The implicit-association test (IAT) is a measure within social psychology designed to detect the strength of a person's automatic association between mental representations of objects (concepts) in memory. The IAT was introduced in the scientific literature in 1998 by Anthony Greenwald, Debbie McGhee, and Jordan Schwartz. The IAT is now widely used in social psychology research and, to some extent, in clinical, cognitive, and developmental psychology research. The IAT is the subject of much controversy regarding precisely what it measures, and the lack of reproducibility of many of its results.

Emotion and prejudice:

In 1872, Charles Darwin published The Expression of the Emotions in Man and Animals and theorized that humans had universal emotions that functioned to motivate specific behaviors. Paul Ekman, in 1971, published cross-cultural research supporting Darwin's predictions. People in both pre-literate and literate societies recognized distinct emotions (fear, anger, disgust, sadness, happiness, surprise), which Ekman suggested were universal and socially functional adaptations. Cottrell and Neuberg (2005) found that threats are functionally different for different individuals and predictably activate different emotions, which motivate unique behavioral responses.
2018 Philip Morris accused of hypocrisy over anti-smoking ad. One of the world's biggest tobacco firms, Philip Morris, has been accused of 'staggering hypocrisy' over its new ad campaign that urges smokers to quit.

The Marlboro maker said the move was 'an important next step' in its aim to 'ultimately stop selling cigarettes'.
But Cancer Research UK said the firm was just trying to promote its smoking alternatives, such as heated tobacco.
'This is a staggering hypocrisy,' it said, pointing out the firm still promotes smoking outside the UK.
'The best way Philip Morris could help people to stop smoking is to stop making cigarettes,' George Butterworth, Cancer Research UK's tobacco policy manager said.
The charity said smoking was the leading preventable cause of cancer and it encouraged people to switch away completely from smoking, including through the use of e-cigarettes.

- Is the vape shop boom about to end?
- Vapers rise 'to more than three million'

Health charity Action on Smoking and Health (Ash) also criticized the campaign - which is called Hold My Light and has been launched in a four-page wraparound on Monday's Daily Mirror - saying it was a way for Philip Morris to get around the UK's anti-tobacco advertising rules.
There is also a campaign video, which shows a young woman negotiating a Mission Impossible-style room in order to hand her cigarette lighter over to a group of friends, who are supporting her in a bid to give up smoking.
Most forms of tobacco advertising and promotion in the UK are banned, and rules introduced mean cigarettes and tobacco must be sold in plain green packets.
Deborah Arnott, chief executive of Ash, said Philip Morris was still advertising its Marlboro brand wherever globally it was legal to do so.

'The fact of the matter is that it can no longer do that in the UK, we're a dark market where all advertising, promotion and sponsorship is banned, and cigarettes are in plain packs.
'So instead Philip Morris is promoting the company name which is inextricably linked with Marlboro,' she said.
Philip Morris has said previously that it wants to achieve a 'smoke-free' future.

Like many tobacco firms, Philip Morris is moving towards a focus on new products to replace cigarettes as the number of smokers in the UK continues to decline.
In the UK, it markets several alternatives to cigarettes, including a heated tobacco product, Iqos.
It also owns the Nicocig, Vivid and Mesh e-cigarette brands.
'It takes time'
The firm's managing director Peter Nixon said its new advertising campaign was 'about supporting smokers in finding alternatives'.

Asked why, if Philip Morris was so keen for smokers to quit, it did not simply stop making cigarettes and focus entirely on alternative products, he said it was because smokers would just switch to a rival product.

'Cigarettes still generate 87% of our business. We want to get to [smoke-free] as soon as possible, and we want to be selling alternatives, but it does take time,' he said.
Mr Nixon said the firm had invested over £4bn in developing alternative products to cigarettes.
The campaign suggests four ways to give up cigarettes, including going cold turkey, using nicotine patches, vaping and using heated tobacco products.

In an unusual move, the Daily Mirror made a reference in its editorial column to the advertising feature which envelops the paper. It said it was 'pleased to back the campaign'.
It added: 'Yes, we were surprised too that this is a campaign created by Philip Morris Ltd. But it can only be a good thing that they are now trying to encourage people to quit cigarettes.'
In July last year, the government set out a plan to make England, in effect, smoke-free in the next few decades.
The new Tobacco Control Plan aimed to cut smoking rates from 15.5% to 12% of the population by 2022.
Rather than depending on my luck by playing the national lottery and claiming welfare payment which would, I prefer which one would anybody prefer being born in the UK to claim welfare benefit is it by chance or by luck if it seems the case is this what most of us call life. What is chance and what is luck?

I do not go for the Epiya, Obonkun, liver, heart, cow leg in my African Asian food store since am of an opinion you cannot replicate the act and rituals of the Ogboni's not even if you are the son, daughter or relative of its fraternity cult. It becomes even more difficult within the existence of Rastafarian's while in other scenarios as a child coming from the same parent you might have step brothers or sisters including step Mums or a Dad. Based with the existence of Rastafarianism and the omens of the gods or goddess it becomes so obvious science with its experiments can detect anomalies to cure and treat diseases in humans and animals. It's the members of the cult who can replicate members of their own family or friends.
Living my life to the will of God my aura may be found in the dry or fresh Epiya, prawns, crayfish or Obonkun in the

market place it might sound as if I see myself as a fish a sign to depict it should be my choice to buy. It might beam my star or what am up to by playing the national lottery other people can buy them and likely become what I am or want to become. Now consider and wonder at the same time why, in the Holy Bible there were time, when God instructed the children of Israel if they conquered a city they should not loot where does this leave me at the mercy of my chance or luck but what is chance and what is luck? What is my chance of winning in such a lottery game it's just a machine what can be a philosophy behind it what if you put philosophy into it how possible can this be achieved. Is it more likely that you will win what about psychology since they use our sense of gambling as well?

What about if it's written in your star how, can it be written in your star? In time we might learn we, have to program certain things to occur. What might be written in my star is to win the lottery so I can publish my books is this possible it's just something I want or hope it will happen. If I go further, to say that I also want to win the national lottery so I will no longer live on welfare benefit. In this instance it will mean am taking the blue pill while in the first instance am taking the red pill which could mean something to astrologers. While in my own terms as a philosopher stone wining £10.000 or £15.000 in the national lottery I will not use it in buying food stuffs, furniture's not even clothing's. Could it be likely I would win playing a group of compiled numbers won through lucky dip?

To become lucky can sometimes cloud our life it can make us go beyond boundaries of what it is and what it should not be while in some case we hardly realise it. Astrologers do not look this far except that they might see a tragic thing happening. So how much do we know about the philosopher stone how do astrologers treasure the philosopher stone infarct how did they come about it or get hold of it in the first place and how do they, use it?

How strange can humans be what cause one to be strange what is considered as being strange I have come about 24 motivational quotes about being a wired person? What is it that could lead me to my star, fortune, luck or chance should usually come with strange events true or false? It has something to do about being shy, strange or manic. Something can be wonderful at the same time strange. Most real successful business man and woman usually went into strange success.

If we have places of worship we have a God and we say prayers are there anything as luck or chance? Dose wisdom, knowledge and obedience give us chance or luck nevertheless one can imply that everyone, a country, a nation including every continent have chance and luck in such a case we are implying Gods wisdom in his creativity whereby we can talk about being giving the grace, blessing the chance or luck to do things or come about things.
If God has not given me legs how would I have walked out of my flat to buy the lottery ticked but someone who is physically disable without the ability to do the same thing might say they have the chance and luck as well it does not been they cannot buy or get hold of a lottery ticket which would win e.g. someone else can buy it for them so what is the chance or what is the luck? Chance or luck comes once in a blue moon while the chance or luck of winning a huge sum of money from the national lottery game comes once in a blue moon for gamers. So far in writing this book can it come to me in, my mind to be left with if I do not win the national lottery the game has nothing to do with God?

- ✓ Why do people have beliefs
- ✓ How do beliefs come about
- ✓ What do most people want out of beliefs.

Writing and publishing my books I have in the past been duped of over £1.000 by a publisher to get two of my books published and met with Mr. Jason Pegler at Chipmunka publishing whom I am some worth compelled to stay with because at least he got some of my books published. Writing a book now and publishing it is through foresight the same thing applies to reading books it might mean a lot in the future.

How do we know what we really deserve?
How do we know what other people deserve?
How do we know what God deserves from us?
Within ambiguity what is consideration
Do we always get what we deserve?
For what reasons do we know we deserve something?
How do we get to know we do not deserve something?
We know we deserve or do not deserve something through evidence.

Why do we going through pain, evil and suffering for example to derive evidence.

For most of us, science arrived in our lives packaged neatly as fact. But how did it become this way? Science is an active process of observation and investigation. Evidence: How Do We Know What We Know or deserve examines that process, revealing the ways in which ideas and information become knowledge and understanding?

In certain case study in human origins, they explore how scientific evidence is being used to shape our current understanding of ourselves: What makes us human and how do we go about the way we do?

If you are schizophrenic you are born with an affinity against witchcraft if you are a bipolar you are born with an affinity against magic. Consider I have an affinity against witchcraft as a schizophrenic I go through phase am, a deity known as Orunmila and I have lived under the Ogboni fraternity I sometimes sneeze when a cat is nearby right from within me sometimes the experience makes me feel my airway and whole internal being becomes clear with a tingling sensation. You see I would rather consider going for the Squirrel than going for the Rabbit am very much intrigued by the Squirrel any time it comes close to my blocks of flat it means something has occurred in my own world. A great female would rather go for the Rabbit she would be one who has excel over witchcraft, magic, sorcery but to become more human, defined in her ways in excellence she has to liaires with me who would rather go for the Squirrel the creature naturally makes me feel sometimes am in control of my life and destiny.

There are certain things people do to get where they are a truth and reality is when you come out with it it's like telling them God exist and their reply would be he does not exist. Yes we all have different knowledge and affinity to life there is basically right and wrong we leave each day to admit them in our lives it's not our won doing but that of God himself. There are thing which makes us happy and there are things which makes us sad in the real sense, we all want to be happy. We are the aims we hope to achieve.

Voodoo is a thing within Jamaicans, Caribbean's, Barbados, Trinidad a Jamaican or Caribbean woman said to me she is a Christian and preach the Gospel she does not practice Voodoo. I suffer from symptoms of Schizophrenia she says through our African juju step relatives are living through me at the same time living through her. We know some of the nature of schizophrenic scientifically how much do we know about its spiritual symptoms whether positively or negatively I have written my books which has a lot to say about my life skill in managing my illness.

Was it all just about slavery that brought about Jamaica, Caribbean etc. What if it had, had something to do with creation or with Flash Gordon? The hero of a space opera adventure comic strip created by and originally drawn by Alex Raymond first published January 7, 1934, the strip was inspired by, and created to compete with, the already established Buck Rogers adventure strip. The Flash Gordon comic strip has been translated into a wide variety of media, including motion pictures, television, and animated series. The latest version, a Flash Gordon television series, appeared on the Syfy channel in the United States in 2007–2008.

How did, juju came into our world?
What spirituality do we gain from it?
How does it correlate with science?
What makes a bird fly in correlation to a spell of witchcraft?
What makes us believe in such things?

How are they meaningful to us in our ways of life?
What life skills do we gain from it?
How does it correspond to our Ori or Oriki e.g. Ifaneye means the oracles of juju have wings. Tomori means one who have had or natured a child before. Abeni means we have informed, begged or asked you beforehand.
What makes us human?

What sort of life skill can be relied on to make it more exuberant, breath taking fulfilling in a way which encapsulated our whole being. If it's about writing it depends on what you write about, how you have written it the benefit it brings may be yours to look into which would naturally be a life skill a sort of memorabilia for your effort in life to be focused regardless of pain, suffering or evil it might at the end of the day bring you joy or happiness.

Certain things we hope which, might bring us happiness sometimes bring us sadness if we suffer from involuntary movement e.g. Jacky leg or hand movement what does it mean. Could the working of the mind be sometimes different from the working of the human physical body? Why do we have to concentrate sometimes or meditate and why or how do some people suffer from hallucination.

Can it be said and accepted that hallucination is somehow a way to look into the future of course if I may add, for the would be sceptic that's if, we train the mind. If someone has an ability to concentrate why should they suffer from hallucination? I must confess I have used a unique ability to hallucinate at the same time concentration to have written my books projecting my thoughts, feeling on a computer which means hallucination can be cured by projecting your thoughts, concentration in movements.

Election is the eternal fountain head of grace and salvation. It is the eternal good pleasure granted from God according to which, for His own name's sake and with absolute sovereignty, He chose out of the whole human race a church ordained unto eternal life and glory.

The Word of God in II Peter 1: 10 admonish believers to make their calling and election sure. In fact, it exhorts them to give diligence to do so. And it emphasizes the importance of this spiritual diligence on the part of believers by adding, first, that by doing this they shall never stumble, and, secondly, that thus the entrance into the eternal kingdom of our Lord Jesus Christ shall be richly supplied unto them.

It is evident, then, that we have something to do with election. There are those who would not deny this. They do not deny the truth of this doctrine. On the other hand, they understand very well that the Word of God teaches it; and they profess to believe that God has chosen those who are to be saved from before the foundation of the world. It is not an impracticable doctrine.

It is a mystery. It belongs to those things which are hidden from us, that are for the Lord our God, to us. The more we think about it, the better for us. And by all means it should be preached occasionally to remind us that there is such a truth. Above all, we should never ask ourselves the question whether we are of God's elect, lest we become confused. Our calling is to preach and to believe the gospel, to accept Jesus Christ, and the things to God.

How do we come about?

- ✓ Assurance of God
- ✓ The will of God
- ✓ The grace of God
- ✓ Is it by being ignorant to some of the things around us
- ✓ Or just push them aside
- ✓ I have demonstrated some of the issues of taking the red or blue pill
- ✓ You can't live your life without facing reality or you would be confused in life, goal set or do just your own thing this might make one seem judgmental, self-imposing which might not be the will of God
- ✓ Faith works with grace but can be sometimes daunting in a world of the good the bad and the ugly
- ✓ Therefore we often make a stance through which we come about chance, luck when we come about grace, assurance it means it has been granted - A positive declaration intended to give confidence; on a promise.

If Christ is the blood and bread of life is the vessels e.g. is he the cup and plate it was placed on? We his disciples from all religion and belief system are those things and the table itself why do we have rainfall, fluctuation from the sun how do the clouds contribute spiritually for this to occur. May be in a short time we might become more aware of the programming taking place to reveal a new world that has already been mentioned since before time began.

Can it not ironically be a reality for this to be understood if every home has a mirror and a computer? They are both very important for every home to have then we can understand where science, engineering, technology and architecture might be leading us to in relation to the new world that is coming. Through a mirror you can see from time immemorial even before time began our world revolving from where it all started and where it takes a new turn. You can view yourself in a past life you can see all your trails or happiness, joy or sadness or even your pain and suffering.

Examine you mind, soul, thoughts and emotions why do you have them just focus on them as if that's the only part of you, you have and understand welcome to the world of meditation. In respect of this think of having your whole body, the things around you and then there is not more suffering, pain and evil in our world in our everyday life this, is what we should be aiming for in everything we do. It's something for centuries even before time began we have always been conscious of.

It has kept us moving in view of the programming entering the 21st century it has gone past asking questions. Asking question when it's too late has gone past reality it becomes a consequence having to do with another level of reality to bear. We are being called upon to take a real view of ourselves know every man by the works of his or her hand what, comes out of it in relation to such a difficult time. We should know why it's a difficult time it's, all part of our own doing through the works of our hands, let each of us give a testimony of ourselves in everything we do. Pain, suffering and evil since time began had been leading us somewhere.

In this present time an irony is your relatives and friends ought to know you better but it's as if they do not know you therefore it's time to know thyself.

In most cases as a schizophrenic sufferer anything we buy or use is about going out to tell in most cases the negative aspects retailers do not seem to like us.

But if we really like or enjoy something the whole world would know about it or want it.

As a mental health sufferers try always to know or understand that inner part of you no matter our strange they might seem or come to you.

Cares should express more about the difference within physical and emotional pain. How do they confirm with each other to make life more bearable when it comes to pain or suffering maybe we can understand things better as we seek understanding to the problem of evil one cannot only suffocate under water it can happen anywhere even in space.

We correlate anomalies by knowing or by understanding ourselves better while each day seems as if we are just beginning to understand ourselves.

In this present time and scenarios within small businesses and big businesses who among them can suffer most about not doing things the right way.

If something goes wrong, as a customer which one of them can compensate you most or give you more or less reassurance.

Dose it depends that if you have a physical disability you might or could lose the chance of winning a lottery ticket compered to someone who doesn't have a physical disability?

Can it not be right to say that for those who do not believe in God if so, then they can agree it means to all race, background, culture history we are all an abuse to each other?

Then what would we call a race, ethnic background, culture who say that they are better than others, e.g. one race should not exist they should be wiped out of the entire human race in view of this it might seems like a child's talk in reality, even a child should not have such an opinion.

History can repeat itself but it cannot actually replicate itself since I believe in reincarnation it's the people who come in that it really bears on mostly people who like change who will not imitate history to repeat itself in unfriendly ways. We are often called on, to compromise or blood would have no reason to regenerate itself. You have to live your life in a way your blood replicates you so that you can understand more about yourself spiritually.

It's one reason we have mixed race. Race who do not give support to such life would fight for territory e.g. thinking they are the best others are outcast. What then is a man who practice celibacy it might coincides with I am the fruit of life, Jesus is the fruit of life, I am the boy as lovely as a true where can one give birth to such a child as lovely as a tree on a planet such as Krypton. October 2018 I went through phase I should no longer eat fruits.

23rd October 2018 following a referral received from my Dentist at Woolwich for an appointment at Guy's and St Thomas NHS foundation Trust who, would want me to contact them to agree on a suitable time and date for the appointment I was put off I knew what problem it would be getting in touch with them on the phone to book the appointment. I then realized what it means to know other people. There were only two people I know or can rely on who can accompany me Mr. Dax known as Dotun Sobowale and my brother Omagbemi they are both working.

I was also due for an appointment at the Cardiac Department at Queen Elizabeth Hospital for a 24 hour tape on the 15th of November at 02.15pm. Two weeks before this date I had a fall in my council block of flat had a bruise by my left rib just under my hand it was very painful. I thought of rescheduling the appointment until the next year at least, I would have felt much better and the bruise would have healed it was as if, I was stricken by a moving airplane infarct I thought of rescheduling all appointments until the coming 2019.

I have been referred back by my GP to the Greenwich East Locality mental health Team at Ferryview Health Center Primary care Plus/ADAPT Team since I began talking to myself out loud. They have tried to contact me but were unable to speak with me I should contact them within 14 days from the date of a letter by 12th November if I still wish to speak with them.

If, they do not hear from me they will assume I do not wish to engage with their service and will discharge me back to my GP. I wonder how I can contact them by making telephone calls with no credit on my mobile phone the year before, I disconnected my land line feeling I will not be unwell again but just looking for a part time job. I can hardly phone my brother in other to save money he calls me ones in while for which, am grateful.

I wanted to write in regards to my appointments to inform them about alternatives e.g. postpone or extend the appointments until next year book them for other time more convenient when am feeling much better. If I felt or, expect to be unwell, I do not dwell on it anymore since it always occur on certain peculiar time I wanted to get familiar with such scenarios or the more I will feel am very unwell or feel am being replicated to become unwell.

If I take my stance not to be unwell I later feel calm the symptom will erase itself so when I make myself feel much stronger, courageous, do things in the right order I overcome the symptoms. The worst thing I would do is let fear set in or so be it that am overtaken by the symptoms it's when it gets really unbearable I tend to see my GP.

But I was worried about writing e.g. it will replicate my computer or printer the letter posted to me from the mental health team was in an envelope addressed by hand.
I just felt like being on my own as if everything will get better if, I remain calm it was all part of my assessment it depends on how I respond within myself but I have to commit myself to what is already expected of me.

Something was distinct, but seems ambiguous on the other hand if, I do not attend I would be disappointing other people at the same time make myself as if the letters in relation to the appointments were not distinct but ambiguous. I felt it was something just happening all around me I was not the only one who felt this way. I heard voices as well saying I should not attend the appointments but something intriguing was uncertain on which I have to be committed to respond to the appointments in one way or the other.

I had to wait until my employment and support allowance comes in before I can top up my mobile phone if I have an opportunity to respond by e-mail it would have been much easier for me to respond. But it did not stop me from buying a blender and grinder on a Sunday for religious awareness asking if it was right for me to buy my Egusi, Ogbono ungird or already ground after which I was left with less money to top up my mobile phone therefore, I had to wait until my nest payment comes in which fortunately enough it was in good time for me to either respond or not respond.

It was on the second week of December 2018 my brother Mr. Omagbemi visited me I become aware I can speak more freely registering for WhatsApp account on my mobile phone which he did for me before he left my flat. It did not mean I could use my phone through WhatsApp reschedule my appointment but I can easily get in touch with him if need be. He brought food for me and gave me £50.00 as Christmas gift. I realized something of a strange phenomenon related to taking money from other people even a close relative whilst living in the UK.

Now how would I respond by feeling sulky I might not be certain of what I wanted I wanted to hear voices gearing me into right and definite directions but they were all voices dropping on me. I tried word process I felt it would give me reassurance it would keep me in the right frame of mind at least if I can manage to do just that it mean am moving on.

I did expect to hear voices taunting me about my being able to word process as usual and at the same time having pain in my ribs from my fall in the bathroom. I felt at some point, if I no longer feel the pain severely I would attend my appointment at the Cardiac department. I did not fail to notice I didn't hear voices asking me how I felt in some cases asking question or for information. I wanted to respond but cannot respond to my feelings at the same time do not want to be confused and not putting myself in a position in which I was not doing the right thing and it was near Christmas and a coming new year.

As I word process to some level I felt the pain in my ribs why should I at such a time and a scenario wear a tag around my neck which would be handed to me at the hospital to take home later on. I felt aware airplanes flying in the air around my neighborhood also have effects on just the pain alone among other effects e.g. opening the entrance door to my flat walking in and walking out in one case I had to check the door of the bathroom and entrance door which also induced the pain to be felt more leaving me, as if I had closed or not close the doors which I also go through about airplanes flying in the air even some cars parked or moving in front of my flat have an effect. I did not want to complicate the bruise I received from my fall in the bathroom in respect to my appointment at the Cardiac department.
When I had the fall in my bathroom a voice said even if, it's to computerize my experience I would not be able to word process anymore.

My GP E-mail the mental health team right above her regarding my referral I was expecting I would be posted a letter of appointment and date-time saying I should come and see them but they wanted to speak to me on the phone.

When I walk outside voices revolve all around me my feet, body is encapsulated with the voices and my movement early man use to place their ear on the ground to listen to a point tremors. Its only when, am sometimes talking to other people voices are not inside me maybe it's because then, am no longer conscious of the voices or concentrating my mind on something else.

It's been years since I traveled on train or by private car except by bus bumps have been placed in my neighborhood I still have to be very careful when walking if I had won the national lottery when I expect I would win all this might have been fewer problems. I can think of going for my appointments alone it can encourage me to move on. Airplanes also have effect when am word processing may be through the internet as well at least at this point my readers might see some reason why I have not traveled to Nigeria or any other part of the world outside Great Britain. Physically I have cracked a little especially on my leg and feet. Gone, bald but my body, skin is still fresh.

Anytime I feel unwell it means something terrible has happened or is going to occur 24th December 2018 Indonesia tsunami: Death toll from Anak Krakatau volcano rises meanwhile before this period I had cancelled my dental appointment due on Thursday January the 3rd 2018 at 11.00pm to Monday 18th March 2019 at 12.30. I went for my Cardiac appointment and did as I was told.

It should not necessarily mean a matter of I do not Believe in God: What is it some atheist do not like about God if you have such in mind are there anything you do not like about yourself or about other people what dose religion teaches us it, teaches us the way of living what are the knowledge and wisdom behind faith what dose life teach us or represent. Religion teaches us sheared values which are important to each and every one of us and not to make us more different. But how! We make war or create conflict out of Gods value.

If you value God it means something to you e.g. commitments to you and God and the rest of the world. Other people in such matters are your observers while God is our ultimate observer. He made it this way for his own personal reasons.

How dose religions help us it connects us to God. Whatever be the religion, it doesn't really matter as far as it connects us to God. Every religion believes in a God, believes in a Creator, and believes in living with ethics, values compassion and love. Therefore, a religion helps us to live ethical, moral and happy lives to a point we are what we eat, do or understand about our ways religion, teaches us different things in an ever changing world we are basically what we practices when it comes to this.

In secular usage, religious education is the teaching of a particular religion (although in the United Kingdom the term *religious instruction* would refer to the teaching of a particular religion, with *religious education* referring to teaching about religions in general) and its varied aspects: its beliefs, doctrines, rituals, customs, rites, and personal roles. In Western and secular culture, religious education implies a type of education which is largely separate from academia, and which (generally) regards religious belief as a fundamental tenet and operating modality, as well as a prerequisite for attendance.

The secular concept is substantially different from societies that adhere to religious law, wherein 'religious education' connotes the dominant academic study, and in typically religious terms, teaches doctrines which define social customs as 'laws' and the violations thereof as 'crimes', or else misdemeanors requiring punitive correction.

The free choice of religious education by parents according to their conviction is protected by Convention against Discrimination in Education.

Religious education is controversial worldwide. Some countries, such as the United States, do not publicly fund religious education nor make it part of compulsory schooling. In other contexts, such as the United Kingdom, an 'open' religious education has emerged from Christian confessionals' that it is intended to promote religious literacy without imparting a particular religious perspective. This kind

of religious education has drawn criticism because, it is argued, there is no neutral perspective from which to study religions and any kind of compulsory schooling is likely to impact on the formation of a student's religious identity.
Running a business now is what people do to look after themselves and their own family and friends. To some of us we are yet realizing it's when we buy a bag of rice, grind it ourselves in a grinder to make ground rice to consume with prepared Egusi soup that's when we would feel much better. What difference does this make having a wife and practicing celibacy as a celibate what I do I also do for other people related to how they bear on me within a multicultural nation. For personal reasons I do not wear perfumes as much as I would enjoy wearing perfumes. Couples still together after gender reassignment they are determined to stay together after one of them undergo gender reassignment.

November 2018 India man-eating tigress killed after huge hunt. A tigress in India which is said to have killed 13 people has been shot dead after a major hunt, officials say.
The six-year-old tigress had evaded capture in the jungles of the western state of Maharashtra for two years.
Last month wildlife officials deployed perfume in a bid to lure the animal.
Activists had campaigned to save the tiger, but India's Supreme Court said it would not interfere if forest rangers were forced to shoot it.
A team armed with a tranquiliser gun and a firearm was stationed in a vehicle on a road where the tigress, known as T-1, had been spotted by villagers, a Forestry Department statement said.
A patrol team went to an area near Borati village on Friday evening, after receiving reports of the tigress' presence.
A tranquilliser dart was fired at the animal. Once hit, the tigress charged the patrol's vehicle and she was killed by a single shot from a distance of between eight and 10 metres (26-33 ft), the statement said.
A post-mortem was to be performed on the beast.

- Can Calvin Klein scent catch a 'killer' tiger?
- Why India should not get complacent over its tiger population
-

In August the tigress and her two nine-month-old cubs killed three people in the area around the town of Pandharkawada in Yavatmal district and left more than 5,000 residents fearing for their lives.
Farmers and graziers were told to return early from the fields and forest, venture out only in groups, and not defecate in the open fields, a common practice in the villages.
All creatures are observers of humans take for example you went into a food chain store included in what you bought was a bottle of small whisky the casher mistakenly or knowingly did not take off the security knob on top of the bottle. Unlucky you took your receipt home getting indoors, you immediately got rid of the rubbish bin inside your flat in a new type of bin, and you cannot go back and get your receipt back from. How would you react?
If you take the bottle of whisky back without the receipt it might be taken you stole it one two, you have not got the receipt for the purchased bottle of whisky. I have the feeling police officer are programing themselves in things like these in our community. If you brock the bottle of whiskey and drank it even, just the security knob the police officer or security officer would say it's tagged and they tagged you until you got into your flat.

If a creature becomes aware of this how would the creature react? Not long ago you had this current type of bin tenants living in the council blocks of flat cannot open to retrieve things back from even a voodoo, a witch can instigate such an act just because e.g. they do not like you. Race relation makes creature react they guide those who are peace makers. Do police officer, council staff know of juju or voodoo in some case politics people do to get single council flat?

As a schizophrenic sufferer this is a time we have to be grateful for the hands and legs we have an occurrence of such an issue like these can be very much heartfelt and can lead to instigation there is a security entrance how would the person explain or make a case it did not pip when walking out of the food chain store. At this hour you do not have to be a schizophrenic sufferer to be grateful for the hands and leg you have it's a time it means so much to all of us for which we all should be grateful to God. Being watchful and being directed by God is different from being direct by the devil it's a time the walks of our hands the word of our mouth spells who we are.

The black history you might not learn at school Black History Month is celebrated in the UK every October. As the year's celebration comes to an end, here are four lesser-known historical figures who helped shape multicultural Britain.
Una Marson - 'She was a real trailblazer'
Poet, dramatist, and broadcaster Una Marson made history by becoming the first black woman to be employed by the BBC.

Born in Jamaica, Marson moved to the UK in the early 1930s and took up her first position at the BBC as a programme assistant in March 1941.
'She was a real pioneer in giving voice to black women's experience, as well as generously creating a platform for other contemporary black voices,' historian Robert Seatter says.

'Sparked resentment'

At the BBC, Marson worked alongside writers TS Eliot and George Orwell before establishing her own weekly feature within the Calling the West Indies radio programme, called Caribbean Voices.
She went on to become the first black producer at the BBC.
'This choice sparked resentment, but Marson was described as an extremely intelligent, loyal and lively person,' Prof James Procter, at Newcastle University, wrote in 2015.
Robert Seatter says her ability to persevere despite prejudice highlights why 'she was a real trailblazer' and should be remembered.
The people embracing their disabilities for Halloween for some, with physical disabilities Halloween has become an

opportunity to embrace their bodies and celebrate difference.

A number of people are sharing photographs of their creative costumes which highlight and incorporate their disability.
April, from Chicago, US, shared a photo of herself dressed up with the caption 'Halloween is Christmas for us amputees', an image that has been up-voted more than 115,000 times on Reddit.
April told the BBC that she wanted to 'share some portion of my experience' to help others with disabilities see their bodies more positively.

The YMCA hostel accused of failing the young homeless
This BBC investigation reveals claims that the YMCA North London is failing the young people that live there.
As the largest provider of supported and safe accommodation in England for young people, the YMCA plays a big role in tackling youth homelessness in the UK.
However, the BBC has spoken to a variety of former and current residents and staff members who told us what life was like in the hostel, with some reporting personal stories of crime and poor conditions.

The YMCA North London states it is a charity and has spent £500,000 on refurbishing the facilities in the building over the past two years.

How do we make angels out of ourselves such are the true realities of what lies before us. Both couples were virgins when they met each other raised children both, living together God be praised they are both from the same race. Another couple were both virgins but they were from different race it's what a celibate might learn something from would it be more ambiguous if as a celibate you have once made love before maybe with two different opposite sex. If you become a smoker could it reduce an effect of you suffering from an ear infection?

But if one had always been a virgin practicing celibacy its likely you will never suffer from an ear infection. If you did it might have, had something to do with your parent giving birth to you or it runs in your family what would you do if your step brother was born with an ear infection. Aviation, pharmacies the NHS should make studies into this before people with physical disability in wheelchairs are given access to fly on airplanes.

How do we explain why a person born, grow up and who always looks immaculate, refined gradually or suddenly deteriorates, emaciates how do we relates this to being distinguish. I can know more about traits, behavior, life goals no wonder when there is life, there is hope we can remember the good times and the bad times what it means to us and how we can move on.

Its sin, our sins piles up and fumes it's why we have illness infection and disease it concerns all race and creed.
This coming from food chain stores e.g. to do things their family way even schools to do things their own family way one thing I must add is that this, is not a time for the science of medicine to harass the world or a community infarct not in a place like Britain what really goes inside their most of us know but our mouths are sealed we would always want to trust and look –up to them.

I and my wife have been together with children for years never quarrel or divorce is a case for patronizing each other on every level, category- moral justification, what did you get out of it? If it not gratification. Am managing, outliving my illness of schizophrenia by practicing celibacy who cares! So I have this relationship with God. Knowing him I feel is good for me it gratifies and justifies a feeling in me. Who cares, is this what some people want imply?

What is expected of a leader, do not make commitments, pleasing one party and leave the other? The same thing applies to police officers people do anything now to pave their own way when you scrap birth right citizenship right what does it make out of people like me or my niece Miss. Lydia Omagbuse Megbele. Life is for the living we just sometimes have to live our life as things come to us. A person who does not believe in God will not leave things in the hands of God. My purpose in life is to face my mistakes and suffering, to better my chance when I have opportunities life is an opportunity. How I do this spells that I am not somebody else we are all meant to be different. How is life affecting us these days words cannot recite? Let us come out with what is really in the closet we are left to behave matured.

I observe mental health issues since after 2017 it was all quite, disciplined inwardly we are suffering more. We know what the stakes are. It seems we have been put in the closet. Some people tend to tell you how to live your life it should not be all that viewed with enigmas when this is being done through hearing voices.
November 2018 the plane of being referred back by my GP to the Ferryview view mental health centre might have been welcomed since I was talking out loud to myself, people inside me are talking out loud to me through my own voice I also observed most voices I hear outward are no longer with me. Can it be said when one distance themselves from voice bearers the voices goes away or become reduced.
Scraping birth citizenships is like telling all Rastafarians to shave off the hair on their heads, It's like telling Asians to stop selling our African food we Africans would do it ourselves. It's like calling some people outcast in a world were some people practice celibacy, mixed marriages, homosexuality. The more euthanasia becomes popular. Or it might be a move to make some people react more sensibly.

If it should become the case it might re-shape religiosity, life complexity, social complexity it would probably repeat history e.g. Windrush migration in respect to any significant positive changes taking place in Nigeria since 1988 why am I in Great Britain I hope in time most people might understand what the Krypton factor means. How would I know and understand e.g. from where dose my help comes? How do airplanes fly what are its philosophical effect do that creates enigmas?

If it all gives rise to a global conflict it would be a matter of the world's universal aliens' after the Nazi Aliens.
Iron Sky (2012): a science fiction black comedy about Nazis who left Earth from their hidden base in Antarctica and established a secret fortress on the dark side of the Moon. After Germany's defeat in 1945, the Nazis vowed to return to Earth 'in peace,' and they finally return in the year 2018, but with a full invasion force of flying saucers in order to finally defeat the Allies and restore Nazi Germany. During my years in Africa I am very happy Nigeria has crude oil before I left it ought to have been at least Kerosene or petroleum from where I stand this, is all I can say.
All I can add at this present time is Nazis alien has a lot do with all race, culture, origin and creed they do not thrive on magic and juju they rather make it useless or to lie eggs. Their present stances in this century are those, who were before and during the Second World War began but reincarnated. They have young baby face you can hardly tell their age you would know if they have been on uniform or not.

Do not portray yourself with your powers or ability you can control or outwit them because what you will receive is infuriation. With phenomena's you can outwit them through the help or act of witchcraft through, race juju, the help of the gods and prophets while you remain steadfast in God and your beliefs system in a way which postulates its rightness and goodness. We are our history, our beliefs and cultures we should not be found useless in there respect. We are also the reasons behind the works of our hands and we happen to know most of the reasons behind the works of our hands what greater good can this bring us than the reality of the works of our hands and mind.

We are blessed since we have talent it's those who try to manage or outlive e.g. schizophrenia or bipolar illness who would benefit more from the contents of my books. Your features may change e.g. Facially but not too drastically inside, you are still who you are e.g. very human and considerate you might worry a lot because you do not understand certain things it's a journey you have to understand. Make sure you are all right with your medication e.g. that they are working realize it yourself when you are being hunted.

As for me, I am a ghost hunter when it comes to such matters parts of a reality you go through you want other people around you to understand. Not only cares should make us trust them more we all should be amiable we are all actually displaying our true self at this present time. We only tend to follow ourselves were its more amicable. The effect could be self-centeredness which depolarize relationship with no apologies in a way it does really matter, make sense, more consideration is given to what really matters.
They were around in in 1989, 2007 and 2018 they are in all race to the point of through reincarnation before and after the Second World War they wanted to rule it was then, the human race might have realized they themselves are built with or on the basis of science and technology in every step they make all this while. Why when it comes to issues of mental health I can't wash my teeth, have my bath, wear tidy cloths even if I can afford them and drink alcohol or smoke like a fish under water
They look odd but can also make you look, feel odd or uncertain. You never know where to place your fingers on them they have impacts on magic and juju on a basis they can make one generally feel weakened. More food chain stores like Iceland frozen foods plc ought to spring-up. When they are put on prescriptions it wears-off in time prescriptions ought not to wear-off or leave residuals in humans they would be the wrong sort of people to work in the medical field except if, they have been thoroughly screened to produce positive effects against a more drastic anomaly.
They can create un-pleasantries to achieve their own goals or make their mark. They can be contained through rituals or witchcraft no wonder we are personally becoming ritualistic in our own way we are yet, to ask ourselves why we do certain things or are computers now more knowledgeable than humans? If so, it would be when they begin to execute that's when it makes meaning or more sense because rationally it will makes us more certain that's what Spock in

Star Trek series wants or find problems with to make us understand.
They seem to have a strange strong, determine seemly sublime, personality which, they do not really have while, their spirit level is slightly visible they customary invite themselves into strange and quire situation easily through doing so can they have chance to gain dominance and control. One thing I must mention is that you easily know if they like you or not if they like you, it means they want something from you. If care is not taken they can engulf the whole human race.

From their body to their head when they walk pass you are like standing high like a thread from the sky they sometimes seems like shadows walking by with a star on their head if you look closer, it suddenly fades away. A ritual to avoid them is to prepare a meal within two day it must be consumed and using old or already used furniture's for certain race or culture this method could be quite different for other race and culture. For some other race and culture it would be more applicable to use recent made furniture's of the 21st century. In the real sense of their characteristics and nature they only tend to appeal within themselves in reality all such descriptions are camouflage.

In view of these in relation to my background, culture, religious beliefs and creed I personally feel those with tribal marks on them are not alienated to Rastafarianism while they hardly realize this among themselves. Or why do people have god marks. A god mark which might be affecting a step brother or sister born of another parent by either different father or mother what can this effect has on children who are born premature or Suzerain is what cares need to take note of. No wonder, I endeavored to study BA in business studies at Greenwich university because there was accounting involve on which I could not do well in my studies. Rather for me to have studied psychology or psychiatrist but too close a topic in my care since I had already been diagnosed as a paranoid schizophrenic. I might be much better off with economics but have not the ability to cram in my head.

Likely a grandparent from e.g. Nigeria for example who reincarnates with his or her secrets into Great Britain would be the property and affair of a Jamaican or a Caribbean, While a child who travels to dwell in Great Britain would be an affair for Trinidad or Barbados if, I were to make my choice as one with strong African background and if I might reincarnate I definably might end up in the hands of **Hawaii Five-0.**

I would guess we all from Africa, Jamaica, Caribbean, Trinidad and Barbados have spent more of our lives in and out of Great Britain to ascertain or realis such an occurrence while it would not be left, for a step parent, to realis such an occurrence first if, it should be a similar occurrence somewhere e.g. Africa. If money does not grow on trees, how can I be in one place and feel am in a different place I have been before, dose it really mean culture can be frog under water? Its people and the surroundings which make it seem that way they make you feel good or bad. it's when it speaks to our mind and body that's when we feel, we are welcome you will meet different people, different things if it looks familiar and we have not been there before in a past life it might be our next journey into life. Grand parents should move closer to their grandchildren its where reality of a family lies based on the unknown and that which should not be forgotten.

Hawaii Five-O is an American police procedural drama series produced by CBS Productions and Leonard Freeman. Set in Hawaii, the show originally aired for 12 seasons from 1968 to 1980, and continues in reruns. At the airing of its last episode it was the longest-running police drama in American television history.

It's so obvious after being able to write my books I enjoy watching *Little House on the Prairie and Murder, She Wrote* an American crime drama television series starring Angela Lansbury as mystery writer and amateur detective Jessica Fletcher on television. I do not feel so bad being on free-view only which was installed by the Royal Borough of Greenwich Council just, sometime after I left a contract for free-view with cable and wireless. I was working at the

Woolwich Gala Club at the time technology is improving at what pace and at what cost even to our quality of health there are changes.
Mr. Brian Archer I took over from as cleaning supervisor for initial cleaning service had a previous job with British Rail his son Mr. Martin who is my age group also once a staff at the Club as a cleaner left probably married to an Asian after leaving the job and worked for cable and wireless. Mr. Martin's girlfriend who I first met at the club had a job working at a Chemist. I and Miss Lorain O'Connor a friend of mine where at the club after a night out partying there, was no excuse I wasn't going to be at the club that morning for work so I took Lorain with me to work. If am a sort of person who make or give flimsy excuses with my illness of paranoid schizophrenic I wouldn't have been able to come this far.
Now when someone over reacts, goes off his or her head you make the person cough out, calm he or her down do not do anything to make the person explode then you are being human not only that you are being considerate to a human. On the other hand it would or could be my lord said to my lord. But with me, I have placed an indemnity on the leaders' that's why, I somehow see myself as Balaam (Tori obi mi kose je fun awon Oba). Its how, I always walk into this world no matter how hard and difficult it is with some delicate simplicity relating to facts. (Because leaders cannot eat my Kola nut) While am always ready to face the consequence which bears on me this might be a reason why, I enjoy having goat meat.

When a goat gives you an assurance a tree or leafs is good for its consummation (Oti di idilere niooo..!) (It has become its focus like a home and something personal). It's an adage. It's an adage heaven and the works of humans would always advertise us. I wonder how many people have such beliefs about themselves it does not necessarily mean because I do not have material wealth but am famous in intricate issues only visible to the wise and diligent for which I feel, am wealthy. The Freemasons have a symbol of an eye inside the cloud. Why do we suffer, do each other wrong, why do we tend to set things right now, if we have these and much more, what can stop anyone from being

recognized. Whatever makes the giraffe have a long neck to do what it does to tress or it leaves the goat also knows?
Any plant or tree of any form or kind humans consume are instigated by creatures humans feed on they both have mythical meaning to each other. What is death why do we have death how much do we know about death before we die psychologically, philosophically, spiritually and by our beliefs in some ways out of the boundaries of science. What are our true feelings, emotions or thoughts about death?
Such is always a personal thing and has to do with us getting together therefore, it bears on all of us e.g. the way we live our lives, the food and cloths we wear, how we do things. We all try to avoid death but it's inevitable if there is evil, pain and suffering some of us might understand death and life. All the small gods and goddess at the end of the day will be called Adam or Eve. Meanwhile they should not only know how to address but also authenticates themselves in their reincarnations, trials, less submission to just their own will, address themselves throughout the course of each life to the one and only supreme being and architect of the Universe in a way which makes they them Universal.
Some people might have come into this world with beautiful or handsome face or bodies taken from the gods and goddess in reality of really getting to know them it would be when you have touched their hearts and mind that is when you actually to know them or they reveal themselves. Why do we have pain and suffering in our world, what does it do to us?

Some people always cause trouble or problems they would not contribute in solving this creates a good a leader because that's where they make their mark that's where they truly show and demonstrate who, they are. But somehow that's how certain people lose out. Do not intimidate anyone for being, a fallout. We all exist for different reason. If we all are peace loving people we might not need too much of leadership or make leaders explode or frustrated. If they become frustrated where would our position lie? It's time to know those, who are governed by greed, self-centeredness, conceitedness and for power.
We are meant to exist for God if life really matters to most of us it's a time for reasoning it's time to know who we really

are what we mean to each other not for suffocating each other. From the way people feel it's not time for making excuses any excuse is a rip-off.

November 2018 Americans are voting in nationwide elections that are being seen as a referendum on Donald Trump's presidency.

Polling stations opened at 06:00 (11:00 GMT) on the East Coast, as Republicans and Democrats battle for control of the two houses of Congress.

Governor posts and seats in state legislatures are also up for grabs.
The mid-term elections come halfway through Mr Trump's four years in office and follow a divisive campaign.
All 50 states and Washington DC are going to the polls, and experts say voter turnout could be the highest for a mid-term election in 50 years.

Mr. Trump attended three rallies on the final day of campaigning on Monday, telling his supporters: 'Everything we have achieved is at stake tomorrow.'
Barack Obama - on the campaign trail for the Democratic party - said 'the character of our country is on the ballot'.
What is at stake?

Americans are voting for all 435 seats in the House of Representatives and 35 of 100 seats in the Senate - the two bodies that make up Congress. Governors are also being chosen in 36 out of 50 states.
If Republicans maintain their hold on both the Senate and the House of Representatives, they could help President Trump press on with his agenda.

But if the Democrats wrest control of one or both chambers, they could stymie or even reverse Mr. Trump's plans.
Pollsters suggest Democrats may win the 23 seats they need to take over the House of Representatives, and possibly 15 or so extra seats.

In the Senate, the Democrats are expected to fall short: They would need to keep all their seats and claim two Republican ones to win control.

Asked on Monday how he would handle a lower chamber controlled by his political opponents, the president appeared to concede it was a risk.

'We'll just have to work a little bit differently,' he told reporters.

Trump's invincible but, for how much longer?
Presidents have always commanded attention. Theodore Roosevelt called the White House his 'bully pulpit' - the place from which he could demand attention and advance his agenda.
But Donald Trump has his own bully pulpit, 55 million Twitter followers and a penchant for saying the outrageous.
You feel that everything in American life is a reaction to what Donald Trump has said: his followers adoring it, his opponents deploring it and the candidates actually on the ballot trying to get a word in edgeways.
And this has generated real excitement in these elections - both for and against him.
What happens on Election Day?
After months of campaigning, speculation, and billions of dollars spent on adverts, leaflets and bumper stickers, voters finally have their say.
Democratic candidates for the House of Representatives have raised $649m (£500m) from individual donors, more than double the $312m tally for the Republicans.
Democrats are hoping to achieve a 'mid-term wave' - a sweeping victory that changes the shape of the political map in the US.

What you need to know about mid-terms:

- Why US mid-term elections matter The big issues explained
- Hour-by-hour guide to election night What to expect when

- Can we tell yet who has the edge? Analysis of what we know so far
- Follow the US election on the BBC How to keep up with the results

More than 38 million people have cast early ballots and the official number is probably higher, according to the US Elections Project, a University of Florida-based information source. That figure in 2014 was just 27.5 million.
In Texas, early voting has exceeded the entire turnout in 2014.
As the president observed at a rally in Cleveland, Ohio: 'The mid-term elections used to be, like, boring. Now it's like the hottest thing.'
However, thunderstorms are forecast for Tuesday along the eastern coast, as well as snowstorms in the Midwest, which could affect turnout.
The first polls close at 18:00 EST (23:00 GMT) in Kentucky, and the state could provide some early indications of where the night is heading.
The race for the 6th district is between third-term Republican Rep Andy Barr and the Democrats' retired Marine fighter pilot Amy McGrath.
Mr. Trump won there comfortably two years ago, so a Democrat victory would be a worrying sign for Republicans.
Florida's governorship
A left-wing progressive, Andrew Gillum, and a Trumpist conservative, Ron DeSantis, are battling to become Florida's governor.

It's a tight race in a state that is usually evenly divided, so the result will also be looked at as a sign of things to come.
Georgia's governorship
Democratic candidate Stacey Abrams will become the first female African-American governor in the US if she wins.
Republican opponent Brian Kemp's office has been accused of voter suppression, one of the hot-button issues this year.

Texas Senate

This contest has received national media attention, with high-profile Republican Ted Cruz being closely challenged by Democrat Beto O'Rourke.
Mr O'Rourke is viewed as a rising star in the party and, if he wins, would become the first Democratic senator in Texas for more than two decades.
Arizona Senate
This race is as close as they come.
Martha McSally, a two-term Republican representative from Arizona, is running against Democrat Kyrsten Sinema.
Whoever wins will make history by becoming the first woman to represent the state in the Senate.
What are the key issues?
During his final campaign rallies in Ohio, Indiana and Missouri, Mr Trump returned to his key campaign issues, insisting that Democrats would damage the economy and allow more illegal immigration.
Democratic candidates, meanwhile, have tended to avoid directly confronting the president, focusing instead on so-called 'kitchen table' issues, such as healthcare and economic inequality.

The party hopes younger voters, suburban moderates and minorities will be drawn to the polls to react against the president's rhetoric.

- The most surprising candidates in US mid-terms
- The celebs who want to influence the US elections
- Democrats dazzled by rising star in Texas
-

Mr. Trump has faced widespread criticism for his divisive language.

What we understand definably about our religion becomes like food in its practice food is sustaining without food can mean lots of things anger, frustration, crime the will to follow God is not there but to query him but in some cases it might seems like instinct. Parables comes from the wise and experience people out of e.g. sometimes old age we are in a world where some children can be said to have exceptional

abilities we all need a perception of grace so we have pain, evil and suffering that we do not only depend on our abilities and become arrogant since it has to grow on a basis of fulfilment while, there is beauty, ugliness and death. Only God can have been so exceptional to have created such a scenario.
How do we identify ourselves and the things around which as varied and huge as they are we still need to advance but the time is ticking it now seems time wants to have the propensity to stop for the sake of something we are yet to understand or know yet, we do not want to header to. On the other hand, to question is based on e.g. our spirituality, the works of our hands, the direction we are taking, what we think of ourselves and how they call for a sense of discipline e.g. we ought to know better, think better and it does not seems based on all we are going through is not like the wind.

It's time to hear the stories of those who are suffering what they think or make out of life and it's not time to make bald judgement or bald remarks. For a long time humans have been capable of making Nuclear war heads capable of destroying planet earth and still blame God for the presence of pain, suffering and evil in their world.

- Holding on to the worth of our experience
- Losing the worth of our experience
-

What do you hold to be true? Why did you choose the belief? Do you act according to those beliefs? Perhaps you believe in particular widely-held values that provide an excellent standard learning from right and wrong, good and bad. Perhaps you have other values or believe in something else. Knowing yourself requires a careful examination of your own values and beliefs. What are they, how did they originate, What are they based on, why do you hold such beliefs, Are they based on reliable evidence, are your goals and actions consistent with your beliefs, how do your beliefs align with your values, how have they evolved over your lifetime and how do they help you live a gratifying life?

Assumption is an unfounded belief. Assumptions are unchallenged, unquestioned, unexamined, and very often untrue. Many terms describe unfounded beliefs including: rumours, myths, legends, folk-lore, blind-faith, and wives-tales. Our bias, prejudices, ignorance, and experiences manifest in our assumptions. Apply your theory of knowledge to challenge rumours and assumptions before basing decisions on them. Stay curious. Don't be gullible, don't be fooled.
Possibilities and speculations may become firm beliefs after curiosity, inquiry, and exploration transform assumptions into opinions and opinions into facts. This is the substance of wisdom.

Each of us approaches a new idea, information, rumour, proposal, or explanation with a particular presumption. This presumption can range from a very unlikely, dismissive, and skeptical stance to a very likely and accepting stance.

To determine the truth of a belief we assess the correspondence of this belief with reality. As we become more curious about the proposal we can learn more about the evidence that supports or contradicts its accuracy. Our understanding of the evidence begins to increase as a result of our inquiry and exploration. As more and more information becomes available, we become better informed and create a more accurate understanding and assessment of the situation.

Holding on to the past should not limit us, put us down or we would lack the true values of our experience for its then we are meant to congratulate our experience in several ways related to our perception.

The Lord's recovery today is also a recovery program from alcoholism, substance abuse, or any other kind of vice. In the name of reality the Lord's recovery is the return to what God intended from the beginning, as revealed in His word. To understand him and the meaning of life, we first need to acknowledge him as a precious hymn of praise concerning life. As believers in Christ our faith grows by our appreciation of Christ in His many aspects. Christ's life, in His fine humanity, is one aspect that we need to remember, to appreciate, again and again.

As human beings, we all have our own values, beliefs and attitudes that we have developed throughout the course of our lives. Our family, friends, community and the experiences we have had all contribute to our sense of who we are and how we view the world. Working with people who are vulnerable and or who may live a lifestyle that mainstream society views as being different or unacceptable. To provide a service that meets the needs of the target groups and help them feel empowered, cares need to be aware of their own personal values, beliefs and attitudes and be prepared to adopt the professional values of their industry.

I wrote my books for something distinct it's something am yet to explain but relates to a world that is to come. Your experience are you we all have our own opinions for our reward for being good or bad. Humans have a tendency to judge in a world where there is pain, evil and suffering it means their own free will is vast but on a basis for consideration how do you look beyond what something is e.g. I have an illness of paranoid schizophrenia and can only manage to write my books may be writing my books are a hang-up sign. Why should I be in so much difficulty yet writes my books since there is a motive for everything I must admit it means something to me into the supernatural and paranormal but how do I explain it without creating fallacy so, I merely tried to create an awareness.

Sharing professional opinions with co-workers is an integral part of workplace teamwork efforts. Discussing different points of view promotes brainstorming, generates new ideas and leads to more effective project planning. Sharing opinions related to best practices and different or better ways of doing things can also increase the viability of teamwork, build cohesion and encourage communication and collective efforts.

Be respectful. Part of sharing opinions with colleagues involves being gracious in the way you state your feelings and validate your positions. You can be effective in giving your opinion without putting down the thoughts or feelings of others, which can lead to tension and hostility. For example, 'I think your idea about instituting a customer appreciation program is really on track for improving repeat business. Maybe we could take it one step further and introduce a loyalty rewards program at the same time.'

In an average week, one-in-five Americans share their religious faith online, about the same percentage that tune in to religious radio talks, watch religious TV programs or listen to Christian rock music. And nearly half of U.S. adults see someone else share their religious faith online in a typical week.

These are among the key findings from a survey conducted in May and June of 2014 which asked 3,217 adults from the Pew Research Center's nationally representative American Trends Panel whether they had engaged in various kinds of religious activities during the previous week.

What are your religious beliefs and why do you hold these beliefs? Some people might think or feel am struggling with depression.

In my opinion religion is always a solid topic no religion is wrong the things with different religions is that different cultures throughout time have identified them in different ways. But they do have one thing in common, they all have God the only different thing about them is that every culture has different names and meaning for God. As long as we behave a certain way here on earth we will have a spot where ever it is that we deserve to be but for a long time before that time our opinions would be we. Why should a livid chicken or goat just be put down for food?

People working, in the process of working they, brag, lie, cheat, befriend for reason e.g. to have aid within the goals they hope to achieve. They talk, behave and address each other for peculiar reasons.

People work for all sorts of reasons spiritual, psychological, befriending, social or because of their beliefs. We learn from hard work my late mother once told me hard work doesn't kill it contributes to who you are and what your beliefs are. It's when we feel bad about something that's where there is problem it should be dealt with. We should be happy in what we do for it would contribute in prolonging our life.

If we feel bad about gambling, smoking or being an alcoholic we should find solution to them. You might blame or shame yourself, let down because of what you do try to be philosophical erase all those sneers of hating yourself try to learn from it. We sometimes learn a great deal from our mistake. We might learn at that point what is most crucial to who we are. 90% of those who are destined to win do not especially if you have a strong belief you might win.

I might think gambling first started with people who wanted to make easy money. Both parties want easy money it does not comes easily with reason to win money to do something what while what you are doing is quite different from gambling.

There are banks, credit loan providers, relatives or friends are there. If for example I play and win it only come through chance which is luck but such luck rarely happens yet, it could go beyond luck depending on our beliefs, knowledge of gambling, how much we know of ourselves, relevance of our being deterministic which is the difficult part because it might depend on how wise we are or foolish.

Nevertheless the situation you find yourself in can play with your faith or believes such, is life. If you are a gambler know what you are doing it's the only right thing to do gambling can take you off course or you may find yourself in a situation where the route or direction followed by a ship, aircraft, road, or river knows its course better than you. A paradigm of the Tower of Babel is meant, to lead us further into our own maturity. Words alone are not enough to make some of us reason therefore action sometimes speak louder than voice. It gets to a point in everyone's life we realize, life is not a gamble.

When it comes to what you believe in, you hardly hesitate there are paradox within gambling and hesitation can hesitation result to wining a lottery ticket for the jackpot? I might feel if, I hesitate too often playing the national lottery I can, hardly be a winner. Hesitation and luck means there is something behind the hesitation resulting to the wining. Call it an angel, the luck itself, a belief or prophesy. Not hesitating to something uncertain can result to bad luck how can such a paradigm result to good luck or good fortune except, there are mysteries behind whatever it is.

There is much to gambling than it, just being a game. Hesitation is part of mystic which might need to be correlated with beliefs. If you are not a person who hesitates, you can easily run into debt or gambling addiction. The game providers ought to make room for our hesitation as a matter of fair play not to our own detriments, disbelief, and dis-benefit at the same time, not all that too solemnly to their own favor. Nevertheless we are both an opportunist.

Being an opportunist can cost one a lot so, it's better to be careful rather than being carefree nobody is 'happy go lucky' except if, they are careful if, it contributes to relieving one of smoking or alcohol addiction it would be less complicated. Hesitation can lead to confusion if not well handled; it could lead to mental health issues related to paranoias. Except one has the mystic, a strong belief in something else could help to smooth things out.

Luke 17:33: whoever tries to save his life will lose it, but whoever loses his life will preserve it.

Luke 17:32:
Remember Lot's wife.
Genesis 19:16:
But he hesitated. So the men seized his hand and the hand of his wife and the hands of his two daughters, for the compassion of the LORD were upon him; and they brought him out, and put him outside the city.
Genesis 19:26:
But his wife, from behind him, looked back, and she became a pillar of salt.

Exodus 3:11: But Moses said to God, 'Who am I, that I should go to Pharaoh, and that I should bring the sons of Israel out of Egypt?'

Acts 10:14-20:
But Peter said, 'By no means, Lord, for I have never eaten anything unholy and unclean.' Again a voice came to him a second time, 'What God has cleansed, no longer consider unholy.' This happened three times, and immediately the object was taken up into the sky. Now while Peter was greatly perplexed in mind as to what the vision which he had seen might be, behold, the men who had been sent by Cornelius, having asked directions for Simon's house, appeared at the gate; and calling out, they were asking whether Simon, who was also called Peter, was staying there. While Peter was reflecting on the vision, the Spirit said to him, 'Behold, three men are looking for you. 'But get up, go downstairs and accompany them without misgivings, for I have sent them myself.'

Numbers 13:31-33:
But the men who had gone up with him said, 'We are not able to go up against the people, for they are too strong for us.' So they gave out to the sons of Israel a bad report of the land which they had spied out, saying, 'The land through which we have gone, in spying it out, is a land that devours its inhabitants; and all the people whom we saw in it are men of great size. 'There also we saw the Nephilim (the sons of Anak are part of the Nephilim); and we became like grasshoppers in our own sight, and so we were in their sight.'

Numbers 14:1-4:
Then the entire congregation lifted up their voices and cried, and the people wept that night. All the sons of Israel grumbled against Moses and Aaron; and the whole congregation said to them, 'Would that we had died in the land of Egypt! Or would that we had died in this wilderness! 'Why is the LORD bringing us into this land, to fall by the sword? Our wives and our little ones will become plunder;

would it not be better for us to return to Egypt?' So they said to one another, 'Let us appoint a leader and return to Egypt.'

1 Kings 18:21:
Elijah came near to all the people and said, 'How long will you hesitate between two opinions? If the LORD is God, follow Him; but if Baal, follow him.' But the people did not answer him a word.

God made us in a way we would believe in lots of other things apart from wining a gambling ticket but it has become obvious gambling now has a lot to do with beliefs. It should have something to do with beliefs, your horoscope, being able to get hold of your star and knowing what perspectives to hold or bear if you win.

- 'Life on earth is being wiped out by humans' Tuesday 30October 2018
- It's time to overhaul our lives to save the planet, there is a lot we can do to make sure we keep the planet on track for a lower temperature rise but we need to act now.
- Sea levels warning as scientists find larger part of massive Totten Glacier floating. The Totten Glacier is one of the fastest-flowing and largest glaciers in Antarctica and could raise sea levels by three meters.

WHO - Gaming addiction 'a mental health condition. For most people gaming is an enjoyable hobby and a way to spend time with friends. But for some it can become more than that. Gaming addiction has been listed as a mental health condition for the first time by the World Health Organization. For information designed to help children with their online lives has contributed to my writing this book. What do you do to limit the amount of time your children spend gaming.
Snake bites are now a 'global health priority' according to a new resolution passed by the World Health Organization (WHO) on Friday. The WHO says complications linked to attacks make the phenomenon one of the most neglected of tropical diseases. The world health body will now develop a

global plan of action to tackle the issue, which will include providing cheaper antidotes and training.
Between 81,000 and 138,000 people are killed by snake bites each year.
The resolution aims to ensure that countries follow a common strategy in dealing with such attacks.
Amazing science behind fatal snake bites

How big is the problem?

According to the World Health Organization (WHO), around five million snake bites occur each year, although venom is only injected in just over half of cases.
From blindness to amputations, hundreds of thousands of people are left with permanent disability after being attacked by snakes. The WHO describes such cases as among the most neglected tropical diseases.
The majority of snake bites take place in densely populated areas of sub-Saharan Africa, South Asia and South-East Asia, where humans and snakes often come into contact.
Poor, rural populations are at particular risk from snake bites, as they often lack access to antidotes or may turn to traditional treatments in the absence of modern medical facilities.
Many of the worst affected countries do not have their own facilities for producing antivenoms, which must be quickly administered to prevent or halt the damage caused by toxins.
The World Health Assembly's new resolution will ensure that countries follow a common strategy in the prevention, treatment and management of snake attacks.
What happens when a venomous snake bites?
Venomous snakes generally fall into two categories.
Snakes with fixed fangs usually use neurotoxic venom which affects the nervous system and breathing, while other species have folded fangs which are only used when attacking prey or threats. Their toxin usually destroys skin tissue and causes internal bleeding.
Which snakes have the most toxic venom?

It is important to distinguish between the snakes with the most potent venom and those which pose the greatest threat to humans.
The most toxic venom of any land snake is found in Australia's inland taipan.
But while the snake is said to have enough venom in one bite to kill 100 men, there are no recorded human deaths from a bite by the species, thanks to its shy and reclusive nature, its remote location and the widespread availability of antivenom in Australia.
Sea snakes are also highly venomous, but because of their limited contact with humans, bites are relatively rare.
The less-venomous but still highly dangerous black mamba and the coastal taipan (native to Australia) pose a more immediate threat to humans.
Both come from the same family of snakes and their venom is more fast-acting than that of other snakes, meaning that without treatment a bite victim can die in less than half an hour.
The black mamba is in fact brown or olive, but gets its name from the colour of the inside of its mouth. It is found in much of Sub-Saharan Africa and grows to over 10ft (3 metres) in length.

The coastal taipan, meanwhile, is very aggressive compared to its inland cousin.
Which snakes cause the most deaths?
In terms of numbers of snakebite cases and fatalities, the relatively small saw-scaled viper is one of the most deadly snakes. It is found from West Africa to parts of South Asia and most often bites after dark.
In India, where around half of snake bite deaths worldwide are thought to take place, the saw-scaled viper is one of four species which together account for the highest number of human fatalities.

The other members of the so-called 'big four' are:

- The common or Indian krait: Although normally docile during the day, it becomes very aggressive at night, and can grow up to 1.75m (5ft 9in) in length

- Russell's viper: It is a generally aggressive snake and is widespread across India and South Asia. It feeds on rodents and so is often found near human settlements, both in urban and rural areas
- The Indian cobra is found across South Asia. It is widespread in areas without modern medical facilities and attacks after dark, and causes internal bleeding
-

What should you do if you're bitten by a snake?
The NHS advises the following steps if you or someone else is bitten by a snake:

- Remain calm and seek immediate medical attention.
- Keep the affected part of the body as still as possible, and remove jewellery or watches
- Loosen, but do not remove, clothing

Do not try any of the following steps:

- Sucking the venom out of the bite
- Cutting the venom out of the bite or making it bleed
- Applying anything to the wound, including ice, heat or chemicals
- Leaving the person alone
-

The NHS also advises against putting anything around the limb, such as a tourniquet, as it could make any swelling worse and lead to amputation. The World Health Organization advises the use of the Australian Pressure Immobilisation Bandage (PIB) method only for neurotoxic snake bites, which do not cause swelling.
It is also important not to try to handle or capture a potentially venomous snake. Even dead snakes should be handled with caution, as the nervous system of recently killed specimens may still be active and can deliver a venomous bite.

An earlier version of this story referred to an incident in India in which a child was reported to have died because her breastfeeding mother had been bitten by a snake. The incident was reported by Indian police but experts have cast doubt on the manner of transmission of the venom.

Other Related Topics:

Vaping - the rise in five charts
For travellers looking forward to their summer holidays, what to pack can be a source of stress. But did you know that taking an e-cigarette with you to countries such as Thailand could land you with a fine - or even time in jail?
Countries including the Seychelles and Brazil have also banned the sale of e-cigarettes, but spending on them globally is going up.
These charts tell the story of a growing industry - but how many people vape, how much is being spent on e-cigarettes and why do people buy them?

1. Vaping is increasingly popular
According to the latest statistics from the World Health Organization, there has been a small but steady decrease in the estimated number of smokers globally since 2000 - from 1.14 billion then to about 1.1 billion now.
But it's a different matter when it comes to vaping.
The number of vapers has been increasing rapidly - from about seven million in 2011 to 35 million in 2016.
Market research group Euromonitor estimates that the number of adults who vape will reach almost 55 million by 2021.

2. Spending on e-cigarettes is growing
The e-cigarette market is expanding, as the number of vapers rises.
The global vapour products market is now estimated to be worth $22.6bn (£17.1bn) - up from $4.2bn just five years ago.
The United States, Japan and the UK are the biggest markets. Vapers in the three countries spent a combined $16.3bn on smokeless tobacco and vaping products in 2016.
European countries such as Sweden, Italy, Norway and Germany also feature in the top 10.

3. Open-system e-cigarettes are the most popular
There are two main types of e-cigarette - open and closed system, also known as open and closed tank.
In an open system, the liquid that is vapourised can be refilled manually by the user. There is also a removable mouthpiece.
Closed system e-cigarettes use ready-made refills, which screw directly on to the e-cigarette's battery.
Since 2011, the gap in spending between them has been gradually widening.
It is reckoned that this year, vapers will spend an estimated $8.9bn on open system e-cigarettes, also known as vape pens - more than double the spend on closed-system products.

4. Most e-cigarettes are purchased in-store
Most e-cigarette users buy their devices in specialist shops, according to a report published by Ernst & Young.
In 2015, 35% of e-cigarette users surveyed across the UK, France, Germany, Poland, Italy, Russia and South Korea bought their devices in e-cigarette shops.
Of the 3,000 users surveyed by Kantar for Ernst & Young, 21% said they had purchased their devices online.
It's thought that consumers might make their first e-cigarette purchase in person, to build familiarity with a relatively new product, or to seek advice on which type of device might suit them best.
In the UK, Europe's largest e-cigarette market, there are an estimated 2,000 vaping outlets.

5. Why do people vape?
Across the countries surveyed for Ernst & Young, the most common reason for using an e-cigarette was that they are 'less harmful than regular cigarettes'.
About 49% of regular users said that they used e-cigarettes in order to curb their smoking habit.
Public Health England's latest report on vaping highlighted evidence that e-cigarettes are less harmful than regular cigarettes, and that there was no evidence so far to suggest that e-cigarettes might encourage young people to take up smoking.

The agency has also recommended that e-cigarettes should be available on prescription, because of their role in helping people give up smoking.

However, the World Health Organization has cited several health concerns associated with vaping, pointing out that:

- The long-term effects are unknown
- Nicotine in the liquid that is vapourised in an e-cigarette is addictive
- Users replacing the liquid in refillable e-cigarettes might spill the product on their skin, possibly leading to nicotine poisoning
- Some sweeter flavours of e-cigarettes are irritants, potentially causing inflammation of the airways.

Sunday E. Tuoyo ('Sunny') is a retired Nigerian Brigadier General who served as the Military Governor of Ondo State (July 1978 - October 1979) during the military regime of General Olusegun Obasanjo. He is of Itsekiri origin. His son-in-law is Emmanuel Uduaghan, elected governor of Delta State in April 2007.

Emmanuel Eweta Uduaghan (born 22 October 1954) was the 3rd Governor of Delta State from 2007 to 2015. He assumed office via an inconclusive election on May 29, 2007 and is a member of the People's Democratic Party (PDP). A medical doctor by profession, prior to becoming governor he was the Commissioner for Health, Delta State and the Secretary to the State Government. Uduaghan ran again for governor in the 26 April 2011 elections, and was reelected.

Emmanuel Eweta Uduaghan was born on 22 October 1954 in Warri North Local Government Area in Delta State of Itsekiri origin. He attended Federal Government College, Warri (1968–1974), and the University of Benin (1975–1980) earning a Bachelor of Medicine and Surgery (MBBS) degree, and a Diploma in Anaesthesia. He is married, with two children. His wife, Roli, is the daughter of Brig. General Sunny E. Tuoyo (Rtd), at one time Military Administrator of Ondo State.

Emmanuel Uduaghan began work in 1983 at the Delta Steel Company, as a medical officer. From 1989 to 1994, he worked in a number of hospitals including Westend Hospital, Warri; Benoni Hospitals, Benin City and Shell Hospital, Ogunu, where he was a Consultant Anaesthesiologist. In 1994 he set up a private medical practice. He was held the positions in the Nigerian Medical Association in Warri, Bendel State and Delta State. He was also active in the Junior Chamber International (Jaycees) leadership development organization.

Cannabis war 'comprehensively lost', says William Hague
Former Conservative leader Lord Hague has called for a 'decisive change' in the law on cannabis - suggesting that the Tories should consider legalizing recreational use of the drug.
Writing in the Daily Telegraph, he said 'any war' has been 'irreversibly lost'.
Lord Hague goes further than senior Tories who have suggested a law change after a boy with epilepsy was given a special license to use cannabis oil.
The government is creating an expert panel to look into individual cases.

It will not be looking at the legalization or decriminalization of the drug for recreational use, something Prime Minister Theresa May has ruled out 'because of the impact that [it has] on people's lives'.
She said a system was already in place for medicinal use, and that government policy would be driven by 'what clinicians are saying'.

A Home Office spokesman said: 'Any debate within government about the efficacy and therapeutic use of cannabis-based medicines emphatically does not extend to any review regarding the classification of cannabis and the penalties for the illicit possession, cultivation and trafficking of cannabis will remain the same.'
The cops and politicians joining Canada's cannabis business
29 December 2017As Canada moves towards legalizing

recreational cannabis, there's a surprising group of entrepreneurs jumping into the market: cops and politicians. Canada unveils plans to legalize recreational marijuana Canada has laid out its plan to legalize the sale of recreational marijuana by June 2018.

If it passes, the country will be the largest developed nation to end marijuana prohibition.
The law was tabled on Thursday, and would allow adults over 18 to possess up to 30g of dried marijuana.
The proposed legislation would allow the federal government to license producers, but provinces would be in charge of regulating consumer sale.
Other issues, such as pricing, taxation and packaging must still be worked out.
'This is a very important day, I've spent most of my adult life keeping children and communities safe,' said MP Bill Blair during a press conference shortly after the legislation was presented to parliament.
The former police chief had chaired the government's cannabis task force, which laid out a blueprint for legal recreational pot in Canada
Hereditary: The 'scariest film for years' is coming It's been described as 'the singularly most terrifying horror film in years' and 'a new generation's The Exorcist'.
Horror movie Hereditary has become one of 2018's most eagerly anticipated releases after scaring and impressing critics in equal measure.
Actress Toni Collette is coming in for particular praise as a woman whose family has demons in its DNA.
Bustle said it's 'truly unlike anything you've seen before', while The AV Club called it 'pure emotional terrorism'.
The film is released in the US on 8 June and in the UK a week later.

In his five-star review for The Guardian, Peter Bradshaw wrote: 'Hereditary tripled my heart rate, prickle-massaged my scalp, cured my hiccups - and pretty much terrified me.'
Collette's 'operatic, hypnotic performance seals the deal every second she's on the screen', he said.

Referring to next year's film awards season, he added: 'Surely this magnificent actor will get some silverware next February.'
The film's New York-based first-time writer-director Ari Aster has also received acclaim.
Writing in Vox, Alissa Wilkinson said: 'The first time I saw Hereditary I yelped a lot, and very nearly crawled under my seat once or twice.
'What you feel from the start is a sense of real horror, some kind of cross between dismay and disgust, which starts out almost undefinable and builds to a (literal) crescendo by the end.'

The Independent's Clarisse Loughrey wrote: 'The fact Hereditary is being (rightly) talked of as one of the most singularly terrifying, singularly disturbing horror films in years speaks to its unique sense of mood.
'Secrecy, guilt, anguish: Hereditary breeds its own phantoms. Ones which like hang around, to boot. Weeks later, you may step into a dark room, and that chilled feeling will come rushing back: am I truly alone right now?'
How trying to stay cool could make the world even hotter
Air conditioning systems that keep homes, offices and shops cool on hot days are rapidly gaining in popularity in a warming world. But is all the extra electricity they use going to exacerbate climate change or can design efficiencies prevent this?
The world is getting hotter; indeed 16 of the 17 warmest years on record have occurred since 2001, say climatologists.
It's no wonder demand for air conditioning systems is going through the roof. The energy they consume is likely to triple between now and 2050, the International Energy Agency (IEA) says.
This would mean that by 2050, the world's air conditioners would be using the current electricity capacity of the US, the European Union and Japan combined.
Scientists and tech companies are trying, to make cooling systems more efficient.

Researchers at Stanford University, for example, have developed a system that uses cutting edge materials and 'nano-photonics'.

They've invented a wafer-thin, highly reflective material that radiates heat even in direct sunlight. The infrared, thermal energy is radiated at a wavelength that slips through the Earth's atmosphere into space, rather than being absorbed by it.

June 2018 Debenhams warns on profits for third time that year Debenhams said full-year profits will be lower than expected - the third time it has issued a profit warning this year.

The department store blamed 'increased competitor discounting and weakness in key markets' for the profit shortfall.

It said annual pre-tax profits would come in between £35m and £40m, below previous estimates of £50.3m.

Debenhams' latest profit warning comes despite a turnaround plan designed to cut costs and boost sales.

Chief executive Sergio Bucher pointed to 'exceptionally difficult times in UK retail'.

Shares in Debenhams fell as much as 16% in early trading before recovering slightly.

Debenhams runs 182 stores in the UK, Republic of Ireland and in Denmark.

Regular excess drinking can take years off your life, study finds

Regularly drinking above the UK alcohol guidelines can take years off your life, according to a major report.

The study of 600,000 drinkers estimated that having 10 to 15 alcoholic drinks every week could shorten a person's life by between one and two years.

And they warned that people who drink more than 18 drinks a week could lose four to five years of their lives.

The 2016 UK guidelines recommend no more than 14 units a week, which is six pints of beer or seven glasses of wine.

Authors of the Lancet study said their findings backed up the new guidelines and also said they did not find an increased risk of death for light drinkers.

- Your guide to alcohol drinking limits
- Alcohol limits cut to reduce risks
- Booze calculator: What's your drinking nationality?
-

Scientists, who compared the health and drinking habits of alcohol drinkers in 19 countries, modelled how much life a person could expect to lose if they drank the same way for the rest of their lives from the age of 40.

They found people who drank the equivalent of about five to 10 drinks a week could shorten their lives by up to six months.

The study's authors also found drinking increased the risk of cardiovascular illness, with every 12.5 units of alcohol people drank above the guidelines raising the risk of:

- Stroke by 14%
- Fatal hypertensive disease by 24%
- Heart failure by 9%
- Fatal aortic aneurysm by 15%
-

Drinking alcohol was linked with a reduced risk of non-fatal heart disease, but scientists said this benefit was wiped out by a higher risk of other forms of the illness.

Previous studies have suggested that drinking red wine can be good for our hearts, although some scientists have suggested these benefits may be overhyped.

Another Danish study found drinking three to four times a week was linked to a lower risk of type 2 diabetes.

'This study makes clear that on balance there are no health benefits from drinking alcohol, which is usually the case when things sound too good to be true,' said Tim Chico, professor of cardiovascular medicine at the University of Sheffield, who was not involved in the research.

'Although non-fatal heart attacks are less likely in people who drink, this benefit is swamped by the increased risk of other forms of heart disease including fatal heart attacks and stroke.'

Recommended limits in Italy, Portugal, and Spain are almost 50% higher than the UK guidelines, and in the USA the upper limit for men is nearly double this.

But Victoria Taylor, senior dietician at the British Heart Foundation, which partly funded the study, said this did not mean the UK 'should rest on its laurels'.
'Many people in the UK regularly drink over what's recommended' she said.
'We should always remember that alcohol guidelines should act as a limit, not a target, and try to drink well below this threshold.'
Dr Angela Wood, from the University of Cambridge, lead author of the study, said: 'The key message of this research is that, if you already drink alcohol, drinking less may help you live longer and lower your risk of several cardiovascular conditions.'
Genes behind deadly heart condition found, scientists say
Scientists say they have identified genes that cause a deadly heart condition that can only be cured by transplants of the heart or lungs.
Pulmonary arterial hypertension kills 50% of those affected within five years, but little was known about what caused the condition in some people.
Now experts say they have discovered five genes that cause the illness.

The findings could lead to earlier detection of the disease and ultimately new treatments, researchers say.

- Thousands 'unaware of sudden death risk'
- New blood test to spot heart conditions
-

Pulmonary arterial hypertension (PAH) currently affects around 6,500 people in the UK and causes the arteries carrying blood from the heart to their lungs to stiffen and thicken, ultimately leading to heart failure.
It is often diagnosed in people, who have other heart or lung conditions, but it can affect people of any age and in about a fifth of people there is no obvious cause.
The only 'cure' is a transplant of the heart and particularly the lungs, but there is a waiting list for organ transplants and the body will often ultimately reject them, particularly in the case of lungs.

For this latest research, published in Nature Communications, scientists carried out the largest ever genetic study of the disease by analysing the genomes - the unique sequence of a person's DNA - of more than 1,000 PAH patients for whom the cause of the illness was unknown.

They found that mutations in five genes were responsible for causing the illness in these people, including in four genes that were not previously known to be involved in the disease.

In people with the condition these genes fail to effectively produce the proteins that are required for the structure, function and regulation of the body's tissues, researchers found.

Nick Morell, the lead author of the paper and professor at the British Heart Foundation, told BBC News: 'Identifying the nature of these new genes and mutations in the new genes tells you what causes the disease.

'It allows you to design and come up with potential new ways of treating the disease because you have really well-grounded knowledge about what's actually causing it in cases where you find these mutations,' he explained.

Wendy Callaghan, from west London, was diagnosed with PAH in 2013 after doctors became concerned about her persistent chest infection.

Her sister died from the condition 27 years ago at the age of 36, and her grandmother also died from a similar heart condition.

Wendy, who participated in the trial, has been told she has the genetic version of the illness and is now waiting to learn if her daughters and grandchildren have inherited the same deadly condition.

The 58-year-old said: 'Even children can get it. People should be more aware of it and look out for the signs and persist with it if they think their child is not well.

'Especially as it does run in families, some people if they don't know they've got it could be passing those genes on to the next generation,' Wendy added.

The research was part of a pilot study for the 100,000 Genomes Project - a huge initiative focused on understanding the genetics of cancer and rare diseases.

Prof Morell said such genetic studies were helping to transform our understanding of rare diseases.

He said: 'Often people with rare diseases go to lots of different specialists, everybody is scratching their head a bit, we don't know what the cause is, and therefore it's hard to find a treatment for it.

'Now being able to [genetically] sequence people with rare diseases at scale allows you to push the genetics into the clinic and into the families, and it also gives you a cause for the disease which you can potentially do something about,' he said.

Darren Griffin, professor of genetics at the University of Kent, who was not involved in the study, said the research was 'one of the big successes' of the 100,000 Genome Project.

He said: 'By studying the role of rare genetic variation in diseases, we come to a better understanding of the disease pathology itself, which can aid in early diagnosis and in tailoring treatment regimes.'

'Wake-up call' over liver disease risks due to weight

One in eight middle-aged adults in the UK could have a potentially serious form of liver disease - because they are overweight.

Scans of nearly 3,000 individuals from the UK Biobank research project showed that 12% had inflamed fatty livers.

The British Liver Trust said the 'very alarming' findings were a 'wake-up call' because the condition can lead to cirrhosis, liver failure and death.

Hepatologists said there was a silent epidemic of fatty liver disease.

This is especially worrying because symptoms often do not emerge until permanent damage is done - but the condition is reversible if caught in time.

The results of the MRI scanning study, led by scientists in Oxford, were announced at the International Liver Congress in Paris.

They were made possible by an innovative software analysis tool called LiverMultiScan, developed by Perspectum Diagnositics, a spin-out company from the University of Oxford.

Dr Rajarshi Banerjee, CEO of Perspectum Diagnostics said: 'LiverMultiScan is a great example of a smart health technology discovered and developed by UK clinicians and scientists with clear benefits for patients, the NHS, and taxpayers.

'Whilst liver biopsy remains an important part of hepatology practice, clearly we need better non-invasive tools at our disposal to evaluate the nature and severity of liver disease.'

Needle biopsies are the gold standard for assessing liver disease, but they are costly, invasive, painful and carry some health risks.

The software tool can be used in any MRI scanner but is not yet in routine clinical practice.

Southampton General is the first NHS hospital to use the new system outside of research.

David Breen, associate professor of radiology at University Hospital Southampton believes it could reduce the need for biopsies.

He said: 'The scan gives a map of the entire liver as opposed to a needle-core biopsy which samples just one area and can be unpleasant.

'It also allows us to re-scan patients over time and see if they improve.'

Previous studies had suggested that around one in 20 adults might have the potentially serious form of fatty liver disease known as NASH (non-alcoholic steatophepatitis).

This is where there is inflammation in and around the liver cells liver which, over time, can lead to the build-up of scar tissue known as fibrosis - eventually this can lead to cirrhosis.

But the scanning study suggests the proportion could be much higher.

Steve Ryder, consultant liver specialist in Nottingham said: 'This study accords with what we are seeing on the ground - a lot of people are coming to hospital with significant liver disease because they are overweight.'

Ninety per cent of liver disease is reversible if caught in time.

Judi Rhys, chief executive of the British Liver Trust said: 'Reducing alcohol is important which most people already know, but for fatty liver disease the key things are having a healthy weight and doing exercise.'
The charity has an online screening tool to assess your risk of liver disease.
Why some cancers are 'born to be bad'
A ground-breaking study has uncovered why some patients' cancers are more deadly than others, despite appearing identical.
Francis Crick Institute scientists developed a way of analysing a cancer's history to predict its future.
The study on kidney cancer patients showed some tumours were 'born to be bad' while others never became aggressive and may not need treating.
Cancer Research UK says the study could help patients get the best care.
'We don't really have tools to differentiate between those that need treatment and those that can be observed,' said researcher and cancer doctor Samra Turajlic.
One cancer could kill quickly while a patient with a seemingly identical cancer could live for decades after treatment.

It means uncertainty for both the patient and the doctor.
It is most common in people in their 60s and 70s. Symptoms include:

- Blood in your pee
- Persistent pain in the lower back or side
- Sometimes a lump or swelling in your side
-

The work published in three papers in the journal Cell, analysed kidney cancers in 100 patients.
The team at the Crick performed a sophisticated feat of genetics to work out the cancer's history.
It works like a paternity or ancestry test on steroids.
As cancers grow and evolve, they become more mutated and, eventually, different parts of the tumour start to mutate in different ways.

Researchers take dozens of samples from different parts of the same tumour and then work out how closely related they are.

It allows scientists to piece together the evolutionary history of the whole tumour.
'That also tells us where the tumour might be heading as well,' said Dr Turajlic.

Chance to change care

The researchers were able to classify kidney cancer into one of three broad categories:

- Born to be bad
- Benign
- Intermediate
-

The 'born to be bad' tumours had rapid and extensive mutations and would grow so quickly they are likely to have spread round the body before they are even detected.
Surgery to remove the original tumour may delay the use of drugs that can slow the disease.
The benign tumours are at the complete opposite and are likely to grow so slowly they may never be a problem to patients and could just be monitored.
The intermediate tumours were likely to initially spread to just one other location in the body and could be treated with surgery.

Sugar tax: Will paying more for fizzy drinks and alcohol make us healthier?

An anti-obesity drive is about to see a tax introduced on sugary drinks across the UK, while Scotland is set to impose a minimum price on alcohol to target problem drinking.
But do making unhealthy products more expensive persuade people to make 'better' choices? And what are the trade-offs associated with doing so?

Everybody will pay more

The price increases being introduced could lead to significant health improvements, but they will be felt by everybody, not just those with the unhealthiest lifestyles.
From 6 April, the UK's tax on sugary drinks will see shoppers asked to pay 18p or 24p more a litre, depending on just how much has been added to their drinks. The price of a 1.75-litre bottle of cola bought from a supermarket could increase by about 25%.
In Scotland, from May, alcohol will not be allowed to be sold for less than 50p per unit, which could see a four-pack of cider cost 10% more, while a pack of 20 cans could double in price. Wales is looking at similar measures.
This is happening because sugar and alcohol are associated with problems that impose a substantial cost on society.
Animals' popularity 'a disadvantage'
The world's most popular animals are in more danger than we realise, according to a new study.
A survey of the public's perceptions suggests many people are unaware that the animals they consider 'charismatic' are under threat in the wild.
These include lions, elephants, tigers and other animals which frequently appear in branding and advertising.
Researchers suspect the animals' media ubiquity may lead people to think they are prospering in the wild.
The findings were published by an international team of scientists in PLOS Biology.

Charismatic species

The notion of 'charismatic' species has cropped up recently in conservation biology, explains Dr. Franck Courchamp, the study's lead author.
'There is a regular claim that the most charismatic species are diverting most of the time and resources [in conservation]. I started wondering whether this was true and followed by better results in conservation,' he told BBC News.
Dr. Courchamp and his team set out to determine exactly which species these might be.

Using an online survey available in four languages, supplemented by classroom questionnaires in English, Spanish and French primary schools, researchers asked the public to name the wild species they considered most charismatic.
They also looked at how frequently animals were represented on zoo websites, and on the covers of Disney and Pixar animated films.

The ten most 'charismatic' animals:

- Tiger
- Lion
- Elephant
- Giraffe
- Leopard
- Panda
- Cheetah
- Polar bear
- Wolf
- Gorilla

Virtual wildlife

Additionally, the team had volunteers in France catalogue their encounters with 'virtual' populations of the 10 animals over the period of a week.
They encountered an average of 4.4 lions in logos, cartoons, magazines and other sources each day, implying that people are likely to see two to three times as many 'virtual' lions in a year as there are lions in West Africa.
Dr. Courchamp thinks this may have a subconscious impact, though there is no direct evidence as of yet.
'Mostly I think because people see giraffes and lions every day of their life, they unconsciously think they are in abundance,' he said.
Despite their abundant media representation, nine of the animals on the list are classed as vulnerable, endangered or critically endangered on the International Union for the Conservation of Nature (IUCN) Red List.

When researchers asked survey participants whether they thought these animals were endangered, explaining that they were not using IUCN terminology, they were surprised by the results.

Almost half of respondents thought that critically endangered gorillas were not under threat.

But conservation biologist Dr Sarah Durant cautions that this doesn't yet establish ‘a causal relationship between seeing the species frequently in society and whether that relates to our bias perception of their endangerment.’

Other factors may influence people's understanding of a species' status, and their participation in conservation efforts.

‘We don't know that much about the psychology behind conservation. It's a very new field. I think a lot of people often feel overwhelmed as well, because the problems are so huge,’ added the Zoological Society of London researcher, who was not involved in the study.

‘It would be an interesting area for further research,’ she said.

Dr. Courchamp proposes an innovative solution; funding conservation by ‘copyrighting’ the image of vulnerable or endangered species.

Companies would donate money to NGOs in return for using the animals in their branding or advertising.

‘I think it's not so unrealistic,’ says Dr. Courchamp.

‘There are already some companies that do that. Jaguar are in partnership with Panthera.

‘Lacoste... also made a campaign recently where they replaced their logo with silhouettes of endangered species.’

Dr Durant observes that it would likely be difficult to execute, but is an interesting suggestion.

‘This is just the first step,’ she commented, ‘putting this idea out there. Hopefully it will open a discussion about the use of these species and how it relates to their conservation.’

Time is certainly short for some of the animals on the list. Ecologists predict that, without sustained conservation efforts, elephants will become extinct in the wild within a century.

Cheetah are facing an imminent population decline of up to 70%, and are already confined to just 9% of their historical territory in Africa.
Dr. Courchamp feels that more needs to be done. 'At the moment we are doing first aid on species that are on the verge of dying. We are just pushing the day they go extinct in the wild, we are not saving them.'

How bacteria are changing your mood

By James Gallagher Presenter, The Second Genome, BBC Radio 4
If anything makes us human it's our minds, thoughts and emotions.
And yet a controversial new concept is emerging that claims gut bacteria are an invisible hand altering our brains.
Science is piecing together how the trillions of microbes that live on and in all of us - our microbiome - affect our physical health.
But even conditions including depression, autism and neurodegenerative disease are now being linked to these tiny creatures.
We've known for centuries that how we feel affects our gut - just think what happens before an exam or a job interview - but now it is being seen as a two-way street.
Groups of researchers believe they are on the cusp of a revolution that uses 'mood microbes' or 'psychobiotics' to improve mental health.
The study that ignited the whole concept took place at Kyushu University in Japan.
The researchers showed that 'germ-free' mice - those that never came into contact with microbes - pumped out twice the amount of stress hormone when distressed than normal mice.
The animals were identical except for their microbes. It was a strong hint that the difference was a result of their micro-organisms.

'We all go back to that first paper for the first wave of neuroscientists considering microbes,' says Dr Jane Foster, a neuropsychiatrist at McMaster University in Canada.

'That really was very powerful for those of us who were studying depression and anxiety.'
It was the first hint of microbial medicine in mental health.

How could bacteria be altering the brain?

The brain is the most complex object in the known universe so how could it be reacting to bacteria in the gut?

- One route is the vagus nerve; it's an information superhighway connecting the brain and the gut.
- Bacteria break down fibre in the diet into chemicals called short-chain fatty acids, which can have effects throughout the body.
- The microbiome influences the immune system, which has also been implicated in brain disorders.
- There is even emerging evidence that gut bugs could be using tiny strips of genetic code called microRNAs to alter how DNA works in nerve cells.
- There is now a rich vein of research linking germ-free mice with changes in behaviour and even the structure of the brain.
-

But their completely sterile upbringing is nothing like the real world. We're constantly coming into contact with microbes in our environment; none of us are germ-free.
At Cork University Hospital, Prof Ted Dinan is trying to uncover what happens to the microbiome in his depressed patients.
A good rule of thumb is a healthy microbiome is a diverse microbiome, containing a wide variety of different species living all over our bodies.
Prof Dinan says: 'If you compare somebody who is clinically depressed with someone who is healthy, there is a narrowing in the diversity of the microbiota.
'I'm not suggesting it is the sole cause of depression, but I do believe for many individuals it does play a role in the genesis of depression.'
And he argues some lifestyles that weaken our gut bacteria, such as a diet low in fibre, can make us more vulnerable.

The microbiome

- You're more microbe than human - if you count all the cells in your body, only 43% are human
- The rest is our microbiome and includes bacteria, viruses, fungi and single-celled archaea
- The human genome - the full set of genetic instructions for a human being - is made up of 20,000 instructions called genes
- But add all the genes in our microbiome together and the figure comes out at between two million and 20 million microbial genes
- It's known as the second genome and is linked to diseases including allergy, obesity, inflammatory bowel disease, Parkinson's, whether cancer drugs work and even depression and autism
-

It's an intriguing concept - that an imbalance in the gut microbiome could be involved in depression.
So scientists at the APC Microbiome centre, at University College Cork, started transplanting the microbiome from depressed patients to animals. It's known in the biz as a trans-poo-sion.

It showed that if you transfer the bacteria, you transfer the behaviour too.

Prof John Cryan told the BBC: 'We were very surprised that you could, by just taking microbiome samples, reproduce many of the features of a depressed individual in a rat.'
This included anhedonia - the way depression can lead to people losing interest in what they normally find pleasurable.
For the rats, that was sugary water they could not get enough of, yet 'when they were given the microbiome from a depressed individual, they no longer cared', says Prof Cryan.
Listen to The Second Genome on BBC Radio 4. In 2018
The next episode airs at 11:00 BST on Tuesday April 24, repeated 21:00 BST Monday April 30 and on the BBC iPlayer

Similar evidence - linking the microbiome, the gut and the brain - is emerging in Parkinson's disease.
It is clearly a brain disorder. Patients lose control over their muscles as brain cells die and it leads to a characteristic tremor.
But Prof Sarkis Mazmanian, a medical microbiologist from Caltech, is building the case that gut bacteria are involved.
'Classical neuroscientists would find this as heresy to think you can understand events in the brain by researching the gut,' he says.

He has found 'very powerful' differences between the microbiomes of people with Parkinson's and those without the disease.
Studies in animals, genetically hardwired to develop Parkinson's, show gut bacteria were necessary for the disease to emerge.
And when stool was transplanted from Parkinson's patients to those mice, they developed 'much worse' symptoms than using faeces sourced from a healthy individual.
Prof Mazmanian told the BBC: 'The changes in the microbiome appear to be driving the motor symptoms, appear to be causal to the motor symptoms.
'We're very excited about this because it allows us to target the microbiome as an avenue for new therapies.'
The evidence linking the microbiome and the brain is as fascinating as it is early.
But the pioneers of this field see an exciting prospect on the horizon - a whole new way of influencing our health and wellbeing.

If microbes do influence our brains then maybe we can change our microbes for the better.
Can altering the bacteria in Parkinson's patients' guts change the course of their disease?
There is talk of psychiatrists prescribing mood microbes or psychobiotics - effectively a probiotic cocktail of healthy bacteria - to boost our mental health.
Dr. Kirsten Tillisch, at University of California, Los Angeles, told me: 'If we change the bacteria can we change the way we respond?

But she says we need far bigger studies that really probe what species, and even sub-species, of bacteria may be exerting an effect on the brain and what products they are making in the gut.

Dr. Tillisch said: 'There's clearly a connection here, I think our enthusiasm and our excitement is there because we haven't had great treatments.

'It's very exciting to think there's a whole new pathway that we can study and we can look and we can help people, maybe even prevent disease.'

And that's the powerful idea here.

The microbiome - our second genome - is opening up an entirely new way of doing medicine and its role is being investigated in nearly every disease you can imagine including allergies, cancer and obesity.

I've been struck by how malleable the second genome is and how that is in such stark contrast to our own DNA.

The food we eat, the pets we have, the drugs we take, how we're born... all alter our microbial inhabitants.

And if we're doing that unwittingly, imagine the potential of being able to change our microbiome for the better.

Prof Cryan said: 'I predict in the next five years when you go to your doctor for your cholesterol testing etc., you'll also get your microbiome assessed.

'The microbiome is the fundamental future of personalised medicine.'

Follow James on Twitter.

Illustrations: Katie Horwich

More than half your body is not human

By James Gallagher Presenter, the Second Genome, BBC Radio 4

More than half of your body is not human, say scientists.

Human cells make up only 43% of the body's total cell count. The rest are microscopic colonists.

Understanding this hidden half of ourselves - our microbiome - is rapidly transforming understanding of diseases from allergy to Parkinson's.

The field is even asking questions of what it means to be 'human' and is leading to new innovative treatments as a result.

'They are essential to your health,' says Prof Ruth Ley, the director of the department of microbiome science at the Max Planck Institute, 'your body isn't just you'.

No matter how well you wash, nearly every nook and cranny of your body is covered in microscopic creatures.

This includes bacteria, viruses, fungi and archaea (organisms originally misclassified as bacteria). The greatest concentration of this microscopic life is in the dark murky depths of our oxygen-deprived bowels.

Prof Rob Knight, from University of California San Diego, told the BBC: 'You're more microbe than you are human.'

Originally it was thought our cells were outnumbered 10 to one.

'That's been refined much closer to one-to-one, so the current estimate is you're about 43% human if you're counting up all the cells,' he says.

But genetically we're even more outgunned.

The human genome - the full set of genetic instructions for a human being - is made up of 20,000 instructions called genes.

But add all the genes in our microbiome together and the figure comes out between two and 20 million microbial genes.

Prof Sarkis Mazmanian, a microbiologist from Caltech, argues: 'We don't have just one genome, the genes of our microbiome present essentially a second genome which augment the activity of our own.

'What makes us human is, in my opinion, the combination of our own DNA, plus the DNA of our gut microbes.'

Listen to The Second Genome on BBC Radio 4.

Airs 11:00 BST Tuesday April 10, repeated 21:00 BST Monday April 16 and on the BBC iPlayer

It would be naive to think we carry around so much microbial material without it interacting or having any effect on our bodies at all.

Science is rapidly uncovering the role the microbiome plays in digestion, regulating the immune system, protecting against disease and manufacturing vital vitamins.

Prof Knight said: 'We're finding ways that these tiny creatures totally transform our health in ways we never imagined until recently.'
It is a new way of thinking about the microbial world. To date, our relationship with microbes has largely been one of warfare.

Microbial battleground

Antibiotics and vaccines have been the weapons unleashed against the likes of smallpox, Mycobacterium tuberculosis or MRSA.
That's been a good thing and has saved large numbers of lives.
But some researchers are concerned that our assault on the bad guys has done untold damage to our 'good bacteria'.
Prof Ley told me: 'We have over the past 50 years done a terrific job of eliminating infectious disease.
'But we have seen an enormous and terrifying increase in autoimmune disease and in allergy.
'Where work on the microbiome comes in is seeing how changes in the microbiome, that happened as a result of the success we've had fighting pathogens, have now contributed to a whole new set of diseases that we have to deal with.'
The microbiome is also being linked to diseases including inflammatory bowel disease, Parkinson's, whether cancer drugs work and even depression and autism.
Obesity is another example. Family history and lifestyle choices clearly play a role, but what about your gut microbes?
This is where it might get confusing.
A diet of burgers and chocolate will affect both your risk of obesity and the type of microbes that grow in your digestive tract.
So how do you know if it is a bad mix of bacteria metabolising your food in such a way, which contributes to obesity?

Prof Knight has performed experiments on mice that were born in the most sanitised world imaginable.
Their entire existence is completely free of microbes.

He says: 'We were able to show that if you take lean and obese humans and take their faeces and transplant the bacteria into mice you can make the mouse thinner or fatter depending on whose microbiome it got.'
Topping up obese with lean bacteria also helped the mice lose weight.

'This is pretty amazing right, but the question now is will this be translatable to humans'
This is the big hope for the field, that microbes could be a new form of medicine. It is known as using 'bugs as drugs'.
Goldmine of information
Dr. Trevor Lawley at the Wellcome Trust Sanger Institute, where he is trying to grow the whole microbiome from healthy patients and those who are ill.
'In a diseased state there could be bugs missing, for example, the concept is to reintroduce those.'
Dr. Lawley says there's growing evidence that repairing someone's microbiome 'can actually lead to remission' in diseases such as ulcerative colitis, a type of inflammatory bowel disease.
And he added: 'I think for a lot of diseases we study it's going to be defined mixtures of bugs, maybe 10 or 15 that are going into a patient.'
Microbial medicine is in its early stages, but some researchers think that monitoring our microbiome will soon become a daily event that provides a brown goldmine of information about our health.
Prof Knight said: 'It's incredible to think each teaspoon of your stool contains more data in the DNA of those microbes than it would take literally a tonne of DVDs to store.
'At the moment every time you're taking one of those data dumps as it were, you're just flushing that information away.
'Part of our vision is, in the not too distant future, where as soon as you flush it'll do some kind of instant read-out and tells you are you going in a good direction or a bad direction.
'That I think is going to be really transformative.'
Follow James on Twitter.
Illustrations: Katie Horwich

Listening to your heartbeat can help with your feelings
'I wish I could feel happy or excited' - Tom is trying a new treatment that could help people with autism to better recognize their emotions.
Research shows the more someone can tune into their own heartbeat, the better they can relax and calm themselves down.
The treatment has also been able to help people respond better to other emotions.
Horses 'fly-tipped and left to die', says RSPCA
By Louis Lee RayVictoria Derbyshire programme
Horses are regularly being 'fly-tipped' and left to die by irresponsible owners, the RSPCA has told the Victoria Derbyshire programme.
One mare had been dumped by the side of the road while trying to give birth, it said. The mother and foal both died.
The charity said the problem was partly that horses were cheap to buy but expensive to maintain, especially if they needed veterinary care.
It said prosecution cases involving horses had risen by 25% since 2015.

'Horse crisis'

RSPCA chief inspector Sam Garvey said it had taken care of horses that had been 'literally dumped down dirt tracks along with the rubbish'.
'[The owners had] taken their rubbish out to fly-tip and at the same time taken a sick and injured horse along with it,' she explained.
'And we've gone out to calls and not been able to see the horse until we've literally rifled through the rubbish.'
Almost 1,000 horses were rescued by the RSPCA in England and Wales last year, the highest number for four years.
The animal welfare charity described it as a 'horse crisis' and said some owners felt it was not worth paying a vet to treat an ill horse, or put the animal to sleep and dispose of the body.

Ms. Garvey said she had also rescued a Shetland pony from a 19th floor flat in London, whose owner had taken it there via the lift.

A report published in 2015 estimated that there were nearly 800,000 horses in the UK.

'Horses for free'

The RSPCA runs private stables which nurses rescued horses back to health. It is currently caring for more than 850.

One of those currently being treated is Adie, who was found collapsed and covered in mud on a footpath on New Year's Eve.

It is thought he had become ill, so his owner had dumped him there to die.

'It took five people to try and get him up.

'It was very touch and go - often when a horse goes down it's the end, so you have to put a lot of hard work and time and effort to get them back on their feet,' said Ms Garvey.

Ms Garvey said she had seen horses being sold online 'cheaper than a kitten'.

'There were horses for as cheap as £25, horses for free, 'buy the mare, get the foal for free'. [It's] horrifying.'

She compared this with the cost of treating a horse with colic, which can be as much as £4,000 to £5,000.

Prosecutions involving horses have risen by 25% in the last two years, to 225 in 2017.

The charity said people who were finding their animals too expensive to look after should seek professional advice, from either local instructors or charities.

Watch the BBC's Victoria Derbyshire programme on weekdays between 09:00 and 11:00 on BBC Two and the BBC News Channel.

Co-living in London: Friendship, fines and frustration

By Winnie Agbonlahor

More than three quarters of 18 to 34-year-olds living in Britain say they feel lonely. So could co-living be the answer? The BBC stayed in two different communes to find out if a living space shared is a social problem solved.

Communal living in the 21st Century is a far cry from the hippie movement of the 1960s counterculture: there is no singing of protest songs around the campfire, vegetarianism is optional and group nudity would raise a few eyebrows.

Co-living is a bit like inhabiting well-appointed student halls for working people. For prices ranging from about £1,000 to nearly £3,000 a month, residents get an en-suite room and access to communal facilities such as a gym, TV room and kitchen.

The only co-living options in the UK are currently in London. To gain an idea of what it's like to live this way, I spent a total of six days at the Collective in North Acton and Roam in Chelsea.

In terms of private living space, there's no denying the Collective is cramped.

For Lucilia Wuillaume, a translator and interpreter from Brazil, the main drawback to living here is the size of the rooms.

She has a point: at just over eight square metres, my bedroom didn't even provide enough space for my osteopath-prescribed back stretches.

Two residents I meet during my three-day stay say this is the reason they are moving out, while Markaiu Mason, who left the Collective in 2017, says: 'At the end of the day, you're stuck between a cupboard and a door.'

The vibe here can perhaps best be described as like a high-end youth hostel.

The development houses up to 550 residents, with prices starting at £240 a week.

Its communal facilities are extensive: six kitchens, three themed dining rooms, a terrace, cinema room, games room, large industrial-style co-working area and a gym and spa, all spread over 10 floors in a modern building block that was in fact originally meant to be student accommodation.

As I walk down the long dark corridors, I notice various food smells emanating from the private rooms - curry, garlic, fried onions, and pizza. Someone is baking a cake and there's also the aromatic scent of basmati rice.

But it is on the other side of these doors that the Collective offers the opportunity for the social interaction that can help fend off feelings of loneliness.

One resident, Matty Pepprell, even credits living here with saving him.
The 33-year-old IT consultant from Torquay is finally on the mend after undergoing four organ transplants over 10 years. He says his self-esteem took a hit after years of feeling tired, ill and isolated.
A rare kidney disorder left him feeling 'like a dead man walking', but living at the Collective has made him more confident.
'In a way, living here brought me back to life,' he says.
Being around people who 'ask me how I am all the time' has helped him with his mental recovery after a long illness, and he says he's made lots of friends.
Lucilia, 58, who moved to London from France with her family, says she's made more friends in three months at the Collective than she did in Paris 'over three whole years', while Abel Tedros, a 21-year-old entrepreneur from Ealing, says he loves meeting new people at the organised events here.

However, there are drawbacks to this style of living: finding basic utensils in the kitchen on my floor was not easy, with many dirty or broken. Dotted around the building are signs urging people to clean up after themselves.
(The development's planning and design manager Ollie Spragley says the Collective stopped providing items in shared spaces at the end of 2017 but offers residents the option of buying 'kitchen packs'.)
At a 'town hall meeting', general manager Roberto Russo tells residents that anyone breaking house rules, such as keeping communal spaces tidy, faces fines of up to £250.
And it's not the case that everyone at the Collective sees the social upside to living here, with a handful of residents saying the majority of people aren't interested in meeting anyone.
'It's always the same 50 to 60 people you see and the community feel is missing,' 28-year-old Jérémie Mora says.
One resident, who asked to stay anonymous, goes as far as saying he was mis-sold what the Collective would be like. Because he believes its 'unique selling point' - a sense of community - is missing, he says the building is 'not much more than a glorified student dorm'.

DISTINCT

The Collective says it is 'constantly working to understand how we can help improve the growth of community - not something one can turn up and buy'.

The Collective became the UK's first large-scale co-living space when it opened in 2016.

Since then, developers have submitted plans for 700 co-living units in Canary Wharf, 220 in Stratford, 320 in Ilford and 170 in London Bridge.

And for the first time, the Greater London Authority (GLA) has acknowledged co-living as a form of accommodation in its draft London Plan - an overarching policy document providing guidance to London councils.

This was necessary because these schemes 'haven't historically come forward', according to London's deputy mayor for housing and residential development James Murray.

PLP, the architects behind the Collective, say they have been asked to advise on and design a number of co-living projects 'not only in London or elsewhere in the UK but all over the world'.

But it's a complex picture, with many of those responsible for housing in the capital remaining to be convinced of the social benefits of such developments.

There's a different atmosphere at my next home, Roam, in upmarket Chelsea, which is more boutique hotel than youth hostel.

The feel is intimate, with just 34 rooms, all en-suite and most of which boast a kitchenette. There's also access to a communal kitchen, a TV area, and a co-working space that feels like the living room of a tastefully decorated townhouse.

At a somewhat eye-watering £2,800 a month, Roam is 'not the cheapest option, but worth it', says Laura Meier, who moved here from Germany.

She had only planned to stay for three months but ended up here for a year because she 'really enjoyed being part of the community, having a house full of life and the opportunity to work from home and talk to other people'.

- Up to a third of millennials 'face renting their whole life'

- Life as a tenant: 'I felt like I was cursed'
- How Tower Hamlets council is tackling loneliness
-

Moving to a new country without knowing anyone can be hard, she says, describing Roam as the 'perfect place to make friends'.

Roam's community manager Michelle Sims says its customers 'pay for ease, convenience, flexibility and the opportunity to stay at our unique spaces all over the world, which have everything they need to feel at home the moment they arrive', including an 'integrated community and community manager'.

Compared to the price of a local boutique hotel or a comparable one-bed apartment, she says 'you can easily see the value in our pricing'.

An online search for furnished one-bedroom flats on a short let in Chelsea shows properties available from about £2,000 a month - although this sum covers none of the amenities associated with co-living.

And as Kristina Barger, a 37-year-old psychologist from New York City, explains, if people are used to rents in San Francisco, New York or Seoul, as a lot of these globetrotters are, £2,800 a month 'seems reasonable'.

Loneliness, depression and anxiety are a growing problem globally, Michelle says, with people travelling more and feeling 'disconnected'. Roam has four branches around the world and is planning to open more - thus building a 'community without borders' and offering what she sees as a solution to loneliness and isolation.

Web designer Todd Steinhilber tells me that life in his line of work indeed can be lonely.

But thanks to Roam, he says he has access to an instant community of 'like-minded people with a similar worldview' in London and Roam's other locations around the world.

He says that while it's possible to make friends in bars or by playing sports, nothing comes close to the relaxed and natural way of striking up conversations with the people 'you live with'.

But as I go up the creaky steps of this 1930s building, I can't help but think that it's a little less luxurious than I expect at almost three grand a month. There is no gym, no separate

TV or living room and the kitchen isn't big enough for more than three people to cook in.

In terms of communal activities, most seem to involve going out and spending yet more money, although Michelle tells me there are usually events for 'diverse budgets', including book and running clubs and free 'pop-up mini couch concerts'.

The rooms also vary. Some boast lots of natural light and lovely views of London. But mine is in the basement and quite dark as a result.

The bed and kitchen unit are part of the same square living space, and there's no wardrobe. My bathroom, just big enough to hold a small sink and shower cubicle, has a leak in the ceiling.

The leak isn't a safety risk, I'm assured, and repairs won't be carried out since Roam is soon moving to a new and more spacious location.

The lack of space and operational issues are the reasons Roam decided to leave the Chelsea building, which 'did not match the quality' of its properties around the world, Michelle says.

So while it's clear this way of living suits some people very well, it's uncertain what the future holds.

A development like the Collective would 'never' get planning permission now, according to Alex Springer, who is working on a co-living project in Ilford. He says he was told by the GLA that the size of the Collective's rooms would rule out backing from planners.

And while the GLA's James Murray concedes that co-living might provide 'suitable accommodation for a very specific group of people with a very specific need', he believes it is 'not the answer across the board in any way'.

An application for 170 co-living units is currently being considered by Southwark Council, which says it remains 'to be convinced' of the concept, as people should not be 'forced through economic necessity to live in very small flats'.

As Mark Williams, the council's cabinet member for regeneration and new homes says: 'Why can't developers deliver standard housing?'

But with the housing crisis in the capital showing no sign of abating, it seems likely further co-living developments will spring up.
So would I be prepared to spend more than three days in one? In a different city or country - perhaps. In a different phase of my life - definitely.
If I were single or lonely (I'm aware there's a difference), I could envisage enjoying the co-living experience. But as I'm ready to settle down, living like this would feel like a step backwards - as though I were returning to a phase of my life I've left behind.

Dementia risk linked to some medicines

A study links the long-term use of some drugs with a higher risk of dementia.
In England, 1.5 to two million people are likely to be taking anticholinergics for depression, Parkinson's and bladder problems.
University of East Anglia researchers found more cases of dementia in patients prescribed larger quantities of particular anticholinergics.
But experts said patients should not stop taking them, as their benefits may outweigh any risk.
The study found no risk with other anticholinergic medicines used to treat common conditions such as hay fever, travel sickness and stomach cramps.
What did the study look at?
The research, funded by Alzheimer's Society and published in the British Medical Journal, looked at the medical records of 40,770 patients aged from 65 to 99 with a diagnosis of dementia between April 2006 and July 2015 and compared them with those of 283,933 people without dementia.
It also analysed more than 27 million prescriptions - making it the biggest study of its kind into the long-term impact of anticholinergic drugs in relation to dementia.
What are anticholinergic drugs?
They block acetylcholine, a chemical messenger that carries signals across the nervous system.
Some are available on prescription only.
What should patients do if they take any of these drugs?

The most important thing is 'not to panic', according to Dr. Ian Maidment, from Aston University.

'Don't do anything suddenly. Don't stop taking your medication,' he told the BBC.

'As a patient, if you are concerned about it, go and speak to your doctor or your pharmacist. You don't have to see them urgently.'

Not taking prescribed drugs could have serious consequences, Dr. Maidment said.

'Having untreated depression is also a risk as people can die from that, so it is a question of balancing risks,' he added.

How have experts reacted?

Alzheimer's Society head of research Dr James Pickett told the BBC that compared with the risk of dementia being caused by an unhealthy lifestyle, the potential risk of an anticholinergic drug contributing to the onset of the disease was 'quite small'.

'We don't exactly know within those that are taking these drugs, who are at the increased risk and who aren't,' he said.

Dementia Research national director Prof Martin Rossor said: 'It is important to be cautious about associations as they do not prove causation.'

Alzheimer's Research UK research director Dr. Carol Routledge said: 'The study didn't investigate what might cause this link between anticholinergics and dementia risk, and researchers will need to build on these findings in future studies.'

Rob Howard, professor of old age psychiatry at University College London, said: 'It is possible that use of some of these drugs may have actually been to treat the very earliest symptoms of Alzheimer's disease, which can be associated with low mood and lower urinary tract infections, many years before the development of dementia.'

Dr. Parastou Donyai, associate professor of social and cognitive pharmacy at the University of Reading, said: 'This type of study imagines that patients actually take their drugs as they were prescribed for them.

'But we know from other research that people with long-term health conditions really only take their medication as prescribed around half of the time - the other half, people either take more or less of their medication or not at all.'

History of Introspection in Psychology:

Wundt:

Wilhelm Wundt, the father of modern psychology, was the first to adopt introspection as a tool for use in the context of experimental psychology research. Wundt was influenced by notable physiologists, such as Gustav Fechner, who used introspection as a means to study human sensory organs. Building upon this preexisting use of introspection in physiology, Wundt imposed exacting control over the use of introspection in his experimental laboratory at the University of Leipzig. By requiring this stringent control, it became possible for other scientists to replicate Wundt's experiments elsewhere, and this advent would prove essential in the development of psychology as a modern, peer-reviewed scientific discipline.

Titchener:

Edward Titchener was an early pioneer in experimental psychology and student of Wilhelm Wundt. After earning his doctorate under the tutelage of Wundt at the University of Leipzig, Titchener made his way to Cornell University where he established his own laboratory and research. At the time of Titchener's arrival at Cornell, psychology was still a fledgling discipline, especially in the United States.

This being the case, Titchener was a key figure in bringing Wundt's ideas to America; however in the capacity Titchener was also responsible for misrepresenting some of Wundt's ideas to the American psychological establishment. This misrepresentation was especially evident in Titchener's conception of introspection. Titchener taught that introspection only served a purpose in the qualitative analysis of consciousness into its various parts.

This viewpoint stood in stark relief against Wundt's notion of introspection as a means to quantitatively measure the whole of conscious experience. In other words, Titchener was exclusively interested in the individual components that comprised conscious experience, while Wundt, seeing little purpose in the analysis of individual components, focused on the synthesis of these constituent parts as a whole.

Ultimately, Titchener's ideas would form the basis of the short-lived psychological theory of structuralism.

Further Developments in Psychology:

Behaviorism claimed that introspection was unreliable and that the subject matter of scientific psychology should be strictly operationalized in an objective and measurable way. This then led psychology to focus on measurable behavior rather than consciousness or sensation. Cognitive psychology accepts the use of the scientific method, but often rejects introspection as a valid method of investigation for this reason, especially concerning the causes of behavior and choice. Herbert Simon and Allen Newell identified the 'think aloud protocol', in which investigators view a subject engaged in a task, and who speaks his thoughts aloud, thus allowing study of his thought process without forcing the subject to comment on his thinking.

On the other hand, introspection can be considered a valid tool for the development of scientific hypotheses and theoretical models, in particular in cognitive sciences and engineering. In practice, functional (goal-oriented) computational modeling and computer simulation design of meta-reasoning and metacognition are closely connected with the introspective experiences of researchers and engineers.

Inaccessible mental processes and confabulation:

Main article: Introspection illusion

Psychological research on cognition and attribution has asked people to report on their mental processes, for instance to say why they made a particular choice or how they arrived at a judgment. In some situations, these reports are clearly confabulated. For example, people justify choices they have not in fact made. Such results undermine the idea that those verbal reports are based on direct introspective access to mental content. Instead, judgements about one's own mind seem to be inferences from overt behavior, similar to judgements made about another person. However, it is hard to assess whether these results only apply to unusual experimental situations, or if they reveal something about everyday introspection.

The theory of the adaptive unconscious suggests that a very large proportion of mental processes, even 'high-level' processes like goal-setting and decision-making, are inaccessible to introspection.

Even when their introspections are uninformative, people still give confident descriptions of their mental processes, being 'unaware of their unawareness'. This phenomenon has been termed the introspection illusion and has been used to explain some cognitive biases and belief in some paranormal phenomena. When making judgements about themselves, subjects treat their own introspections as reliable, whereas they judge other people based on their behavior. This can lead to illusions of superiority.

For example, people generally see themselves as less-conformist than others, and this seems to be because they do not introspect any urge to conform. Another reliable finding is that people generally see themselves as less biased than everyone else, because they are not likely to introspect any biased thought processes. These introspections are misleading, however, because biases work sub-consciously. One experiment tried to give their subjects access to others' introspections.

They made audio recordings of subjects who had been told to say whatever came into their heads as they answered a question about their own bias. Although subjects persuaded themselves they were unlikely to be biased, their introspective reports did not sway the assessments of observers. When subjects were explicitly told to avoid relying on introspection, their assessments of their own bias became more realistic.

The position of many contemplatives is that while introspection does have its limitation in identifying thoughts, it can be used to accurately identify states of consciousness. Thus, humanistic and transpersonal psychology, as well as existential-phenomenology, finds great value in introspection despite the role of introspective illusion.

Observation

Observation in science:

The scientific method requires observations of nature to formulate and test hypotheses. It consists of these steps:

1. Asking a question about a natural phenomenon
2. Making observations of the phenomenon
3. Hypothesizing an explanation for the phenomenon
4. Predicting a logical consequence of the hypothesis
5. Testing the hypothesis by an experiment, an observational study, or a field study
6. Creating a conclusion with data gathered in the experiment

Observation plays a role in the second and fifth steps of the Scientific Method. However the need for reproducibility requires that observations by different observers can be comparable. Human sense impressions are subjective and qualitative making them difficult to record or compare. The idea of measurement evolved to allow recording and comparison of observations made at different times and places by different people.

Measurement consists of using observation to compare the thing being measured to a standard; an artifact, process or definition which can be duplicated or shared by all observers, and counting how many of the standard units are comparable to the object. Measurement reduces an observation to a number which can be recorded, and two observations which result in the same number are equal within the resolution of the process.

Senses are limited, and are subject to errors in perception such as optical illusions. Scientific instruments were developed to magnify human powers of observation, such as weighing scales, clocks, telescopes, microscopes, thermometers, cameras, and tape recorders, and also translate into perceptible form events that are unobservable by human senses, such as indicator dyes, voltmeters, spectrometers, infrared cameras, oscilloscopes,

interferometers, geiger counters, x-ray machines, and radio receivers.
One problem encountered throughout scientific fields is that the observation may affect the process being observed, resulting in a different outcome than if the process was unobserved. This is called the observer effect. For example, it is not normally possible to check the air pressure in an automobile tire without letting out some of the air, thereby changing the pressure. However, in most fields of science it is possible to reduce the effects of observation to insignificance by using better instruments.
Considered as a physical process itself, all forms of observation (human or instrumental) involve amplification and are thus thermodynamically irreversible processes, increasing entropy.

Alternative definitions:

In some specific fields of science the words 'observer' and 'observation' have to be redefined to take into account factors that don't seem so important in everyday observation:

- Relativity: In relativistic physics which deals with velocities close to the speed of light, it is found that different observers may observe different values for the length, time rates, mass, and many other properties of an object, depending on the observer's velocity relative to the object. Therefore an observation must always be qualified by specifying the state of motion of the observer, his reference frame.
- Quantum mechanics: In quantum mechanics, which deals with the behavior of very small objects, it is not possible to observe a system without changing the system, and the 'observer' must be considered part of the system being observed. In isolation, quantum objects are represented by a wave-function which often exists in a superposition or mixture of different states. However, when an observation is made to determine the actual location or state of the object, it always finds the object in a single state, not a 'mixture'. The interaction of the observation process

appears to 'collapse' the wave-function into a single state. So any interaction between an isolated wave-function and the external world that results in this wave-function collapse is called an observation or measurement, whether or not it is part of a deliberate observation process.

Biases:

Observational bias:

An observational bias occurs when researchers only look where they think they will find positive results, or where it is easy to record observations. This is called the 'streetlight effect'.

Confirmation bias:

Human observations are biased toward confirming the observer's conscious and unconscious expectations and view of the world; we 'see what we expect to see'. In psychology, this is called confirmation bias. Since the object of scientific research is the discovery of new phenomena, this bias can and has caused new discoveries to be overlooked. One example is the discovery of x-rays. It can also result in erroneous scientific support for widely held cultural myths, for example the scientific racism that supported ideas of racial superiority in the early 20th century, and creation science today. Correct scientific technique emphasizes careful recording of observations, separating experimental observations from the conclusions drawn from them, and techniques such as blind or double blind experiments, to minimize observational bias.

Cargo cult' science:

Another bias, which has become more prevalent with the advent of 'big science' and the large rewards of new discoveries, is bias in favor of the researcher's favorite hypothesis; we 'see what we want to see'. Called pathological science and cargo cult science, this is different from deliberate falsification of results, and can happen to good-faith researchers. Possible examples of mistaken discoveries caused by this bias are Martian 'canals', N rays, polywater, and cold fusion.

Recent decades had seen scientific scandals caused by researchers playing 'fast and loose' with observational methods in order to get their pet theories published. This type of bias is rampant in pseudoscience, where correct scientific techniques are not followed. The main defense against this bias, besides correct research techniques, is peer review and repetition of the experiment, or the observation, by other researchers with no incentive to bias. For example, an emerging practice in the competitive field of biotechnology is to require the physical results of experiments, such as serums and tissue cultures, be made available to competing laboratories for independent testing.

Processing bias:

Modern scientific instruments can extensively process 'observations' before they are presented to the human senses, and particularly with computerized instruments, there is sometimes a question as to where in the data processing chain 'observing' ends and 'drawing conclusions' begins. This has recently become an issue with digitally enhanced images published as experimental data in papers in scientific journals.
The images are enhanced to bring out features that the researcher wants to emphasize, but this also has the effect of supporting his conclusions. This is a form of bias that is difficult to quantify. Some scientific journals have begun to set detailed standards for what types of image processing are allowed in research results. Computerized instruments often keep a copy of the 'raw data' from sensors before processing, which are the ultimate defense against processing bias, and similarly scientific standards require preservation of the original unenhanced 'raw' versions of images used as research data.

Observations in philosophy

'Observe always that everything is the result of a change, and get used to thinking that there is nothing Nature loves so well as to change existing forms and to make new ones like them.'

Meditations. iv. 36. – Marcus Aurelius

Observation in philosophical terms is the process of filtering sensory information through the thought process. Input is received via hearing, sight, smell, taste, or touch and then analyzed through either rational or irrational thought. You see a parent beat their child; you observe that such an action is either good or bad. Deductions about what behaviors are good or bad may be based in no way on preferences about building relationships, or study of the consequences resulting from the observed behavior. With the passage of time, impressions stored in the consciousness about many related observations, together with the resulting relationships and consequences, permit the individual to build a construct about the moral implications of behavior.

The defining characteristic of observation is that it involves drawing conclusions, as well as building personal views about how to handle similar situations in the future, rather than simply registering that something has happened. However, observation according to Jiddu Krishnamurti does not necessarily imply drawing conclusions and building personal views. Instead of the accumulation of knowledge, a time-based, conditioning function he identified with the past, he stressed observation as a continuous process of learning, a timeless process that happens always in the present. Such observation, he asserted, frees the mind of its conditioning by discarding psychological dependence on the past.

List of cognitive biases

A cognitive bias describes a replicable pattern in perceptual distortion, inaccurate judgment, illogical interpretation, or what is broadly called irrationality. They are the result of distortions in the human mind that always lead to the same pattern of poor judgment, often triggered by a particular situation. Identifying 'poor judgment,' or more precisely, a 'deviation in judgment,' requires a standard for comparison, i.e. 'good judgment'. In scientific investigations of cognitive bias, the source of 'good judgment' is that of people outside the situation hypothesized to cause the poor judgment, or, if possible, a set of independently verifiable facts. The existence of most of the particular cognitive biases listed below has been verified empirically in psychology experiments.

Cognitive biases are influenced by evolution and natural selection pressure. Some are presumably adaptive and beneficial, for example, because they lead to more effective actions in given contexts or enable faster decisions, when faster decisions are of greater value for reproductive success and survival. Others presumably result from a lack of appropriate mental mechanisms, i.e. a general fault in human brain structure, from the misapplication of a mechanism that is adaptive (beneficial) under different circumstances, or simply from noisy mental processes.

Despite several decades of effort, no comprehensive theory of what creates these biases has emerged. This is why it is not straightforward to group and categorize them, and this results in what has been called 'a grab bag of heuristics and biases, with no quantitative psychological theory describing the underlying processes'. A 2012 Psychological Bulletin article suggested that at least eight seemingly unrelated biases can be produced by the same information-theoretic generative mechanism that assumes noisy information processing during storage and retrieval of information in human memory.

Irrationality is cognition, thinking, talking or acting without inclusion of rationality. It is more specifically described as an action or opinion given through inadequate using reason, emotional distress, or cognitive deficiency. The term is used, usually pejoratively, to describe thinking and actions that are, or appear to be, less useful or more illogical than other more rational alternatives.

Irrational behaviors of individuals include taking offense or becoming angry about a situation that has not yet occurred, expressing emotions exaggeratedly (such as crying hysterically), maintaining unrealistic expectations, engaging in irresponsible conduct such as problem intoxication, disorganization, or extravagance, and falling victim to confidence tricks. People with a mental illness like schizophrenia may exhibit irrational paranoia.

These more contemporary 'normative' conceptions of what constitutes a manifestation of irrationality are difficult to demonstrate empirically because it is not clear by whose standards we are to judge the behavior rational or irrational.

Explanation of occurrence

The study of irrational behavior is of interest in fields such as psychology, cognitive science, economics, game theory, and evolutionary psychology, as well as of practical interest to the practitioners of advertising and propaganda.

Theories of irrational behavior include:

- People's actual interests differ from what they believe to be their interests.
- Mechanisms that have evolved to give optimal behavior in normal conditions lead to irrational behavior in abnormal conditions.
- Situations outside one's ordinary circumstances, where one may experience intense levels of fear, or may regress to a fight-or-flight mentality.
- People fail to realize the irrationality of their actions and believe they are acting perfectly rational, possibly due to flaws in their reasoning.
- Apparently irrational decisions that are actually optimal, but made unconsciously on the basis of 'hidden' interests that are not known to the conscious mind.
- An inability to comprehend the social consequences of one's own actions, possibly due in part to a lack of empathy.
- Some people find themselves in this condition by living 'double' lives. They try to put on one 'mask' for one group of people and another for a different group of people. Many will become confused as to which they really are or which they wish to become.
-

Factors which affect rational behavior include:

- stress, which in turn may be emotional or physical
- the introduction of a new or unique situation
- intoxication

- peers who convey irrational thoughts as necessary idiosyncrasy for social acceptance

Intentional irrationality

Irrationality is not always viewed as a negative. Dada Surrealist art movements embraced irrationality as a means to 'reject reason and logic'. André Breton, for example, argued for a rejection of pure logic and reason which are seen as responsible for many contemporary social problems.

In science fiction literature, the progress of pure rationality is viewed as a quality which may lead civilization ultimately toward a scientific future dependent on technology. Irrationality in this case, is a positive factor which helps to balance excessive reason.

In psychology, excessive rationality without creativity may be viewed as a form of self-control and protection. Certain problems, such as death and loss, may have no rational solution when they are being experienced. We may seek logical explanations for such events, when in fact the proper emotional response is grief. Irrationality is thus a means of freeing the mind toward purely imaginative solutions, to break out of historic patterns of dependence into new patterns that allow one to move on.

Irrationalist:

Irrationalist is a wide term. It may be applied to mean 'one without rationality', for their beliefs or ideas. Or, more precisely, it may mean someone who rejects some aspect of rationalism, variously defined. For example religious faith may be seen as, in part, a rejection of complete rationalism about the world; this would be contested by some religious thinkers, in that the *rational* is a debatable term. On the other hand, it might be considered irrationalist to buy a lottery ticket, on the basis that the expected value is negative.

In contemporary philosophy 'irrationalism' is, inspired by Hindu and Buddhist philosophies, emerging into a new growing school of thought in which the importance of our intuitive capability is stressed. One such young philosopher, Robin Vermoesen (Belgium, 3 November 1978), states in his

Dutch written book *Rationaliteit is vals* (translated: 'Rationality is false') that every conscious is at the same time an individual being and total reality, thus as a consequence our rationalistic capabilities aren't enough if we truly want to understand reality in its truest form. For us to truly know reality we need to become it, we need to become our Self.
He further states that there are four 'knowledge relationships', (in growing order of *intimacy*: knowing, sensing, realizing and being) a being can experience, and all true knowledge of the Self, thus reality, must eventually grow into the most intimate of the four: *being*. Since rationalistic knowledge can bring us only *knowing*, it is, although a necessary tool, not enough to uncover reality. It needs to be balanced by other capabilities and framed in a patchwork that gives positive meaning to personal commitment.
Irrational thought was seen in Europe as part of the reaction against Continental rationalism. For example Hamann is sometimes classified as an irrationalist.

In literature

Much subject matter in literature can be seen as an expression of human longing for the irrational. In Romanticism irrationality was valued over the sterile, calculating and emotionless philosophy brought about by the Age of Enlightenment and the Industrial Revolution. The Dadaists and Surrealists later used irrationality as a basis for their art. The disregard of reason and preference for dream states in Surrealism was an exaltation of the irrational and the rejection of logic.
Mythology nearly always incorporates elements of fantasy and the supernatural; however myths are largely accepted by the societies that create them, and only come to be seen as irrational through the spyglass of time and by other cultures. But though mythology serves as a way to rationalize the universe in symbolic and often anthropomorphic ways, a pre-rational and irrational way of thinking can be seen as tacitly valued in mythology's supremacy of the imagination, where rationality as a philosophical method has not been developed.

On the other side the irrational is often depicted from a rational point of view in all types of literature, provoking amusement, contempt, disgust, hatred, awe, and many other reactions.

In psychotherapy

The term *irrational* is often used in psychotherapy and the concept of irrationality is especially known in rational emotive behavior therapy originated and developed by American psychologist Albert Ellis. In this approach, the term *irrational* is used in a slightly different way than in general. Here irrationality is defined as the tendency and leaning that humans have to act, emote and think in ways that are inflexible, unrealistic, absolutist and most importantly self- and social-defeating and destructive.

Also

- Amygdala hijack
- Behavioral economics
- Bounded rationality
- Cognitive Bias
- Dysrationalia
- Irrationalism and Aestheticism
- Logical Fallacy
- Optimism bias
- Rationality and power
- Self-serving bias
-

Rational emotive behavior therapy (REBT), previously called rational therapy and rational emotive therapy, is a comprehensive, active-directive, philosophically and empirically based psychotherapy which focuses on resolving emotional and behavioral problems and disturbances and enabling people to lead happier and more fulfilling lives. REBT was created and developed by the American psychotherapist and psychologist Albert Ellis who was inspired by many of the teachings of Asian, Greek, Roman and modern philosophers. REBT is one form of cognitive behavior therapy (CBT) and was first expounded by Ellis in the mid-1950s; development continued until his death in 2007.

History

Rational Emotive Behavior Therapy (REBT) is both a psychotherapeutic system of theory and practices and a school of thought established by Albert Ellis. Originally called *rational therapy*, its appellation was revised to *rational emotive therapy* in 1959, then to its current appellation in 1992. REBT was one of the first of the cognitive behavior therapies, as it was predicated in articles Ellis first published in 1956, nearly a decade before Aaron Beck first set forth his cognitive therapy.

Precursors of certain fundamental aspects of REBT have been identified in various ancient philosophical traditions, particularly Stoicism. For example, Ellis' first major publication on rational therapy describes the philosophical basis of REBT as the principle that a person is rarely affected emotionally by outside things but rather by 'his perceptions, attitudes, or internalized sentences about outside things and events.' He adds,

This principle, which I have inducted from many psychotherapeutic sessions with scores of patients during the last several years, was originally discovered and stated by the ancient Stoic philosophers, especially Zeno of Citium (the founder of the school), Chrysippus [his most influential disciple], Panaetius of Rhodes (who introduced Stoicism into Rome), Cicero, Seneca, Epictetus, and Marcus Aurelius. The truths of Stoicism were perhaps best set forth by Epictetus, who in the first century A.D. wrote in the Enchiridion: 'Men are disturbed not by things, but by the views which they take of them.' Shakespeare, many centuries later, rephrased this thought in Hamlet: 'There's nothing good or bad but thinking makes it so.'

Theoretical assumptions

One of the fundamental premises of REBT is that humans, in most cases, do not merely get upset by unfortunate adversities, but also by how they construct their views of reality through their language, evaluative beliefs, meanings and philosophies about the world, themselves and others. This concept has been attributed as far back as the Greek Philosopher Epictetus, who is often cited as utilizing similar ideas in antiquity.

In REBT, clients usually learn and begin to apply this premise by learning the *A-B-C*-model of psychological disturbance and change. The A-B-C model states that it normally is not merely an *A*, *a*dversity (or *a*ctivating event) that contributes to disturbed and dysfunctional emotional and behavioral *C*s, *c*onsequences, but also what people *B*, *b*elieve about the *A*, *a*dversity. *A*, *a*dversity can be either an external situation or a thought or other kind of internal event, and it can refer to an event in the past, present, or future.

The *B*s, beliefs that are most important in the *A-B-C* model are explicit and implicit philosophical meanings and assumptions about events, personal desires, and preferences. The *B*s, *b*eliefs that are most significant are highly evaluative and consist of interrelated and integrated cognitive, emotional and behavioral aspects and dimensions. According to REBT, if a person's evaluative *B*, *b*elief about the *A*, *a*ctivating event is rigid, absolutistic and dysfunctional, the *C*, the emotional and behavioral *c*onsequence, is likely to be self-defeating and destructive. Alternatively, if a person's evaluative *B*, *b*elief is preferential, flexible and constructive, the *C*, the emotional and behavioral *c*onsequence is likely to be self-helping and constructive.

Through REBT, by understanding the role of their mediating, evaluative and philosophically based illogical, unrealistic and self-defeating meanings, interpretations and assumptions in upset, people often can learn to identify them, begin to *D*, *d*ispute, refute, challenge and question them, distinguish them from healthy constructs, and subscribe to more constructive and self-helping constructs.

The REBT framework assumes that humans have both innate rational (meaning self- and social-helping and constructive) and irrational (meaning self- and social-defeating and un-helpful) tendencies and leanings. REBT claims that people to a large degree consciously and unconsciously construct emotional difficulties such as self-blame, self-pity, clinical anger, hurt, guilt, shame, depression and anxiety, and behaviors and behavior tendencies like procrastination, over-compulsiveness, avoidance, addiction and withdrawal by the means of their irrational and self-defeating thinking, emoting and behaving.

REBT is then applied as an educational process in which the therapist often active-directively teaches the client how to identify irrational and self-defeating beliefs and philosophies which in nature are rigid, extreme, unrealistic, illogical and absolutist, and then to forcefully and actively question and dispute them and replace them with more rational and self-helping ones. By using different cognitive, emotive and behavioral methods and activities, the client, together with help from the therapist and in homework exercises, can gain a more rational, self-helping and constructive rational way of thinking, emoting and behaving.

One of the main objectives in REBT is to show the client that whenever unpleasant and unfortunate activating events occur in people's lives, they have a choice of making themselves feel healthily and self-helpingly sorry, disappointed, frustrated, and annoyed, or making themselves feel unhealthily and self-defeatingly horrified, terrified, panicked, depressed, self-hating, and self-pitying. By attaining and ingraining a more rational and self-constructive philosophy of themselves, others and the world, people often are more likely to behave and emote in more life-serving and adaptive ways.

Albert Ellis- posits three major insights of REBT:

Insight 1 - People seeing and accepting the reality that their emotional disturbances at point C only partially stem from the activating events or adversities at point A that precede C. Although A contributes to C, and although disturbed Cs (such as feelings of panic and depression) are much more likely to follow strong negative As (such as being assaulted or raped), than they are to follow weak As (such as being disliked by a stranger), the main or more direct cores of extreme and dysfunctional emotional disturbances (Cs) are people's irrational beliefs — the absolutistic musts and their accompanying inferences and attributions that people strongly believe about their undesirable activating events.

Insight 2 - No matter how, when, and why people acquire self-defeating or irrational beliefs (i.e. beliefs which are the main cause of their dysfunctional emotional-behavioral consequences), if they are disturbed in the present, they tend to keep holding these irrational beliefs and continue upsetting themselves with these thoughts. They do so not because they held them in the past, but because they still actively hold them in the present, though often unconsciously, while continuing to reaffirm their beliefs and act as if they are still valid. In their minds and hearts they still follow the core 'musturbatory' philosophies they adopted or invented long ago, or ones they recently accepted or constructed.

Insight 3 - No matter how well they have achieved insight 1 and insight 2, insight alone will rarely enable people to undo their emotional disturbances. They may feel better when they know, or think they know, how they became disturbed - since insights can give the impression of being useful and curative. But, it is unlikely that they will actually get better and stay better unless they accept insights 1 and 2, and then also go on to strongly apply insight 3: There is usually no way to get better and stay better but by: continual work and practice in looking for, and finding, one's core irrational beliefs; actively, energetically, and scientifically disputing them; replacing one's absolutist musts with flexible preferences; changing one's unhealthy feelings to healthy, self-helping emotions; and firmly acting against one's dysfunctional fears and compulsions. Only by a combined cognitive, emotive, and behavioral, as well as a quite persistent and forceful attack on one's serious emotional problems, is one likely to significantly ameliorate or remove them — and keep them removed.

Regarding cognitive-affective-behavioral processes in mental functioning and dysfunctioning, originator Albert Ellis explains:

'REBT assumes that human thinking, emotion, and action are not really separate or disparate processes, but that they all significantly overlap and are rarely experienced in a pure state. Much of what we call emotion is nothing more nor less than a certain kind a biased, prejudiced, or strongly evaluative kind of thought. But emotions and behaviors significantly influence and affect thinking, just as thinking influences emotions and behaviors. Evaluating is a fundamental characteristic of human organisms and seems to work in a kind of closed circuit with a feedback mechanism: Because perception biases response and then response tends to bias subsequent perception. Also, prior perceptions appear to bias subsequent perceptions, and prior responses appear to bias subsequent responses. What we call feelings almost always have a pronounced evaluating or appraisal element.'

REBT then generally proposes that many of these self-defeating cognitive, emotive and behavioral tendencies are both innately biological and indoctrinated early in and during life, and further grow stronger as a person continually revisits, clings and acts on them. Ellis alluded to similarities between REBT and General Semantics in explaining the role of irrational beliefs in self-defeating tendencies, citing Alfred Korzybski as a significant modern influence on this thinking.

REBT differs from other clinical approaches like psychoanalysis in that it places little emphasis on exploring the past, but instead focuses on changing the current evaluations and philosophical thinking-emoting and behaving in relation to themselves, others and the conditions under which people live.

Psychological dysfunction

One of the main pillars of REBT is that irrational and dysfunctional ways and patterns of thinking, feeling and behaving are contributing to much, though hardly all, human disturbance and emotional and behavioral self- and social defeatism. REBT generally teaches that when people turn flexible preferences, desires and wishes into grandiose, absolutistic and fatalistic dictates, this tends to contribute to disturbance and upsetness.

Albert Ellis has suggested three core beliefs or philosophies that humans tend to disturb themselves through.

REBT commonly posits that at the core of irrational beliefs there often are explicit or implicit rigid demands and commands, and that extreme derivatives like awfulizing, frustration intolerance, people deprecation and over-generalizations are accompanied by these. According to REBT the core dysfunctional philosophies in a person's evaluative emotional and behavioral belief system, are also very likely to contribute to unrealistic, arbitrary and crooked inferences and distortions in thinking. REBT therefore first teaches that when people in an insensible and devout way overuse absolutistic, dogmatic and rigid 'shoulds', 'musts', and 'oughts', they tend to disturb and upset themselves.

Further REBT generally posits that disturbed evaluations to a large degree occur through over-generalization, wherein people exaggerate and globalize events or traits, usually unwanted events or traits or behavior, out of context, while almost always ignoring the positive events or traits or behaviors. For example, awfulizing is partly mental magnification of the importance of an unwanted situation to a catastrophe or horror, elevating the rating of something from bad to worse than it should be, to beyond totally bad, worse than bad to the intolerable and to a 'holocaust'.

The same exaggeration and overgeneralizing occurs with human rating, wherein humans come to be arbitrarily and axiomatically defined by their perceived flaws or misdeeds. Frustration intolerance then occurs when a person perceives something to be too difficult, painful or tedious, and by doing so exaggerates these qualities beyond one's ability to cope with them.

Essential to REBT theory is also the concept of secondary disturbances which people sometimes construct on top of their primary disturbance. As Ellis emphasizes:

'Because of their self-consciousness and their ability to think about their thinking, they can very easily disturb themselves about their disturbances and can also disturb themselves about their ineffective attempts to overcome their emotional disturbances.'

Mental wellness

As would be expected, REBT argues that mental wellness and mental health to a large degree results from an adequate amount of self-helping, flexible, logico-empirical ways of thinking, emoting and behaving. When a perceived undesired and stressful activating event occurs, and the individual is interpreting, evaluating and reacting to the situation rationally and self-helpingly, then the resulting consequence is, according to REBT, likely to be more healthy, constructive and functional. This does not by any means mean that a relatively un-disturbed person never experiences negative feelings, but REBT does hope to keep debilitating and un-healthy emotions and subsequent self-defeating behavior to a minimum. To do this REBT generally promotes a flexible, un-dogmatic, self-helping and efficient belief system and constructive life philosophy about adversities and human desires and preferences.

REBT clearly acknowledges that people, in addition to disturbing themselves, also are innately constructivists. Because they largely upset themselves with their beliefs, emotions and behaviors, they can be helped to, in a multimodal manner, dispute and question these and develop a more workable, more self-helping set of constructs.

REBT generally teaches and promotes:

- That the concepts and philosophies of life of unconditional self-acceptance, other-acceptance, and life-acceptance are effective philosophies of life in achieving mental wellness and mental health.
- That human beings are inherently fallible and imperfect and that they had better accept their and other human being's totality and humanity, while at the same time not like some of their behaviors and characteristics. That they are better off not measuring their entire self or their 'being' and give up the narrow, grandiose and ultimately destructive notion to give themselves any global rating or report card. This is partly because all humans are continually evolving and are far too complex to accurately rate; all humans do both self- and social-defeating and self- and social-helping deeds, and have both beneficial and un-beneficial attributes and traits at certain times and in certain conditions.

REBT holds that ideas and feelings about self-worth are largely definitional and are not empirically confirmable or falsifiable.

- That people had better accept life with its hassles and difficulties not always in accordance with their wants, while trying to change what they can change and live as elegantly as possible with what they cannot change.

REBT Intervention:

As explained, REBT is a therapeutic system of both theory and practices; generally one of the goals of REBT is to help clients see the ways in which they have learned how they often needlessly upset themselves, teach them how to un-upset themselves and then how to empower themselves to lead happier and more fulfilling lives. The emphasis in therapy is generally to establish a successful collaborative therapeutic working alliance based on the REBT educational model. Although REBT teaches that the therapist or counsellor had better demonstrate unconditional other-acceptance or unconditional positive regard, the therapist is not necessarily always encouraged to build a warm and caring relationship with the client. The tasks of the therapist or counsellor include understanding the client's concerns from his point of reference and work as a facilitator, teacher and encourager.

In traditional REBT, the client together with the therapist, in a structured active-directive manner, often work through a set of target problems and establish a set of therapeutic goals. In these target problems, situational dysfunctional emotions, behaviors and beliefs are assessed in regards to the client's values and goals. After working through these problems, the client learns to generalize insights to other relevant situations. In many cases after going through a client's different target problems, the therapist is interested in examining possible core beliefs and more deep rooted philosophical evaluations and schemas that might account for a wider array of problematic emotions and behaviors. Although REBT much of the time is used as a brief therapy, in deeper and more complex problems, longer therapy is promoted.

In therapy, the first step often is that the client acknowledges the problems, accepts emotional responsibility for these and has willingness and determination to change. This normally requires a considerable amount of insight, but as originator Albert Ellis explains:

'Humans, unlike just about all the other animals on earth, create fairly sophisticated languages which not only enable them to think about their feeling, their actions, and the results they get from doing and not doing certain things, but they also are able to think about their thinking and even think about thinking about their thinking.'

Through the therapeutic process, REBT employs a wide array of forceful and active, meaning multimodal and disputing, methodologies. Central through these methods and techniques is the intent to help the client challenge, dispute and question their destructive and self-defeating cognitions, emotions and behaviors.

The methods and techniques incorporate cognitive-philosophic, emotive-evocative-dramatic, and behavioral methods for disputation of the client's irrational and self-defeating constructs and help the client come up with more rational and self-constructive ones. REBT seeks to acknowledge that understanding and insight are not enough; in order for clients to significantly change, they had better pinpoint their irrational and self-defeating constructs and work forcefully and actively at changing them to more functional and self-helping ones.

REBT posits that the client must work hard to get better, and in therapy this normally includes a wide array of homework exercises in day-to-day life assigned by the therapist. The assignments may for example include desensitization tasks, i.e., by having the client confront the very thing he or she is afraid of. By doing so, the client is actively acting against the belief that often is contributing significantly to the disturbance.

Another factor contributing to the brevity of REBT is that the therapist seeks to empower the client to help himself through future adversities. REBT only promotes temporary solutions if more fundamental solutions are not found. An ideal successful collaboration between the REBT therapist and a client results in changes to the client's philosophical way of evaluating him- or herself, others, and his or her life, which will likely yield effective results. The client then moves toward unconditional self-acceptance, other-acceptance and life-acceptance while striving to live a more self-fulfilling and happier life.

Limitations and critique:

REBT and CBT in general have a substantial and strong research base to verify and support both their psychotherapeutic efficiency and their theoretical underpinnings. A great quantity of scientific empirical studies has proven REBT to be an effective and efficient treatment for many kinds of psychopathology, conditions and problems. A vast amount of outcome and experimental studies support the effectiveness of REBT and CBT recently, REBT randomized clinical trials have offered a positive view on the efficacy of REBT.
In general REBT is arguably one of the most investigated theories in the field of psychotherapy and a large amount of clinical experience and a substantial body of modern psychological research have validated and substantiated many of REBTs theoretical assumptions on personality and psychotherapy.
Some critiques have been given on some of the clinical research that has been done on REBT both from within and by others. For instance originator Albert Ellis has on occasions emphasized the difficulty and complexity of measuring psychotherapeutic effectiveness, since many studies only tend to measure whether clients merely feel better after therapy instead of them getting better and staying better. Ellis has also criticized studies for having limited focus primarily to cognitive restructuring aspects, as opposed to the combination of cognitive, emotive and behavioral aspects of REBT. As REBT has been subject to criticisms during its existence, especially in its early years, REBT theorists have a long history of publishing and addressing those concerns. It has also been argued by Ellis

and by other clinicians that REBT theory on numerous occasions has been misunderstood and misconstrued both in research and in general.
Some have criticized REBT for being harsh, formulaic and failing to address deep underlying problems. This has been cogently refuted by REBT theorists who have pointed out that a careful study of REBT shows that it is both philosophically deep, humanistic and individualized collaboratively working on the basis of the client's point of reference.
They have further pointed out that REBT utilizes an integrated and interrelated methodology of cognitive, emotive-experiential and behavioral interventions. Others have questioned REBTs view of rationality, both radical constructivists who have claimed that reason and logic are subjective properties and those who believe that reason can be objectively determined. REBT theorists have refuted these claims by maintaining that REBT raises objections to clients' irrational choices and conclusions as a working hypothesis and through collaborative efforts demonstrate the irrationality on practical, functional and social consensual grounds. In 1998 when asked what the main criticism on REBT was, Albert Ellis replied that it was the claim that it was too rational and not dealing sufficiently enough with emotions. He repudiated the claim by saying that REBT on the contrary emphasized that thinking, feeling, and behaving are interrelated and integrated, and that it includes a vast amount of both emotional and behavioral methods in addition to cognitive ones.

Ellis has himself in very direct terms criticized opposing approaches such as psychoanalysis, transpersonal psychology and abreactive psychotherapies in addition to on several occasions questioning some of the doctrines in certain religious systems, spiritualism and mysticism.
Many, including REBT practitioners, have warned against dogmatizing and sacredizing REBT as a supposedly perfect psychological cure-all and panacea. Prominent REBTers have promoted the importance of high quality and programmatic research, including originator Ellis, a self-proclaimed 'passionate skeptic'.

He has on many occasions been open to challenges and acknowledged errors and inefficiencies in his approach and concurrently revised his theories and practices. In general, with regard to cognitive-behavioral psychotherapies' interventions, others have pointed out that as about 30-40% of people are still nonresponsive to interventions, that REBT could be a platform of reinvigorating empirical studies on the effectiveness of the cognitive-behavioral models of psychopathology and human functioning.

REBT has generally in quite many ways been developed, revised and augmented through the years as understanding; knowledge and science about psychology and psychotherapy have progressed. This includes both its theoretical concepts but also its practices and methodology. Inherent in REBT as an approach has been the teaching of scientific thinking, reasonableness and un-dogmatism and these ways of thinking have been part of REBT's empiricism and skepticism.

Applications and interfaces:

Applications and interfaces of REBT are used with a broad range of clinical problems in traditional psychotherapeutic settings such as individual-, group- and family therapy. It is used as a general treatment for a vast number of different conditions and psychological problems normally associated with psychotherapy.

In addition, REBT is used with non-clinical problems and problems of living through counselling, consultation and coaching settings dealing with problems including relationships, social skills, career changes, stress management, assertiveness training, grief, problems with aging, money, weight control etc.

REBT also has many interfaces and applications through self-help resources, phone- and internet counseling, workshops & seminars, workplace and educational programmes, etc. This includes Rational Emotive Education (REE) where REBT is applied in education settings, Rational Effectiveness Training in business and work-settings and SMART Recovery (Self-Management And Recovery Training) in supporting those in addiction recovery, in addition to a wide variety of specialized treatment strategies and applications.

Stress management refers to a wide spectrum of techniques and psychotherapies aimed at controlling a person's levels of stress, especially chronic stress, usually for the purpose of improving everyday functioning.

In this context, the term 'stress' refers only to a stress with significant negative consequences, or distress in the terminology advocated by Hans Selye, rather than what he calls eustress, a stress whose consequences are helpful or otherwise positive.

Stress produces numerous symptoms which vary according to persons, situations, and severity. These can include physical health decline as well as depression. According to the St. Louis Psychologists and Counseling Information and Referral, the process of stress management is one of the keys to a happy and successful life in modern society. Although life provides numerous demands that can prove difficult to handle, stress management provides a number of ways to manage anxiety and maintain overall well-being.

Despite stress often being thought of as a subjective experience, levels of stress are readily measureable using various physiological tests, similar to those used in polygraphs.

Many practical stress management techniques are available, some for use by health practitioners and others for self-help, which may help an individual to reduce stress, provide positive feelings of being in control of one's life and promote general well-being.

The effectiveness of the different stress management techniques can be difficult to assess, as few of them have received significant attention from researchers. Consequently, the amount and quality of evidence for the various techniques varies widely. Some are accepted as effective treatments for use in psychotherapy, whilst others with less evidence favoring them are considered alternative therapies. Many professional organizations exist to promote and provide training in conventional or alternative therapies.

There are several models of stress management, each with distinctive explanations of mechanisms for controlling stress.

Much more research is necessary to provide a better understanding of which mechanisms actually operate and are effective in practice.

Historical foundations:

Walter Cannon and Hans Selye used animal studies to establish the earliest scientific basis for the study of stress. They measured the physiological responses of animals to external pressures, such as heat and cold, prolonged restraint, and surgical procedures, then extrapolated from these studies to human beings.

Subsequent studies of stress in humans by Richard Rahe and others established the view that stress is caused by distinct, measureable life stressors, and further, that these life stressors can be ranked by the median degree of stress they produce (leading to the Holmes and Rahe Stress Scale). Thus, stress was traditionally conceptualized to be a result of external insults beyond the control of those experiencing the stress. More recently, however, it has been argued that external circumstances do not have any intrinsic capacity to produce stress, but instead their effect is mediated by the individual's perceptions, capacities, and understanding.

Models

Transactional model:

Richard Lazarus and Susan Folkman suggested in 1984 that stress can be thought of as resulting from an 'imbalance between demands and resources' or as occurring when 'pressure exceeds one's perceived ability to cope'. Stress management was developed and premised on the idea that stress is not a direct response to a stressor but rather one's resources and ability to cope mediate the stress response and are amenable to change, thus allowing stress to be controllable.

In order to develop an effective stress management programme it is first necessary to identify the factors that are central to a person controlling his/her stress, and to identify the intervention methods which effectively target these factors. Lazarus and Folkman's interpretation of stress focuses on the transaction between people and their external environment (known as the Transactional Model). The model contends that stress may not be a stressor if the person does not perceive the stressor as a threat but rather as positive or even challenging. Also, if the person possesses or can use adequate coping skills, then stress may not actually be a result or develop because of the stressor. The model proposes that people can be taught to manage their stress and cope with their stressors. They may learn to change their perspective of the stressor and provide them with the ability and confidence to improve their lives and handle all of types of stressors.

Health realization/innate health model:

The health realization/innate health model of stress is also founded on the idea that stress does not necessarily follow the presence of a potential stressor. Instead of focusing on the individual's appraisal of so-called stressors in relation to his or her own coping skills (as the transactional model does), the health realization model focuses on the nature of thought, stating that it is ultimately a person's thought processes that determine the response to potentially stressful external circumstances. In this model, stress results from appraising oneself and one's circumstances through a mental filter of insecurity and negativity, whereas a feeling of well-being results from approaching the world with a 'quiet mind'.

This model proposes that helping stressed individuals understand the nature of thought especially providing them with the ability to recognize when they are in the grip of insecure thinking, disengage from it, and access natural positive feelings will reduce their stress.

Techniques:

High demand levels load the person with extra effort and work. A new time schedule is worked up, and until the period of abnormally high, personal demand has passed, the normal frequency and duration of former schedules is limited.

Many techniques cope with the stresses life brings. Some of the following ways induce a lower than usual stress level, temporarily, to compensate the biological tissues involved; others face the stressor at a higher level of abstraction:

- Autogenic training
- Social activity
- Cognitive therapy
- Conflict resolution
- Exercise
- Getting a hobby
- Meditation
- Mindfulness (psychology)
- Deep breathing
- Yoga Nidra
- Nootropics
- Reading novels
- Prayer
- Relaxation techniques
- Artistic Expression
- Fractional relaxation
- Progressive relaxation
- Spas
- Somatics training
- Spending time in nature
- Stress balls
- Natural medicine
- Clinically validated alternative treatments
- Time management
- Planning and decision making
- Listening to certain types of relaxing music, particularly:
    - New Age music
    - Classical music
    - Psychedelic music
    - Christian music
    - Liquid funk
    - ambient music
    - Sleep Music

- Spending quality time with pets

Techniques of stress management will vary according to the philosophical paradigm.

Measuring stress:

Levels of stress can be measured. One way is through the use of psychological testing: the Holmes and Rahe Stress Scale is used to rate stressful life events, while the DASS contains a scale for stress based on self-report items. Changes in blood pressure and galvanic skin response can also be measured to test stress levels, and changes in stress levels. A digital thermometer can be used to evaluate changes in skin temperature, which can indicate activation of the fight-or-flight response drawing blood away from the extremities.

Effectiveness:

Stress management has physiological and immune benefits. Positive outcomes are observed using a combination of non-drug interventions:

- treatment of anger or hostility,
- autogenic training
- talking therapy (around relationship or existential issues)
- biofeedback
- cognitive therapy for anxiety or clinical depression

Also

- Biofeedback
- Burnout (psychology)
- Distress
- Eustress
- Occupational health psychology
- People skills
- Psychological resilience
- Stress (biological)
- Reachback
- Relaxation technique

- Work-life balance
- I hardly turn on the TV and at the same time write with my hand on a piece of notebook with a pen
- The washing machine cannot be in use while at the same time the television is on
- The airplanes fly with electric current and configuration aligned with my computers
- I have my bath not too early in the morning when I will not have to turn the lights in the bathroom on
- Wavelengths are now in configuration with the meridians
- Dose the supernatural and magic still have much to do with our world
- Dose our world still has much to do with the laws of nature in this present Millennium
- How do we go about it by not complicating our culture, tradition, history or belief system
- We are being tuned to epitomize ourselves related to the way we do things
- Could it be possible using your hearing voices skills to ward off evil magical spells
- How likely is this possible or is it all just part of an hallucination
- How are we left to be in our new world with or after the use of electricity
- What would be the aftereffects of magic, juju, voodoo and witchcraft spells if not another level of reality into the supernatural. For example realizing why humans grow hairs on their head or why dose the human head stand out when they have seen a ghost
- If we know so much about children how much do we know of grandparent secrets
- An understanding of grandparents secrets means 1) you might have likes for mysteries 2) you might be a very outgoing sort of person always get what you want or 3) An outlandish sort of person. In whichever case, there is always a mystery behind that person
- How far do we know of how if the male genital is likely linked to the firmament in the sky

- It might have a link to one of the third eye probably in the head
- **Third eye.** The third eye (also called the mind's eye or inner eye) is a mystical and esoteric concept of a speculative invisible eye which provides perception beyond ordinary sight
- When with the issue of time would humans become immortals because only time will tell while time alone can sometime, make one feel that we are immortal or meant to be immortal
- Innovation in this present time can do our world lots of good with inner vision reflecting a true picture of reality
- How can we come about with such powers
- It's all around us in view of negativity, to configure a situation to make it look itself or much at its best
- It might have a lot to do with our life skills

The supernatural (Medieval Latin: first used: 1520–30 AD) is that which is not subject to the laws of nature, or more figuratively, that which is said to exist above and beyond nature. With neoplatonic and medieval scholastic origins, the metaphysical considerations can be difficult to approach as an exercise in philosophy or theology because any dependencies on its antithesis, the natural, will ultimately have to be inverted or rejected. In popular culture and fiction, the supernatural is whimsically associated with the paranormal and the occult, this differs from traditional concepts in some religions, such as Catholicism, where divine miracles are considered supernatural.

In Catholicism, while the meaning of the term and its antithesis vary, the 'Supernatural Order' is the gratuitous production, by God, of the ensemble of miracles for the elevation of man to a state of grace, including the hypostatic union (Incarnation), the beatific vision, and the ministry of angels. Divine operation, 'spiritual facts' and 'voluntary determinations' are consistently referred to as 'supernatural' by those who specifically preclude the 'extrinsic concurrence' of God or by those espousing a materialist or determinist worldview that excludes immaterial beings or free will. Barring disingenuous intent, there is no objection to this manner of speaking.

Catholic theologians sometimes call supernatural the miraculous way in which certain effects, in themselves natural, are produced, or certain endowments (like man's immunity from death, suffering, passion, and ignorance) that bring the lower class up to the higher though always within the limits of the created, but they are careful in qualifying the former as accidentally supernatural and the latter as relatively supernatural. For a concept of the substantially and absolutely supernatural, they start from a comprehensive view of the natural order taken, in its amplest acceptation, for the aggregate of all created entities and powers, including the highest natural endowments of which the rational creature is capable, and even such Divine operations as are demanded by the effective carrying out of the cosmic order.

The supernatural order is then more than a miraculous way of producing natural effects, or a notion of relative superiority within the created world, or the necessary concurrence of God in the universe; it is an effect or series of effects substantially and absolutely above all nature and, as such, calls for an exceptional intervention and gratuitous bestowal of God and rises in a manner to the Divine order, the only one that transcends the whole created world... It is obvious also that this uplifting of the rational creature to the supernatural order cannot be by way of absorption of the created into the Divine or of fusion of both into a sort of monistic identity, but only by way of union or participation, the two terms remaining perfectly distinct.

Divine revelation of the supernatural order is considered to be a matter of fact, contingent upon proper evidence of such, (miracle, prophecy etc.). 'The revelation and its evidences are called extrinsic and auxiliary supernatural, the elevation itself retaining the name of intrinsic or, according to some, theological supernatural.' The supernatural order was analyzed primarily by scholastic and post-Tridentine theologians. Theories denying or belittling the supernatural order, are historically classified into three groups:

1. present *de facto* condition (Pelagianism, Beghards, Stoic influence),
2. the original status of man (Reformers such as Baius, Protestant and the Jansenist School),
3. possibility and evidence (Rationalist School, from Socinus to the present Modernists).
4.

Rosmini ... unwittingly, [may] have paved the way for them in the following vaguely Subjectivist proposition: 'The supernatural order consists in the manifestation of Being in the plenitude of its reality, and the effect of that manifestation is a God-like sentiment, inchoate in this life through the light of faith and grace, consummate in the next through the light of glory' (36th Rosminian proposition condemned by the Holy Office, 14 Dec., 1887).

Preserving the dogmatic formulæ while voiding them of their contents, the Modernists constantly speak of the supernatural, but they understand thereby the advanced stages of an evolutive process of the religious sentiment. There is no room in their system for the objective and revealed supernatural: their Agnosticism declares it unknowable, their Immanentism derives it from our own vitality, their symbolism explains it in term of subjective experience and their criticism declares non-authentic the documents used to prove it.

'There is no question now,' says Pius X, in his Encyclical 'Pascendi' of 8 Sept., 1907, 'of the old error by which a sort of right to the supernatural was claimed for human nature. We have gone far beyond that. We have reached the point where it is affirmed that our most holy religion, in the man Christ as in us, emanated from nature spontaneously and entirely. Than this, there is surely nothing more destructive of the whole supernatural order.' ...From the commonly received axiom that 'grace does not destroy but only perfects nature' they establish between the two orders a parallelism that is not mutual confusion or reciprocal exclusion, but distinction and subordination.

The Schoolmen spoke freely of nature's possibilities and even conations towards the supernatural. To those traditional methods and views some Christian writers have,

of late, endeavored to add and even substitute another theory which, they claim, will bring the supernatural home to the modern mind and give it unquestionable credentials.
The novel theory consists in making nature postulate the supernatural. Whatever be the legitimacy of the purpose, the method is ambiguous and full of pitfalls. Between the Schoolmen's and the Modernist tenet according to which the supernatural 'emanates from nature spontaneously and entirely' there is space and distance; at the same time, the Catholic apologist who would attempt to fill some of the space and cover some of the distance should keep in mind the admonition of Pius X to those 'Catholics who, while rejecting immanence as a doctrine, employ it as a method of apologetics, and who do this so imprudently that they seem to admit that there is in human nature a true and rigorous necessity with regard to the supernatural order and not merely a capacity and suitability for the supernatural such as has at all times been emphasized by Catholic apologists'.

Process theology

Process theology or *process thought* is a school of thought influenced by the metaphysical process philosophy of Alfred North Whitehead (1861–1947) and further developed by Charles Hartshorne (1897–2000).
It is not possible, in process metaphysics, to conceive divine activity as a 'supernatural' intervention into the 'natural' order of events. Process theists usually regard the distinction between the supernatural and the natural as a by-product of the doctrine of creation *ex nihilo*. In process thought, there is no such thing as a realm of the natural in contrast to that which is supernatural. On the other hand, if 'the natural' is defined more neutrally as 'what is in the nature of things,' then process metaphysics characterizes the natural as the creative activity of actual entities.

In Whitehead's words, 'It lies in the nature of things that the many enter into complex unity' (Whitehead 1978, 21). It is tempting to emphasize process theism's denial of the supernatural and thereby highlight what the process God cannot do in comparison to what the traditional God can do (that is, to bring something from nothing). In fairness, however, equal stress should be placed on process theism's denial of the natural (as traditionally conceived) so that one may highlight what the creatures cannot do, in traditional theism, in comparison to what they can do in process metaphysics (that is, to be part creators of the world with God).

Contrasting views

In relation to: The nature of God in Western theology, Anthropology of religion, and Biblical cosmology
One complicating factor is that there is no universal agreement about the definition of 'natural' or the limits of naturalism. Concepts in the supernatural domain are closely related to concepts in religious spirituality and occultism or spiritualism. Additionally, by definition anything that exists naturally is not supernatural.
For sometimes we use the word *nature* for that *Author of nature* whom the schoolmen, harshly enough, call *natura naturans*, as when it is said that *nature* hath made man partly corporeal and partly immaterial. Sometimes we mean by the *nature* of a thing the *essence*, or that which the schoolmen scruple not to call the *quiddity* of a thing, namely, the *attribute* or *attributes* on whose score it is what it is, whether the thing be corporeal or not, as when we attempt to define the *nature* of an *angel*, or of a *triangle*, or of a *fluid* body, as such.

Sometimes we take *nature* for an internal principle of motion, as when we say that a stone let fall in the air is by *nature* carried towards the centre of the earth, and, on the contrary, that fire or flame does *naturally* move upwards toward heaven. Sometimes we understand by *nature* the established course of things, as when we say that *nature* makes the night succeed the day, *nature* hath made respiration necessary to the life of men. Sometimes we take *nature* for an aggregate of powers belonging to a body, especially a living one, as when physicians say that *nature* is strong or weak or spent, or that in such or such diseases *nature* left to herself will do the cure.

Sometimes we take nature for the universe, or system of the corporeal works of God, as when it is said of a phoenix, or a chimera, that there is no such thing in *nature*, i.e. in the world. And sometimes too, and that most commonly, we would express by *nature* a semi-deity or other strange kind of being, such as this this book and its discourse examines the notion of. And besides these more absolute acceptations, if I may so call them, of the word *nature*, it has divers others (more relative), as *nature* is wont to be set or in opposition or contradistinction to other things, as when we say of a stone when it falls downwards that it does it by a *natural motion*, but that if it be thrown upwards its motion that way is *violent*.

So chemists distinguish vitriol into *natural* and *fictitious*, or made by art, i.e. by the intervention of human power or skill; so it is said that water, kept suspended in a sucking pump, is not in its *natural* place, as that is which is stagnant in the well. We say also that wicked men are still in the state of *nature*, but the regenerate in a state of *grace*; that cures wrought by medicines are natural operations; but the miraculous ones wrought by Christ and his apostles were *supernatural*. The term 'supernatural' is often used interchangeably with paranormal or preternatural — the latter typically limited to an adjective for describing abilities which appear to exceed the bounds of possibility. Epistemologically, the relationship between the supernatural and the natural is indistinct in terms of natural phenomena that, *ex hypothesi,* violate the laws of nature, in so far as such laws are realistically accountable.
Many supporters of supernatural explanations believe that past, present, and future complexities and mysteries of the Universe cannot be explained solely by naturalistic means and argue that it is reasonable to assume that a non-natural entity or entities resolve the unexplained. Proponents of supernaturalism regard their belief system as more flexible, allowing more diversity in terms of intuition and epistemology.

Views on the 'supernatural' see it, for example, as:

- Indistinct from nature. From this perspective, some events occur according to the laws of nature, and others occur according to a separate set of principles external to known nature. For example, in Scholasticism, it was believed that God was capable of performing any miracle so long as it didn't lead to a logical contradiction. As a pedagogical exercise, a physics university instructor might ask what the aftermath would be, as nature returns to normal, following a hypothetical miraculous intervention by God, similar to a modern thought experiment. Some religions posit immanent deities, however, and do not have a tradition analogous to the supernatural; some believe that everything anyone experiences occurs by the will (occasionalism), in the mind (neoplatonism), or as a part (nondualism) of a more fundamental divine reality (platonism).

- Incorrect attributed to nature. Others believe that all events have natural and only natural causes. They believe that human beings ascribe supernatural attributes to purely natural events, such as lightning, rainbows, floods, and the origin of life.
-

Magical thinking is thinking that one's thoughts by themselves can bring about effects in the world or that thinking something corresponds with doing it. It is a type of causal reasoning or causal fallacy that looks for meaningful relationships of grouped phenomena between acts and events. In religion, folk religion, and superstition, the correlation posited is between religious ritual, such as prayer, sacrifice, or the observance of a taboo, and an expected benefit or recompense. In clinical psychology, magical thinking is a condition that causes the patient to experience irrational fear of performing certain acts or having certain thoughts because they assume a correlation with their acts and threatening calamities.

'Quasi-magical thinking' describes 'cases in which people act as if they erroneously believe that their action influences the outcome, even though they do not really hold that belief'.

Prominent Victorian theorists identified 'associative thinking,' (a common feature of practitioners of magic) as a characteristic form of irrationality. As with all forms of magical thinking, association-based and similarity-based notions of causality need not involve the practice of magic by a magician. For example, the doctrine of signatures held that similarity between plant parts and body parts indicated their efficacy in treating diseases of those body parts, and was a part of Western medicine. This association-based thinking is a vivid example of the general human application of the representativeness heuristic.

Edward Burnett Tylor coined the term 'associative thinking', characterizing it as pre-logical, in which the 'magician's folly' is in mistaking an ideal connection with a real one. The magician believes that thematically-linked items can influence one another by virtue of their similarity. For example, in E. E. Evans-Pritchard's account, amongst the Azande tribe members rub crocodile teeth on banana plants to invoke a fruitful crop. Because crocodile teeth are curved (like bananas) and grow back if they fall out, the Azande observe this similarity and want to impart this capacity of regeneration to their bananas. To them, the rubbing constitutes a means of transference.

Sir James Frazer later elaborated upon this principle by dividing magic into the categories of 'contagious' and 'homeopathic' magic, both of which are forms of 'sympathetic' magic. The former is based upon the law of contagion or contact, in which two things that were once connected retain this link and have the ability to affect their supposedly related objects, such as harming a person by harming a lock of his hair. Homeopathic magic operates upon the premise that 'like affects like', or that one can impart characteristics of one similar object to another. Frazer believed that these individuals think the entire world functions according to these mimetic, or homeopathic, principles.

In *How Natives Think* (1925), Lucien Lévy-Bruhl describes a similar notion of mystical, 'collective representations'. He too sees magical thinking as fundamentally different from a Western style of thought. He asserts that in these representations, 'primitive' people's 'mental activity is too little differentiated for it to be possible to consider ideas or images of objects by themselves apart from the emotions and passions which evoke those ideas or are evoked by them.' Lévy-Bruhl explains that natives commit the *post hoc,*

ergo propter hoc fallacy, in which people observe that x is followed by y, therefore y has been caused by x. He believes that this fallacy is institutionalized in native culture and is committed regularly and repeatedly.
Despite the view that magic is less than rational and entails an inferior concept of causality, in *The Savage Mind* (1966), Claude Lévi-Strauss suggested that magical procedures are relatively effective in exerting control over the environment. This outlook has generated alternative theories of magical thinking, such as the symbolic and psychological approaches, and softened the contrast between 'educated' and 'primitive' thinking: 'Magical thinking is no less characteristic of our own mundane intellectual activity than it is of Zande curing practices.'

Other forms

Bronisław Malinowski's *Magic, Science and Religion* (1954) discuss another type of magical thinking, in which words and sounds are thought to have the ability to directly affect the world. This type of wish fulfillment thinking can result in the avoidance of talking about certain subjects ('speak of the devil and he'll appear'), the use of euphemisms instead of certain words, or the belief that to know the 'true name' of something gives one power over it, or that certain chants, prayers, or mystical phrases will bring about physical changes in the world. More generally, it is magical thinking to take a symbol to be its referent or an analogy to represent an identity.
Sigmund Freud believed that magical thinking was produced by cognitive developmental factors. He described practitioners of magic as projecting their mental states onto the world around them, similar to a common phase in child development. From toddlerhood to early school age, children will often link the outside world with their internal consciousness, e.g. 'It is raining because I am sad.'
Symbolic approach to magic
Another theory of magical thinking is the symbolic approach. Leading thinkers of this category, including Stanley J. Tambiah, believe that magic is meant to be expressive, rather than instrumental. As opposed to the direct, mimetic

thinking of Frazer, Tambiah asserts that magic utilizes abstract analogies to express a desired state, along the lines of metonymy or metaphor.

An important question raised by this interpretation is how mere symbols could exert material effects. One possible answer lies in John L. Austin's concept of 'performativity,' in which the act of saying something makes it true, such as in an inaugural or marital rite. Other theories propose that magic is effective because symbols are able to change internal psycho-physical states. They claim that the act of expressing a certain anxiety or desire is reparative in itself.

These theories can seem limited in that they do not account for the various explicitly instrumental magical practices. Many magical cultures have produced extensive rationalizations for magic's potential lack of efficacy; this indicates that magical routines are invoked to bring about physical results. As stated by Gilbert Lewis, 'if magicians performed spells for explicitly symbolic or metaphorical purposes, then we wouldn't consider them magic at all…'

A healing ritual (the laying on of hands):

Some scholars believe that magic is effective psychologically. They cite the placebo effect, psychosomatic disease, etc., as prime examples of how our mental functions exert power over our bodies. Similarly, Robert Horton suggests that engaging in magical practices surrounding healing can relieve anxiety, which could have a significant positive physical impact. In the absence of advanced health care, such impacts would play a relatively major role, thereby helping to explain the persistence and popularity of such practices.

According to theories of anxiety relief and control, people turn to magical beliefs when there exists a sense of uncertainty and potential danger and little to do about it. Magic is used to restore a sense of control. In support of this theory, research indicates that superstitious behavior is invoked more often in high stress situations, especially by people with a greater desire for control.

Another potential reason for the persistence of magic rituals is that the rituals prompt their own use by creating a feeling of insecurity and then proposing themselves as precautions.

Boyer and Liénard propose that in obsessive-compulsive rituals — a possible clinical model for magical thinking — focus shifts to the lowest level of gestures, resulting in goal demotion. For example, an obsessive-compulsive cleaning ritual may overemphasize the order, direction, and number of wipes used to clean the surface. The goal becomes less important than the actions used to achieve the goal, with the implication that magic rituals can persist without efficacy because the intent is lost within the act.

Phenomenological approach:

Ariel Glucklich tries to understand magic from a subjective perspective, attempting to comprehend magic on a phenomenological, experientially-based level. Glucklich seeks to describe the attitude that magical practitioners feel which he calls 'magical consciousness' or the 'magical experience.' He explains that it is based upon 'the awareness of the interrelatedness of all things in the world by means of simple but refined sense perception,'
Another phenomenological model is Gilbert Lewis's, which is that 'habit is unthinking.' He believes that those practicing magic do not think of an explanatory theory behind their actions any more than the average person tries to grasp the pharmaceutical workings of aspirin. When the average person takes an aspirin, he does not know how the medicine chemically functions. He takes the pill with the premise that there is proof of efficacy. Similarly, many who avail themselves of magic do so without feeling the need to understand a causal theory behind it.

Idiomatic difference:

Robin Horton maintains that the difference between Western and non-Western people's thinking is predominantly 'idiomatic.' He asserts that both cultures employ the same practical common-sense, and both science and magic are ways in which people delve into theory, into what occurs beyond that basic logic. When modern farmers desire, for example, to ensure plant growth, they would turn to scientific theory and might purchase fertilizer or consult an agronomist. However, non-western cultures possess the idiom of magic or spiritual figures and would therefore turn to magical practices or an expert in that idiom. Horton sees both western and native cultures as possessing the same logic and common-sense, but simply different ontological idioms, which may contribute to seemingly illogical practices on either part. He explains, 'the layman's grounds for accepting the models propounded by the scientist is often no different from the young African villager's ground for accepting the models propounded by one of his elders.'

Along similar lines, Michael F. Brown argues that the Aguaruna of Peru see magic as merely a type of technology, no more supernatural than their physical tools. He argues that the Aguaruna utilize magic in a very scientific manner, for example, discarding magical stones which they have observed to be ineffective. It seems, that to Brown, too, magical thinking merely differs in idiom.

These theories tend to blur the lines between magic, science, and religion, asserting the similarities between magical, technical, and spiritual practices. Brown even notes that he is tempted to claim that 'magic' does not exist.

Substantive difference:

One theory of substantive difference is that of the open versus closed society. Horton describes this as one of the key dissimilarities between traditional thought and Western science. He suggests that the scientific worldview is distinguished from a magical one by the scientific method and by skepticism, requiring the falsifiability of any scientific hypothesis. He notes that for native peoples 'there is no developed awareness of alternatives to the established body of theoretical texts.' He notes that all further differences between traditional and Western thought can be understood as a result of this factor, for example, the fact that African thought both lacks impersonal theory, or objectivity, and clings to the past as opposed to looking towards the future. Because there are no alternatives in magically-thought based societies, a theory does not need to be objectively judged to be valid, and each moment that passes draws them further away from a once undiluted relationship with the spiritual and natural world.

It's said in religion do not think of what you will eat, wear but if I should it will be by every words and commandments of God nevertheless its right having the good things in life nobody wants to be lonely, feel rejected, always in need of help. How would I know if and when am entitled to the boiler chickens in my African Asian food store. When and how do I know when God commands me to do something? Sometimes I can understand it when a situation arrives that 'you have been framed' in a world of the good the bad and the ugly it would not be rather daunting if I hear voices from the boiler chicken telling me before I go out of my flat to the shops if its 3 for £5.00 or 2 for £5.00 I should buy infarct sometimes how I will get it prepared also realizing's while doing the cooking it reflects on the meal and how it will go down well in my stomach. And that's when I customary feel hungry.
How sensitive are we eating food from within our own origin and culture within us personally do we find means correlating it to food of other culture, tradition and creed? Did it come about through how I handled and cultured myself on a basis of my life experience or was it part of my relationship with God or just part of being human.

While bearing in mind the heart and mind is where things take shape its left for each man to shape his or her own heart and mind this is why in the present age innovation comes very handy it demonstrate that in reality you have earned whatever you have in life. I have in time discovered my reproductive organ holds the centre of my own inspiration linked with my third eye I might in the future see what's in the heavenly bodies or beyond the heavenly bodies I might even become immortal where time has or no longer have meaning.

I. I cannot be preparing a meal at the same time watching TV
II. I cannot be preparing a meal at the same time word process
III. It has to be one thing at a time
IV. Would any of the above have anything to do with magic

V. Or they are solemnly just ways of taking caution, being attentive to a particular course

VI. While at the same time am exploring my inner vision based on what am going to write about in my books

VII. Do not feel a crucifix can no longer do squirt, you will do squirt because it's all inside you therefore it's still ok to having a crucifix.

My books have been written based on something from within my own native background I call it my 'native scrolls' with inner meaning and relevance to juju partly from the food I eat, the way I prepare it.

It's now left for my bloodline correlating its meaning or definition based on my own personal life experience and that of their. Also correlate its contents from within my native background and the Western world or was it that I was bound going into something near stereotyping? Suffering is based on reality it's a basis on which science makes its mark when correlated with experiments.

Did it come about through how I handled the course of my life experience or what is all about having something to do with my relationship with God or was it all part of my just being human knowing right from wrong. It could have meant for me to shape a life for me to be me.

Now is a time for those of us who have been doing things by nature our natural instinct gives us an opportunity to be square in the things we do, to adjust easily in difficult time. The truth and reality is worth it for we, are truly ourselves.

Doing by nature the things of the law are humans, born with a set of basic laws already written on their hearts laws which they do not have to learn but know instinctively in their conscience? What does it mean to 'do by nature the things contained in the law'? Romans 2:14.

- The great things about nature Romans 2:14-15. For when Gentiles who don't have the law are doing by nature what the law requires, they are a law to themselves, even though they don't have the law. They show that the work of the law is written on their hearts their conscience bears witness, and their thoughts accuse or excuse them' Romans 2:14-15.

- Ephesians 2:3**:** We all once lived among the disobedient, in the passions of our flesh, obeying the desires of body and mind. We were by nature children of wrath, like the rest of mankind.

Isn't nature part of instinct? My instinct can instruct me about disciplines when I become unreasonable my instinct instructs me to take caution and be wise therefore I might have been born with a set of laws, disciplines to adder to so that I can do things and abide by nature. Instinct can be positive or negative. Nature throws some nasty things at us. We are called to be governed by law, rules, virtues and morals that we contain ourselves to enable us obey the commandments of God, express who, we truly are as much as we would define who we are.

Being Human aims to engage us with the very best of innovations attached to humanity. Being human consist of lot of things e.g. being sensible, being natural is another one. Humans in themselves possess all the natural basic elements of the Universe. The main difference between human being and being human is that 'human being' is generally defined as being a member of Homo sapiens race, while 'being human' means displaying characteristics that are unique to human beings.

It's not easy to abide by our own laws not, to imply those of God he made it this way because he wants to nature us, create a relationship. our eyes more or less choose to be closed towards him and his commandments probably because of the pleasure's, pain and suffering involved, not having a determined life to our own taste or that his commandments are difficult to abide by. Or it's all just part of our being self-centered, particular about ourselves. on the other hand since there is evil, pain and suffering in our world it can simply be put down as justified nevertheless this makes him truly God his commandments ought to be obeyed or we fail to realize our true self in the real sense of humanity or our worth.

It's part of what makes us humans. We are meant to strive; strife to be who we are a question would be for what? We are meant to understand not only ourselves but also life. As long as our world exist, we would also strife to understand life even ourselves for as long as we do so we would want to know God the creator and architect of the Universe.

If we depart ourselves from doing so we wallow in our own self in a world of the good the bad and the ugly, beauty, ugliness and death and then, we expire.

In a world where only good needs to prevail for us to really live and survive, also to express and experience our true worth God will always still prevail.

If this is what makes God who he is what makes you, who you are e.g. being human you have life, a job, one or two children, few friends and relatives. You eat, you sleep you do lots of things to wonder about God do his will he is in every human and we have read about the parable of the sower.

The Parable of the Sower was told to the crowd that had gathered around Jesus. Jesus tells a story of a sower who scattered seeds on four different types of soil. The first type of ground was hard and the seed could not sprout or grow at all and became snatched up instantly. The second type of ground was stony. The seed was able to plant and begin to grow, however it could not grow deep roots and withered in the sun. The third type of ground was thorny and although the seed could plant and grow, it could not compete with the amount of thorns that overtook it. The fourth ground was good soil that allowed the seed to plant deep, grow strong, and produce fruit. Who then his the sower?

Jesus used this parable to explain to his followers and the disciples how there are different responses to the saving Gospel of Jesus Christ. The sower in the parable is Jesus and the seed is the word of God. The hard ground represents someone with a hardened heart full of sin that hears the word of God but does not accept it. Satan is able to keep this person from growing at all. The stony ground is someone who shows interest and awareness in the Gospel, yet his heart isn't fully convicted so that when trouble comes his faith is not strong enough to stand.

The thorny ground is a person who receives the Gospel but who has many other idols and distractions in life - worries, riches, and lusts, which take over his mind and heart and he cannot grow in the truth of God's Word. The good soil is someone who has heard and received the Word of God and allows it to take root and grow within his life. This person represents true salvation that bears good fruit.

Jesus spoke the Parable of the Sower to teach how important the state of our heart is to receiving the Gospel and how our salvation is proved by our choices and actions.

There is greed, hat and lies in a world of pain, evil and suffering listen and follow thy conscience which is a person's moral sense of right and wrong, viewed as acting as a guide to one's behavior.

Conscience is a cognitive process that elicits emotion and rational associations based on an individual's moral philosophy or value system. Conscience stands in contrast to elicited emotion or thought due to associations based on immediate sensory perceptions and reflexive responses, as in sympathetic CNS responses. In common terms, conscience is often described as leading to feelings of remorse when a person commits an act that conflicts with their moral values.

An individual's moral values and their dissonance with familial, social, cultural and historical interpretations of moral philosophy are considered in the examination of cultural relativity in both the practice and study of psychology. The extent to which conscience informs moral judgment before an action and whether such moral judgments are or should be based on reason has occasioned debate through much of modern history between theories of modern western philosophy in juxtaposition to the theories of romanticism and other reactionary movements after the end of the Middle Ages.

Religious views of conscience usually see it as linked to a morality inherent in all humans, to a beneficent universe and/or to divinity. The diverse ritualistic, mythical, doctrinal, legal, institutional and material features of religion may not necessarily cohere with experiential, emotive, spiritual or contemplative considerations about the origin and operation of conscience. Common secular or scientific views regard the capacity for conscience as probably genetically determined, with its subject probably learned or imprinted as part of a culture.

Commonly used metaphors for conscience include the 'voice within', the 'inner light', or even Socrates' reliance on what the Greeks called his 'daimōnic sign', an averting inner voice heard only when he was about to make a mistake. Conscience, as is detailed in sections below, is a concept in national and international law, is increasingly conceived of as applying to the world as a whole, has motivated numerous notable acts for the public good and been the subject of many prominent examples of literature, music and film

Reason is a term that refers to the capacity human beings have to make sense of things, to establish and verify facts, and to change or justify practices, institutions, and beliefs. It is closely associated with such characteristically human activities as philosophy, science, language, mathematics, and art, and is normally considered to be a definitive characteristic of human nature. The concept of reason is sometimes referred to as rationality and sometimes as discursive reason, in opposition to intuitive reason.

Reason or 'reasoning' is associated with thinking, cognition, and intellect. Reason, like habit or intuition, is one of the ways by which thinking comes from one idea to a related idea. For example, it is the means by which rational beings understand themselves to think about cause and effect, truth and falsehood, and what is good or bad.

In contrast to reason as an abstract noun, a reason is a consideration which explains or justifies some event, phenomenon or behavior. The ways in which human beings reason through argument are the subject of inquiries in the field of logic.

Reason is closely identified with the ability to self-consciously change beliefs, attitudes, traditions, and institutions, and therefore with the capacity for freedom and self-determination.

Psychologists and cognitive scientists have attempted to study or explain how people reason e.g. which cognitive and neural processes are engaged, and how cultural factors affect the inferences that people draw. The field of automated reasoning studies how reasoning may or may not be modeled computationally. Animal psychology considers the controversial question of whether animals can reason.

In the English language and other modern European languages, 'reason', and related words, represent words which have always been used to translate Latin and classical Greek terms in the sense of their philosophical usage.

Philosophy can be described as a way of life based upon reason, and in the other direction reason has been one of the major subjects of philosophical discussion since ancient times. Reason is often said to be reflexive, or 'self-correcting' and the critique of reason has been a persistent theme in philosophy. It has been defined in different ways, at different times, by different thinkers.

For many classical philosophers, nature was understood teleologically, meaning that every type of thing had a definitive purpose which fit within a natural order that was itself understood to have aims. The cosmos is even said to have reason. Reason, by this account, is not just one characteristic that humans happen to have, and that influences happiness amongst other characteristics.

Reason was considered of higher stature than other characteristics of human nature, such as sociability, because it is something humans share with nature itself, linking an apparently immortal part of the human mind with the divine

order of the cosmos itself. Within the human mind or soul, reason was described as being the natural monarch which, rules over the other parts, such as spiritedness and emotions. Human beings as rational animals, emphasis reason as a characteristic of human nature. The highest human happiness or well-being of life lived consistently, excellently and completely is done in accordance with reason.
Having read this book this far what would my readers, myself and a carer think God, would expect from me? After withdrawing from drinking alcohol, I wanted to give up smoking or should I also stop playing the national lottery or rather play it with reason and concepts. God wants some important thoughts from me am not putting my stance to judge but seriously the situation am in, might lead to some dilemmas if I do not take care or caution myself.

If am willing on the right path God will definably show me the way so that am not lost in view that I seek through his own plan, path and directions. E.g. I would make myself safe from gambling, smoking excessively or going back to drinking alcohol and if I give all these up in view of my need to have my books published what path or reward will come out of it. So I opened a savings account rather than using money to buy tobacco I save part of it at the same time reduce the amount of tobacco I smoke.

Deuteronomy 29:29 Secret things belong unto the Lord our God. That is the counsels and purposes of God concerning persons or nations, and the reasons of his dispensations toward them, together with the time and manner of inflicting judgments or showing mercy, are hidden in his own bosom, and not to be pried into, much less fathomed, by us.

Some dilemmas humans can leave themselves in is left, for them to be damned or take caution thinking it over and deciding to save some money nevertheless with difficulty but very thoughtful and considerate in view of what lies before me are true digital projections of myself in the real world. What makes it so difficult for I have to find escape routes that I make life and this digital projection of myself not only found to be unbearable to become decisive?

At least if it's just having this book published on E-book only is a decisive move and a projection of what I feel about the use of windfarm or Solar energy in the new heaven this are what religious leaders should strive into with knowledge from the holy scriptures in religions in this present time we have to move in a way that we understand, feel the presence of the new heaven it might be a spiritual projection of myself in a way correlated with science and technology. Has science and technology have anything to do with the new heaven?

The relationship between religion and science is the subject of continued debate in philosophy and theology. To what extent are religion and science compatible? Are religious beliefs sometimes conducive to science, or do they inevitably pose obstacles to scientific inquiry? The interdisciplinary field of 'science and religion' also called 'theology and science', aims to answer these and other questions. It studies historical and contemporary interactions between these fields, and provides philosophical analyses of how they interrelate.

In several was correlated to: What are science and religion, and how do they interrelate?

- A brief history of the field of science and religion
- What is science, and what is religion?
- Models of the interaction between science and religion
- The scientific study of religion
- Religious beliefs in academia
- Divine action and creation
- Human origins
- Evolutionary ethics
- Implications of cognitive science of religion for rationality of religious beliefs

Science and religion are closely interconnected in the scientific study of religion, which can be traced back to seventeenth-century natural histories of religion. Natural historians attempted to provide naturalistic explanations for human behaviour and culture, for domains such as religion, emotions, and morality.

Our beliefs, sometimes our wish are preceded by phenomena's we can hear voices with directions based on what we should do in view of a given scenario how we should conduct ourselves e.g. spiritually, emotionally or morally.

Just weeks before 12th November 2018 I played the national lottery with just one game of £2.00 in three different game draws I won lucky deep three times. With the game which fell around 12th of November 2018 I resort to play £8.00 on that day in just one draw within the week. It rained as I was, walking out of my flat to play the games at WH Smith Woolwich. Immediately I walked back into my flat the rain stopped on that day, thunders trick occurred. It leaves room not only for spiritual consideration and also some psychological and emotional thinking which I would not, go into because I do not want to leave room for hallucinations or paranoias in this book. I also heard voices. I did not win at all for the game I spend £8.00 on but in view of the scenario I would have thought that I would win and if, I did not win take a step back and think things over.

On Monday the 3rd of December 2018 something similar took place it rained I went to buy my lottery ticket at the same place for a Wednesday game. I cannot think of another proper place for money to come in to publish a book like this or other books I hope to get word process for publication. It comes to mind that the book could be a number of something but of what? I was yet to reason it out or make out its full and real significance in reality as I look forward to win on the Wednesday draw. If, I do not win, it means the lottery game controllers are aware that it is not easy to prepare a meal but it's very easy to feel free and eat it when it's prepared. But at least if I put myself into it, it should be a choice that yields result. I need not go into gambling addiction realising later that I have been making a great mistake. Gambling should make gamers happy not sad we all know if wishes are horse beggars would rise.

If you are a gamer and let's say religious as well at each time you play a game and it's as if you and your spirituality is sipping out of you whenever you lose you should reconsider.

Gambling is something that should put a smile on your face. Now a secret of gambling is they do not make anything certain for example you are rewarded by your skills if it does not match which doesn't always match or you later on feel bias what do you do. Do I have to wait for my beliefs to be justified on such a game? Should I consider gambling within a scope of my beliefs? But it's possible! The only thing right I can receive by having any belief relating to gambling is to be wise on their own part they, are very crafty while, God in his own creation is more than crafty.

There are tricks gamers use or can use to win the national lottery games draw such as putting money by the side of a road or just where somebody could pick it up in other to get hold of their star because its written on them probably they also play the lottery it has to do with whose hand is higher and the star that follows you. Once the money is picked up they play the game further to this if they drive a vehicle put the ticket inside the car closet next to the driver's front seat. Furthermore drive the car when the game draw is being played.

Mysteries of gambling is you have got hold of your star with the winning ticket the money are all you and your life while having, a huge amount of money won through gambling is for throwing about. You are left to realize if holding on to your star and life brings you something favorable or what while apart from a winning ticket you might have to make a choice this, was what lies before me. E.g. can it make me lose my talent for writing books would, it make me care less for giving up smoking or alcohol would it, make me want to gamble more? What are my best options and way out that's life it's what it's all about to definably make me who I am, to realize my true self, it makes me aware of my consciousness, feelings and emotions apart from my physical self.

What can this number of something be? It's when a certain number of people have read my book that is when, I will return back through birth into this planet. It's about time we ought to realize what it takes to hold on to the pillars of the

Universe so that in Gods recreation we are part and parcel of it in its real sense.
I have been bringing issues out which could make some of us destroy ourselves if it would save humanity would anyone care without a world government related to technology it might destroy us.

Difference within gambling and investing **gambling,** is all about risk and the odds cannot be lowered by further research (except for those who can modify the odds of blackjack by card counting or something like that). The goal of investing is to build up a company and portfolio.
Britain's biggest gambling companies have voluntarily agreed to a 'whistle-to-whistle' television advertising ban.
The Remote Gambling Association (RGA), which includes Bet365, Ladbrokes and Paddy Power, has struck a deal to stop adverts during live sports broadcasts.
It follows political pressure about the amount of betting advertising on TV.
More than 90 minutes of adverts were shown during the football World Cup and anti-gambling campaigners say sport's use of adverts 'normalises' betting.
There are also fears it contributes to the rise in the amount of problem gamblers - with a Gambling Commission report suggesting 430,000 Britons can be described as such - and helps fuel under-age gambling.
The deal follows extensive talks between firms - also including SkyBet, Betfred, Betfair, Stan James, Gala Coral and William Hill - to ensure no adverts will be broadcast for a defined period before and after a game is broadcast.
Three online casino companies will pay penalties of £14m and one has been prevented from operating in the UK following a crackdown by the industry regulator.
The Gambling Commission said the three firms did not have 'effective safeguards' to prevent money laundering and harm to customers from gambling.
God gave us leaders whereas he had made each of us to be our own leader we make and correct our own mistakes; we are either justified or not justified by our own actions, stricken by the brunt of our action if we want peace, we seek peace, if we want favour we seek favour. We are pleased by the works of our hands if it is good it can make us feel

remarkable become more diligent while, we face repercussions to make us mend our ways through our conscientiousness. We have been created in the image of God we might without knowing be consuming the image of God in so doing, every man becomes his or her own distinct nature or attributes.

Diligence is one of the seven heavenly virtues. Diligent behavior is indicative of a work ethic; a belief work is good in itself. Diligence is carefulness and persistent effort or work diligence in a student is defined as an effort he or she puts towards balanced and holistic development in mental, physical, social and spiritual dimensions.
Diligence, in Christianity, is the effort to do one's part, while keeping faith and reliance in God. In other words, diligence and faith are two sides of a mystery. One doesn't know how, despite one's effort, it all works out. But diligence when combined with faith assures spiritual success. Diligence as one of seven virtues describes thoroughness, completeness and persistence of an action, particularly in matters of faith.
We want each of you to show this same diligence to the very end, in order to make your hope sure. We do not want you to become lazy, but to imitate those who through faith and patience inherit what has been promised.
Hebrews 6:11-12
Conscientiousness is the personality trait of being careful, or vigilant. Conscientiousness implies a desire to do a task well, and to take obligations to others seriously. Conscientious people tend to be efficient and organized as opposed to easy-going and disorderly. They exhibit a tendency to show self-discipline, act dutifully, and aim for achievement; they display planned rather than spontaneous behavior; and they are generally dependable.

It is manifested in characteristic behaviors such as being neat, and systematic; also including such elements as carefulness, thoroughness, and deliberation (the tendency to think carefully before acting.) Conscientiousness is one of the five traits of both the Five Factor Model of personality and is an aspect of what has traditionally been referred to as having character.

Conscientious individuals are generally hard-working, and reliable. They are also likely to be conformists. When taken to an extreme, they may also be 'workaholics', perfectionists, and compulsive in their behavior. People who score low on conscientiousness tend to be laid back, less goal-oriented, and less driven by success; they also are more likely to engage in antisocial and criminal behavior.
Personality psychology is a branch of psychology that studies personality and its variation among individuals. It is a scientific study which aims to show how people are individually different due to psychological forces. Its areas of focus include:

- construction of a coherent picture of the individual and their major psychological processes
- investigation of individual psychological differences
- investigation of human nature and psychological similarities between individuals
-

'Personality' is a dynamic and organized set of characteristics possessed by a person that uniquely influences their environment, cognitions, emotions, motivations, and behaviors in various situations. The word *personality* originates from the Latin *persona*, which means 'mask'.

Personality also refers to the pattern of thoughts, feelings, social adjustments, and behaviors consistently exhibited over time that strongly influences one's expectations, self-perceptions, values, and attitudes. Personality also predicts human reactions to other people, problems, and stress. Gordon Allport (1937) described two major ways to study personality: the nomothetic and the idiographic. *Nomothetic psychology* seeks general laws that can be applied to many different people, such as the principle of self-actualization or the trait of extraversion. *Idiographic psychology* is an attempt to understand the unique aspects of a particular individual.
The study of personality has a broad and varied history in psychology with an abundance of theoretical trad. The major theories include dispositional (trait) perspective, psychodynamic, humanistic, biological, behaviorist,

evolutionary, and social learning perspective. However, many researchers and psychologists do not explicitly identify themselves with a certain perspective and instead take an eclectic approach. Research in this area is empirically driven, such as dimensional models, based on multivariate statistics, such as factor analysis, or emphasizes theory development, such as that of the psychodynamic theory. There is also a substantial emphasis on the applied field of personality testing. In psychological education and training, the study of the nature of personality and its psychological development is usually reviewed as a prerequisite to courses in abnormal psychology or clinical psychology.

The nature of God:

1. God
a. A being conceived as the perfect, omnipotent, omniscient originator and ruler of the universe, the principal object of faith and worship in monotheistic religions.
b. The force, effect, or a manifestation or aspect of this being.

2. A being of supernatural powers or attributes, believed in and worshiped by a people, especially a male deity thought to control some part of nature or reality.

3. An image of a supernatural being; not an idol.

4. One that is worshiped, idealized, or followed.

Nature, in the broadest sense, is the natural, physical, or material world or universe. 'Nature' can refer to the phenomena of the physical world, and also to life in general. The study of nature is a large, if not the only, part of science. Although humans are part of nature, human activity is often understood as a separate category from other natural phenomena.
The word *nature* is derived from Latin 'essential qualities, innate disposition', and in ancient times, literally meant 'birth'. *Natura* is a Latin translation of a Greek word, which originally related to the intrinsic characteristics that plants,

animals, and other features of the world develop of their own accord. The concept of nature as a whole, the physical universe, is one of several expansions of the original notion; it began with certain core applications of pre-Socratic philosophers, and has steadily gained currency ever since. This usage continued during the advent of modern scientific method in the last several centuries.
Within the various uses of the word today, 'nature' often refers to geology and wildlife. Nature can refer to the general realm of living plants and animals, and in some cases to the processes associated with inanimate objects the way that particular types of things exist and change of their own accord, such as the weather and geology of the Earth. It is often taken to mean the 'environment' or wilderness wild animals, rocks, forest, and in general those things that have not been substantially altered by human intervention, or which persist despite human intervention. For example, manufactured objects and human interaction generally are not considered part of nature, unless qualified as, for example, 'human nature' or 'the whole of nature'. This more traditional concept of natural things which can still be found today implies a distinction between the natural and the artificial, with the artificial being understood as that which has been brought into being by a human consciousness or a human mind. Depending on the particular context, the term 'natural' might also be distinguished from the unnatural or the supernatural.

1 What is an example of attribute?
Attribute is defined as a quality or characteristic of a person, place or thing. Intelligence, charm and a sense of humor are each an example of an attribute.

2 What is personal attribute?
An attribute is a quality or characteristic of a person, place or thing. Personal attributes are character traits or personality traits.

3 What are some good qualities?
Opinions of good leadership qualities varies however, honesty, good communication, confidence and the ability to inspire are some qualities commonly attributed to good

leadership. Additional qualities include creativity, a positive attitude and commitment.

4 What are personality traits examples?
The definition of a personality trait is a quality or characteristic that distinguishes the character, action and attitude of a person, animal or geographical location.

When we talk of attributes recently it's about metadata, computing, file attributes, field name, HTML hyper-text makeup language. This **attribute** was used to **define** a region for hyperlinks to create an image map. The values are circle, default, polygon, and rect. The format of the coords **attribute** depends on the value of shape. We also have biological attributes the basis for my implying this, is what kind of attributes would have prompted me to write this book. You will have to read it to come up with answer in my case in a simple way I have been correlating science conscientiously with religion. In computing, an attribute is a specification that defines a property of an object element or file it may also refer to or set the specific value for a given instance of such.

Behavioral attributes is defined as individual characteristics that may be measured by the performance measured that is considered effective. An example of a behavioral attribute is discipline. An individual who has good discipline can make wise choices with positive benefits.

A positive attribute in a person is that quality that other people may find likeable and worthy of emulation. Positive attributes are what makes other people enjoy being with someone.

A value is a **belief, a mission, or a philosophy that is meaningful.** Whether we are consciously aware of them or not, every individual has a core set of personal values. Values can range from the commonplace, such as the belief in hard work and punctuality, to the more psychological, such as self-reliance, concern for others, and harmony of purpose.

As human beings, we all have our own values, beliefs and attitudes that we have developed throughout the course of our lives. Our family, friends, community and the experiences we have had all contribute to our sense of who we are and how we view the world.

Dose values really unite while beliefs divide there is a significant difference between values and beliefs but one must value both. Beliefs are assumptions we hold to be true. When we use our beliefs to make decisions, we are assuming the causal relationships of the past, which led to the belief, will also apply in the future. We could have nursing beliefs and values, business beliefs and values or educational beliefs and values. If you take a real and carefully look into the contents of this book you will realize why beliefs and values join hands.

Mysteries of the Rosary:

The Church has used three sets of mysteries for many centuries. In 2002 Pope John Paul II proposed a fourth set of mysteries—the Mysteries of Light, or Luminous Mysteries. According to his suggestion, the four sets of mysteries might be prayed on the following days: the Joyful Mysteries on Monday and Saturday, the Sorrowful Mysteries on Tuesday and Friday, the Glorious Mysteries on Wednesday and Sunday, and the Luminous Mysteries on Thursday

Mysteries of the gold crucifix:
Joyful
Sorrowful
And Glorious

And mysteries of the silver crucifix:
Devotion to the rosary is one of the most notable features of popular Catholic spirituality. Pope placed the rosary at the very center of Christian spirituality and called it 'among the finest and most praiseworthy traditions of Christian contemplation.

The Rosary has been featured in the writings of Roman Catholic figures from saints to popes and continues to be mentioned in reported Marian apparitions, with a number of promises attributed to the power of the rosary.

The overwhelming majority of adults in England are so unhealthy they put their lives at risk, a survey suggests.

The data from the Health Survey for England showed nearly nine in 10 had at least one unhealthy trait.

That was classed as those who smoke, drink more than 14 units of alcohol, eat fewer than five portions of fruit and vegetables, are obese or have low rates of physical activity.

Half of adults have two or more of these risk factors.

Although there are signs some people are giving up some of the unhealthy traits.

A violent storm on the Sun could cripple communications on Earth and cause huge economic damage, scientists have warned. Why are solar storms such a threat?

In 1972, dozens of sea mines off the coast of Vietnam mysteriously exploded.

It was recently confirmed the cause was solar storms, which can significantly disrupt the Earth's magnetic field.

Today, the effects of a similar event could be much more serious - disrupting the technology we rely on for everything from satellites to power grids. The cost to the UK economy alone of an unexpected event has been estimated at £16bn.

There are good reasons why we are vulnerable to events taking place millions of miles from Earth.

What causes an extreme solar event?

The Sun is a star, a seething mass of electrified hydrogen. As this fluid moves around, it builds up energy within its complex magnetic field.

This magnetic energy is released through intense flashes of light known as solar flares and through vast eruptions of material and magnetic fields known as coronal mass ejections or solar storms.

While flares can disrupt radio communication on Earth, solar storms pose the greatest threat.

Each storm contains the energy equivalent to 100,000 times the world's entire nuclear arsenal, although this is spread throughout an enormous volume in space.

What does all these in today and tomorrows' world mean? If believing it might be Gods wish for me to win the national lottery to aid me in publishing my books because am on the dole with financial problem it might mean, God wants me to build a statue or an Alter for him through the help of my winning the national lottery. But the Gambling agent would also claim to be part of the help at the end of the day while not everybody might accept such a notion that its Gods wish.

On the other hand, I might be obliterated from the Alter through consequences unknown e.g. I might be stroked by thunder struck or lightning through my own course e.g. still going back to drinking alcohol or smoking why not I include myself definably by reducing or giving up smoking to actually build the Alter for the name if God based on life repercussion's? And then what would this book mean based on its content if not an Alter.

Our world is changing a mystery behind this book is why should it be written as an e-book only time and change waits for no one you can use them wisely or waist it the choice is yours how do we notice our strength and weakness. When the day is over it once again entails time waits for no one while life goes on and that every day in life people separate for different reason until one day the reality really sets in that they are gone for good hopefully leaving us with a positive, negative or loving memory.

It's not to exist by condemning things, things one can easily make sense out of if we are really ready to confront reality which can be positive or negative if, I have existed by condemning things about life to a point of you are a sinner, you do things I do not like am not God it does not and dose stop us from making our world more convenient and beautiful to live in its just about how we do it so to imply if I have lived by passing condemnation on myself and other people I would not have been in any stance to have written this book. I would have been too direct, rude or one sided.

Life is what we make out of it; it should not solemnly always be about am on the right while the nest person is wrong. It depicts I am my mind a person, who speaks from his mind in a world of pain, evil, suffering within the good, the bad and the ugly. A world of beauty, ugliness and death I do not solemnly exist for myself alone but for other people as well in a world where time and change waits for no one.

We often talk of one form of disability or the other and let's correlate them to e.g. programing through a computer for example infarct what are there in science or technology in relation to human health? Let's take someone for example who has a physical disability who is likely unable to have a child for life to continue, what good, or enhancement can the effect of a book published as e-book or paperback have on them through recent human advancements in technology, science, engineering or infrastructures.

What could it mean in view of the supernatural e.g. a mystic within the heavenly bodies and those within our planet? Without pain or suffering humans are likely to seems bionic whilst any technological object would be viewed as bionic. What would be the effect of programing a book that can be read on a computer or a tablet? What are the real effect of someone being on medication for a long time what is the meaning of residual e.g. residual image are there mystic involved in science what cause some wired feeling or emotions.

Being born premature at birth I might have been lucky if I wasn't placed in an incubator I have somehow completed my life time and era with an illness of paranoid schizophrenia to have written and published my books on a computer before handing them to my publisher Mr. Jason Pegler at Chipmunkapublishing.co.uk. Correlating my experience with someone who has been placed in an incubator because they were born premature I feel they will do well if I publish my book as e-book only. Nevertheless, those who, were born before me as premature might want to read my books on paperback.

Growing up to this stage, it doesn't beguiles me that two objects my late mother took me and herself away back to our native land Nigeria in the mid 1960's where a gramophone and what, I would call a primordial television which one has to open and close the screen it was later as at 1970' modified. A Mr. Barrister Aromolarun at Lagos and a school principal at Ibadan Mr. Osibowale owns the current modification at that time. The one my mother took from London was much older in its model. My parents separately sheared accommodation with both of them and their family. The version of the one my mother took back was black and white while the recent version own by them where coloured.

2019 if I should decide to change my present television whilst living in London, it would be a plasma model when, I first arrive back to Great Britain the first television I bought was from a fellow tenants who just moved in after me at number 1 Searles house within Elephant and Castel and Old Kent road who, asked me if I would like to buy a second hand television from him for £40.00. I priced it down to £20.00 which he accepted. It was a small black and white television white in colour.

Why should I want to do a thing like this I myself was just settling down in my new accommodation at the time? It's apparent that sometimes we do certain unusual things and later realis why we have done so which pose a stronger reality to our existence. The next day at work during my lunch break I went straight to the post office at Lewisham to buy, my first TV licence could both have been triggered by fear flight, curiosity, self-actualisation or was it that at that time, I had an intention of programing myself. At East Street Market very close to Searles house I would have got myself a coloured TV for probably under £40.00.

With my illness as a diagnosed paranoid schizophrenia since 1995 I have been the author of five books this would be my sixth book to be published with the use of a computer, how could I have managed to do this it's because I was born with something, something I could feel my late mother under pressure slavishly did for me and my father when it comes to father and son relationship which, am grateful when I realised its worth and true significance in my life especially at this present time. I grow up under my father's dwelling with the television not under my late mothers dwelling.

Implying something about programing I go through feelings computers would become more user friendly when dates depicted on computer screens is programed for example as 23rd April 2019 and not 23/04/2019. It would create a feeling of sustaining us in reality of being concurrent to nature in e.g. daily, weekly or monthly activities. It would contribute making computers more of a sense of being precise not tiring our brain or to suffer from memory lethargy.

Another aspect of my life in the UK is that I should rather be feeding on English meal but if am to return to dust from which I came I should also feed on meals of African diet. So long, but I hope to hear more from some people who want bronze in a museum back in their land of origin it would all lead to operation polymer wettier. More thought should be given to dose suffering from schizophrenia or any other form of mental illness. It's like saying Rastafarians who were born and bred in other parts of the glob should not come and live there.

Realisation of the effect of the new polymer currency should be taken into consideration by developing nations the more, they develop the more the real significance would sink in. May be they are just implying they are part and parcel of the country in which the Bronze where kept in view of the worlds situation related to cultural assimilation and what lies before us. We all have something in common when it comes to currency therefore I do not see anything wrong why we should not shear our culture. In another sense we can put it this way that money embezzled by people from its culture where the bronze are being taken back to, should be returned back to its respective nation would this solve the problem of embezzlements? Or why bring children born in Great Britain from other nations back into Britain. Come winter when I should be drinking tea I find myself drinking wine, beer or flimsy drink coca cola.

Is it always better applying wisdom in what is beyond our reach who, among us can play with such intelligence in given scenario's about life to play betrayal in matters which are related to issues beyond our reach.

As young as seven years old I witness the circumcision of my uncle Mr. Sony Goldpin Megbele at the age of 12 or 13 years under the roof of my late father at Lawani Street Yaba Lagos carried out by his own father who was my own grandfather while my late uncle Mr. Temitayo Akinlami infer something of an enigma about me and his daughter Layiwola Akinlami he gave birth to in America. The circumcision occurred before my uncle from America with his family moved in the same house with my father and his own family.

Male circumcision is the removal of the foreskin from the human penis. In the most common procedure, the foreskin is opened, adhesions are removed, and the foreskin is separated from the glans. After that, a circumcision device may be placed and then the foreskin is cut off. Topical or locally injected anesthesia is sometimes used to reduce pain and physiologic stress. For adults and children, general anesthesia is an option and the procedure may be performed without a specialized circumcision device. The procedure is most often an elective surgery performed on babies and children for religious or cultural reasons.

The only drawback I have living in the United Kingdom is about living a life which seems rather withdrawn in quietude. I do not feel lonely inside or outside I just want to be happy money now seems; like something which could buy happiness but it's not the case for all people.

Wyrd is a concept in Anglo-Saxon culture roughly corresponding to fate or personal destiny. The word is ancestral to Modern English *weird*, which retains its original meaning only dialectically.

Destiny, sometimes referred to as fate is a predetermined course of events. It may be conceived as a predetermined future, whether in general or of an individual.

Although often used interchangeably, the words 'fate' and 'destiny' have distinct connotations.

- Traditional usage defines fate as a power or agency that predetermines and orders the course of events. Fate defines events as ordered or 'inevitable' and unavoidable. This is a concept based on the belief that there is a fixed natural order to the universe, and in some conceptions, the cosmos. Classical and European mythology feature personified 'fate spinners,' known as the Moirai in Greek mythology, the Parcae in Roman mythology, and the Norns in Norse mythology. They determine the events of the world through the mystic spinning of threads that represent individual human fates. Fate is often conceived as being divinely inspired.

- Destiny is used with regard to the finality of events as they have worked themselves out; and to that same sense of 'destination', projected into the future to become the flow of events as they will work themselves out.
- Fatalism refers to the belief that events fixed by fate are unchangeable by any type of human agency. In other words, humans cannot alter their own fates or the fates of others.
-

Fortune differs terminologically from destiny and fate in that it has more to do with specific occurrences and outcomes, whereas destiny ultimately revolves around death rather than the events of one's life. In Hellenistic civilization, the chaotic and unforeseeable turns of chance gave increasing prominence to a previously less notable goddess, Tyche (literally 'Luck'), who embodied the good fortune of a city and all whose lives depended on its security and prosperity, two good qualities of life that appeared to be out of human reach. The Roman image of Fortuna, with the wheel she blindly turned, was retained by Christian writers, revived strongly in the Renaissance and survives in some forms today.

Philosophy on the concepts of destiny and fate has existed since the Hellenistic period with groups such as the Stoics and the Epicureans.

The Stoics believed that human decisions and actions ultimately went according to a divine plan devised by a god. They claimed that although humans theoretically have free

will, their souls and the circumstances under which they live are all part of the universal network of fate.
The Epicureans challenged the Stoic beliefs by denying the existence of this divine fate. They believed that a human's actions were voluntary so long as they were rational.
In daily language, 'destiny' and 'fate' are synonymous, but with regard to 19th-century philosophy, the words gained inherently different meanings.
For Arthur Schopenhauer, destiny was just a manifestation of the Will to Live, which can be at the same time living fate and choice of overrunning fate, by means of the Art, of the Morality and of the Ascesis.
For Friedrich Nietzsche, destiny keeps the form of *Amor fati* (Love of Fate) through the important element of Nietzsche's philosophy, the 'will to power' (der *Wille zur Macht*), the basis of human behavior, influenced by the Will to Live of Schopenhauer. But this concept may have even other senses, although he, in various places, saw the will to power as a strong element for adaptation or survival in a better way. Nietzsche eventually transformed the idea of matter as centers of force into matter as centers of will to power as humanity's destiny to face with *amor fati*. The expression *Amor fati* is used repeatedly by Nietzsche as acceptation-choice of the *fate*, but in such way it becomes even another thing, precisely a 'choice' destiny.

Determinism is a philosophical concept often confused with fate, it can be defined as the notion that all intents/actions are *causally* determined by the culminations of an agent's existing circumstances; simply put, everything that happens is determined by things that have already happened. Determinism differs from fate in that it is never conceived as being a spiritual, religious, nor astrological notion; fate is typically thought of as being 'given' or 'decreed' while determinism is 'caused.' Influential philosophers like Robert Kane (philosopher), Thomas Nagel, Roderick Chisholm, and A.J. Ayer have written about this notion.
The idea of a god controlled destiny plays an important role in numerous religions.

- Followers of Ancient Greek religion regarded not only the Moirai but also the gods, particularly Zeus, as responsible for deciding and carrying out destiny, respectively.
- Those who followed Gnosticism believed in fate as something strict and unchangeable, resulting in salvation only for the 'chosen ones.'
- Followers of Christianity consider God to be the only force with control over one's fate and that he has a plan for every person. Many believe that humans all have free will, which is contrasted with predestination, although naturally inclined to act according to God's desire.
- In Islam, fate or *qadar* is the decree of Allah.

Whoever says or have a notion we all should learn, understand what it is for each and every one of us to be our own psychiatrist should also understand and accept that dose of us through the process of being our own psychiatrist in positive ways should and ought to be rewarded positively. Balaam was questioned by his donkey And he beat his donkey and beat it and the donkey spoke master how many times have you beaten me have you seen me behave like this before. Another incident Zacchaeus a tax collector climbed a climbed a sycamore trees. As he was teaching how come in another incident one implied how can my lord said to my lord he was told to come down from the tree they all knew what's written in the scriptures.

Not everyone that saith unto me, **Lord, Lord**, shall enter into the kingdom of heaven; but **he** that doeth the will of **my** Father who is in heaven. Many will **say** to me on that day, **Lord, Lord**, have we not prophesied in thy name? And in thy name have cast out devils? And in thy name done many wonderful works? Why use that phrases my lord said to my lord? On another level, its science and technology which is having its say in relation to this matter. In short after coming this far through history, culture, creed, tradition after centuries, we need not ask why Jesus Christ died on the cross but, that we also reflect our mind and views we ought to know what brought forth pain and suffering and what to do about the problem of evil.

From £250.00 a fortnight having employment and support allowance each fortnight am paying my internet provider £32.00 each month, £20.00 on housing and for electricity each and £10.00 on gas. How much choice do I have in what I buy and eat what is the enigmas relating to smoking and drinking alcohol? For the sake of my own health it's left for me to understand the spirituality of publishing my books as e-book, paperback or both.

Dose science and technology have more than what they offer when it comes to money language. What does it take to know what e.g. simple medications one could be on would be a huge step forward? I might be experiencing money for value our effort always outweigh the value for money. Why do people do or say crazy things. I laboured through series of endeavour's to have written and published my books because I want my voice, feelings and experiences heard. It's also part of making experience count for me and those who really care having more avenues to do more through gaining inside information on how to make such related issues easier to bear.

14th December 2018:-

Brexit: More assurances for MPs possible says May
Theresa May has said it is still possible to get the assurances MPs need to back her Brexit deal, despite EU leaders ruling out any renegotiation.
At a summit in Brussels, the UK PM said there was 'work to do' but talks on 'further clarification' would continue.
Tourist pound now down at close to just one dollar Travellers at some UK airports are barely being offered one US dollar for each of their pounds, following a month of Brexit uncertainty.
Those exchanging pounds at the UK's biggest airport, Heathrow, are finding as little as $1.05 coming back across the counter.
Since 16 April the pound has fallen by 11.77% against the US dollar.

In places, sterling buys less than a euro, with tourists being offered just 92 cents for every pound.
Against the dollar, the pound is now at its weakest since April 2017, although it has recovered slightly since Theresa May won her vote of confidence.
In March 2008 the pound was briefly worth more than $2.00.
Brexit: No-deal will near-bankrupt UK, says Branson Sir Richard Branson warned that the UK will be left 'near bankrupt' in the event of a hard Brexit.
He told the BBC he was 'absolutely certain' that leaving the EU without a deal would lead to the closure of 'quite a few British businesses'.
He said Prime Minister Theresa May had admitted that her version of Brexit was not as good as staying in the EU.
Meanwhile, a pro-Brexit business group has urged the government to adopt a 'managed no-deal' approach.
Brexit: No visa but Britons will pay €7 to travel to EU countries Britons will have to pay €7 (£6.30) every three years to travel to EU countries, as a consequence of Brexit.
The European Commission has confirmed that while UK travellers will not need a visa, they will need to apply for and buy another document.

It is called an ETIAS (European Travel Information and Authorization System) and although not launched yet, is expected to come into force in 2021.
The travel requirement is not just for the UK but for many non-EU countries.
Why are people spending less this Christmas? There are discounts galore on the High Street, and online retailers have also started discounting products, 12 days before Christmas. Sales usually rise in the run-up to Christmas, so why are consumers spending less this year?
Half of UK homes could get faster broadband One in seven homes could be paying more than they need to for broadband and could get faster services for the same or less money, Ofcom has said.
New research suggests that half of UK homes have not taken up faster services even though they are available.

Ofcom has launched a campaign dubbed Boost Your Broadband to let people know about what options are available.
It follows years of effort to ensure that fast internet reaches as much of the country as possible.
A website to accompany the campaign will allow people to check what broadband they can receive in their area, as well as providing independent information on how to get the best deal.
The regulator also announced proposals to force broadband and mobile firms to tell customers about their best available deal, both when their deals are coming to an end, and every year after that if they don't change them.
It also plans to investigate broadband firms' pricing practices to examine why some customers pay more than others.
It is particularly keen to look at introductory offers that run out. It estimates that customers who take a landline and broadband service together are paying an average of 19% more once their discounted deal has expired.
It is currently reviewing how mobile operators charge their customers for handsets when bundled with airtime in a single contract.
If one has a birthmark from bath or an insignia from history or culture they hardly win when it comes to gambling am not implying witchcraft related to this because it's something else e.g. sale it to the devil and win or obtain something materialistic those are just to be used as advocates towards insurrection. Let's talk an insignia from a pharaoh's tomb for example, god or from a goddess. You hardly win if you win considerably the insignia has been rubbed off or stolen from you someone else, becomes the heir, likely you can no longer pass it on to children.

Or with the wining the money becomes either something of an enigma no longer governed by the insignia. Is gambling therefore a thing of God or the gods they are not things to gamble with because they have their own insignia and domain infarct what it means is that before the wining the final conflict is already over they have moved somewhere else because they themselves are searching for something. Money, material things where not their game wisdom, talent, creativity, knowledge of the earth and the unknown,

courage, resilience, to defend are their game, what would I do with such an amount of many as being creative when humans for example can be cloned.
The insignia is for them to find you or for you to find them to shed light. Now can the insignia have anything do to with finding wealth to find them? Advocates are used for such purposes not you while they are never the genuine replica. In some cases one needs to hold on to the insignia for life to take shape, for meaning to occur or to be translated. It might be once insignia to correlate existence within the heavenly body's right here from earth.
Giving up smoking or alcohol there are certain technicalities we have to use or rely on being who, we are to give them up completely or be more considerate in giving them up it's the feel, thoughts and emotions if, you have it inside you, you can give them up. Other things will lead you or pave the way for you to do as your thoughts, feelings and emotions in doing the right things that's if, you are considerate towards your thoughts feeling or emotion. When, it comes to your considering giving them up.
At the time of writing this book, I was at the verge of giving up smoking after giving up alcohol. A query is why go back to it when, I have made up my mind infarct have stopped it? What triggers this to occur again? How do I, arrest the situation and the effigies involved completely. Why should it be a thing that it's all about trying? Or why wait until when fear about something terrible strikes.
Living in a world of constant debate and disagreement, evaluating your own position on an issue of special importance is sometimes straightforward when based on to your beliefs, values, and general knowledge. However, other times it is much harder to make up your mind about an issue because the territory is somewhat complicated e.g. worrying or troublesome involving lots of other competing or controversial values and ideas that go into forming the issue under discussion or in dispute.

When making up your own mind about the issue, it's important to have studied the varied perspectives before reaching your own conclusion. Even then, you are best served by keeping an open mind about future directions and understand as new information transpires. I cannot ignore my gut instinct but, I can clarify my values I have made my research related them to the facts of the issues and I want to go beyond my stance e.g. make it certain e.g. I have made up my mind.

But how do I go beyond forming my opinion and ask myself how would I defend my stance on the issue if someone were to question me in the wrong direction while I have already advocated on my behalf should I remain open minded or not. I realize am either trying to close my mind or open my mind to certain things e.g. may be understanding what makes me draw a fag and light up will do much better if, I were to explore other factors I do not smoke or drink alcohol because it's something other people do if so why do I do it I realize it's about in certain ways to understand myself and what lies before me.

I do not have to wait until I suffer from cancer or hear somebody close to me had died of cancer that's when I consider giving it up based on fear flight it's also about taking care and consideration in view that we all react in different ways cares should endeavor more allowing those they are caring to come out openly with their own experience they might be taken with the surprise that it's all just too different! Or is there anything related to eating smoking for example and surviving?

Am raising up an issue here, where its coupled with schizophrenia one can hear voices instructing one should go out and buy alcohol, tobacco or preventing one from giving them up meanwhile from every positive things one dose from having my bath to brushing my teeth at a particular time they are the once who are telling me to have my bath, brush my teeth or wash my cloths they need to understand what I went through to have managed to save some money to buy myself a washing machine but no mention was made about it in the voices I heard instead, I experience spirit levels in relation to the money I was saving trying to prevent me from saving.

In earnest I endeavored to have written this book and got it published probably in time they would leave me alone to live my life as it best suits me. I do not feel am the one creating the bias or negativity because I think of doing everything I want to do in the right perspective in some case I do not get on well with the voice bearers what I mean is that we do not have a close relationship.

They just seems to be infringing on me while there are several ways they can make it more amicable e.g. they do not create this feeling that am no good, I need to be told what to do or that they are in authority while explanation for their reactions or motive need to reach me if I should listen to their voices and do as they say. Then, it might be considered a relationship more friendly or without bias. Doing what the voice bearer's tells me to do I realize in certain case I have to do some editing in relation to what the voices say?

It goes a long way as driving me out of my rationale. In my opinion we still have a long way to go in understanding the human architecture and it's not all going to go down well just putting it downs as related to mental health issues.

After reading this book, do please, consider it a probability if, at the end of the day, I would take life or the experience as a gamble even after I have won a considerable amount of money through gambling.

Had I won the national lottery and use my wining to publish this book could anybody or organizations willingly implied that, they piped me in which might create other paradigms in conflict to its content nevertheless some organization or individuals might be interested based on the relevance of the content of this book if, they are interested in seeking a way forward for other people to move on through which, I can come to learn more or understand other related issues concerning the relevance of this book.

While I wish, very much the meaning of the word 'paradigm' ought to be made much clearer and relevant when, it comes to what the word means. In this present time the word has relevance to a lot of things that has been going on in not only our daily lives but what have been from the past. To my knowledge of understanding, the word paradigm is a progressive word with a magical touch with reference to essence. I guess I ought to have tilted this book 'social experiment' since am a diagnosed paranoid schizophrenic in constant observation.

End

www.ingramcontent.com/pod-product-compliance
Lightning Source LLC
La Vergne TN
LVHW090301210926
848480LV00001B/92
* 9 7 8 1 7 8 3 8 2 4 9 3 9 *